COGNITIVE SCIENCES
**Basic Problems, New Perspectives,
and Implications
for Artificial Intelligence**

COGNITIVE SCIENCES
Basic Problems, New Perspectives, and Implications for Artificial Intelligence

MARIA NOWAKOWSKA

Machine Intelligence Institute
Iona College
New Rochelle, New York

1986

ACADEMIC PRESS, INC.

Harcourt Brace Jovanovich, Publishers
Orlando   San Diego   New York   Austin
London   Montreal   Sydney   Tokyo   Toronto

ACADEMIC PRESS, INC.
Orlando, Florida 32887

United Kingdom Edition published by
ACADEMIC PRESS INC. (LONDON) LTD.
24–28 Oval Road, London NW1 7DX

Library of Congress Cataloging in Publication Data

Nowakowska, Maria.
  Cognitive sciences.

  Bibliography: p.
  Includes index.
  1. Social sciences—Methodology.   I. Title.
H61.N64   1985   300'.72   83-9957
ISBN 0–12–522620–9
ISBN 0–12–522621–7 (paperback)

PRINTED IN THE UNITED STATES OF AMERICA

86 87 88 89   9 8 7 6 5 4 3 2 1

To the memory of my parents,
Jan and Anna Kowal

CONTENTS

PREFACE

This book presents certain new models and theories that are designed to describe and analyze some selected topics in the cognitive sciences. These topics range from the relatively unexplored, such as problems of observability and its restrictions or distortions of the subjective perception of time, to those that are traditionally analyzed by cognitive scientists, such as visual perception, memory, and communication. In each case, the main efforts are directed at a new conceptual representation of the phenomenon analyzed, with appropriate mechanisms postulated and explanatory hypotheses formulated.

The book treats cognitive processes through a set of interrelated theories, from different perspectives and on different levels of generality. The main purpose is to deepen and extend the theoretical apparatus of cognitive processes so that they can become an "interdiscipline" useful for a wider class of sciences. Thus, the book abandons the information-processing paradigm and searches instead for new concepts and solutions in psychological intuitions and mechanisms. It stresses the problems of cognitive limitations and distortions on the one hand and the generative, controlled, and dynamic character of cognition on the other. The best example here is the interactional model of perception, in which one distinguishes four basic mechanisms assumed to be under partial control of the subject.

As already stressed, the book is based on a multimodel conception of analysis of cognition. The possibilities of a unification through more general models, such as formal theory of actions and formal semiotics (theory of object and sign) have been presented in earlier books of the author: "Quantitative Psychology: Some Chosen Problems and New Ideas" (Nowakowska, 1983) and "Theories of Research" (Nowakowska, 1984). These books form an important context and are complementary to the present book. It is also worthwhile to mention that both theories may be of direct interest for planning in robotics and knowledge representation of situation structure for Artificial Intelligence and Expert Systems (representation of knowledge about situation structure).

The book ends with some stochastic models of expertise formation, opinion change, and learning. These models allow a deeper connection between problems of the cognitive sciences and expert systems and AI.

The book is entirely original and is not intended to be a review of the literature on the subject. Therefore only those works that were actually used are referenced.

For other approaches, especially those related to the information processing paradigm in the cognitive sciences, see, for instance, Anderson (1980,1983), Grossberg (1982), Hayes (1978), Kosslyn (1980), Lindsay and Norman (1977), Minsky (1975), Neisser (1967), Newell and Simon (1972), Norman and Rumelhart (1975), Posner (1973), Rumelhart (1975), Shank and Abelson (1977), Shepard and Cooper (1982), Sowa (1984), or Townsend and Ashby (1983).

The book is intended for all those who deal with cognitive processes in their research and teaching; hence it should be of interest not only to social scientists but also to information scientists, artificial intelligence specialists, logicians, philosophers, psycholinguists, neurobiologists, and system specialists and engineers interested in cognitive problems.

The book assumes some mathematical background; in particular, a basic knowledge of the theory of relations, fuzzy set theory, and probability theory. To facilitate reading, the Appendix contains basic information about these theories and references to the literature; in addition, the theorems are explained on an intuitive level whenever possible and their proofs are given in appendixes to the chapters.

The work on this book was partially supported by the Information Sciences branch of the National Science Foundation (IST-84-304), for which the author wishes to express her deep gratitude.

The author gratefully acknowledges the copyright release from North-Holland Publishing Company for Chapters 3 and 4, which appeared in *Mathematical Social Sciences,* Volumes 9 and 10, 1985, under the common title "Fundamentals of Expert Systems" (Part 1 "Judgment Formations and Problems of Description," and Part 2 "Communication").

The author was formerly associated with the Laboratory of Psychology and Action Theory, Polish Academy of Sciences, Warsaw, Poland.

INTRODUCTION

The premise of this book is my firm conviction that advancement of all sciences that owe their foundations to the cognitive processes depends on an extension, a deepening, and an exactness of description within the cognitive dialogue between the perceiver and objective reality. This tenet is well served by the choice of topics highlighted in the chapter titles in this book: (1) *A New Theory of Time*, (2) *Events and Observability*, (3) *Multidimensional Units and Languages: Verbal and Nonverbal Communication*, (4) *Judgment Formation and Problems of Description*, and (5) *Memory and Perception: Some New Models*, (6) *Stochastic Models of Expertise Formation, Opinion Change, and Learning*.

From the content of the chapters it may be seen that the book puts stress on concepts such as time and observability underlying all cognitive processes, as well as processes that constitute fundamentals of expert systems (Chapters 2, 3, and 4). The aim of Chapter 6 is also to more deeply connect the cognitive sciences with the topics of expert systems and AI. One can hope that such an approach will—to some extent at least—allow us to overcome the difficulties in communication and conceptual incompatibility of the cognitive sciences and the dynamically developing AI field [for information on the latter see, e.g., Barr and Feigenbaum (1982), Heyes-Roth et al. (1983), Nilssen (1980), Pearl (1984), or Winston (1983)]. Formal semiotics and formal theory of actions [see Nowakowska, "Quantitative Psychology: Some Chosen Problems and New Ideas" (1983), and "Theories of Research" (1984)] constitute an important extension of the problem of representation of knowledge about structure and change of situation/object, and actions admissible for this situation.

Each chapter presents a new theory or set of theories. Each begins with an extensive introduction outlining the theory's content and its relationship to other theories. At the same time, to facilitate reading, all formal considerations are accompanied by an intuitive informal explanation and most proofs are

1

given in chapter appendices.

Extensive use is made of fuzzy set theory, which allows a more flexible and realistic description; throughout the text some foundational problems of this theory are shown. These problems are connected with the properties and distortions of judgment formation.

Chapter 1 allows relatively deep penetration into the process of observation, the problems of construction of such an abstract concept as time, and (among others) the reconsideration of James's concept of stream of consciousness. However, the crucial topic in this chapter is the distortion of time perception and the relationship between objective and subjective time. An explanatory concept used here is that of a pre-event (being a candidate for an event to be stored in memory) and the concept of a dynamic event-representation of an object (events on events) generated by the perceiver in the process of perceptual work.

Moreover, the boundedness of memory and attention, which leaves many events outside the scope of consciousness, leads to subjective discontinuity of time and space caused by competition of internal and external processes in consciousness. The principle of semantic continuity allows us to overcome the discreteness of consciousness and to pass relatively smoothly from one semantic system to another. Theory of time is, in fact, an extension of the theory of measurement [for information about this important domain of mathematical psychology, see, e.g., Nowakowska (1983)], to the problems of time, where such considerations were simply absent. The theory of time combines in one formal system the problems of objective and subjective time and memory. This is a theoretical novelty in measurement theory, being the first analysis of its kind in the literature. One can expect that further development of the theory of measurement will go towards construction of new class of models that are not only descriptive but also explanatory, thus bringing it closer to cognitive processes, and allowing us to rely less on physical models. The notion of time is of fundamental importance not only for measurement from the theoretical, philosophical, or physical point of view, it is also crucial for AI (simulation of cognitive processes), mathematical theory of programming (restrictions of satisfiability and truth in time), and in studies of structure and coding of information, especially for the new generation of super fast computers for which information is to be coded in molecular structures. The chapter also contains a discussion of other theories of time, mainly causal in nature.

In the social sciences one often deals with changing objects of a fuzzy character (e.g., attitudes, inflation); the fuzziness may concern either the spatial or temporal boundaries of the object or even its definition. The theory of such objects, as well as their observability and the related concept of a fuzzy event, are introduced in Chapter 2. The latter is different from the concept of event studied in fuzzy set theory (Zadeh, 1965) and in probability theory, in which the events are identified with subsets of the sample space. The basic notions in this chapter are those of preobjects, their temporal cores and carriers, as well as observability networks. They allow us to define the concept of an object and the concept of the separation of two objects. Of crucial importance here are the considerations of restrictions of observability, in particular the constraints on joint observability, which are often overlooked in cognitive, behavioral, and social sciences. Thus, two attributes may be observable, but not jointly; that is, if we observe one of them, the other cannot be observed. We have to decide then what to observe, and pay for it by being unable to observe the value of the other attribute. This is common in physics, biology, etc., but it also appears in cognitive and social sciences, when the observation may modify the subject irreversibly. In other words, the choice of what to observe has some immediate consequences on what one does, by limiting the scope of legitimate inference.

Various types of observability constraints, as related to fuzziness or physical impossibility of joint observations, are analyzed. Also considered are the effects of outside interference on observability, called *filters*, and the constraints imposed by the observer's choice of temporal patterns when taking observations, called *masks*.

The importance of constraints on observability reaches far beyond the obvious cases of measurement errors or grouping of data. The concepts introduced may have considerable usefulness in the social and cognitive sciences as a foundation for a formal theory of experiments. The most important contribution of observability theory, however, is the ontology of random fuzzy objects, which is encountered so often in the social and cognitive sciences. Some examples of such objects include "epidemics," "inflation," "human attitude," "intelligence," etc.

Theory of objects and observability, combined with theory of formal semiotics, may allow us to enrich, deepen, and revise the theoretical and methodological foundations of the social and cognitive sciences. Moreover, it may also be of importance for AI, in simulation of research. In systems theory, it allows us to introduce a new class of systems, namely, those of semirandom and random objects, with various kinds of distinguishability and changeability. Such systems may have interesting applications in physics (linear random systems, random fields, etc.), as well as in computer sciences and biology.

Chapter 3 shows how one can incorporate into one system a formal description of simultaneous communication events and actions occurring in everyday life. The concepts of multimedial fuzzy units and languages not only describe communication phenomena but may also be useful in modeling and simulation of some neuropsychological processes in the brain. Another important concept for the same purpose might be that of networks with randomly varying nodes and edges (appearing and disappearing, according to suitable stochastic mechanisms). For this approach, the reader is referred to Chapter 3 of "Theories of Research" (Nowakowska, 1984), where it was used to model social networks in science. This would allow simulation studies of knowledge acquisition and learning, in particular if one accepts a new learning model (shown in the last chapter), in which the increases in knowledge about a given topic occur at random moments in the form of enlightenments, not only during effective learning of a given topic but also during learning of some other topics. This happens because of the existing semantic relationships between topics, and because of delayed learning due to perseverance of previous topics in memory that are not sufficiently understood, as well as some tendency of restructuring, re-representing and re-interpreting of the perceived and learned material. The above ideas may lead to some new approaches in machine learning, dominated thus far by sequential models [see, for instance, Michalski *et al.* (1983)] and computer architecture.

In this chapter we consider not only the structural constraints (such as enforcing or exclusion) of these units but also their fuzzy semantics. For the multimedial languages, for example, one analyzes, among others, pragmatic semantics, that is, problems of expressibility of certain meanings in situations in which some media are excluded from use (the media in this case being verbal medium, medium of gestures, medium of facial expressions, etc.). These considerations are used later (in Chapter 5) for a heuristic model of memory, which introduces the notions of internal action languages.

As regards communication problems, one considers planning and re-alization of a unit in a given context by the sender, as well as expectations concerning kinds of units, from the viewpoint of the receiver, especially under temporal constraints.

The notion of a standard fuzzy unit is introduced, and the importance of particular media for a given meaning is analyzed through the concept of recognition weights (based on voting coalition theory). These recognition weights play an important role when the exposition time is limited.

As a result, the unit as a whole expresses various meanings in varying degrees, depending on the meanings expressed on particular media and the degrees of expressions of these meanings.

The meaning of a unit is treated as an invariant of a certain class of transformations, and composite meaning is obtained as a result of a certain semantic calculus, with operations such as supporting and inhibiting. This analysis is also applied to strings of units, especially those that appear in dialogues. The latter are treated in the last section of the chapter, with special emphasis put on the meanings expressed by nonverbal media.

At present, an increasing number of researchers appreciate the advantage of analyzing behavior in terms of strings of discrete units, in particular, communication behavior. Chapter 3 provides not only a theory but also a convenient methodological tool for empirical research.

One of the most important media in communication is quite obviously the verbal medium. The psychological, logical, and linguistic analyses of various aspects of judgment formation and description are presented in Chapter 4. Emphasis is put on the role of ambiguity (and unavoidability of the latter) connected with such properties of perception as the ability of discrimination and identification. It is shown how these properties of perception constrain the logical values such as truth, which lead to their uncertainty and vagueness.

The models of judgment formation are relevant for social sciences, linguistics, and fuzzy set theory.

The models of question answering show, among other things, those psychological mechanisms that are responsible for distortions of answers. These models allow for reconstruction of the statistical characteristics of answers in the population, in the sense of variability. This, in turn, leads to estimation of the magnitude of a bias. The models have been successfully tested empirically and are the first of this type in the psychological and sociological literature. For fuzzy set theory, they bring attention to certain important inherent cognitive problems concerning negative bounds on the possibility of removing uncertainty and vagueness. These bounds restrain to some extent the development of fuzzy set theory, especially its applications, and show the necessity of concentrating efforts on the foundational aspects of the theory.

Chapter 4 also deals with a theory of descriptions called *verbal copies*. The subject evaluates an object within its various semantic dimensions, that is, classifies it according to relevant categories, thus performing a multiple linguistic measurement [for the latter concept, see Nowakowska (1979d)].

The main problem analyzed here concerns the structural aspects of such descriptions and their relations to reality, especially truth (referred to as faithfulness, in case of fuzzy attributes) and exactness. This leads to exhibiting various cognitive limitations on descriptions, especially those connected with the choice of the language of descriptors.

For describing a dynamically changing object, the notion of generative verbal structures (verbal copies enriched by temporal and motivational variables) is introduced and connected with the algebra of goals and means [for a description of motivational linguistic variables, see Nowakowska (1973)].

The algebra of goals and means (Nowakowska, 1976a) allows us to analyze the attainability of composite goals (in this case, the descriptions of future states).

The study of composite descriptions leads in a natural way to theories of texts and knowledge. A very rich system of concepts is introduced for analysis of text properties, especially the semantic relations between the text parts.

These relationships may be analyzed from logical, linguistic, and statistical viewpoints; in addition, a model for change of topics is introduced.

Among the many ways in which a text may be viewed, two are analyzed in more detail: as a sequence of responses to a hypothetical string of questions and as a representation of some body of knowledge. The latter analysis may be of some wider significance and applicability, since it combines not only the factual knowledge but also the evaluations of propositions as regards their credibility, possibility, and so on. The suggested theory of α-bility provides the rules of combining the degrees of credibility, possibility, and so on, of constituent parts of a text into an overall judgment.

The last section of Chapter 4 deals with the dynamics of discourses, that is, with the analysis based again on the algebra of goals and means. The latter leads to treating the generation of a discourse as a function of the planned composite goal. These considerations show, from a somewhat different viewpoint, the previously discussed topics of knowledge generation and structure.

Chapter 5 deals with certain important aspects of two closely interrelated psychological processes: memory and perception. Several models are offered, some treating these processes separately, some treating them jointly as two components of a larger process.

Regarding memory, the book offers some novel approaches that capture the effects of control of memory storage time. Generally, this model tries to reconcile two seemingly opposing facts: (1) that the process of information loss in memory (forgetting) is to some extent random and beyond conscious control and (2) that one may control memory storage by conscious efforts to remember given information, at least until a specified target time.

The model is based on the idea that in order to enhance the probability of remembering information at some future time one may simply increase the number of memory units that store this information (so to speak, "copy" the information several times).

The control of memory results from the operation of metamemory, which issues "metainstructions" concerning not the content of the message to be remembered, but the message itself. This idea of memory operation raises a number of interesting questions. It is clear that producing several copies of information will enhance the probability of remembering (existence of at least one copy at target time) if the processes of losing information are to some extent independent.

The models offered in Section 5.2 explore this problem. First, they offer two alternative mechanisms of "copying" (called *internal recalls*): one in which an internal recall produces an additional copy and another in which an internal recall causes doubling of the number of copies.

Regarding the process of losses, the assumptions cover the case of total independence as well as the case in which the process of forgetting is "self-accelerating" (i.e., loss in one memory unit enhances the chances of loss in other memory units).

Another problem of considerable interest concerns optimization. Given the target time (when the information is to be recalled) and given a limitation on the number of internal recalls that one can make, the question arises of their optimal location in time. Here the analysis leads to some rather unexpected results, showing (among others) that the optimal placement of two internal recalls differs in essential aspects from the optimal placement of three internal recalls.

The model of memory with internal recalls is used in Section 5.3 to analyze the process of memory of sentences. Here the internal recalls are induced spontaneously by some of the subsequent words of the sentence (due either to the structure of the sentence or to some semantic relations between the words). The model offered explains the empirical data, which show the phenomenon of better recall of the initial and terminal words of the sentence.

The discussion closing Chapter 5 shows a heuristic dynamic model of memory (Nowakowska, 1981b; the first version of this model was presented in 1978 at the Berlin Symposium on Cognition and Memory) that uses the theories presented earlier in this book. Among others, crucial here are multidimensional units and languages and the algebra of meanings, which lead to parallel, distributive, and hierarchical concepts of memory.

It is worth stressing that this conception, in combination with that of metamemory determine the strength, direction, and horizon of storage, preceded by only a few years the actual interests of memory theoreticians in multidimensional units having internal structure and capable of simultaneous processing, as well as in control processes [see, e.g., Hinton and Anderson (1981)].

The notion of metamemory and multidimensional units may play a crucial role in artificial intelligence, where it may serve as a basis for the greatly needed model of the structural program of memory founded on new cognitive and economic principles.

One of the functions of metamemory may not only be the choice of horizon time, but also the degree of faithfulness and exactness of represent of the object in memory.

The novelty of the dynamic model of perception lies in introducing the models of some basic mechanisms and in treating the process of perception as a mixture of these mechanisms. Additionally, it assumes partial control over the perceptual process, and, moreover, it is based on the concept of an event-representation of the object formed in the perceptual work of the eye. The basic unit of perception is a glance, which involves both jumping and fine eye movement.

The models of various perceptual mechanisms complement the more global approach to perception and recognition in Chapter 3. Four main mechanisms are distinguished:

(a) *The model of building event-representations of the object* deals with changing pre-events into events. The model (shown in Chapter 1 in connection with temporal phenomena) describes the statistical features of what is being perceived, in the sense of storage of the material to be processed later. It is shown that one may derive the distribution of the temporal spacings between consecutive stored events (which constitute approximately the Poisson process).

(b) *The model of attraction mechanism* introduces the function representing the changes of attractiveness of various domains of focal points on the inspected picture. This function determines the probability of jumping to another focal point. Roughly stated, the areas of various focal points "compete" for attention of the eye, creating a sort of conflict resolved according to the principle of stochastic attraction to the most attractive domain.

(c) *The model of optimal glance path* treats (as opposed to purely random movements of the eye, resulting from competing attractions by various domains) consecutive glances as a goal-oriented process that optimizes some criterion, for example, recognition or identification time. The model uses the notion of weights [see Nowakowska (1967)], measuring the importance of fragments for recognition of meaning (this extends the notion of weight introduced in Chapter 3 for multimedial units). The optimal path is determined by a solution of the Bellman equation. The actual glance process is a mixture of purely random walk governed by attractions and purely purposeful inspection governed by the desire to attain some specific goal.

(d) *The model of mechanisms of transportation* is related to the glance process, which leads to inspection of some fragments, which must then be compared with some other fragments according to certain attributes. Such a comparison involves "transporting" a fragment to the location of another for purposes of comparison (the results of comparisons may be regarded as pre-events or raw data about the relational structure of the picture). The process of transportation leads to a fuzzification of the stimulus trace in memory and hence to a loss of precision in comparison. The probabilities of error provide means of estimating the parameters of the model and testing the hypotheses of parallel versus serial processing.

This model leads in a natural way to formulating some conjectures about mental operations on certain stimuli (both conceptualizable and unconceptualizable) and designing means of testing these conjectures.

Interactions of mechanisms of attractiveness, purposeful inspection, and transportation may determine various perceptual pressures and conflicts. The notion of conflict allows us to analyze the perceptual distortions that, in the simplest forms, appear as optimal solutions to conflicts (in visual illusions). Two sections of Chapter 5 are devoted to explanations of visual illusions. One presents a stochastic model based on fine eye movements to explain the Müller–Lyer illusion. This explanation consists simply of showing that there must be a difference in sizes of memory traces of the "outward" and "inward" arrow. In another explanation of the mechanisms of visual illusions, it was assumed that, on a relatively low level of cognition, there appears some specific type of modeling. The explanation of illusion is based on the notion of competing perceptual semantic systems (basic and contextual) that give different evaluations of some observed values of attributes. The resultant constructivistic system is the optimal solution for diverging and conflicting values.

Another section of Chapter 5 discusses the relationship between the structure of an object and its verbal copy [see also Nowakowska (1967)]. Various strategies of description connected with the conditional weight structure of an object are considered, conditional weight being defined as the recognition weight in situations in which a part of the object is already known.

The concept of weights, incidentally, enables us to define formally some concepts of Gestalt theory, for example, good figure and normalization.

A sequential decision model for recognition is also introduced. The important feature of this model is that it allows the information to be drawn from outside the object, for example, from one's own knowledge.

Chapter 5 ends with two short sections. One of them is devoted to a general heuristic model of memory, which builds an explanation of the mechanisms of memory on the basis of the notions such as (1) multidimensional units and the language of communication with dynamic fuzzy semantics in the form of semantic calculus, (2) the ideal of an object and of a concept defined through a class of meaning-preserving transformations, (3) the multidimensional gnostic unit, which memorizes the ideals of the objects and of the concepts, (4) the algebra of goals and means showing a method of constructing composite goals through logical operations on simpler goals, to which there correspond set-theoretical operations on sets of means of attaining these goals, (5) the representation of situation understood as a description or linguistic measurement of situation, also containing motivational evaluations, and (6) the metamemory, understood as a certain subspace of cognitive or motivational space supplying modal frames over some motivational frames (e.g., "I want X" and "I ought to remember that I ought to X").

The last section of Chapter 5 presents a model of allocation of visual control among the tasks that cannot be controlled simultaneously (e.g., tasks performed by two hands, with locations so distant one from another that one is forced to shift attention from one hand to the other). The model postulates that the required hand (or arm) motions are representable by appropriate differential equations, which (in the absence of visual control) involve a stochastic component. For given times of attention shift one obtains a solution, which deviates from the motion that would result under continuous visual control. Given such an expression, one can use various known optimization techniques to find the optimal shift times, and, consequently, open up the empirical possibilities of analysing the magnitudes, sources, etc. of deviations from optimality in real human behavior. The model combines the problems of multimodal perception with the knowledge of structure of situation and action, and may be useful in cognitive foundations of robotics.

The last chapter of the book presents some models of processes involved in forming an opinion (in particular an expertise), and learning.

As regards expertise, the model concerns a plausible mechanism of arriving at one's "true" opinion (which need not coincide with the opinion actually expressed). Such an analysis is an obvious necessary prerequisite for any study of biases in expert opinions, since the very concept of bias presupposes a difference between the opinion actually expressed, and the opinion that would be revealed if there were no bias. The latter opinion may be identified with the "true" conviction of the expert.

The model presupposes that an opinion (about some object of expertise) is representable, at any given time, as a state-vector with a certain number of coordinates (representing various aspects, or evaluations on some attributes, of the opinion object). The state vector is subject to changes, one coordinate at a time. Moreover, the process of changes is assumed discrete, so that each coordinate is an integer, and the coordinates change by the value 1 up or down only. Consequently, the process of arriving at the final opinion is a multidimensional one, with components changing up or down by 1.

The model consists of postulating the form of transition intensities, that is, probabilities of changes of a given variable by unit value up or down at any given time. These probabilities depend on a number of factors: first, on the state at a given time, and also on control parameters, as well as on the "environment" process.

The latter represents (in the context of the opinion forming process) the arrival of any new data, changes in theoretical knowledge, etc. or anything else that may affect opinion. On the other hand, the control parameters represent those features of the situation that can be manipulated.

Two models of the above type are specified in some detail. In both cases, the control parameters are assumed constant, while the environmental process is generated by a stream of events of some kind (for instance, arrivals of some items of information that affect opinion). The difference between these two models lies in treatment of memory, that is, the effect of an event of a given kind and changes of this effect in time.

The next section concerns a model of learning. Here it is assumed that acquisition of knowledge (of a set of interrelated topics) consists of a sequence of "enlightenments"—instances of sudden realization of some truth, grasping some relationship, etc. The state of the knowledge is then representable as a vector, whose components are numbers of enlightenments concerning particular topics. The question asked is as follows: how many hours, within some fixed total, should be allocated to instructions on each of the topics, so as to maximize the expected acquired knowledge?

Here the control variable is the vector of allocated times, while the "environmental" process is relatively simple: it represents different abilities in the class of students.

Finally, the last section concerns the possibility of testing the "synergy" hypothesis, underlying both models. Each of them presupposes that the coordinates of the process under study interact in some way. More precisely, they increase in a way "enhanced" by the growth of other coordinates. In an obvious sense, this type of growth involves synergy effects.

Although such an effect is quite plausible on purely intuitive grounds, it is worthwhile to be able to test it empirically. The last section suggests how such a test may be carried out in the context of teaching.

This introduction gives only a brief outline of the rich network of concepts and theories, and their mutual interrelations, presented in the book. In the choice of topics, the accent was placed on certain domains relatively little explored in the social and cognitive sciences. One can hope that this book's interdisciplinary approach will prove fruitful and stimulating for reader interested not only in the social and cognitive sciences but also in logic, philosophy, linguistics, psycholinguistics, neurobiology, artificial intelligence, computer science, and engineering (especially those who use the fuzzy set theory).

1 A NEW THEORY OF TIME

1.1 INTRODUCTION

The problems of the structure of situations and events, as well as their perception and evaluation, are receiving more and more attention within the social sciences. The theory of time presented here allows not only for deepening the dynamic analysis of events but also for analyzing the distortions of perception and judgment formation that are so important in the decision-making processes.

The shift of emphasis from structural to dynamic analysis makes problems of time of primary importance, because—as will be demonstrated later—the notion of time is inherently connected with the perception of a stream of events. In other words, we shall regard time as an abstraction from the order of events. Because of the properties of perception and memory, time may be susceptible to subjective distortions.

To make the intuitive understanding of the concept of time more precise, its measurement-theoretical definition will be shown, with special emphasis put on identifying those properties that are responsible for the ordinal properties of time, and those that account for its cardinal properties.

It is well known from science and from everyday life that time can be measured on an interval scale, so that the durations of time intervals are measurable on a ratio scale (we neglect here the relativistic phenomena connected with time and restrict the analysis to one inertial system). Thus a 2-hour period is twice as long as a 1-hour period, and so on. The question arises, as usual in measurement problems, of finding some simpler, more basic relations that are, in a sense, "responsible" for time being what it is.

The new theory of time suggested in this chapter clarifies, among others, the following points. First, the *ordinal* properties of time are a consequence of some elementary and self-evident properties of the relation "occurs earlier than" in the class of all events. What is worth stressing is the fact that this relation may be fuzzy; that is, it may not be possible to unambiguously determine which of two events occurred earlier. However, as long as the degree of fuzziness meets certain regularity properties, the overall temporal order of events may still be recovered.

Second, for the *cardinal* properties of time, that is, the measurability of time distances on a ratio scale, one needs something more, namely, a homomorphism into some appropriate empirical relational system with concatenation and comparisons. This occurs because intervals of time can never be repeated and, for comparison with other intervals, must be represented in some form (e.g., as the angle swept by the hand of the clock).

Thus two intervals of time with identical representations (e.g., two intervals occurring on different days during which the hour hand of the clock makes one full circle) are of the same length. However, they often do not seem such, and the question arises to account for such phenomena.

Imagine one afternoon during which a person waits for some important event such as a call from a friend. Nothing much is happening, and even if it is, it remains largely unnoticed by the person concentrating on the phone. Imagine now that on some other day this person spends a hectic afternoon, full of activity of some sort, when one event follows another in quick succession. The first afternoon will seem long while it lasts; the second will pass quickly, often with the observer surprised: "How late it is already!" But a year later, in retrospect, the first afternoon will appear shorter than the second.

To explain this phenomenon of deformation of the subjective perception of time, it is first necessary to explore the construction of subjective time. This theory provides such a construction, based again on the fuzzy relation "occurs earlier than."

It is clear that the main factor responsible for the distortion of the person's perception of the duration of the elapsed time between events a and b is the events that occurred in between. It is the memory of these events that makes the distance between a and b longer or shorter in retrospect.

There are numerous events occurring (both external and internal) all the time, and only some of them enter the long-term memory. In other words, not all "pre-events" become events, in the sense of being noticed and stored in memory. The choice here is partially subjective. This theory offers us a model, based on the notion of "linkage" between events. Roughly, an event enters the memory (and remains there for a random time) if at the moment of its occurrence it is linked to another event in memory. The notion of linkage is a primitive concept and may only be informally explicated, as any causal, logical, semantic, or emotional relation between two events.

The considerations outlined above concern "long" intervals of time, so the events that mark the beginning and the end of the interval enter the person's long-term memory. In Section 1.4 another model will be offered concerning the perception of short-term time intervals, for example, durations of some signals lasting for approximately a second.

This model is based on the same ideas used in Section 1.2 to construct cardinal time, namely, that of mapping time intervals into some objects. The latter in this case are the memory traces of stimuli. The sizes of these memory traces will be analyzed later to compare the durations of stimuli.

Because everyday life experience indicates that people are capable of differentiating the durations of stimuli, at least if both their lengths and the ratios of their length exceed certain thresholds, it appears that the "internal clock" that produces memory traces may somehow be "set" to make traces with uniform speed.

Our model postulates that the memory traces are subject to specific deformations. This allows us to derive the formulas giving probabilities for the correct and incorrect decisions when dealing with the relationships between lengths of stimuli. Given such formulas, one may use the experimental results to estimate the relevant parameters of the model, thus learning about the memory traces and the rate of their "fuzzification."

Time between two consecutive occurrences of events of some kind is inversely related to the frequency of these events. The relation between two frequencies, in turn, is reflected in the probability that (counting from some fixed moment) an event from one stream will occur earlier than an event from the less frequent stream. It turns out that under some assumptions about the nature of the processes, this probability allows us to determine the ratio of frequencies of the events in both streams, hence also the ratio of inter-event times. Consequently, given a family of such streams of events, one could (at least in principle) build a ratio scale for time intervals, given all probabilities that provide comparisons between pairs of streams.

Finally, Section 1.9 is devoted to the following problem. From simple introspection we know that people are capable of ordering the events that occurred in the past. This means that when an event is stored in memory, it must be stored with some kind of "label" that allows us to later tell when it occurred, at least in ordinal sense, that is, to tell which of the two events occurred earlier. These comparisons are also subject to errors, and one may say that a *reversal* occurs if in retrospection the person is convinced that *a* occurred earlier than *b*, while, in fact, the order was just the opposite.

This section offers a simple model of reversals, which explains that a reversal is less likely to occur if the distance between the events is large. Also, a reversal is less likely to occur if there are many events that occurred between the events to be reversed.

The model consists of a simple "shuffling" scheme of a sequence of events, where the reversals between two more distant events are obtained as a result of a series of successive reversals of neighboring events.

1.2   THE OBJECTIVE AND SUBJECTIVE TIME SCALES

The formal system introduced in this section will allow us to define the notion of *time*, both objective and subjective, and derive its basic properties (e.g., the type of scale on which time is measured). We shall proceed slowly, starting from the simplest framework and enriching it gradually.

1.2.1   The Ordinal Objective Time

The basic system, which will serve as a starting point, is an ordered pair

$$\langle Z, W \rangle, \tag{1.1}$$

where Z is a set and W a family of partial fuzzy relations in Z. Before we formulate the assumptions about system (1.1), it will be best to spell out the intended interpretation.

First, Z is a set of *events*, understood as instantaneous changes of state of some fragment of reality. Thus the notion of event, as used here, is somewhat more restrictive than in everyday usage, since we require that events have the unique times of their occurrences. Note that this is an informal requirement, since formally we do not have the notion of time as yet; it will be defined later, in terms of system (1.1).

According to this interpretation, hiking trip, flood, war, and so on, are *not* events, even though they are usually referred to as such in everyday language. However, the beginning and end of a hiking trip, flood, and so on are events in the sense considered here. This distinction between the term "event" in everyday language and as used here (as an element of Z) is essential for understanding the subsequent constructions. The elements of Z will be denoted $a, b, c, \ldots$ with identifying subscripts if necessary.

The second element of system (1.1) is a class of fuzzy partial relations in Z. The elements of W will be denoted $w, w', w'', \ldots$, again with identifying subscripts if necessary.

Let $w \in W$, and let

$$A(w) \subset Z \times Z \tag{1.2}$$

be the set on which w is defined. Thus w is a function

$$w: A(w) \rightarrow [0, 1] \tag{1.3}$$

which to every pair of events (a, b) in $A(w)$ assigns the number $w(a, b)$. The value $w(a, b)$ will be interpreted as the *degree to which event a precedes event b*.

The order of events is visualized as judgments being made by an observer at any one time. His memory may be imperfect, and, moreover, his recollection may change in time. The latter effect will be represented by the assumption that different functions w reflect the judgments made at various times.

To better appreciate the subsequent formal constructions, we shall first give an informal, intuitive sketch of formal derivations.

Let us consider the judgments as described by a function w. These judgments are allowed (make sense) for the pairs of events in the domain $A(w)$ of the function w.

Consider now a pair of events a and b, and the comparison of their order of occurrence. The events a and b will always be comparable if they occurred in the past. Another situation in which a and b are comparable is when one of them is in the past and the other in the future (i.e., did not occur as yet). However, when both are in the future, they may not be comparable.

It is worth stressing that noncomparability of events in the future is a possible, but not necessary, property of such events. In other words, some events in the future are comparable and some are not. For example, suppose that Mr. X has at present no children. Then the event $a = $ birth of Mr. X's first son and $b = $ birth of Mr. X's second son are comparable: b cannot precede a. However, with a as above and $b = $ birth of Mr. Y's first son (assuming Mr. Y has no children at present either), the events a and b are not comparable *at present*.

This general idea of comparability and noncomparability of events will allow us to use the sets $A(w)$ of pairs on which w is defined to separate those events in Z that are still in the future, counting from the time of comparison w.

By imposing appropriate conditions on the mutual relations between sets $A(w)$ for various w, we shall be able to order the comparison functions w. This order will be taken as a representation of the objective time scale. Intuitively, if $F(w)$ and $F(w')$ are the sets of events that are still in the future at comparisons w and w', then w must be earlier than w' if $F(w)$ is larger than $F(w')$. In other words, the class of events that are in the future should decrease with the passage of time.

After generating the objective time scale in the manner described above (i.e., through the sets of events belonging to various futures), we shall explore the properties of orderings w. Intuitively, we shall generate an order for each w in the class of events in the past of w. This order will reflect the subjective time according to "recollection" function w. Consequently, for various w we shall have various time scales, or even various orders of events, in agreement with the empirical fact that the recollection of time may change and is subject to various distortions.

Let us now proceed formally. First, we make the following assumption.

ASSUMPTION 1.1   For any $w \in W$ and $a, b \in Z$ we have

$$(a, a) \in A(w); \tag{1.4}$$

$$if \quad (a, b) \in A(w), \quad then \quad (b, a) \in A(w). \tag{1.5}$$

This assumption is of a rather technical nature. It asserts simply that one can always compare, relative to the order of occurrence, any event a with itself (the results of such comparisons will be postulated later). Moreover, if a is comparable with b, then b is comparable with a.

Let us now define the class of events, denoted $F(w)$, to be interpreted as the class of all events that belong to the future according to the comparison function w.

DEFINITION 1.1   The *future of* w is defined as

$$F(w) = \{a \in Z : (\exists b) \quad \text{such that} \quad (a, b) \notin A(w)\}. \tag{1.6}$$

The properties of sets $F(w)$ and $Z - F(w)$ are given in the following theorem.

THEOREM 1.1   If $a \in F(w)$ and $(a, b) \notin A(w)$, then $b \in F(w)$.

THEOREM 1.2   If $a \in Z - F(w)$, then $(a, b) \in A(w)$ for every $b \in Z$.

The first theorem asserts that, if an event belongs to the future and is not comparable with some other event, then the latter event must also belong to the future.

The second theorem asserts the converse: if an event does not belong to the future (i.e., belongs to the past or present), then it is comparable with any other event, from the past, present, or future.

We shall now introduce the next assumption, which will allow us to introduce the notion of the ordinal time.

ASSUMPTION 1.2   For any $w, w' \in W$ we have either $A(w) \subset A(w')$ or $A(w') \subset A(w)$.

We shall first prove the following theorem.

THEOREM 1.3   If $A(w) \subset A(w')$, then $F(w') \subset F(w)$.

For the proof, let $a \in F(w')$. Then there exists b with $(a, b) \notin A(w')$; hence, also $(a, b) \notin A(w)$. But the last condition means that $a \in F(w)$, which proves the proposition.

Thus, the increase of sets $A(w)$ is accompanied with the decrease of the corresponding futures $F(w)$.

We shall now introduce the notion of the objective ordering in time.

DEFINITION 1.2   For $w, w' \in W$, we put $w \leq w'$ iff $A(w) \subset A(w')$; we then say that the comparison w occurs *earlier* than the comparison w.

From Assumption 1.2 it follows that the relation $\leq$ is connected in W: for each w and w' we have either $w \leq w'$ or $w' \leq w$. Moreover, this relation is also transitive in W (since the relation of set inclusion has this property). One can then define the relations of equivalence: $w \sim w'$ iff $w \leq w'$ and $w' \leq w$; and strict order: $w < w'$ iff $w \leq w'$ and not $w' \leq w$.

We shall now make an assumption of a rather technical nature, which will allow a representation of the system $\langle W, \leq \rangle$ on an ordinal type scale.

ASSUMPTION 1.3   *There exists a countable set $W' \subset W$ that is order-dense in W: for every $w, w'' \in W - W'$ with $w < w''$ there exists $w' \in W'$ such that $w \leq w' \leq w''$.*

We then have [see Roberts (1979)] the following theorem.

THEOREM 1.4   *There exists a function $t \colon W \to R$ (the real line) such that*

$$t(w) \leq t(w') \qquad iff \quad w \leq w'. \tag{1.7}$$

Moreover, if t^* is any other function satisfying condition (1.5), then there exists an increasing function $f \colon R \to R$ with

$$t^*(w) = f(t(w)) \tag{1.8}$$

for all $w \in W$.

We shall refer to function t as to a time scale (objective), interpreting $t(w)$ as the time at which comparison w is made. From Theorem 1.3 it follows that, as time increases, the corresponding futures decrease.

The conceptual construction carried out thus far was based on a very simple system (1.1). It is therefore not very surprising that the conclusions derived fall short of what we are accustomed to as an inherent property of time, namely, its measurability on an interval type scale. So far, time has only ordinal properties connected with occurrences of events: out of two moments of time, the one that has more events in its past must come later.

In subsequent parts of this chapter we shall enrich system (1.1) to obtain that measurability of objective time on an interval scale. Before that, however, we shall further explore system (1.1) by imposing some conditions on relations w and building the subjective time scales corresponding to comparisons made at various times $t(w)$.

1.2.2   The Subjective Time

First, let us fix some ordinal time scale $t(w)$ and introduce the following definition.

DEFINITION 1.3   For each event $a \in Z$, its *time of occurrence* $T(a)$ is defined as

$$T(a) = \inf\{t(w): a \notin F(w)\}. \tag{1.9}$$

As will be shown by the propositions below, this definition yields the concept of time of occurrence that has all the properties one might intuitively expect.

Indeed, time of occurrence of an event a is defined as the earliest moment at which a is not in the future of comparison relations pertaining to this moment. Since the futures are decreasing (Theorem 1.3), if an event is not in the future for some time t, it is not in the future for any subsequent moments. Equivalently, once an event occurs, it belongs to the past from that moment on. This is a self-evident property of the real time, hardly requiring any comment, but one should remember that our time scale is derived formally, and it is always necessary to verify that it has the properties that are known to hold for real time.

If $t = t(w)$, we shall write F_t instead of $F(w)$ for the future at time t. Similarly, let the *past* at t (denoted P_t), and *present* at t (denoted N_t, from "now") be defined as

$$P_t = \{a \in Z : T(a) < t\} \tag{1.10}$$

and

$$N_t = \{a \in Z : T(a) = t\}. \tag{1.11}$$

We then have the following theorem.

THEOREM 1.5   For any event $a \in Z$ we have $T(a) > t$ iff $a \in F_t$.

This theorem follows directly from the definition of $T(a)$ and from the assumption that $t = t(w)$.

We shall now proceed with the assumptions concerning function w.

ASSUMPTION 1.4   Let $t = t(w)$, and let $a, b \in P_t \cup N_t$. Then

$$w(a,b) + w(b,a) \leq 1. \tag{1.12}$$

First observe that relation (1.12) makes sense from the formal point of view: if $a, b \in P_t \cup N_t$, then $a, b \notin F_t = F(w)$; hence, by Theorem 1.2, $(a, b) \in A(w)$, i.e., the value $w(a, b)$ is defined. By Assumption 1.1, we also have $(b, a) \in A(w)$, so that $w(b, a)$ is defined.

The difference

$$q_w(a, b) = 1 - w(a, b) - w(b, a) \tag{1.13}$$

is the degree to which events a and b occur simultaneously.

Define now

$$w^*(a, b) = w(a, b) + \tfrac{1}{2} q_w(a, b). \tag{1.14}$$

Clearly, we then have

$$w^*(a, b) = \tfrac{1}{2} + \tfrac{1}{2}[w(a, b) - w(b, a)], \tag{1.15}$$

and therefore

$$w^*(a, b) + w^*(b, a) = 1. \tag{1.16}$$

We now make the following assumption.

ASSUMPTION 1.5   *For any* $t = t(w)$ *and any* $a, b, c \in P_t \cup N_t$, *whenever* $w^*(a, b) \geq \tfrac{1}{2}$ *and* $w^*(b, c) \geq \tfrac{1}{2}$, *then*

$$w^*(a, c) \geq \max[w^*(a, b), w^*(b, c)]. \tag{1.17}$$

This assumption means simply that function $w^*(x, y)$ satisfies the so-called *strong stochastic transitivity* [see, e.g., Luce (1959)]. The role of this assumption will be to ensure the transitivity of the order of events in subjective time. Let us introduce the following definition.

DEFINITION 1.4   Let $t = t(w)$, and let $a, b \in P_t \cup N_t$. The relation $\leq_t$ on $P_t \cup N_t$ is defined by

$$a \leq_t b \qquad \text{iff} \qquad w^*(a, b) \geq \tfrac{1}{2}. \tag{1.18}$$

Moreover, let $a \sim_t b$ if $a \leq_t b$ and $b \leq_t a$, while $a <_t b$ if $a \leq_t b$ and not $b \leq_t a$. We then have the following theorem.

THEOREM 1.6   *Relation* $\leq_t$ *is connected and transitive on* $P_t \cup N_t$. *Relation* $\sim_t$ *is an equivalence in* $P_t \cup N_t$, *while* $<_t$ *is a strict ordering on the set of equivalence classes of* $\sim_t$.

Thus, for each t, the events that occurred not later than t are ordered by relation $\leq_t$. As before, this ordering is representable on an ordinal scale, say, by some function s_t. Actually, we shall assume more and accept the following condition.

ASSUMPTION 1.6   Let $t = t(w)$. Function $w^*(x, y)$ on $P_t \cup N_t$ is such that there exists a function

$$s_t: P_t \cup N_t \to R \tag{1.19}$$

satisfying the conditions

$$s_t(a) \leq s_t(b) \qquad \textit{iff} \quad a \leq_t b \tag{1.20}$$

and

$$\textit{if} \quad 0 < w^*(a, b) = w^*(c, d) < 1,$$

$$\textit{then} \quad s_t(b) - s_t(a) = s_t(d) - s_t(c). \tag{1.21}$$

Moreover, if s_t^* *is any other function satisfying* (1.20) *and* (1.21), *then for some* $\alpha > 0$ *and* β *we have*

$$s_t^* = \alpha s_t + \beta. \tag{1.22}$$

Thus, s_t is a representation of subjective time on an interval type scale, and Assumption 1.6 replaces, in fact, a series of assumptions known from the literature [see, e.g., Debreu (1958); Luce (1959); Pfanzagl (1968); Kranz *et al.* (1971); Roberts (1979)] concerning the existence of interval-type scales induced by choice probabilities.

1.2.3 Interval Scale for Objective Time

One of the main goals in these considerations is to characterize various types of distortions of time perception. In other words, the problem will be to study the relations between the subjective time and the objective time. For this purpose we need the latter to be measurable on the same type of scale as the former.

Now, one of the reasons that the real time is measurable on an interval scale is simply that intervals of time may be mapped into objects of some relational system that admits the appropriate measurability, such as angles (in clocks) or lengths. This mapping is very important to ensure (indirect) comparability and concatenations. Direct comparisons of nonoverlapping intervals of time are impossible because intervals of time *occur just once* and cannot be repeated. Also, unless two time intervals are adjacent, they cannot be concatenated directly. Thus, it is the possibility of "freezing" the lengths of time intervals by mapping them into some other objects that ultimately enables us to concatenate and compare the lengths of time intervals.

We shall begin by stating the conditions that must be met by the class of objects that will serve as representations of time interval durations. Keep in mind that our ultimate goal is to measure time through measurement of some auxiliary objects. Intuitively, this means that we have a set, say D, of objects d, d', d'',..., which could be combined by some operation, denoted here by $\oplus$, corresponding to addition, so that one can form new objects, such as $d \oplus d''$. Also, the objects in D may be compared according to some relation $\prec$ with properties of "less than." The System $\mathscr{D} = \langle D, \oplus, \prec \rangle$ should satisfy the appropriate assumptions, allowing measurement on a ratio scale. This means, among others, that to every $d \in D$ there corresponds a value $f(d)$ such that $f(d) < f(d')$ whenever $d \prec d'$ and $f(d \oplus d') = f(d) + f(d')$.

Next, there must be a mapping of time intervals, that is, pairs of the form (w, w') with $w \leq w'$, into elements of D. Thus, to each (w, w') with $w \leq w'$ there corresponds an element $F(w, w')$ of D, and its measure $f[F(w, w')]$ is taken as a representation of the duration of the time interval (w, w').

The best-known example is when elements of D are angles measured on a clock. The angles are measurable on a ratio scale, and the duration of a time interval is simply taken as the measure of the angle swept by the hand of the clock during the interval in question (in this case, even the units of angle measurement have temporal connotations, being called minutes and seconds).

To proceed formally, the above outline suggests that we have to extend the basic system (1.1) to a quadruplet

$$\langle Z, W, \mathscr{D}, F \rangle, \tag{1.23}$$

Where Z and W are as before and satisfy Assumptions 1.1–1.6 and $\mathscr{D}$ is a relational system forming the so-called *extensive structure* [see Roberts and Luce (1968)]

$$\mathscr{D} = \langle D, \oplus, \prec \rangle, \tag{1.24}$$

where $\oplus$ is a binary operation and $\prec$ a binary relation in D such that $\mathscr{D}$ satisfies the following assumptions with the definition

$$dEd' \quad \text{if neither} \quad d \prec d' \quad \text{nor} \quad d' \prec d. \tag{1.25}$$

ASSUMPTION 1.7   For all $d, d', d'' \in D$

$$[d \oplus (d' \oplus d'')]E[(d \oplus d') \oplus d'']. \tag{1.26}$$

This assumption asserts associativity of the operation $\oplus$. This means that when one takes a number of elements of D in some specific order and performs the operation $\oplus$ on them, the result does not depend on the way in which one groups the elements to perform the operation.

ASSUMPTION 1.8   Relation $\prec$ is asymmetric and negatively transitive, that is, for all $d, d', d'' \in D$,

$$\text{if} \quad d \prec d', \quad \text{then not} \quad d' \prec d; \tag{1.27}$$

$$\text{if} \quad d \prec d', \quad \text{then either} \quad d \prec d'' \quad \text{or} \quad d'' \prec d'. \tag{1.28}$$

The term *negative transitivity* for property (1.28) was used by Roberts (1979). Observe that it is equivalent to the property: if not $d \prec d'$ and not $d' \prec d''$, then not $d \prec d''$, which explains the term.

ASSUMPTION 1.9   *For all d, d′, d″ ∈ D,*

$$d \prec d' \Rightarrow [(d \oplus d'') \prec (d' \oplus d'') \Leftrightarrow (d'' \oplus d) \prec (d'' \oplus d')]. \qquad (1.29)$$

This assumption simply states that if $d \prec d'$, then one can concatenate an arbitrary element d'' to both sides of the inequality from either direction and still preserve the inequality.

Now inductively define nd as

$$1d = d, \qquad nd = (n-1)d \oplus d. \qquad (1.30)$$

ASSUMPTION 1.10   *For all $d_1, d_2, d_3, d_4 \in D$, if $d_1 \prec d_3$, then there exists a positive integer n such that $(nd_1 \oplus d_2) \prec (nd_3 \oplus d_4)$.*

This assumption is known as the Archimedean axiom. Roughly, it asserts that multiples nd_3 grow faster than multiples nd_1 and that the difference in the rate of growth may compensate for any initial difference.

One can prove [see Roberts and Luce (1968)] the following theorem.

THEOREM 1.7   *Under Assumptions 1.7–1.10, there exists a real-valued function f on D such that*

$$d \prec d' \qquad iff \quad f(d) < f(d'), \qquad (1.31)$$

and

$$f(d \oplus d') = f(d) + f(d'). \qquad (1.32)$$

Moreover, if f^* is any other function satisfying (1.31) and (1.32), then $f^* = \alpha f$ for some $\alpha > 0$.

Returning to system (1.23), there remains the last element of it, namely, F. Denote

$$W^* = \{(w_1, w_2) \in W \times W : w_1 \leq w_2\}. \qquad (1.33)$$

Letting

$$D^* = \{d \in D : f(d) \geq 0\}, \qquad (1.34)$$

then

$$F: W^* \to D^* \qquad (1.35)$$

is a function that assigns to every pair w, w' with $w \leq w'$ the value $F(w, w')$ in D^*.

Function F is interpreted as the mapping that "records" time intervals in that form of elements of D, or, more precisely, as those elements of D that have nonnegative measure f. What remains now is only to specify the assumptions that must be met by the function F.

The general idea here is such that the time interval from w to w' (with $w \leq w'$) will be, on the one hand, assigned the measure $t(w') - t(w)$ and, on the other hand, the measure $f[F(w, w')]$ of the element $F(w, w')$ in D. Such an assignment must be consistent in the sense that shorter time intervals must be assigned smaller (in the sense of measure f) elements of D, and the concatenations of intervals must be assigned the concatenations (in the sense of operation $\oplus$) of the corresponding elements in D. We formulate this as the following assumption.

ASSUMPTION 1.11   *Function* $F: W^* \to D^*$ *is such that for every* $w_1 \leq w_2 \leq w_3 \leq w_4$ *we have*

$$F(w_2, w_3) \preccurlyeq F(w_1, w_4) \tag{1.36}$$

and

$$F(w_1, w_3) = F(w_1, w_2) \oplus F(w_2, w_3). \tag{1.37}$$

To complete the construction of the objective time, we define the function $t(w)$ on W by choosing some arbitrary w_0 and setting

$$t(w_0) = 0 \tag{1.38}$$

and

$$t(w) = \begin{cases} f[F(w_0, w)] & \text{if} \quad w_0 \leq w, \\ -f[F(w, w_0)] & \text{if} \quad w \leq w_0, \end{cases} \tag{1.39}$$

where function $t(w)$ gives the time measurement on an interval-type scale.

1.3   PSYCHOLOGICAL MODELS OF FORMATION OF JUDGMENTS $w(a, b)$

In this section we shall return to the fuzzy relation w discussed in Sections 1.2.1 and 1.2.2. It will be convenient to use the notation $w_t(a, b)$ whenever $t = t(w)$, so that w_t stands for the judgments about the order of occurrence of events a and b made at time t.

We shall now try to formulate some plausible and psychologically justifiable hypotheses about the properties of the function $w_t(a, b)$, depending on t and on the true times $T(a)$ and $T(b)$ of occurrence of a and b.

1.3.1   Chains of Events

We may expect that, as a rule, only some events will be remembered. Some of these events are connected by semantic relations, which determine their order. For instance, the beginning (event a) and end (event b) of a trip are two events whose order is known without any confusion.

Another situation in which the order of events a and b is known without confusion occurs if each of these events is known to have occurred during some period and one remembers without confusion the order of these periods. For instance, one may remember that events a and b occurred in childhood, one during the vacations following fifth grade and the other during the vacations following sixth grade. Such examples suggest introducing the concept of a chain of events.

DEFINITION 1.5   We say that the events $C = \{a_1, a_2, \ldots, a_n\}$ form a *chain* at time t if

$$T(a_1) < T(a_2) < \cdots < T(a_n) \tag{1.40}$$

and

$$w_t(a_j, a_{j+1}) = 1 \qquad \text{for} \quad j = 1, 2, \ldots, n - 1. \tag{1.41}$$

In other words, events form a chain at time t if their true order of occurrence is remembered without confusion at time t.

Generally, the class of events remembered by a given person at time t will contain a number of chains. These may be related in various ways, in particular they may be "linked."

DEFINITION 1.6   Let $C_1 = \{a_1, a_2, \ldots, a_n\}$ and $C_2 = \{b_1, b_2, \ldots, b_m\}$ be two chains at t. We say that C_1 and C_2 are *linked* if there exist i, j, and k such that $1 \le i \le n$ and $1 \le j < k \le m$ with $w_t(b_j, a_i) = 1$, $w_t(a_i, b_k) = 1$, and $T(b_j) < T(a_i) < T(b_k)$.

Linkage between two chains of events means simply that there is one event in one chain that may be unambiguously inserted between two (not necessarily consecutive) events from the other chain.

If chains $C_1 = \{a_1, \ldots, a_n\}$ and $C_2 = \{b_1, \ldots, b_m\}$ are linked, then one can define indices $r'(i)$ and $r''(i)$ as

$$r'(i) = \max\{j : w_t(b_j, a_i) = 1\} \tag{1.42}$$

and

$$r''(i) = \min\{k : w_t(a_i, b_k) = 1\}. \tag{1.43}$$

Then the pair of events $(b_{r'(i)}, b_{r''(i)})$ in chain C_2 is the smallest interval in the chain that covers event a_i in chain C_1.

From Assumption 1.5 the next theorem follows.

THEOREM 1.8   If $j \le r'(i)$ and $k \ge r''(i)$, then

$$w_t(b_j, a_i) = 1 \qquad \text{and} \qquad w_t(a_i, b_k) = 1. \tag{1.44}$$

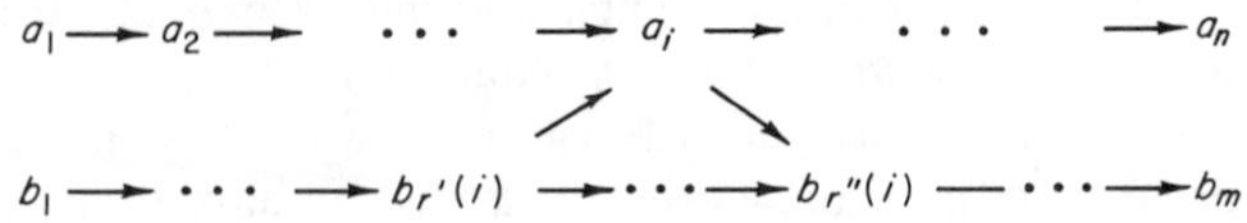

$$a_1 \longrightarrow a_2 \longrightarrow \quad \cdots \quad \longrightarrow a_i \longrightarrow \quad \cdots \quad \longrightarrow a_n$$

$$b_1 \longrightarrow \cdots \longrightarrow b_{r'(i)} \longrightarrow \cdots \longrightarrow b_{r''(i)} \longrightarrow \cdots \longrightarrow b_m$$

Fig. 1.1. Linkage of events.

Indeed, since C_2 forms a chain, we have

$$w_t(b_j, b_{j+1}) = \cdots = w_t(b_{r'(i)-1}, b_{r'(i)}) = 1. \tag{1.45}$$

Moreover, $w_t(b_{r'(i)}, a_i) = 1$ by definition of linkage, hence repeating the condition for strong stochastic transitivity (Assumption 1.5), we obtain the assertion.

The notion of linkage is perhaps best explained by Fig. 1.1, on which the arrows indicate lack of confusion about the order of occurrence of events. From this figure the next theorem is evident.

THEOREM 1.9 *If chains C_1 and C_2 are linked, then the following sequences of events also form chains:*

$$C_3 = \{a_1, \ldots, a_i, b_{r''(i)}, \ldots, b_m\},$$
$$C_4 = \{b_1, \ldots, b_{r'(i)}, a_i, \ldots, a_n\}$$

and

$$C_5 = \{b_1, \ldots, b_{r'(i)}, a_i, b_{r''(i)}, \ldots, b_m\}.$$

Actually, one of the main sources of information about the time of the occurrence of past events is usually a selected chain of some events that serve as a sequence of "pointers." Such pointers allow a person to locate other events between two pointers. In subsequent sections we shall formulate some hypotheses aimed at explaining the mechanisms underlying the creation of pointer chains.

Returning to the problems of linkage of chains of events, one should mention that two chains may be linked several times. As an example of several interrelated chains, imagine a person who, in addition to his job, is involved in some other activities, for example, church or politics. It is then quite possible that there is a sequence of events, all related to the job, that the person in question remembers and can order in relation to time (e.g., his promotions, salary increases). On the other hand, there may also be another sequence, related to the second area of activity, for example, meetings or demonstrations, that form a chain; that is, their order is known. It is psychologically plausible that the person in question may have some difficulties in answering if asked to compare the events from the above-mentioned two chains. However, such comparison may be unambiguous for *some* events from two chains, in which case we have a linkage.

1.3.2 Selection of Events for Memory

We shall now present a model that will attempt to capture the psychological mechanisms underlying the selection of events that enter the long-term memory.

Every person, in his activities, witnesses a stream of events of various kinds. These may be both external events, that is, changes of states of outside world, or internal events, that is, his thoughts, wants, and so forth.

Some of these events will be remembered later, and some will not. To simplify the terminology, let us agree to call the stream of events witnessed by the person in question *pre-events*, so that only some pre-events will become events stored in the memory.

In intuitive terms, the model will be as follows. Suppose that the pre-event e_n occurs at some time t_n. This pre-event may be more or less "important" for the observer; the degree of importance will determine both the probability that e_n will enter the long-term memory and the duration for which it will remain there.

Formally, this idea will be expressed by the assumption that each pre-event e_n is assigned a category, or label, that expresses its importance, curiosity level, and so on.

When the pre-event e_n occurs, it will also be assumed that it activates some kind of readiness for remembering pre-events of some types, depending on the type of the pre-event e_n.

To illustrate how the model operates, suppose that the types (labels) of events are $x, y, z, \ldots$. Suppose that the pre-event e_n (occurring at t) is of type x, say. At that time, the person may be either in the state of readiness for events of type x or not.

In the first case, with the occurrence of e_n two things happen: first, e_n becomes stored in long-term memory, for the period X (i.e., until time $t + X$), where X is random, with the distribution depending on the type of event. Second, the occurrence of e_n (pre-event of type x) causes a possible extension of state of readiness for events of type x and state of readiness for events of some other types (the set of these types depending on x).

In the second case, when there is no state of readiness for events of type x at time t, the pre-event e_n is not stored in long-term memory. However, the modification of state of readiness occurs as in the preceding case.

In more picturesque terms, the pre-event occurs either in "favorable" or in "unfavorable" conditions. In the first case, it becomes stored; in the second case, it is not. However, in both cases, it modifies the conditions by making them more "favorable" for events of certain types.

Let us now formulate the assumptions of the model.

ASSUMPTION 1.12   *There exists a set M of labels (or event types) and a function $g: Z \to M$ that to every event $a \in Z$ assigns the type $g(a) \in M$.*

Now let 2^M denote the class of all subsets of M, including the empty set $\emptyset$. The elements of 2^M will be denoted $A, B, \ldots$, with or without subscripts.

We shall now introduce the notion of a state of receptivity of a person at a given time.

DEFINITION 1.7   The *receptivity* state, or *readiness* state, at time t will be a pair

$$s = (A, \tau), \tag{1.46}$$

where $A \in 2^M$ and $\tau: M \to [0, \infty)$ is a function such that $\tau(x) = 0$ for $x \notin A$ and $\tau(x) > 0$ for $x \in A$.

The interpretation of state $s = (A, \tau)$ at t is as follows. If $x \in A$, then the person is receptive for events of type x, and he will remain receptive to such events until at least the time $t + \tau(x)$.

The role of state (A, τ) is described by the next assumption, which will use two functions, namely,

$$h: M \to 2^M \tag{1.47}$$

and

$$\lambda: M \times M \to (0, \infty). \tag{1.48}$$

ASSUMPTION 1.13   *Suppose that at time t the person is in state (A, τ) and that an event e of type $x = g(e)$ occurs. Then*

(a)   *The state (A, τ) changes to the state (A', τ'), where*

$$A' = A \cup h(x) \tag{1.49}$$

and

$$\tau'(y) = \begin{cases} \tau(y) & \text{if } y \notin h(x), \\ T_{x,y} & \text{if } y \in h(x), \end{cases} \tag{1.50}$$

where $T_{x,y}$ is a random variable with exponential distribution with parameter $\lambda(x, y)$, so that

$$P(T_{x,y} > u) = e^{-\lambda(x,y)u}, \qquad u > 0. \tag{1.51}$$

The random variables $T_{x,y}$ are independent for different pairs (x, y).

(b)   *Event e becomes stored in long-term memory if $x \in A$ and is not stored otherwise.*

The assumption about the appearance of pre-events remains to be specified. Here we shall make a simplifying assumption that pre-events occur at equally spaced time points, and their types are sampled independently from the set M of types with the same distribution.

Before we state this assumption formally and draw some consequences from it, it is worthwhile to give some informal outline of the general perception theory, thus providing a justification of the assumption.

According to the interpretation of the term "event", as specified at the beginning of Section 1.2, events are instantaneous changes of state of some part of the perceived world. This does not mean that a person who remains in a completely stationary environment will not witness any events: in fact, events in such cases are generated by purposive inspection of the organized configuration of objects surrounding the perceiver. The generating factor here is the movement of eyes, head, rotation of the body, or even attention shifts.

For a more precise description, one may introduce a unit of conscious perception, to be referred to as "glance." The subject then makes a sequence of glances, with various combinations of repetitions, at the objects, thus forming some order from the objects distinguished.

In other words, even for a stable configuration of objects, the subject generates a dynamic system of events, due to the process of cognition; he remembers what he saw earlier and what he saw later. Moreover, he has a feeling for the amount of perceptual work that he invested into the construction of knowledge about the object.

One may assume that the parameters of this process are the number of glances, the duration of a glance, and the frequency of revisits. The short-term memory keeps score of not only various values of these parameters but also of the semantic path, generated by perception, rising and decay of some meanings, connected with a glance or a series of glances, and so on. Thus, the subject not only "unfolds" the configuration of objects into a multidimensional dynamic event process, but he also uses this sequence to form subjective temporal evaluations of his own perception.

Consequently, the theory of time introduced in the preceding section applies here. In some sense, one can then speak of local and variable pasts, futures, and presents of the configurations of objects, dynamized by the process of perception.

This process of perception, incidentally, must be distinguished from loose, spontaneous, and passive glances.

In cases in which the situation changes, the perceptual work is very much the same, except that it must be faster, sharper, and more dynamic than in the case of stationary situations. More precisely, the frequency of events (glances) in the process of perception of a given situation results from a control by the observer, the criterion being semantic continuity.

Events, as already mentioned, may also be generated by mental operations on events, that is, by imagining something about them (what would happen if...), inference, and so on.

It is worth stressing that the perception process, as understood here, is partially controllable. The physiological base of this process is as stated, that is, spontaneous eye movement accompanied, if necessary, by body movement, head rotation, and so on. The criterion of semantic continuity allows for economy of perceptual work, in the sense that, even if eye and head movements cannot follow the path, say, of a tennis ball, there exists sufficient supplementary knowledge to allow us to complement the gaps and preserve the semantic continuity and smoothness of the situation, that is, its understanding.

Whether the events are generated by active visual perception or are internal, that is, concerning thoughts, wants, and so on, they may be assumed to occur with sufficient frequency, so that one can reasonably assume that they occur at equally spaced time points.

ASSUMPTION 1.14 *The pre-events occur at equally spaced time points, say,...,* $-1, 0, 1, 2, \ldots$. *If e_n is the pre-event occurring at $t = n$, then its type is $k = g(e_n)$ with probability p_k, $k \in M$. The types of different pre-events are independent.*

Now consider the function h given by (1.47) and the set

$$U_k = \{x : k \in h(x)\} \tag{1.52}$$

of those types that cause modification of the state of readiness for events of type k. Define

$$Q_k = \sum_{j \notin U_k} p_j, \tag{1.53}$$

so that Q_k is the probability that an event will not cause any modification of the state of readiness for type k.

From Assumptions 1.12–1.14 the theorems below follow.

THEOREM 1.10 *Probability $P(k)$ that an event of type k will become stored in the long-term memory is*

$$P(k) = \sum_{i \in U_k} \frac{p_i e^{-\lambda(k,i)}}{1 - Q_k e^{-\lambda(k,i)}}. \tag{1.54}$$

THEOREM 1.11 *The probability that a pre-event will become stored in the long-term memory is*

$$P = \sum_{k \in M} \sum_{i \in U_k} p_k p_i \frac{e^{-\lambda(k,i)}}{1 - Q_k e^{-\lambda(k,i)}}. \tag{1.55}$$

For the proofs of these theorems, see the Appendix at the end of this chapter.

Let us now explore some consequences of Theorems 1.10 and 1.11. The values $\lambda(k, i)$, which appear in formulas (1.54) and (1.55), have the following interpretation: the reciprocal $1/\lambda(k, i)$ is the expected duration of the state of receptivity to events of type k caused by events of type i, provided $i \in U_k$, that is, $k \in h(i)$. This last condition means simply that we take into account here only those types i (for a fixed type k) that cause some change of receptivity to events of type k.

Suppose that $\lambda(k, i) = b(k)$, independently of i. This means that the average duration of state of readiness for events of type k depends only on k, not on the type of pre-event that induces this state. This assumption may perhaps be taken as a reasonable approximation to real situations.

We formulate it as the following condition.

Condition A   For every $k \in M$ we have

$$\lambda(k, i) = b(k) \tag{1.56}$$

for every $i \in U_k$.

In this case formulas (1.54) and (1.55) simplify, and we have the following corollary.

COROLLARY 1.1   *Under Condition A, we have*

$$P(k) = \frac{(1 - Q_k)e^{-b(k)}}{1 - Q_k e^{-b(k)}} \tag{1.57}$$

and

$$P = \sum_{k \in M} \frac{p_k(1 - Q_k)e^{-b(k)}}{1 - Q_k e^{-b(k)}}. \tag{1.58}$$

By simple checking we obtain the next theorem.

THEOREM 1.12   *Under Condition A, probability $P(k)$ decreases with the increase of Q_k and $b(k)$.*

This result agrees with intuition. Indeed, Q_k is the probability that a pre-event *will not* modify the state of readiness for pre-events of type k. Consequently, the higher probability Q_k, the more chances that the state of readiness for events of type k will "wear off" and terminate, thus preventing events of this type to enter the long-term memory.

On the other hand, $b(k)$ is the reciprocal of the average time of readiness for an event of type k, due to one "impulse" (a pre-event of the appropriate type $i \in U_k$). Consequently, as $b(k)$ increases, the average state of readiness for events of type k decreases.

The practical consequences of Theorem 1.12 are as follows. To ensure that more events of a given type will be remembered, one has either to increase the average length of state of readiness for events of this type, when such a state is "triggered" by some other event, and/or increase the class of types of events that trigger such readiness. The first effect may be attained by the conscious effort of keeping the attention directed at events of a given type. The second effect may be enhanced by developing associations that will cause the occurrence of events of other types to direct the attention to events of a given type.

Let us now add some more simplifying assumptions.

Condition B   Assume that the set M consists of a finite number of types, say m, and let $p_k = 1/m$ for $k = 1, 2, \ldots, m$. Moreover, assume that each set U_k consists of the same number r of elements. Finally, let Condition A be satisfied, and let $b(k) = b$ for all k.

We then have the following.

THEOREM 1.13   *Under Condition B, we have*

$$P(k) = \frac{r}{r + m(e^b - 1)} \qquad (1.59)$$

and, consequently, $P = P(k)$.

Since P is the probability that a pre-event, of whatever type, will become stored in the long-term memory, the reciprocal

$$\frac{1}{P} = 1 + \frac{m}{r}(e^b - 1) \qquad (1.60)$$

is the average time between storage of two pre-events. Again, this formula agrees with intuition. Since pre-events occur at a rate of one per unit time, the average time between two pre-events entering long-term memory cannot be less than 1. Next, when the number m of types increases, the average time $1/P$ also increases, since it becomes increasingly seldom that a "matching" pre-event will occur recently enough for the state of readiness to last.

Similarly, as b increases, the average time $1/b$ of state of readiness decreases, which will tend to increase the average time $1/P$ between two storages.

Finally, r is the size of sets U_k. Thus, an increase of r means an increase in the number of types that "trigger" the state of readiness for pre-events of a given type and, consequently, leads to a decrease of the average distance between two remembered pre-events.

Figure 1.2 shows the graphs illustrating changes of the probability P under the change of parameters.

1.3.3   Memory of Event Orders

The main objective of this section is to explain the distortions in the perception of time, that is, differences between objective and subjective time of occurrences of events. One of the forms of such distortions to be analyzed is

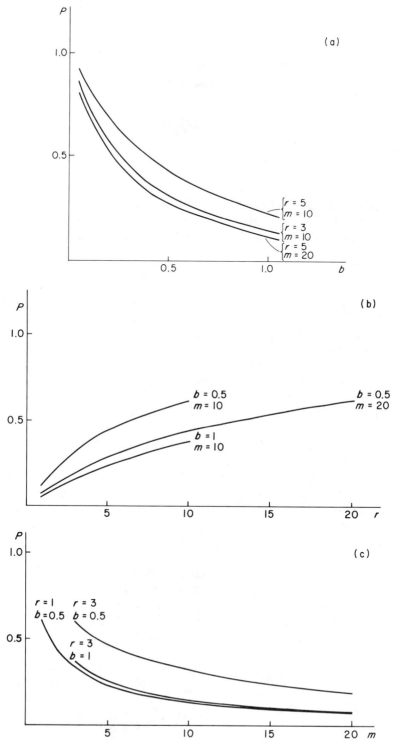

Fig. 1.2. Probability of storage in long-term memory: (a) $b-P$ axis, (b) $r-P$ axis, and (c) $m-P$ axis.

the *reversal*: it occurs if there are two events a and b such that their true times of occurrence satisfy the inequality $T(a) < T(b)$; yet at some time $t > T(b)$ we have $s_t(b) < s_t(a)$, where $s_t(a)$ and $s_t(b)$ are the subjective times of occurrences of a and b perceived at time t. In short, events a and b are reversed at t, if in reality a occurs earlier than b, while according to subjective recollection at time t, the event b occurred earlier than a.

According to the definition of subjective time from Section 1.2.2, we have $s_t(a) < s_t(b)$ if and only if $w_t(a, b) \geq \frac{1}{2}$. Consequently, to explain the distortions of time, it is necessary to present assumptions about the changes of $w_t(a, b)$.

Let S_t be the set of events that occurred prior to t, entered the long-term memory of the person considered, and were still in memory at t. Naturally, the set S_t is time-indexed; that is, with each event $a \in S_t$ there is the associated time $T(a)$ of its occurrence.

The basic ideas introduced are those of *linkage* between events. By "linkage" we mean a connection, causal, logical, emotional, and so on, that helps in remembering the order of two events. We shall assume that the events, as well as linkages between them, are subject to decay in time.

Formally, linkage is a binary relation in S_t, say,

$$L_t \subset S_t \times S_t. \tag{1.61}$$

The condition $(a, b) \in L_t$ will be interpreted as the fact that at t there is a linkage between events a and b. Observe that, if $(a, b) \in L_t$, then both a and b are in S_t; that is, they are present in long-term memory.

We shall assume that the sets S_t and L_t are random. The changes in the set S_t are due to two competing factors: on the one hand, as the time passes, new pre-events occur, and each of them enters the set S_t with probability as given in the preceding section. On the other hand, the events in S_t decay in memory, so that some of them disappear. It will be assumed that the probability that an event $a \in S_t$ will not belong to $S_{t + \Delta t}$ (i.e., will leave the long-term memory between times t and $t + \Delta t$) is

$$\mu(k) \Delta t + o(\Delta t), \tag{1.62}$$

where $\mu(k)$ is a positive constant depending on the type of the event and $o(\Delta t)$ a quantity satisfying the relation $\lim_{\Delta t \to 0} o(\Delta t)/\Delta t = 0$.

It follows that the total "life" X of an event of type k from the moment it enters the long-term memory is exponential:

$$P(X > y) = e^{-\mu(k)y}. \tag{1.63}$$

Consequently, the probability that a pre-event that occurred at time $t - n$ will be in S_t (i.e., will still be in long-term memory at t) may be calculated as follows. If the pre-event is of type $k \in M$, then it will enter the long-term memory with probability $P(k)$ given by (1.54). Thus, the probability that this pre-event will still be present in n long-term memory units of time later equals

$$P(k)e^{-\mu(k)n}. \tag{1.64}$$

Multiplying by p_k, the type k probability, and summing over all possible k we obtain

$$P_{n,t} = \sum_{k \in M} p_k e^{-\mu(k)n} \sum_{i \in U_k} \frac{p_i e^{-\lambda(k,i)}}{1 - Q_k e^{-\lambda(k,i)}}. \tag{1.65}$$

Under Conditions A and B, this reduces to

$$P_{n,t} = \frac{r/m}{r + m(e^b - 1)} \sum_{k \in M} e^{-n\mu(k)}. \tag{1.66}$$

Let us now add the next condition.

Condition C   For all $k \in M$ we have $\mu(k) = \mu$.

Then, under Conditions A, B, and C we have

$$P_{n,t} = \frac{re^{-\mu n}}{r + m(e^b - 1)} = Cq^n, \tag{1.67}$$

where

$$C = \frac{r}{r + m(e^b - 1)}, \qquad q = e^{-\mu}.$$

Let us now try to formulate some assumptions about the appearance of linkage. Consider a pre-event that enters the long-term memory at some time n; assume that it is of type k. At that time, it may become linked with some of the preceding pre-events already in the long-term memory.

Qualitatively speaking, the probability that the new pre-event, say, e, will become linked with a given pre-event e' (which occurred earlier than e) depends on two factors: one is the temporal distance between the occurrences of e and e', and the other is the type of events e and e'. Generally, the longer the difference $T(e) - T(e')$ is, the less chance there is for a linkage. On the other hand, if we have $g(e) = g(e')$, that is, if pre-events e and e' are of the same type, the chances for a linkage are higher.

Formula (1.67) states, in essence, that an event that enters the long-term memory remains there for an exponentially distributed random time (or a mixture of exponentially distributed random variables in the case in which Condition C does not hold).

The necessary conditions for the appearance of a linkage between an event occurring at t and an event occurring at time $t - n$ are mentioned above. If the first of these events is of type k and the second of type j, then the probability of linkage between them is assumed to be

$$u(k, j)P(j)P(k)e^{-n\mu(k)}, \tag{1.68}$$

where $u: M \times M \to [0, 1]$ is a function satisfying the conditions

$$u(k, k) \geq u(k, j) \quad \text{and} \quad u(k, k) \geq u(j, k) \quad \text{for all} \quad j, k \in M. \tag{1.69}$$

This last condition simply states that the probability of linkage is highest when the types of the events agree.

Naturally, Condition C is an idealization. It states that all events, regardless of their type, have the same average duration in the long-term memory. In reality, some events remain in memory for periods comparable in length to the lifetime of the subject, while others disappear from memory after few hours, days, or months.

According to the interpretation of the concept of linkage, its existence between two events ensures that their true order is remembered without ambiguity, and, consequently, the reversal does not occur. Apart from reversal, other deformations of time perception may occur.

Generally, for any two given events a and b with $T(a) < T(b)$, let

$$m_t(a, b) = \frac{s_t(b) - s_t(b)}{T(b) - T(a)}. \tag{1.70}$$

If the reversal does not occur, the value $m_t(a, b)$ is positive. Assuming that both objective and subjective time are measured in the same units, the perception of time may be said to be *positively distorted* if $m_t(a, b) > M$ and *negatively distorted* if $0 < m_t(a, b) < m$, where $0 < m < 1 < M$. Finally, if $m \leq m_t(a, b) \leq M$, we say that perception of time is *distortion-free*, where m and M are suitable constants.

Imagine now that we have some events a and b with $T(a) < T(b)$, which are linked at some time t. We also have a certain number of events that occurred between a and b and became stored in long-term memory.

Clearly, a positive distortion means that the subjective time is "stretched out": it seems longer than it is in reality. On the other hand, in the case of negative distortions, the subjective time is "contracted": it seems to be shorter (flows faster) than in reality.

To formulate the hypotheses, let us introduce one more concept. If $\max(T(a), T(b))$ is close to t, we speak of subjective perception of *local time*, while if $\max(T(a), T(b))$ is considerably less than t (i.e., both events a and b occurred long time before t), we speak of *distant past*.

To formulate the hypotheses, let C_t denote the class of events that occurred between a and b and became stored in long-term memory for such a time that they are still remembered at t.

HYPOTHESIS 1.1   Suppose that the number of events in C_t is small. Then the local time will tend to be positively distorted, and the distant past will tend to be negatively distorted.

As an example, imagine a person who arrives at some place (event *a*) and waits for some event *b* (e.g., arrival of his friend). There are no events of interest occurring between *a* and *b*. Then the real waiting time $T(b) - T(a)$ will seem long during waiting and shortly after. However, in retrospection such waiting periods will seem to be short.

One can also observe a phenomenon opposite to that in the above hypothesis—the case of many events in the set C_t.

HYPOTHESIS 1.2   Suppose that the number of events in the set C_t is large (i.e., the time between a and b is "event-dense"). Then the local time will tend to be negatively distorted, and the distant past will tend to be positively distorted.

As an example, imagine an interesting and eventful period such as vacation at a summer camp. The time "locally" flows fast (i.e., is negatively distorted), while in retrospect, such an eventful vacation may appear longer than in reality.

1.4   MECHANISMS OF COMPARISON OF TIME INTERVALS

One of the important features of the world, which to a large extent influences our perception and memory of time, is the existence of some periodic events. Such periodic events are most often related to the 24-hour period of days and nights; they may also have an annual character (e.g., Christmas), as well as weekly, monthly, and so on, character.

The existence of such events allows us to introduce corrections in the subjectively perceived time. For instance, imagine two 1-week periods of one's life, one full of exciting events and the other dull and uneventful. According to the hypothesis of Section 1.3, after a long time, the first of these weeks will seem longer than the second. However, if the subject knows that both periods were 1 week long, he may force a correction on his subjective judgments.

In the domain of short-time intervals, it is hard to find such universal periodic events, and it is plausible that the memory of the length of time intervals is based on direct mapping of time into something corresponding to length.

The type of situations and questions that will now be explored is illustrated as follows. Suppose that a person receives a certain stimulus that lasts for a short time, for example, a second or a few seconds. The stimulus may be visual, audial, and so on. Imagine now that at some time later there is another stimulus of the same or different kind. The person is then usually able to make the comparison of the durations of the stimuli (this does not mean that he will not make the wrong judgment).

Now, with stimuli duration in the range of fractions of a second to several seconds, one cannot expect to have any well-established periodic events that could serve as a basis for comparisons. It appears reasonable that such stimuli are mapped into some memory traces, with their durations represented in some way by the sizes of these traces. An argument for the existence of such a mapping is also the fact that in real-life (nonexperimental) situations, when there is no motivation to remember the durations of stimuli, one can still answer the question "Which of the two stimuli lasted for a longer time?"

A simple model of remembering and comparison of such stimuli will be presented below, together with the possible experiments. It will be conjectured that the stimuli whose duration falls in a certain range are simply mapped into "internal" traces," the latter being measurable on the absolute counting scale, representing the number of cells.

For a mapping of temporal stimuli into internal traces, in a way enabling later comparisons, a stimulus A that is, say, twice as long as stimulus B must be mapped into a trace that is twice as long as the trace of stimulus B (at least if the duration of A and B does not exceed a certain limit). Clearly, to have a possibility for such mapping, the person must have an "internal clock" that allows him to build a memory trace cell by cell with uniform rate. This "internal clock," incidentally, is a different concept than the internal clock that is set for the 24-hour period.

Suppose that the first stimulus (A) has duration T_A and the second stimulus (B) has duration T_B. Moreover, they are separated by a pause of duration t^*, and finally, the comparison is made at time t_c after the termination of the second stimulus. We shall assume that, during the pause and the period preceding the comparison, the memory traces are subject to random changes, to be described below. Generally, let $x_A(t)$ and $x_B(t)$ denote the sizes of memory traces of stimuli A and B at time t. The temporal configuration of the stimuli is presented on Fig. 1.3. Thus the values compared are actually $x_A(t^* + T_B + t_c)$ and $x_B(t_c)$.

To deduce some testable consequences, one has to formulate some assumptions about the nature of changes of processes $x_A(t)$ and $x_B(t)$ and about the comparison process.

Let us observe that, from the measurement-theory point of view, we are in the situation described by the assumptions of Section 1.2.3 about extensive

T_A $\qquad\qquad$ t^* $\qquad\qquad$ T_B $\qquad\qquad$ t_c

Fig. 1.3. Temporal configuration of stimuli.

structures for representation of time. Now, however, we add some assumptions about the changes of the representations that occur in the passage of time before the comparison.

The model suggested here will be based on the following intuitive conceptualization of the processes that occur in memory. When a stimulus, visual or audial, is perceived, it leaves the trace in memory, which at time of its termination of the stimulus represents its duration faithfully. If $x_S(0)$ is the representation of S at its termination, then this value is assumed to be equal to some measure of S. If $x_S(t)$ were allowed to remain invariant, the stimuli could be preserved for future comparisons without error. In reality, at later time t, the size of representation of S may differ from $x_S(0)$. In other words, we assume that $x_S(t)$ is a certain process that starts with the initial value $x_S(0)$ and is then allowed to vary in a random fashion, thus possibly affecting the comparison. This phase lasts for some time; eventually the trace of the stimulus is either removed from memory or it becomes transformed into some other representation, based on the principle of matching, to be discussed later.

At the beginning, let us consider only the first phase, when the traces of the stimuli to be compared are both present in their original memory compartments.

We shall make the following assumptions.

ASSUMPTION 1.15 *Given the stimulus S, its memory trace* $x_S(t)$, $t \geq 0$, *constitutes a Wiener process, with* $x_S(0) = m(S)$ *where* $m(S)$ *is a measure of the stimulus S on a ratio scale. Moreover, the changes* $x_S(t + u) - x_S(u)$ *have expectation zero and variance* $\sigma^2 t$.

ASSUMPTION 1.16 *At the time of comparison of A and B, the values of the processes* $x_A(t)$ *and* $x_B(t)$ *are compared, and it is asserted that stimulus A had longer duration than B if* $x_A(t) > x_B(t)$.

According to Assumption 1.16, the decision that both stimuli were of the same duration could occur only if $x_A(t) = x_B(t)$; since this event has probability zero, it appears reasonable to modify Assumption 1.16 by allowing the decision of equality of stimuli A and B.

ASSUMPTION 1.16′ *At the time of comparison of A and B, the stimuli are judged to be of equal duration if*

$$|x_A(t) - x_B(t)| \leq d, \tag{1.71}$$

where $d > 0$ *is some threshold. In the opposite case, stimulus A or B is asserted as longer depending on whether* $x_A(t) > x_B(t) + d$ *or* $x_A(t) < x_B(t) - d$.

Let us now calculate the probability, given the initial values of stimuli to be $m(A)$ and $m(B)$, that stimulus A will be judged as longer than stimulus B. We start from calculations according to Assumption 1.16.

Looking at Fig. 1.3, it is clear that, at the comparison time, the memory trace of stimulus A equals $X_A = x_A(t^* + T_B + t_c)$, and hence it has the normal distribution

$$N(m(A), \sigma^2(t^* + T_B + t_c)). \tag{1.72}$$

Similarly, the value of the memory trace of stimulus B at the time of comparison has normal distribution

$$N(m(B), \sigma^2 t_c). \tag{1.73}$$

Finally, since measures $m(A)$ and $m(B)$ represent the durations of stimuli A and B on a ratio scale, we must have

$$m(A) = kT_A, \qquad m(B) = kT_B. \tag{1.74}$$

We have then the following.

THEOREM 1.14 *Under Assumption 1.16', the probability that stimulus A will be perceived as longer than stimulus B is*

$$P_{A>B} = \frac{1}{\sqrt{2\pi}} \int_{-\infty}^{+\infty} e^{-w^2/2} \Phi\left(w\sqrt{\frac{t^* + T_B + t_c}{t_c}} + \frac{k(T_A - T_B) - d}{\sigma\sqrt{t_c}} \right) dw, \tag{1.75}$$

the probability that B will be perceived as longer than A is

$$P_{B>A} = \frac{1}{\sqrt{2\pi}} \int_{-\infty}^{+\infty} e^{-w^2/2} \Phi\left(w\sqrt{\frac{t_c}{t^* + T_B + t_c}} + \frac{k(T_B - T_A) - d}{\sigma\sqrt{t^* + T_B + t_c}} \right) dw, \tag{1.76}$$

and, finally, the probability that both stimuli will be judged as equal is

$$P_{A=B} = 1 - P_{A>B} - P_{B>A}. \tag{1.77}$$

For the proof see the Appendix at the end of this chapter.

The above model involves several parameters and some control variables. The latter are T_A, T_B, and t^*, that is, the durations of stimuli A and B and that of the pause that separates them. The parameters are k, σ, d, and t_c. Regarding k, σ, and d, a look at the formulas in Theorem 1.14 reveals that the values $P_{A>B}$ and $P_{B>A}$ (hence also $P_{A=B}$) remain the same if k, σ, and d are changed in the same proportion. This means that one should take as independent parameters the two ratios obtained by dividing by the third parameters, say, $k' = k/\sigma$ and $d' = d/\sigma$.

Regarding t_c, it is arguable whether it is a controlled variable or a parameter. A way of possibly controlling it would require distracting the subject in some manner, preventing him from making the comparison before the time he is told to do so by the experimenter. Since such a scheme may be hard to achieve, it is better to assume that the subject is instructed beforehand to make the comparison. He is then ready to do so after some physiologically necessary period t_c following the termination of the second stimulus. In this case, t_c is a parameter to be estimated.

Figures 1.4 and 1.5 show the changes of probabilities $P_{A>B}$, $P_{B>A}$, and $P_{A=B}$ under changes of the control variables and parameters of the model. Thus, Fig. 1.4 gives the changes under the change of the duration T_A of the first stimulus. Here the second stimulus B lasts for $T_B = 1$ (second), with the period t^* separating the stimuli equal to 2 seconds. Other parameters are assumed to be $t_c = 0.25$ seconds and the ratios $k/\sigma = 10$ and $d/\sigma = 1$.

This means that after the first stimulus of duration T_A, there is a pause of 2 seconds followed by stimulus B lasting for 1 second, and the comparison occurs 0.25 seconds later. Thus, the comparison occurs at 3.25 seconds after the termination of the first stimulus. It follows that the trace of the first stimulus is subject to random distortions for 3.25 seconds, while the trace of the second stimulus is subject to such distortions only for 0.25 seconds. As a result, the size of the memory trace of the second stimulus represents the size of this stimulus more faithfully than the trace of the first stimulus.

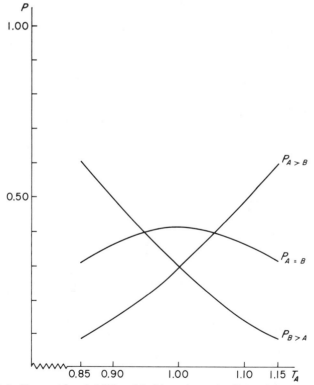

Fig. 1.4. Changes of probabilities of decisions about stimuli A and B. ($T_B = 1.00$.)

Figure 1.4 shows that when the stimuli are equal ($T_A = T_B = 1$), the chances of recognizing them as equal are about 42%, while the chances for each of the decisions $T_A > T_B$ and $T_B < T_A$ are about 29%. When $T_A = 1.15$, hence the first stimulus is 15% longer than the second stimulus, the chances of declaring the stimuli as equal are about 30%, while the probability of a correct decision is about 60%, so that the chances of asserting that $T_B > T_A$, while in fact $T_A/T_B = 1.15$, are less than 10%.

Next, Fig. 1.5 shows the dependence of probabilities of various decisions regarding the stimuli $T_A = 1.2$ seconds and $T_B = 1$ second on the duration of the pause t^*. As may be expected, when t^* increases, probability $P_{A>B}$ of a correct decision decrease, while probability $P_{B>A}$ of incorrect decision increases. Regarding probability $P_{A=B}$ that the stimuli will be judged as equal, it initially increases and then decreases.

The latter phenomenon might be considered as somewhat disquieting. In fact, one can expect that as the duration of the pause increases, the memory of

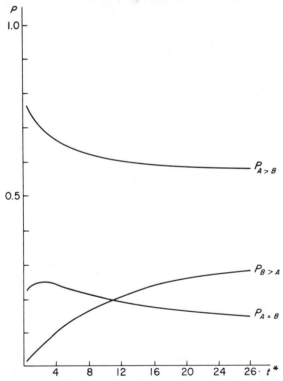

Fig. 1.5. Changes of probabilities of decisions about stimuli A and B, where $T_A = 1.2$, $T_B = 1.00$, and $t_c = 0.25$.

the first stimulus becomes increasingly fuzzy. Consequently, the probability that it will be judged as of the same duration as the second stimulus should increase with an increase in the duration of the pause.

One should remember, however, that the model covers a relatively small range of possible durations of time intervals. In other words, when the length of the pause exceeds a critical value, other mechanisms of remembering begin to operate.

Consequently, for experimental results restricted to short durations of stimuli and the pause, one can use maximum likelihood methods to estimate the values t_c, k/σ, and d/σ.

1.5   SOME PROBLEMS OF EXISTENCE OF EVENTS: AN ALTERNATIVE APPROACH

Thus far we have interpreted events as *instantaneous* changes of state of some fragment of reality. In this interpretation the events had no duration: each event, at the moment of its occurrence, was leaving its "imprint," or "temporal trace," on the time axis. The *present*, being the set of events that occur "now" had no duration; rather it was just a point moving in one direction on the axis of time, sweeping more and more of the future and leaving behind more and more of the past.

When one accepts a somewhat more common interpretation of events, the situation becomes different. In ordinary language, "war," "concert," "rally," and so on, are events, even though their temporal locations take intervals of time, not just single points.

Let us accept this interpretation of events and try to put it into some kind of formal framework. As opposed to the analysis of Sections 1.2 and 1.3, we shall not attempt to define time starting from the notion of an event. Instead, we shall proceed in the opposite direction, taking the time axis as a starting point and trying to find a convenient and fruitful way of representing events.

As a primitive notion, which will not be defined formally, we shall take the idea that for any event a and any time t we may speak of the "degree to which a is at t" or the "degree to which t belongs to a." As an example, take an event such as a = "Rain last Monday." Clearly, if it rained last Monday from 3 to 5 p.m., then time $t = 4$ p.m. belongs to a, while $t = 10$ a.m. does not. Moreover, some times t may belong to the event a only in some degree, which is less than 1 but positive.

Let $f_a(t)$ denote the degree to which the time t is in event a. We assume that

$$0 \le f_a(t) \le 1 \qquad \text{for all } a \text{ and } t, \tag{1.78}$$

with $f_a(t) = 1$ representing full membership.

Thus, $f_a(t)$ may be regarded as the membership function of the fuzzy set of moments when event a occurs. We can then define the usual rules from the algebra of fuzzy set to form an algebra of events such as

$$f_{a \wedge b}(t) = \min(f_a(t), f_b(t)), \qquad (1.79)$$

$$f_{a \vee b}(t) = \max(f_a(t), f_b(t)), \qquad (1.80)$$

and

$$f_{a'}(t) = 1 - f_a(t). \qquad (1.81)$$

Naturally, the function $f_a(t)$ may be defined only for the events that have already occurred. This may be formally described by indexing this function by the "present" and postulating that it is defined for all values t from the past of a given present. Formally, if T stands for the present, then we deal with functions $f_a^T(t)$, defined for all $t \leq T$.

As an idealization, we may accept the following condition of "freezing the past":

$$f_a^T(t) = f_a^{T'}(t) \qquad \text{for all } t \leq T \leq T'. \qquad (1.82)$$

Next, one can introduce the concept of an event being "in" another event or leaving on it a "temporal trace." Suppose that a and b are two events. We say that a occurs *during* b or that a is *in* b, if $f_a^T(t) \leq f_b^T(t)$ for all t for which both sides are defined. In this case, we shall also write $a \subset b$. Obviously, such inclusion may be characterized in the usual way, for example, by the condition $a \wedge b = a$.

Moreover, the relation of inclusion is invariant under changes of T; that is, if it holds for some T, then it also holds for all $T' \leq T$.

Now, one should also distinguish the events that occurred with degree 1 from those that occurred with degree less than 1. Correspondingly, we introduce the concept of *normal* event a, characterized by the condition.

$$\sup_{t \in T} f_a^T(t) = 1. \qquad (1.83)$$

The crucial issue in the theory of events is in the analysis of the relation of causal connection between events. For that purpose it is essential to distinguish classes of events that may occur at different times and yet are acceptable as "exemplars" of the same event. This requires the relation of "sameness" of two events, which holds regardless of their temporal locations (e.g., a *war* is an event whose various copies may occur at various time intervals).

Let us denote the relation of sameness by $\approx$; we shall therefore write $a \approx b$ if a and b are the same events, possibly occurring at different times. The events are, as a rule, preceded, accompanied, and followed by some other events. For instance, the event a such as *earthquake* is preceded by specific readings of various instruments, specific behavior of animals, and so on. It is accompanied by such events as specific noises and followed by still other events.

Such events often occur in conjunction with a given event a. Naturally, such temporal coincidence is a necessary, but by no means sufficient, condition for a causal relation between events (e.g., specific readings of various instruments are not *causes* of an earthquake, even if they should unavoidably precede it).

The generality of the above approach, in which events are represented as fuzzy subsets of the time axis, is its appealing feature; however, it makes formal analysis impossible unless one imposes some structure on the class of all events or, alternatively, distinguishes a class of events that possesses sufficiently rich structure.

We shall follow the second approach, distinguishing a class of events of interest.

DEFINITION 1.8   We say that an event a is *regular* if for all $t_1 < t_2 < t_3 \le T$ we have

$$f_a^T(t_1) > f_a^T(t_2) \Rightarrow f_a^T(t_2) \ge f_a^T(t_3). \tag{1.84}$$

Denote

$$N^T(a) = \{t : t \le T \text{ and } f_a^T(t) = 1\}. \tag{1.85}$$

We have then the following theorem.

THEOREM 1.15   *If $N^T(a) \ne \varnothing$, then $N^{T'}(a) \ne \varnothing$ for all $T' \le T$. Moreover, if the event a is regular and $N^T(a) \ne \varnothing$, then $N^T(a)$ is an interval on the time axis.*

For the proof see the Appendix at the end of this chapter.
We also have Theorem 1.16.

THEOREM 1.16   *The class R of all regular events is closed under conjunction, that is, if $a, b \in R$, then $a \wedge b \in R$.*

For the proof see the Appendix at the end of this chapter.

As opposed to the intersections, the unions of regular events need not be regular. This property holds, however, under some additional assumptions.
Denote

$$M^T(a) = \{t : t \le T \text{ and } f_a(t) = \sup_{t \le T} f_a^T(t)\}, \tag{1.86}$$

so that $M^T(a) = N^T(a)$ if the event a is normal.
We then have the next theorem.

THEOREM 1.17   *Let a and b be regular and let*

$$M^T(a) \cap M^T(b) \ne \varnothing. \tag{1.87}$$

Then event $a \vee b$ is also regular.

For the proof see the Appendix at the end of this chapter.

Observe that the notion of a regular event corresponds to the notion of normal predicates from the following chapter.

1.6 TIME AND FREQUENCY OF EVENTS

Let us return for a while to the relation "occurs earlier than" discussed in Sections 1.2 and 1.3. One may expect that it ought to be closely connected with the relation "less frequent than." The intuitive idea is that when one waits for an occurrence of two events, say, a and b, on average, the more frequent event will occur earlier.

To formulate these intuitive notions in the proper setup, let us proceed as follows. Consider a family of Poisson processes, each with its own "type" of events. Let the types be indexed by some parameter, say, z, so that for each z we have a Poisson process of events $a(z)$; let us denote this process by π^z.

Thus, π^z is a sequence of events, or, equivalently, a sequence of random times of their occurrences

$$T_1^z < T_2^z < \cdots \tag{1.88}$$

such that the successive differences $X_i^z = T_{i+1}^z - T_i^z$ are independent and identically distributed, with exponential distribution

$$P(X_i^z \le x) = 1 - e^{-\lambda_z x}, \tag{1.89}$$

where λ_z is some positive constant characterizing the process π^z. [For information about Poisson processes, see, for instance, Feller (1957) or nearly any other textbook on probability theory.]

It is well known that the expected time between events in the process π^z equals $1/\lambda_z$, i.e.,

$$E(X_i^z) = 1/\lambda_z. \tag{1.90}$$

Moreover, the Poisson process is unique among point processes in the sense of having the "forgetting property": given any t, the waiting time for the next event after t also has the same exponential distribution (1.89). Thus the random variable $Y_z(t)$ defined as

$$Y_z(t) = \min\{T_i^z - t : T_i^z - t > 0\} = \min\{T_i^z : T_i^z > t\} - t \tag{1.91}$$

has the property

$$P(Y_z(t) \le x) = 1 - e^{-\lambda_z x}, \tag{1.92}$$

and, consequently,

$$E(Y_z(t)) = 1/\lambda_z. \tag{1.93}$$

Consider now two independent Poisson processes π^{z_1} and π^{z_2}, and for a fixed t, consider the probability that the nearest event from process π^{z_1} will occur earlier than the nearest event from the process π^{z_2}, that is, that the waiting time, counting from t, for an event from π^{z_1} will be shorter than the waiting time for an event from π^{z_2}. Thus,

$$p(z_1, z_2) = P(Y_{z_1}(t) < Y_{z_2}(t))$$

$$= \int_0^\infty e^{-\lambda_{z_2}x} \lambda_{z_1} e^{-\lambda_{z_1}x}\, dx$$

$$= \frac{\lambda_{z_1}}{\lambda_{z_1} + \lambda_{z_2}} = \left(1 + \frac{1/\lambda_{z_1}}{1/\lambda_{z_2}}\right)^{-1}. \tag{1.94}$$

Using formula (1.90) we may therefore write

$$p(z_1, z_2) = \left(1 + \frac{E(X_i^{z_1})}{E(X_i^{z_2})}\right)^{-1}, \tag{1.95}$$

so that the required probability is expressed through the ratio of the mean inter-event times in the two processes.

If $E(X_i^{z_1}) = E(X_i^{z_2})$, that is, if the average inter-event times in the two processes are equal, then $p(z_1, z_2) = \frac{1}{2}$, as expected. When $E(X_i^{z_1})/E(X_i^{z_2})$ approaches zero, that is, when the events from π^{z_1} tend to occur much more frequently than those from the process π^{z_2}, we have $p(z_1, z_2) \to 1$; that is, it is much more likely that an event from π^{z_1} will occur first.

On the other hand, if $E(X_i^{z_1})/E(X_i^{z_2})$ becomes very large, the situation is opposite: the events from π^{z_2} tend to occur more often than those from π^{z_1}, and hence $p(z_1, z_2) \to 0$: it is unlikely that an event from π^{z_1} will precede an event from π^{z_2} (counting from time t).

The probabilities $p(z, z')$ allow one to construct a time scale, similarly as for relation w from Section 1.2. In fact, we have the following.

THEOREM 1.18   *Probabilities $p(z, z')$ satisfy strong stochastic transitivity, and, consequently, relation $\preccurlyeq$ defined by $z \preccurlyeq z'$ iff $p(z, z') \geq \frac{1}{2}$ is transitive.*

For the proof see the Appendix at the end of this chapter.

We may now construct an interval time scale, by building from increments of the average waiting times $1/\lambda_z$. Indeed, we have

$$E(X_i^{z_1})/E(X_i^{z_2}) = p(z_1, z_2)^{-1} - 1 \tag{1.96}$$

from the basic relation connecting $p(z_1, z_2)$ and the average waiting times. Thus, if we arbitrarily take as a unit of time the mean inter-event time in the process π^{z_1}, that is, put $E(X_i^{z_1}) = 1$, then we obtain

$$E(X_i^{z_2}) = \frac{p(z_1, z_2)}{1 - p(z_1, z_2)} \tag{1.97}$$

as the average inter-event time in the process π^{z2}. Proceeding in this way, all average inter-event times are expressed in the same unit.

The above construction is of a rather theoretical character because of the difficulties and inadequacies in evaluating probabilities by subjective means. In fact, let us imagine a concrete situation of two Poisson processes in real life. Suppose one of the processes is the breakage of china occurring at one's home from time to time. As another process, take, for example, the occurrences of major earthquakes as reported in the news. One can estimate the subjective probability (of a given person) that, from a given moment, the breakage of china will occur earlier than a major earthquake. Given this probability, say, p, the odds $p/(1 - p)$ represent the mean time between major earthquakes expressed in units equal to the mean interbreakage time for china in the household in question.

1.7 FUZZIFICATION OF TIME AND STOCHASTIC PROCESSES

Finally, let us sketch a simple model to show how a fuzzification of time, as reflected in the ordering relations w from Sections 1.2 and 1.3, might arise. The idea is to consider the possibility of a series of consecutive reversals of the "neighboring" events.

Consider a discrete time stochastic process of events of some kind, say, a_1, $a_2, \ldots$. These events may constitute a Markov chain, for example.

Suppose now that each sample path $a_1, a_2, \ldots$ of the process is "shuffled" according to the following random scheme. We first generate an auxiliary process $\{X_n\}$, where the X_i's are independent with

$$P(X_n = 1) = r = 1 - {}^{\bullet}P(X_n = 0), \qquad n = 1, 2, \ldots. \tag{1.98}$$

Then, for $n = 1, 2, \ldots$, events a_k are permuted in such a way that if $X_n = 1$, the events a_n and a_{n+1} are transposed; if $X_n = 0$, the events at these places remain unchanged.

For instance, if the first few events in the original process are ABCDEFG..., and the sequence of successive values of X_k is 0, 1, 1, 1, 0, 0, 1, ..., then the initial elements of the permuted sequence are ACDEBFH....

If a_n is the event that was originally at time n and $a(n)$ is the event at time n after the shuffling is completed, then we have $a(n) = a_{n+1}$ whenever $X_n = 1$; whereas if $X_n = 0$, then $a(n) = a_n$ if also $X_{n-1} = 0$, and in general, $a(n) = a_{n-m}$, $m = 1, 2, \ldots$, if $X_{n-1} = X_{n-2} = \cdots = X_{n-m} = 1$, $X_{n-m-1} = 0$. Consequently, we have

$$P(a(n) = a_{n+1}) = r, \tag{1.99}$$

$$P(a(n) = a_{n-m}) = r^m(1 - r)^2, \qquad m = 0, 1, 2, \ldots. \tag{1.100}$$

The expected shift to the left is then

$$E = -r + \sum_{m=0}^{\infty} mr^m(1-r)^2 = -r + (1-r)^2 r \sum_{m=0}^{\infty} r^m$$

$$= -r + r(1-r)^2/(1-r)^2 = 0, \tag{1.101}$$

which agrees with the fact that for each event shifted to the right by m places, there are m events shifted to the left by one place.

This construction defines the process $a_n, n = 1, 2, \ldots$, of the events as they occur after the time scale is permuted. Since the probability of a change of order of two events whose true distance is k equals r^k, this model captures the property that the chances of a reversal decrease with an increase of the distance between events. A more elaborate model of increase of fuzziness of time, by using a more complex shuffling scheme, may easily be proposed. One could also include in this model the possibility that fuzziness increases as time passes.

1.8 COMMENTS

Besides the problems of subjective perception of time, it is also of interest to know how humans use their internal events as pointer events, how they reconstruct the order of external events, to which degree this reconstruction is correct, and how many of the external events are used in this reconstruction. In particular, it is of interest to determine which of the internal systems are most often used as pointer systems: epistemic, emotional, deontic, or motivational (e.g., "It happened when I wanted to do x," "It happened when I had to do x," "It happened when I was so happy about x").

The perception of time allows us to delve into the structure of the stream of consciousness—when the boundedness of memory and attention leaves many events outside the scope of consciousness, as well as when the events creatively constructed by the perceiver (thinking) do not permit perception of too many external events, thus leading to only a schematic record of the external world.

One of the problems is how consciousness overcomes the subjective discontinuity of time and space caused by competition of external and internal processes in consciousness.

Certainly, we have here a mechanism for complementing those "places" that are cognitively indetermined by knowledge. However, which and how many of such knowledge insertions are necessary to achieve the impression of smoothness of time is very difficult to establish. Perhaps the analysis of formation of judgments concerning perception of time or space may provide the material for analysis of connections among structures of judgment, perception, and knowledge.

1.9 SUMMARY AND DISCUSSION

In analyzing objective time, the two main questions concern the succession or simultaneity of events (and the connection between the order of events and causal relations between them) and the duration of time intervals separating two events. For analysis of the subjective time, the basic questions concern its relation to objective time and the factors that account for distortions of perception of time.

The idea, explored in this chapter, that time is an abstraction of the order of events originates with Leibniz. Next, Kant provides a causal explanation of succession and simultaneity, agreeing with Newtonian physics. He also analyzes the epistemological genesis of the physical temporal order; he seems to be the first to appreciate subjective time and causality and their role in the knowledge of objective time.

Many post-Kantian authors, such as Balmes (1848) and Lotze (1887), studied time; these, however, were mostly analyses of the Kantian interpretation rather than novel ideas.

Lechalas (1896) was the first to base his theory of time on the principle of determinism; he assumed that the states of the system determine one another and that the determining state is, by definition, earlier than the determined one.

Lechalas also stressed the importance of reversibility of physical phenomena for the theory of time; the problem being that of invariance of physical laws under time reversal. More precisely, Lechalas was of the opinion that one may obtain an ordering of events from causal relation: if A determines B, then A must be earlier than B. He noted, however, the difficulty connected with this definition: two observers, applying the causal laws, may order the events in opposite directions, hence inducing opposite directions of time.

Lechalas saw some way of solving this dilemma by replacing the causal relations by semicausal, statistical relations. For Lechalas, only the "true" physical time was genuine as opposed to perceived subjective time.

The relativistic phase of the causal theory of time was inaugurated by Robb (1914), who was called the "Euclid of relativity." He analyzed the causal relations between events, with the temporal order of "before" and "after," which allows one to speak of succession only in the case when there is an invariant succession. For relativistic hypothesis, simultaneity and succession are defined relative to a given decomposition, and the order is required to be invariant with respect to all possible decompositions. In terms of invariant succession, Robb defined metric properties of time and space.

Carnap (1981) showed that the topological properties of space are definable in terms of time. Moreover, time is definable in terms of causal relations. He presented three axiomatic systems. In the first one, for example, he started from two primitives: spatiotemporal coincidence and priority of proper time (time of particle at rest in a measurement system). In terms of these relations he could define the topological properties of space–time, namely, groups of coincident elementary events, each lasting infinitesimally short and occupying infinitesimal amount of space that form the field of fundamental relations. Substantial causal actions operate between sets of coincident elementary events, that is, actions transmitted by successive coincident particles.

Because of a special, narrow meaning of causal relations, Carnap encountered conceptual difficulties, in particular, the impossibility of defining the temporal order of phenomena and their spatial propagation in terms of substantial causal relations. This difficulty vanished when discussing the corpuscular theory of light, but then substantial actions became discontinuous, and one could not speak of temporal order and causality for quantum phenomena.

Probably the most significant contribution to the causal theory of time is due to Reichenbach [see Reichenbach (1969, 1978)]. In 1924 he presented an axiomatization of relativity theory, and one year later he wrote a paper on causal structure of the world and the difference between past and future. He introduced a synthesis of the causal and statistical points of view on physical laws. His system is based on a relation more general than that of causal determination, namely, that of statistical implication. This implication is defined by a set of axioms and is a primitive concept in Reichenbach's theory; intuitively, A statistically implies B if, whenever A occurs, one can infer that B occurs with a nonzero probability.

If X statistically implies Y, but the converse is not true, then one says that X is earlier than Y. With this concept of implication, Reichenbach thus tried to derive the temporal order of events. The difference between past and future may now be explicated as follows: for inference about the future, one needs to know *all* determining causes, and for inference about the past, only some causes are sufficient.

However, even in his very elegant system, Reichenbach did not avoid conceptual difficulties. In particular, from the definition of the implication given above it follows that any part of a phenomenon statistically implies the whole phenomenon, which is contrary to intuition.

Also, Reichenbach did not make clear what is the logical type of the variables linked by statistical implication: are they propositions asserting frequency or do they range over the class of events?

In his book *The Direction of Time*, Reichenbach (1956) dealt with anisotropy of time and advanced the concept of branching time.

Both Carnap and Reichenbach, dealing with the causal explanation of simultaneity and succession, left unexplained the notion of duration. Russell (1927) gave a causal definition of this concept. Roughly, the definition is based on the notion of a continuous string of events representing no change or small changes. Thus, duration is defined through continuity of an object, that is, its duration in time.

Among a number of later works on time, we mention here those of Costa de Beauregard (1965), Watanabe (1966), and Grünbaum (1973), who dealt in particular with time reversal invariants in natural laws. The same topic was studied by Gödel (1949), in particular for relativity theory. One should also mention here the works of Schlegel (1961) and Swinburne (1968), as well as Mehlberg (1981), who, among others, dealt with psychological aspects of time.

This chapter [which is an extension of the theory presented in Nowakowska (1981d, 1982a)] takes as a starting point the lack of invariance of the temporal order of events from an entirely different angle than in relativity theory. The point is that the temporal order of events may change in an observer's memory, depending on such factors as actual proximity of the two events and the temporal distance separating the time of events from the time of judgment. Moreover, the judgments may be uncertain and may vary from occasion to occasion.

Specifically, suppose first that for any pair of events and time of comparison the subject is able to state which of the two events occurred earlier (or that they were simultaneous). If his assertions are consistent, we recover the overall order of the class of events in question, as the subject recalls it (this order need not coincide with the "true" order of these events). Sometimes, however, the subject may be so unsure of his recollection that his judgments are fuzzy, that is, concern only the degree to which one event precedes another. The question then arises: under which regularity assumptions does a class of fuzzy statements allow one to recover the (subjective) order of events?

Formally, we have here a fuzzy (subject-induced) relation (denoted W_t) on events. This relation may represent causal dependence between events, deterministic or not, or just merely accidental order of events. The question is to find formal conditions of consistence of such a relation.

We rely heavily on the theory of fuzzy sets, as introduced by Zadeh (1965). In the context of this chapter, the lack of certainty or the ambiguity of the order of events may be represented as a fuzzy set of pairs of events (A, B) in which the first element of the pair precedes the second. If the subject is uncertain as to whether A or B occurred earlier, both pairs (A, B) and (B, A) may belong to the fuzzy set in question in some degree. This is the meaning of the relation $W_t(A, B)$.

Let us now consider another type of question connected with time, namely, that of duration. Observe that an assertion about the duration of two time intervals (or two pairs of events) is of a different nature, from a logical viewpoint, than an assertion about the order of events. The former is based on a presupposition that time is measurable on an interval scale.

Again, one may ask the same question as before. In the nonfuzzy case, one may consider what conditions have to be met by a class of statements concerning comparison of time intervals to imply measurability of time on an interval scale. This measurability means, roughly speaking, that it is meaningful to say that some temporal distance is "twice as long" as another, etc.

Suppose, however, that we have a class of fuzzy statements about comparison of intervals, elicited from a subject, whose memory is fallible and, moreover, changes in time. Can one still assume measurability of the subjective time of this person on an interval scale? This chapter gives a set of conditions under which this is true.

Finally, let us consider the distortions of time perception. Here one may distinguish two basic types of distortions: those involving reversals, when one remembers event A as preceding event B while in fact the opposite holds, and those without reversals, when the order of events is remembered correctly, but one tends to overestimate or underestimate the real duration. The hypotheses advanced explain all types of distortions, the basic concept used in explanation being that of a pointer event, which serves as a "frame of reference." Some specific models are also devised for explaining which events enter the memory, and the mechanism of comparison of time intervals is offered.

To sum, the main difference between the theory of fuzzy time presented here and previous approaches lies in a unification in one model of the topics of time, perception, and memory. In particular, the problems of time acquire a special significance in semiotics (to be discussed in subsequent chapters), where the signs are produced and reproduced in time. Here the word "produced" is used in a special sense: every recognition and understanding of a sign may be regarded as a production of some other sign, due to specific properties of the perceptual process [for a detailed analysis of this idea, see Nowakowska (1967) as well as Nowakowska (1982b), where some new results in dynamic theory of perception are shown].

Even a static object is dynamized in the process of perception by movements of the eye over its surface. The subject makes a series of glances, thus establishing some order of inspection, hence also generating a series of events (in case of changing situations, one generates events on events).

The process of consecutive glances is partially controllable (see subsequent chapters for some specific hypotheses about this process).

Also, such sign structures as the natural language or various languages of nonverbal communication are temporal structures, subject to special organization constraints. By moving, in the perceiver's conscience from present to future, the sign structures undergo various transformations and deformations. The sequence of such structures ought to satisfy not only specific constraints for a given meaning, through order of words and sentences, but also some temporal constraints on durations of components of such sequences, and relations between these durations. Violations of such constraints lead to changes in meaning structures, more serious in case of more serious deformations. All such deformations and errors in temporal properties of the generated sign structures increase the necessity of additional perceptual work by introducing some conflicting meanings and deoptimizing standard cognitive processes. This, naturally, may be (and is) used in dramaturgy, public appearances, and everyday life. There is, however, a lack of systematic knowledge of semiotic role of time and a goal of one of the subsequent chapters is to originate a new domain of semiotics of time that will be foundational for all branches of semiotics advanced until now. In particular, such a theory might be of importance for the theory of drama, poetry, or dance, as well as for the social sciences and even artificial intelligence.

The process of fuzzification and forgetting of important "parts" of a sign structure has a self-accelerating character to be discussed in detail in the next chapters. After some time, the memory would contain only a "metanote" stating that "I used to know it quite well," "I used to remember it well," and so on.

It is also known that in artificially created multimedial temporal sign structures, such as drama, or in general literature, time is a special actor: it creates and solves conflicts, and the ways of deformation of perception of the past create planned tensions of varying degrees, are subject to interpretations, and so on.

In particular, one often uses the phenomenon of shrinking or lengthening of psychological time, with its layerlike and often only locally ordered character. Thus internal time often precedes objective time or oscillates between past and future, departing from the objective present through a translation or delayed comment of internal events in the present, which enters in turn their own past.

It appears that the semiotics of time suggested here, in view of good perspectives of experimental research and the possibilities of introducing rigorous methodology, may generate a breakthrough for the status of semiotics and its applications to social sciences, artificial intelligence, and foundations of computer sciences.

To conclude, analysis of time shows not a continuous, but a discrete, multidimensional, and often only sketchy structure of consciousness. It embeds discrete and often laconic and fragmentary perceptual events into a semantically complementary structure of internal events, giving the exterior events an impression of relative completeness and continuity of information. Due to a simultaneous partial control of many dimensions of consciousness and certain stochastic properties of the work of the brain (see Stochatic Model of Learning in Chapter 6), even when apparently only one dimension is controlled and subjective unidirectionality of consciousness is perceived, the consciousness is in fact multidimensional.

Economy of consciousness is also deeply related to multimodality of information (see chapter 3 on communication) and to the whole system of temporal and spatial pointers. They relativize external events that are related to other external and also to internal events—that is to other states of consciousness related to observation of events from a class (say) x, with meaning y. Pointer systems also mark internal events. Of course, consciousness very carefully distinguishes information and its carrier from the whole dynamic system of "localizing" pointers. The learning process uses the synergy of information, based both on similarity of the information content (meanings) coded in multimodal system as well as similarity of meta-information, that is, information about information. Repetitiveness of both external and internal events is an additional source of parsimony of the content of consciousness.

One of the attributes of a properly operating consciousness is unambiguous distinction between the situation when a given system plays the role of information carrier, and when it serves as meta-information. Such skill also lies at the foundation of creating intellectual conventions in mathematics and logic.

It seems that the dreams do not so much "debug" the content of consciousness, as—due to suppression of the mainstream of control—show multidimensionality and multidirectionality of consciousness, allowing random realizations of the whole multidimensional process.

Such understanding of consciousness may serve as a convenient starting point for simulation of cognitive processes in AI.

Linguistic representation of time may play an essential role in organization of data bases and knowledge representations. It also has considerable methodological value for computational linguistics.

APPENDIX

PROOF OF THEOREM 1.10

Suppose that a pre-event of type k occurs at some time $t = n$. According to Assumption 1.13, it will enter the long-term memory if there is a state of readiness for events of type k at time n. For the latter condition to exist, an event of type $i \in U_k$ must occur at some time preceding n and trigger the state of readiness to events of type k, which will last at least until the time n.

Let $n - j$ be the last time preceding n at which a pre-event of some type $i \in U_k$ occurs. The probability that at times $n - 1, n - 2, \ldots, n - j + 1$ there occur pre-events from the complement of the set U_k and at $n - j$ there occurs a pre-event of type $i \in U_k$ is

$$p_i Q_k^{j-1},\tag{A.1}$$

with Q_k defined by (1.53). The probability that the state of readiness for events of type k at time n, triggered by an event of type i at time $n - j$ is by Assumption 1.14,

$$e^{-\lambda(k,i)j}.\tag{A.2}$$

Summing over all possible i in U_k and over $j = 1, 2, \ldots$ we obtain

$$
\begin{aligned}
P(k) &= \sum_{i \in U_k} p_i \sum_{j=1}^{\infty} Q_k^{j-1} e^{-\lambda(k,i)j} \\
&= \sum_{i \in U_k} p_i e^{-\lambda(k,i)} \sum_{j=1}^{\infty} [Q_k e^{-\lambda(k,i)}]^{j-1} \\
&= \sum_{i \in U_k} \frac{p_i e^{-\lambda(k,i)}}{1 - Q_k e^{-\lambda(k,i)}},
\end{aligned}
\tag{A.3}
$$

which completes the proof of the theorem.

PROOF OF THEOREM 1.11

Observe that by the law of complete probability, we have, using (A.3),

$$P = \sum_{k \in M} p_k P(k) = \sum_{k \in M} \sum_{i \in U_k} p_k p_i \frac{e^{-\lambda(k,i)}}{1 - Q_k e^{-\lambda(k,i)}}.\tag{A.4}$$

PROOF OF THEOREM 1.14

Denote by X_A and X_B the sizes of memory traces of stimuli A and B at the time of comparison. Since X_A has distribution (1.72) and X_B has distribution (1.23), we may write, under Assumption 1.16′,

$$
\begin{aligned}
P_{A>B} &= P(X_A > X_B + d) = \int_{-\infty}^{+\infty} P(X_B \le z - d) \, dP(X_A \le z) \\
&= \frac{1}{\sigma\sqrt{2\pi t_c}\, \sigma\sqrt{2\pi(t^* + T_B + t_c)}} \int_{-\infty}^{+\infty} \int_{-\infty}^{z-d} \exp\left[-\frac{1}{2}\left(\frac{u - m(B)}{\sigma\sqrt{t_c}} \right)^2 \right] \\
&\quad \cdot \exp\left[-\frac{1}{2}\left(\frac{z - m(A)}{\sigma\sqrt{t^* + T_B + t_c}} \right)^2 \right] du \, dz.
\end{aligned}
\tag{A.5}
$$

Using (1.74) and substituting

$$v = \frac{u - m(B)}{\sigma\sqrt{t_c}},\tag{A.6}$$

we obtain $du = \sigma\sqrt{t_c}\,dv$, and, consequently,

$$P_{A>B} = \frac{1}{\sqrt{2\pi}}\frac{1}{\sigma\sqrt{2\pi}\sqrt{t^* + T_B + t_c}}\int_{-\infty}^{+\infty}\int_{-\infty}^{(z-d-kT_B)/(\sigma\sqrt{t_c})}$$

$$\cdot \exp\left(-\frac{1}{2}v^2\right)\exp\left[-\frac{1}{2}\left(\frac{z-kT_A}{\sigma\sqrt{t^* + T_B + t_c}}\right)^2\right]dv\,dz$$

$$= \frac{1}{\sigma\sqrt{2\pi}\sqrt{t^* + T_B + t_c}}\int_{-\infty}^{+\infty}\exp\left[-\frac{1}{2}\left(\frac{z-kT_A}{\sigma\sqrt{t^* + T_B + t_c}}\right)^2\right]$$

$$\cdot \Phi\left(\frac{z-d-kT_B}{\sigma\sqrt{t_c}}\right)dz. \tag{A.7}$$

where Φ is the distribution function of the normal distribution $N(0,1)$. Substituting

$$z = kT_A + w\sigma\sqrt{t^* + T_B + t_c}, \qquad dz = \sigma\sqrt{t^* + T_B + t_c}\,dw, \tag{A.8}$$

we finally obtain

$$P_{A>B} = \frac{1}{\sqrt{2\pi}}\int_{-\infty}^{+\infty}\exp\left(-\frac{1}{2}w^2\right)\Phi\left(w\sqrt{\frac{t^* + T_B + t_c}{t_c}} + \frac{k(T_A - T_B) - d}{\sigma\sqrt{t_c}}\right)dw, \tag{A.9}$$

which proves formula (1.75). To calculate $P_{B>A}$, i.e., the probability that the second stimulus B will appear longer than the first stimulus A, we may write, by Assumption 1.16′

$$P_{B>A} = P(X_A \leq X_B - d) = \int_{-\infty}^{+\infty}P(X_A \leq z - d)\,dP(X_B \leq z)$$

$$= \frac{1}{\sigma\sqrt{2\pi(t^* + T_B + t_c)}}\frac{1}{\sigma\sqrt{2\pi t_c}}\int_{-\infty}^{+\infty}\int_{-\infty}^{z-d}$$

$$\cdot \exp\left[-\frac{1}{2}\left(\frac{u - m(A)}{\sigma\sqrt{t^* + T_B + t_c}}\right)^2\right]\exp\left[-\frac{1}{2}\left(\frac{z - m(B)}{\sigma\sqrt{t_c}}\right)^2\right]du\,dz. \tag{A.10}$$

As before, substitution of $u = m(A) + v\sigma\sqrt{t^* + T_B + t_c}$, hence $du = \sigma\sqrt{t^* + T_B + t_c}\,dv$, yields

$$P_{B>A} = \frac{1}{\sqrt{2\pi}}\frac{1}{\sigma\sqrt{2\pi t_c}}\int_{-\infty}^{+\infty}\int_{-\infty}^{(z-d-m(A))/(\sigma\sqrt{t^* + T_B + t_c})}\exp\left(-\frac{1}{2}v^2\right)$$

$$\cdot \exp\left[-\frac{1}{2}\left(\frac{z - m(B)}{\sigma\sqrt{t_c}}\right)^2\right]dv\,dz$$

$$P_{B>A} = \frac{1}{\sigma\sqrt{2\pi}\sqrt{t_c}} \int_{-\infty}^{+\infty} \exp\left[-\frac{1}{2}\left(\frac{z - m(B)}{\sigma\sqrt{t_c}}\right)^2\right] \Phi\left(\frac{z - d - m(A)}{\sigma\sqrt{t^* + T_B + t_c}}\right) dz.$$

(A.11)

Finally, substituting $z = m(B) + w\sigma\sqrt{t_c}$, we have

$$P_{B>A} = \frac{1}{\sqrt{2\pi}} \int_{-\infty}^{+\infty} \exp\left(-\frac{1}{2}w^2\right) \Phi\left(w\sqrt{\frac{t_c}{t^* + T_B + t_c}} + \frac{k(T_B - T_A) - d}{\sigma\sqrt{t^* + T_B + t_c}}\right) dw,$$

(A.12)

which completes the proof of the theorem.

PROOF OF THEOREM 1.15

We have $N^T(a) \neq \varnothing$ if and only if there exists $t_0 \leq T$ with $f_a^T(t_0) = 1$. By (1.82), in the latter case we also have $f_a^{T'}(a) = 1$ for $T' \geq T$, which means that $N^{T'}(a) \neq \varnothing$.

To prove the second assertion, assume that a is regular and $N^T(a) \neq \varnothing$, so that $t_0 \in N^T(a)$ for some $t_0 \leq T$. If $N^T(a)$ were not an interval, there would exist points $t_0' \leq t_1 \leq t_0$ with t_0, $t_0' \in N^T(a)$ and $t_1 \notin N^T(a)$. But then, by regularity, we have

$$1 = f_a(t_0') > f_a(t_1),$$

(A.13)

hence also $f_a(t_1) \geq f_a(t_0)$, so that $f_a(t_0) < 1$, contrary to the assumption.

PROOF OF THEOREM 1.16

Denote for simplicity $a(t) = f_a^T(t)$, $b(t) = f_b^T(t)$, and let $c(t) = \min(a(t), b(t))$. Suppose that for some $t_1 < t_2$ we have $c(t_1) > c(t_2)$. Without loss of generality we may assume that $c(t_2) = a(t_2) \leq b(t_2)$. We then have

$$a(t_2) = c(t_2) < c(t_1) = \min(a(t_1), b(t_1)) \leq a(t_1).$$

(A.14)

Since event a is regular, we must have, in view of (A.14),

$$a(t_2) \geq a(t_3).$$

(A.15)

But then we have also

$$c(t_2) = a(t_2) \geq a(t_3) \geq \min(a(t_3), b(t_3)) = c(t_3),$$

(A.16)

which completes the proof.

PROOF OF THEOREM 1.17

As above, let $a(t) = f_a^T(t)$, $b(t) = f_b^T(t)$. Moreover, put $A = \sup_{t \leq T} a(t)$, $B = \sup_{t \leq T} b(t)$.

We have $M^T(a) = \{t : a(t) = A\}$, $M^T(b) = \{t : b(t) = B\}$. Let $t_0 \in M^T(a) \cap M^T(b)$. From the assumption of regularity it follows that both functions $a(t)$ and $b(t)$ are nonincreasing to the right of t_0 and nondecreasing to the left of t_0. Consequently, the same property holds for the function $c(t) = \max(a(t), b(t))$ in the intervals extending to the right and to the left of t_0. This proves the assertion.

PROOF OF THEOREM 1.18

Suppose that $p(z_1, z_2) = a \geq \frac{1}{2}$, $p(z_2, z_3) = b \geq \frac{1}{2}$. We then have $E(X_i^{z_1}) \leq E(X_i^{z_2}) \leq E(X_i^{z_3})$, and we may write

$$p(z_1, z_3) = (1 + E(X_i^{z_1})/E(X_i^{z_3}))^{-1}$$

$$\geq (1 + E(X_i^{z_2})/E(X_i^{z_3}))^{-1} = p(z_2, z_3) = b.$$

In a similar way we show that $p(z_1, z_3) \geq p(z_1, z_2) = a$, which means that

$$p(z_1, z_3) \geq \max(p(z_1, z_2), p(z_2, z_3)),$$

which proves strong stochastic transitivity.

2 EVENTS AND OBSERVABILITY

2.1 INTRODUCTION

In Chapter 1, devoted to the theory of time, a central underlying notion was that of an *event*. This notion was taken as a primitive and served for building the theory, in the sense that time was obtained as an abstraction from the order of events.

In this chapter we shall analyze the notion of an event. It may be argued that this notion is central for science, since scientific observations always concern events.

An "event" means, roughly speaking, a change of state of some fragment of the world. This notion is relatively simple in the physical sciences; in the social sciences, however, the situation is much more complex for the following reason. The concept of change presupposes the more basic concept of *state*: a change occurs if states are different at two different moments.

In the social sciences one often deals with changing objects of a fuzzy character; typical examples may be objects such as human attitudes, social phenomena such as inflation, and so on. A moment of reflection suffices for realizing the inherent difficulties in defining the concept of state necessary to determine whether or not a change occurred.

The analysis of this chapter will start from the simplest case—that of temporal changes of spatial locations of physical objects whose boundaries are not well defined (such as a cloud). The object, at any given time, is then defined through the function that specifies, for any given location, the degree to which an object is present at this location. The set of points at which the object is present in full degree is the *core* of the object, and points at which the object is present with some positive but not full degree, form a fuzzy "cloud" surrounding the object, or its "fuzzy boundary," referred to as the *carrier* of the object.

With this definition of an object, one encounters certain conceptual difficulties connected with explicating the notions such as "being a part of" or "spatial separation" of objects.

A closely related topic, discussed in Section 2.3, concerns the properties of objects, or predicates. Here, both the object and its property may be fuzzy, and the main issue is to separate those properties that are independent of the fuzziness of the object and to explicate the notion that a given object has a given property at some time t. The latter notion plays a central role in the subsequent theory of events: a class of properties of an object (or a set of objects) is a state description for a given time.

Consequently, in Sections 2.4 and 2.5, a theory of events is suggested. It starts with the notion of an "elementary" event, identified with a change of one property, and then proceeds to more complex events, built of elementary ones.

Since the notion of a property is fuzzy, so are the events resulting from changes of such properties. The suggested theory of fuzzy events differs from that advanced in fuzzy set theory [for recent results in this direction, see, e.g., Kwakernaak (1978, 1979); Dubois and Prade (1980); Muir (1981); or Klement (1980)]. It also differs (not only by introduction of fuzziness) from the approach to the theory of events used in probability theory, where events are simply subsets of a sample space (see, e.g., Feller (1957)].

One of the main issues to be discussed is the explication of the notion of an event *preceding* another, as well as the concept of causation between events. In Chapter 1, one section dealt with stochastic processes, that is, descriptions of random phenomena evolving in time, in the case of fuzzy time. In contrast, in this chapter, one section is devoted to the analysis of stochastic processes (specifically, Markov chains) in "crisp" time, but with fuzzy state space.

The remainder of this chapter is devoted to the analysis of the problems of observability. The topics discussed concern not only the constraints on observability related to fuzziness, hence to the degree of ambiguity involved in determining whether a given event occurred, but also constraints due to other causes, for example, the physical impossibility of observing one state variable if another one is observed.

The main issue discussed and formalized is as follows. First, certain combinations of state variables (i.e., values of attributes of some objects) may be jointly observable, and other combinations may be jointly unobservable. The constraints here could be due to various factors; whatever the reason, these constraints reveal some interesting structural regularities.

The constraints on joint observability are of special importance in the social sciences (the impact of them is often overlooked, though). A typical situation concerns the observations of human subjects, which may be changed when observing one characteristic (e.g., by learning, memory, or simply by letting the subject in the "secret"). Such a change may make it impossible to measure some other characteristic.

Another constraint on observability concerns situations when one observes, not the measured value, but a function (usually not one to one) of it. The importance of such constraints reaches far beyond the obvious cases of measurement errors or grouping the data. They are analyzed in some detail for the case of two Poisson processes, when an event in one of them "damps" the events in another.

Finally, the last section concerns the effects of outside interference and observer's decision on observability. The outside interference, in its fuzzified version, is called "filtering" and causes various events to become unobservable with certain probabilities. Such "filters" may be due to various factors. In the social sciences, the typical factors may be connected (e.g., in sampling surveys) with unreliability of interviewers, accessibility of respondents, and so on. Such filters operate jointly, in the sense of becoming superimposed on one another, and it is of interest to analyze the resulting effects.

As regards the observability constraints resulting from the observer's choice, they are expressed as *masks*, that is, temporal patterns of observations of different variables. The theory of masks suggested is an extension and generalization of that proposed by Klir (1972).

Since a mask is a temporal pattern of observation of state variables, one can introduce various notions, such as a horizon of a mask, its anchoring time, and its trace. These describe which data will be collected, hence they also determine the information gathered, thus imposing some constraints on the admissible inference about the phenomenon. Again, in the social sciences, the choice of a mask plays a crucial role in all longitudinal studies.

2.2   SPATIAL AND TEMPORAL FUZZINESS OF OBJECTS

We begin by developing some means to describe the location of an object at time t. The main issue here will be that the object in question may exist only to a certain degree and its location may be fuzzy. To appreciate the nature of the problems analyzed in this section, one may take objects such as "flood" or "epidemic" and try to think what it takes to tell at which precise moments these objects "exist" and where exactly they are located.

At the beginning objects will be understood simply as things that at any given time exist to a given degree and occupy a more or less precise location. To express it precisely, we start by introducing an appropriate conceptual scheme and tools for the description.

In the following, $\xi = (x, y, z)$ will denote the spatial coordinates in some coordinate system in space E and T will stand for the time axis.

Next, let $\mathcal{T}$ be the lattice of all fuzzy subsets of T, so that elements of $\mathcal{T}$ are functions

$$\varphi: T \to [0, 1], \tag{2.1}$$

and $\mathcal{T}$ is a lattice with respect to the operations $\wedge$ and $\vee$ defined by

$$(\varphi_1 \wedge \varphi_2)(x) = \min(\varphi_1(x), \varphi_2(x)), \tag{2.2}$$

$$(\varphi_1 \vee \varphi_2)(x) = \max(\varphi_1(x), \varphi_2(x)). \tag{2.3}$$

Similarly, let $\mathscr{E}$ be the lattice of all fuzzy subsets of the space $\mathscr{E}$, that is, elements of $\mathscr{E}$ are functions

$$g: E \to [0, 1], \tag{2.4}$$

with operations $\wedge$ and $\vee$ defined as above.

Finally, let $\mathscr{F}$ be the class of all mappings

$$f: T \to \mathscr{E}, \tag{2.5}$$

that is, mappings that to every moment $t \in T$ assign a fuzzy subset of E, or, equivalently, a membership function $f_t(\cdot)$ of this subset. The best way to interpret f_t is to think of a fuzzy set in space that changes in time.

Consider now a subset, say $\mathscr{G}$, of the Cartesian product $\mathscr{T} \times \mathscr{F}$, that is, a set of pairs of the form (φ, f) with $\varphi \in \mathscr{T}$ and $f \in \mathscr{F}$.

Before proceeding, it is worthwhile to clarify the intended interpretation of the concepts introduced thus far and also to provide some examples to guide intuition.

Let us first think of a fixed time t and the spatial location of some object at time t. Very often the boundaries of the object are fuzzy, in the sense that for some points it may be impossible to decide whether they belong to the object or not. As an example, imagine an object such as a river. Clearly, a point below the surface in midstream belongs to the river, and a point high on its bank does not. But what about a point that is half the time covered by the water of the river and half the time dry?

As another example, one may consider a flower, for example, a rose, and try to decide whether a point inside the flower but between the petals belongs to the rose.

These examples indicate that one might consider the spatial location of the object as fuzzy and associate with each point ξ in the space the degree to which ξ is "in" the object (or to which the object covers ξ). This degree (at time t) is described by the value $f_t(\xi)$: if this value is 1, the point ξ belongs to the object in full degree; if $f_t(\xi) = 0$, then ξ certainly does not belong to the object. The intermediate cases describe the "fuzziness" of the boundaries of the object: if $0 < f_t(\xi) < 1$, then ξ is neither fully in the object nor fully outside of it.

If the function f_t assumes only the extreme values 0 and 1 and not the intermediate ones, we may say that the boundaries of the object are *sharp* (so that objects with sharp boundaries are special cases of fuzzy objects).

The dependence of the location function $f_t(\xi)$ on t reflects the fact that the object may move, so that its location (whether fuzzy or not) may change in time.

Now, the intended interpretation of the function φ is as follows: the value $\varphi(t)$ represents the degree to which the object under consideration exists at time t. If $\varphi(t) = 1$, the object fully exists at t, whereas if $\varphi(t) = 0$, it does not fully exist, with $0 < \varphi(t) < 1$ representing the intermediate cases.

As an example, consider again an object such as a flower (as opposed to a bud). At some times t we have $\varphi(t) = 0$, for example, when the object is definitely a bud and not yet a flower. Again, at some other times we have $\varphi(t) = 1$, when the bud opens up completely. The intermediate stages $0 < \varphi(t) < 1$ correspond to situations when the object is partially still a bud and partially already a flower, with $\varphi(t)$ representing the degree of "flowerness" at t.

With the above interpretation in mind, we may proceed to introduce some notions. First, the set $\mathscr{G}$ of pairs (φ, f) under consideration, may be assumed to satisfy the following conditions: for every pair (φ, f) in $\mathscr{G}$ we have

$$(\exists t) : \varphi(t) = 1 \tag{2.6}$$

and

$$(\forall t) : \varphi(t) = 1 \Rightarrow [(\exists \xi) : f_t(\xi) = 1]. \tag{2.7}$$

Condition (2.6) simply asserts that the objects under consideration [as represented by pairs (φ, f)] exist at some time in full degree, whereas (2.7) asserts that, if at some time the object exists in full degree, then there exists spatial locations at which the object is located in full degree.

In the terminology of fuzzy set theory, we may say that the set of all times when the object exists is *normal*. On the other hand, (2.7) asserts that at times when the object exists in full degree, the fuzzy set of points in space where the object is located is also normal.

It is natural to introduce the set of moments of time and also the set of points at which the object exists in full degree. Denoting $w = (\varphi, f)$, we may therefore define

$$V(w) = \{t : \varphi(t) = 1\} \tag{2.8}$$

and

$$U_t(w) = \{\xi : f_t(\xi) = 1\}. \tag{2.9}$$

Then (2.6) states simply that $V(w) \neq \varnothing$, and (2.7) asserts the implication $t \in V(w) \Rightarrow U_t(w) \neq \varnothing$.

Roughly speaking, objects will now be defined as equivalence classes of a certain equivalence relation in $\mathscr{G}$; for lack of a better name, the elements of $\mathscr{G}$ will be referred to as *pre-objects*.

First, for any pre-object (φ, f) we define two sets, $V^+(w)$ and $U_t^+(w)$, being, respectively, the sets of all time moments when the pre-object w exists at some positive degree and the sets of locations where the pre-object w exists in some positive degree:

$$V^+(w) = \{t : \varphi(t) > 0\} \qquad (2.10)$$

and

$$U_t^+(w) = \{\xi : f_t(\xi) > 0\}. \qquad (2.11)$$

Obviously, we have here the relations

$$V(w) \subset V^+(w), \qquad U_t(w) \subset U_t^+(w). \qquad (2.12)$$

The sets $V(w)$ and $V^+(w)$ will be called, respectively, the temporal *core* and *carrier* of pre-object w. Similarly, for each t, the sets $U_t(w)$ and $U_t^+(w)$ are called the *spatial* core and spatial carrier at t.

Now let $w = (\varphi, f)$ and $w' = (\varphi', f')$ be two pre-objects.

DEFINITION 2.1   We say that pre-objects w and w' are *temporally* (or *existentially*) *equivalent* if their temporal cores and carriers coincide, that is, if

$$\varphi(t) = 1 \qquad \text{iff} \quad \varphi'(t) = 1 \qquad (2.13)$$

and

$$\varphi(t) = 0 \qquad \text{iff} \quad \varphi'(t) = 0. \qquad (2.14)$$

The existential equivalence will be denoted by $w \sim_T w'$.

We also introduce the analogous concept of spatial equivalence $w \sim_s w'$ by requiring that for all t

$$f_t(\xi) = 1 \qquad \text{iff} \quad f_t'(\xi) = 1$$

and $\qquad\qquad\qquad\qquad\qquad\qquad\qquad\qquad\qquad\qquad\qquad (2.15)$

$$f_t(\xi) = 0 \qquad \text{iff} \quad f_t'(\xi) = 0$$

If $w \sim_T w'$ and $w \sim_s w'$, we simply write $w \sim w'$ and say that pre-objects w and w' are equivalent.

Clearly, if w and w' are equivalent, then the sets representing cores and carriers are equal, which we record as the following.

THEOREM 2.1   *If $w \sim w'$, then $V(w) = V(w'), V^+(w) = V^+(w')$, and for all t we have $U_t(w) = U_t(w'), U_t^+(w) = U_t^+(w')$.*

We now define *objects* as equivalence classes of the relation $\sim$. If $w \in \mathscr{G}$ is a pre-object, then $[w]$ will denote its equivalence class, that is,

$$[w] = \{w' \in \mathscr{G} : w \sim w'\}, \qquad (2.16)$$

and $[w]$ is called the *object* corresponding to the pre-object w.

Thus, w is the set of all pre-objects equivalent to w. Clearly, this definition does not depend on the choice of w, in the sense that, whenever $w \sim w'$, then we have $[w] = [w']$.

The intuitive justification for the above definition is as follows. The values of membership functions φ and f_t are assigned subjectively, consequently, these assignments may vary from person to person and from occasion to occasion, especially as regards the "intermediate" values, that is, values other than 0 or 1. It appears, therefore, that it is reasonable to abstract from these intermediate values and to treat as equal (equivalent) every two pre-objects having the same cores and carriers, even if the membership functions differ in the "doubtful" region.

Figure 2.1 illustrates the situation for the temporal aspects. We have two functions, φ and φ', with the same cores [equal to the interval (t_2, t_3)] and the same carriers [equal to the interval (t_1, t_4)]. These functions differ in the intervals (t_1, t_2) and (t_3, t_4). We have then, denoting the pre-objects by w and w',

$$V(w) = V(w') = (t_2, t_3), \qquad V^+(w) = V^+(w') = (t_1, t_4). \qquad (2.17)$$

Consequently, the objects that are represented by w and w' are temporally equivalent.

The spatial equivalence may be illustrated in a similar way. From the definition of objects as equivalence classes, it follows that they are uniquely determined by the family of pairs of sets

$$(V, V^+), (U_t, U_t^+), t \in T, \qquad (2.18)$$

that is, the core and carrier of the temporal characteristic of existence of the object in question and cores and carriers of the location of object for every t.

From the assumptions about $\mathscr{G}$ it follows that

$$t \in V \Rightarrow U_t \neq \varnothing. \qquad (2.19)$$

In the following, $\mathscr{G}^*$ will denote the class of all objects. Now let $w = (\varphi, f)$ and $w' = (\varphi', f')$ be two pre-objects.

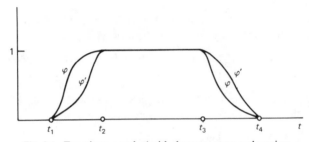

Fig. 2.1. Functions φ and φ' with the same cores and carriers.

DEFINITION 2.2 We say that w is a *part* of w' if the following conditions are met:

$$\varphi'(t) < 1 \Rightarrow \varphi(t) = 0 \qquad (2.20)$$

and

$$(\forall t): f'_t(\xi) < 1 \Rightarrow f_t(\xi) = 0. \qquad (2.21)$$

Observe that the relation of "being a part of" is stronger than the relation of inclusion between fuzzy sets. Indeed, if w is a part of w', then $\varphi(t) \leq \varphi'(t)$, and $f_t(\xi) \leq f'_t(\xi)$, so that w is contained in w'. However, if w is contained in w', there may exist points at which, for example, $0 < \varphi(t) < \varphi'(t) < 1$, so that w is not a part of w'. We may now prove the following theorem.

THEOREM 2.2 *If w is a part of w', then $V^+(w) \subset V(w')$, and for every t, we have $U_t^+(w) \subset U_t(w')$.*

For the proof see the Appendix at the end of this chapter.

The definition of the relation "to be a part of" depends only on the functions φ, φ', f_t, and f'_t being 0 or 1 and not on particular values assumed between 0 and 1. In other words, the definition depends (as asserted in Theorem 2.2) only on the relations between cores and carriers: the carrier of the part must be contained in the core of the whole, as illustrated on Fig. 2.2,

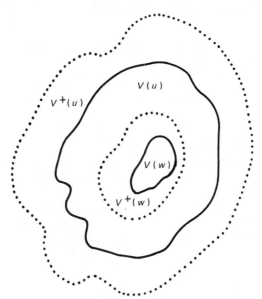

Fig. 2.2. Relation of "being a part of."

where the solid lines indicate the cores and the dotted lines indicate the carriers.

It is easy to see that we must have the following theorem.

THEOREM 2.3   *Let $w \sim w'$ and $u \sim u'$. If w is a part of u, then w' is a part of u'.*

Thus, one may define the relation "to be a part of" for objects: we say that object $[w]$ is a part of object $[u]$ if and only if, whenever $w \in [w]$, $u \in [u]$, then pre-object w is a part of pre-object u.

We have the following theorem.

THEOREM 2.4   *The relation "to be a part of" is transitive, that is, if $[u]$ is a part of $[v]$ and $[v]$ is a part of $[w]$, then $[u]$ is a part of $[w]$.*

If $[w]$ is an object, we shall still use the notation $V(w)$, $V^+(w)$, $U_t(w)$, and $U_t^+(w)$ to denote the cores and carriers of w instead of notations such as $V([w])$, $V^+([w])$.

DEFINITION 2.3   We say that the object w is *existentially fuzzy* if $V(w) \neq V^+(w)$; otherwise, it is called existentially *unambiguous*. Similarly, the object w is called *spatially* fuzzy at time t if $U_t(w) \neq U_t^+(w)$; otherwise it is spatially unambiguous.

We may now state the next theorem.

THEOREM 2.5   *If $[w]$ is a part of itself, then $[w]$ is existentially and spatially unambiguous.*

For the proof see the Appendix at the end of this chapter.

Now let w be a pre-object represented by a pair (φ, f), and let $S = T \times E$ be the time–space. The elements of S will generally be denoted by $\zeta = (t, \xi) = (t, x, y, z)$. Define the function $r_w : S \to [0, 1]$ by

$$r_w(\zeta) = r_w(t, \xi) = \min\{\varphi(t), f_t(\xi)\}. \tag{2.22}$$

The principle of construction of the function $r_w(\zeta)$ is shown in Fig. 2.3, where the variable ξ is one-dimensional. It may be seen that the value $\varphi(t)$ "shaves off" the top of the function $f_t(\xi)$, so that the value $r_w(\zeta) = r_w(t, \xi)$ is the minimum of $\varphi(t)$ and $f_t(\xi)$.

Clearly, the function r_w provides less information than the pair of functions φ and f separately. However, as will be shown below, the information in the function r_w is sufficient for identifying the object. Let

$$R_w = \{\zeta : r_w(\zeta) = 1\} \tag{2.23}$$

and

$$R_w^+ = \{\zeta : r_w(\zeta) > 0\}. \tag{2.24}$$

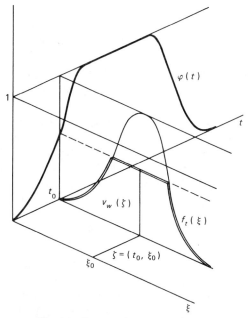

Fig. 2.3. Construction of function r_w.

By the assumption about $\mathscr{G}$, the set R_w is not empty. Indeed, we know that $\varphi(t_0) = 1$ for at least one t_0 and also that $f_{t_0}(\xi_0) = 1$ for at least one ξ_0. Consequently, $(t_0, \xi_0) \in R_w$, which shows that $R_w \neq \varnothing$. The sets R_w and R_w^+ will be referred to as the *core* and the *carrier* in the time–space S.

It appears that the sets R_w and R_w^+ may be constructed using the sets $V(w)$, $V^+(w)$, $U_t(w)$, and $U_t^+(w)$, which shows that R_w and R_w^+ characterize the object. Indeed, define

$$R'_w = \{\zeta = (t, \xi) : t \in V(w), \xi \in U_t(w)\}. \tag{2.25}$$

Then $R_w = R'_w$. In a similar way, define

$$R_w'^+ = \{\xi = (t, \xi) : t \in V^+(w), \xi \in U_t^+(w)\}. \tag{2.26}$$

Similarly, we have $R_w^+ = R_w'^+$.

Thus, pre-object $[w]$ determines a pair of sets (R_w, R_w^+) in time–space. Obviously, for equivalent objects $w \sim w'$ we have $R_w = R_{w'}$ and $R_w^+ = R_{w'}^+$, so that the pair (R_w, R_w^+) characterizes in fact the whole set of equivalent pre-objects, that is, object $[w]$.

The representations of objects as pairs of sets R_w, R_w^+ (where $R_w \subset R_w^+$ always) is very convenient for further analysis. One disadvantage, as compared with the description in terms of the functions (φ, f) is simply that, if

$\zeta \in R_w^+ - R_w$, then all we know is that $0 < r_w(\zeta) < 1$, which is the same as $0 < \min(\varphi(t), f_t(\zeta)) < 1$, and $r_w(\zeta)$ determines the value of one of the functions only, the other value being constrained by the appropriate inequalities. Moreover, one does not (in general) know which of these functions assumes the value $r_w(\zeta)$. This, however, is only a minor problem, since when defining an object it was already decided that the values of membership functions would be disregarded.

The relation "to be a part of" being transitive, it allows us to represent the structure of the object in the form of a tree. This fact is of considerable interest, since both the object and its part are possibly fuzzy, with unclear boundaries.

Naturally, the relation "to be a part of" is not connected, so that there may be objects such that none of them is a part of the other. A special type of such situations, of interest for perception, is described by separation. We say that $[u]$ and $[w]$ are *separated* if

$$R_u^+ \cap R_w^+ = \varnothing. \tag{2.27}$$

This condition simply means that the carriers in the time–space of u and w are disjoint: at any time t, if a point ζ belongs to object $[u]$ in some positive degree, then ζ does not belong at all (at time t) to the object $[w]$.

2.3 PREDICATES

In this section·the analysis will be of predicates of objects and the truth values of predication. Generally, the predicates will be denoted $P, Q, \ldots$ and the objects will be denoted, as in the preceding section, $[u], [v], \ldots$. Sometimes, when we need to speak of an object $[w]$ at time t, the notation $[w]_t$, or simply w_t, will be used.

Predicates $P, Q, \ldots$ may, but need not, be related to spatial or temporal characteristics of the objects, that is, to locations of the sets $V(w)$ on the time axis or locations of the sets $U_t(w)$ in space.

The main issues will concern the truth status of sentences "$[w]$ is P" or "w_t is P" ("w is P at t"). It is especially the latter type of predications that will serve in the next section to define the concept of an event. More precisely, we shall distinguish between predicates that are independent of fuzziness of the object and those that are fuzziness-dependent. To illustrate this distinction, examples of the first type of predicates will be RED, EXPENSIVE, and so on. As an example of the predicate that depends on the fuzziness of the object, one may take OVER 1 INCH IN LENGTH.

The formal distinction between these two types of predicates will be based on the concept of defuzzification of an object. Intuitively, given an object $[w]$, its defuzzification will be any nonfuzzy object whose core (and hence also carrier) is contained in the carrier of [w] and contains the core of [w]. The formal definition is as follows.

DEFINITION 2.4 Let [w] be any object with core R_w and carrier R_w^+. By a *defuzzification* of [w] we shall mean any object [w*] with

$$R_w \subset R_{w*} = R_{w*}^+ \subset R_w^+. \tag{2.28}$$

By definition, a defuzzification of an object is a nonfuzzy object (or, more precisely, a nonfuzzy pre-object).

An important category of defuzzifications of objects is obtained by taking a pre-object characterized by the function r_w and taking as the core the set of points where $r_w(\zeta) \geq \alpha$ for some α with $0 < \alpha \leq 1$. Accordingly, we introduce the following.

DEFINITION 2.5 Let [w] be an object, characterized by the pair (R_w, R_w^+) and let u be its defuzzification (so that $R_u = R_u^+$, with $R_w \subset R_u \subset R_w^+$). We say that defuzzification u is *natural* if there exists a pre-object $w = (\varphi, f) \in [w]$ and a number α with $0 < \alpha \leq 1$ such that

$$(t, \xi) \in R_u \quad \text{iff} \quad \min[\varphi(t), f_t(\xi)] \geq \alpha. \tag{2.29}$$

We may now define the notion of a predicate that is fuzziness-dependent.

DEFINITION 2.6 The predicate P is *fuzziness-dependent*, if there exists an object [w] and its two defuzzifications u' and u'' such that "u' is P" is true and "u'' is P" is false. Otherwise, the predicate P is *fuzziness-independent*.

It follows that, if P is fuzziness-independent, then the following is true. Let [w] be any object and $u, u', \ldots$ its defuzzifications. Then the logical status of all sentences "[w] is P," "u is P," "u' is P," $\ldots$ is the same.

The latter needs some comment. We assume, in general, that the truth is graded, so that a sentence may be true in degree α, where $0 \leq \alpha \leq 1$. If $\alpha = 1$, we have complete truth; if $\alpha = 0$, the sentence is false; and if $0 < \alpha < 1$, the sentence is neither completely true nor completely false.

As with objects, one may (at least for some sentences) abstract from the value α to the extent that the range of α may be partitioned into three categories: $\alpha = 0$, $\alpha = 1$, and the intermediate values $0 < \alpha < 1$ treated jointly. If we call the last category "neither true nor false" (NTNF), then we may say that P is fuzziness-independent if, for all defuzzifications $u, u', \ldots$ of [w], the logical status of all sentences "u is P," "u' is P," $\ldots$ is the same: they are all false, all true, or all are NTNF.

Now let [w] be an object, and for any $u \in [w]$ consider the functions $\varphi^{(u)}(t)$ and $f_t^{(u)}(\xi)$. Let P be a given predicate (fuzziness-independent or not). For any given $u \in [w]$, let the value $\alpha(t, u, P)$ represent the degree of truth of the sentence "u is P at t." We assume that the functions $\alpha(t, u, P)$ satisfy the condition

$$\alpha(t, u, P) \le \min\{\varphi^{(u)}(t), \sup_{\xi} f_t^{(u)}(\xi)\}, \tag{2.30}$$

and define

$$\alpha(t, [w], P) = \inf_{u \in [w]} \alpha(t, u, P). \tag{2.31}$$

We interpret $\alpha(t, [w], P)$ as the degree to which the sentence "$[w]$ is P at t" is true. The meaning of the constraint (2.30) and definition (2.31) is as follows.

First, observe that $\sup_{\xi} f_t^{(u)}(\xi)$ is the degree to which (at time t) the pre-object u is located *somewhere* in space; generally, this value will be 1. Indeed, if it is not 1, then we have a rare situation when the pre-object u is fuzzy to the degree that one cannot indicate even one point that is in the pre-object for sure. This describes a somewhat extreme level of spatial fuzziness of u.

Next, $\varphi^{(u)}(t)$ describes the degree to which u exists at all at time t. Observe that if $\varphi^{(u)}(t) = 1$, then $\sup_{\xi} f_t^{(u)}(\xi) = 1$, according to the basic assumption about pre-objects.

Constraint (2.30) may thus be interpreted as stating that the degree to which it is true that u is P at t cannot exceed the degree to which u exists at t and is located somewhere at t. If $\varphi^{(u)}(t) = 1$, then (2.30) gives no constraint at all, since then the right-hand side of (2.30) is 1.

The interpretation of (2.31) is as follows. The object $[w]$ is defined as the class of abstraction of equivalence relation on pre-objects, hence as a class of pre-objects. Thus, $[w]$ is the set of equivalent pre-objects, and it is natural to assume that $[w]$ is P at t to the degree lowest among all those to which u is P at t for all u in $[w]$. Thus, if $[w]$ is P at t in degree at least α, then the same holds for all pre-objects from $[w]$.

Then we defined the function $\alpha(t, w, P)$, which in a sense describes the evolution of the object $[w]$ in time, as regards predicate P. Now suppose that P_1 and P_2 are two predicates, and let $P = P_1 \,\&\, P_2$ be their conjunction. For any $u \in [w]$ we put

$$\alpha(t, u, P) = \min\{\alpha(t, u, P_1), \alpha(t, u, P_2)\}. \tag{2.32}$$

We then have the same relation if we replace u by $[w]$, so that

$$\alpha(t, [w], P) = \min\{\alpha(t, [w], P_1), \alpha(t, [w], P_2)\}. \tag{2.33}$$

We shall now distinguish an important class of predicates.

DEFINITION 2.7 We say that the predicate P is *normal* for object $[w]$ if for all $t_1 < t_2 < t_3$, we have

$$\alpha(t_1, [w], P) > \alpha(t_2, [w], P) \Rightarrow \alpha(t_2, [w], P) \ge \alpha(t_3, [w], P). \tag{2.34}$$

This condition means that the function α has at most one peak: if it decreases between some points t_1 and t_2, then it cannot increase in any interval (t_2, t_3) to the right of t_2.

Thus, normal predicates are those that the object may possess for some time (perhaps infinite), but when it starts losing this predicate, then it may never regain it.

We have the following important theorem.

THEOREM 2.6   *If P_1 and P_2 are predicates normal for [w], then their conjunction P_1 & P_2 has the same property.*

In other words, the class $N(w)$ of predicates normal for $[w]$ is closed under conjunction: if $P_1, P_2 \in N(w)$, then P_1 & $P_2 \in N(w)$. For the proof, see the Appendix at the end of this chapter.

We have thus far restricted the analysis to the case of predicates normal for a given object w, that is, predicates for which the function $\alpha(t, [w], P)$ has at most one peak. An important subclass is the predicates that are, or become, temporally permanent. The latter concept is defined as follows.

DEFINITION 2.8   The predicate P is said to be *temporally permanent* for object $[w]$, if

(a) $(\exists t): \alpha(t, [w], P) = 1$,
(b) $(\forall t, t'): \alpha(t, [w], P) = 1$ & $t < t' \Rightarrow \alpha(t', [w], P) = 1$.

Thus, a predicate P is temporally permanent if the object eventually acquires P in full degree and then has this predicate forever. It is thus natural to consider the earliest time when $[w]$ acquires P, namely,

$$T(w, P) = \inf\{t : \alpha(t, [w], P) = 1\}. \tag{2.35}$$

Clearly, the class $M(w)$ of all predicates that are temporally permanent for object $[w]$ is a subclass of all normal predicates. One can prove that $M(w)$ is closed under operations of conjunction and disjunction (whereas the class of normal predicates was closed only under conjunction). Indeed, we have the following theorem.

THEOREM 2.7   *If $P_1, P_2 \in M(w)$, then $P_1 \vee P_2$ and P_1 & P_2 are both in $M(w)$. Moreover,*

$$T(w, P_1 \& P_2) = \max(T(w, P_1), T(w, P_2)), \tag{2.36}$$

$$T(w, P_1 \vee P_2) = \min(T(w, P_1), T(w, P_2)). \tag{2.37}$$

These formulas assert, in effect, that the waiting time for the conjunction of two predicates to become permanently true for a given object (i.e., the sentence "w has both P_1 and P_2" to become true) is the longer of the two waiting times for the components of the conjunction. For the alternative, the waiting time is the shorter of the waiting times for the components.

2.4   PREDICATES AND EVENTS

In Chapter 1, the concept of event was used to explicate the notion of time and to derive its properties. For that purpose, the nature of events was quite irrelevant; what mattered was only the temporal aspects of events. Consequently, it was assumed that the exact moment of its occurrence may be connected with each event.

In this and the next sections, we shall analyze the notion of an event in more detail. Intuitively, an event will be treated as "something that happens to an object or objects." Restricting at first the analysis to a single object, the vague term "something happens to an object" may be interpreted as the object in question acquiring or losing an attribute.

It ought to be obvious that the concepts of an attribute of an object and that of a predicate that applies to this object are closely related to one another and may in fact be used interchangeably.

Let us consider a fixed object $[w]$ and its evolution in time, as described by the sets $V(w)$, $V^+(w)$ and $U_t(w)$, $U_t^+(w)$. Let P be a fixed attribute that the object may possess or not at any given time and that it may possess with some degree. Without loss of generality, we may use the same letters for attributes and predicates.

Generally, each pair consisting of an object and an attribute will serve as means for generating events in the following way. Consider the function $\alpha(t,[w],P)$, as defined in the preceding section, describing changes of the degree to which the sentence "$[w]$ is P at t" is true, or, equivalently, describing the changes of object $[w]$ as regards the attribute P. The concept of event, which will be formally explicated below, will be connected with the understanding of the term "event" as a change of state of some fragment of reality, which occurs at some more or less specified time.

Suppose that P is a normal predicate for $[w]$, and suppose that for some points $t_1 < t_2 < t_3$ we have $\alpha(t_1[w],P) = \alpha(t_3,[w],P) = 0$, $\alpha(t_2,[w],P_2) = 1$. Now define

$$T_1 = \inf\{t : \alpha(t,[w],P) > 0\}, \tag{2.38}$$

$$T_2 = \inf\{t : \alpha(t,[w],P) = 1\}, \tag{2.39}$$

$$T_3 = \sup\{t : \alpha(t,[w],P) = 1\}, \tag{2.40}$$

$$T_4 = \inf\{t : \alpha(t,[w],P) = 0\}. \tag{2.41}$$

Then $t_1 \leq T_1 \leq T_2 \leq t_2 \leq T_3 \leq T_4 \leq t_3$, and the function $\alpha(t,[w],P)$ must look as in Fig. 2.4. In other words, for all time between T_2 and T_3, the object $[w]$ must have predicate P in full and also not have P at all prior to T_1 and after T_4.

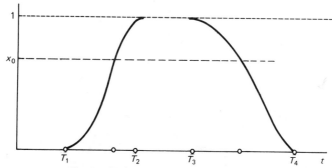

Fig. 2.4. Function α for a normal predicate.

Roughly, by an *event* we mean a change of state of some object or configuration of objects. Considering at first simple objects, we say that an event *occurs* to [w] if [w] either lost or acquired an attribute P, so that the sentence "[w] is P at t" changed its truth value from 0 to 1 or vice versa.

Looking at Fig. 2.4 one readily agrees that the event "[w] acquired P" occurred between T_1 and T_2 and the event "[w] loses P" occurred sometime between T_3 and T_4. Naturally, if $T_1 = T_2$ or $T_3 = T_4$, the moment when the object [w] acquires or loses attribute P is defined in an unambiguous manner. To consider the fuzzy case, assume that $\alpha(t, [w], P)$ varies continuously. In this case we must have $T_1 \neq T_2$ and $T_3 \neq T_4$.

Using the function $\alpha(t, [w], P)$, one can define the fuzzy moment of the occurrence of each of the events "[w] acquires P" and "[w] loses P" as follows. Let h be a function

$$h: [0, 1] \rightarrow [0, 1] \tag{2.42a}$$

satisfying the following conditions:

(a)   *h is continuous,*
(b) $h(0) = h(1) = 0$,
(c)   *there exists a point x_0 with $0 < x_0 < 1$ such that $h(x_0) = 1$,*
(d)   *h is increasing on $(0, x_0)$ and decreasing on $(x_0, 1)$.*

Examples of such functions h are $h(x) = 4x(1 - x)$ and $h(x) = x \log_2(1/x)$.

One can now define the membership function for the fuzzy set of moments when the event "[w] loses P" (or "[w] acquires P") occurs as

$$h(\alpha(t; [w], P)). \tag{2.42b}$$

By assumptions (a)–(d) and the fact that $\alpha(t, [w], P)$ varies continuously between 0 and 1, and then from 1 to 0, it follows that the membership function of the time of the events described above is nonzero only on the intervals

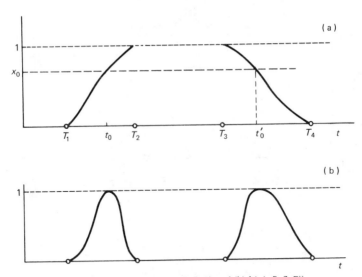

Fig. 2.5. Functions (a) $\alpha(t, [w], P)$ and (b) $h(\alpha(t, [w], P))$.

(T_1, T_2) and (T_3, T_4) and represents a normal fuzzy set (i.e., its supremum is equal to 1).

Figure 2.5 represents function $\alpha(t;, [w]\, P)$ and the corresponding function $h(\alpha(t, [w], P))$. Naturally, the maximum of function $h(\alpha(t, [w], P))$ occurs at the point when $\alpha(t; [w], P) = x_0$, where x_0 is the number appearing in condition (c).

For any interval (a, b) we define now the possibility of the event in question occurring in (a, b) as

$$\text{Poss}(a, b, [w], P) = \sup_{a \leq t \leq b} h(\alpha(t; w, P)). \qquad (2.43)$$

We have then the following theorem.

THEOREM 2.8 *If t_0 is such that $\alpha(t_0; [w], P) = x_0$ then for any a, b with $a \leq t_0 \leq b$ we have $\text{Poss}(a, b, [w], P) = 1$.*

Indeed, if $\alpha(t_0, [w], P) = x_0$, then $h(\alpha(t_0, [w], P)) = 1$, which is also the supremum of values of h for t ranging between a and b.

2.5 THEORY OF EVENTS

In the preceding sections we analyzed events that could be termed "elementary," each of them consisting of an object acquiring or losing an attribute. Since losing an attribute P is the same as acquiring non-P, we may always restrict the analysis to the case of an object acquiring an attribute.

To simplify the notation, the elementary events will simply be denoted e_1, $e_2, \ldots$, where each e_i is the event "object $[w]$ acquires an attribute P" for some $[w]$ and P. With each e_1 we associate a function $g_i(t)$, defined as the possibility that e_i occurs before t, or, in other words, the degree to which $[w]$ has the attribute P at t.

Let $\mathcal{E}$ be the class of elementary events e_i, each characterized by a function $g_i(t)$ which is nondecreasing and such that $g_i(t) \to 1$ as $t \to \infty$. In terms of attributes, elements of $\mathcal{E}$ correspond therefore to objects and attributes such that the object may only increase its degree of possession of the attribute and also such that it will eventually have this attribute in full degree.

Consider now a propositional function involving only the functors of conjunction and disjunction. Moreover, let $\mathcal{F}$ be the class of all such functions satisfying the property

$$f(x_1, \ldots, x_n) = 1 \quad \text{if} \quad x_1 = \cdots = x_n = 1. \tag{2.44}$$

Let $\mathcal{E}^*$ be the class of events obtained as follows:

(i)   *If $e \in \mathcal{E}$, then $e \in \mathcal{E}^*$;*
(ii) *If $f(x_1, \ldots, x_n) \in \mathcal{F}$ and $e_1, \ldots, e_n \in \mathcal{E}^*$, then $f(e_1, \ldots, e_n) \in \mathcal{E}^*$.*
(iii) *$\mathcal{E}^*$ contains only those events formed according to (i) or (ii).*

If g_i is the membership function of e_i and $e = f(e_1, \ldots, e_n)$, then the membership function $g_e(t)$ is obtained by replacing e_i by g_i in function f and also replacing the operations of conjunction and disjunction by fuzzy set-theoretical operations of intersection and union, that is, by minima and maxima.

Suppose, for example, that we have three elementary events e_1, e_2, e_3 and $f(x_1, x_2, x_3) = x_1 \vee (x_2 \,\&\, x_3)$. Then

$$g_e(t) = \max\{g_1(t), \min(g_2(t), g_3(t))\}. \tag{2.45}$$

In words, the event e is "either e_1 or both e_2 and e_3," which may be equivalently expressed as "if not e_1, then both e_2 and e_3," "if neither e_2 nor e_3, then e_1," and so on. We then have the next theorem.

THEOREM 2.9   *If $e \in \mathcal{E}^*$, then $g_e(t)$ is nondecreasing and $\lim_{t \to \infty} g_e(t) = 1$.*

For the proof see the Appendix at the end of this chapter.

This theorem asserts simply that for events from $\mathcal{E}^*$ the degree of possibility of occurrence increases with the passage of time and also tends to 1, that is, the events are bound to occur sooner or later.

One of the very important problems, to be discussed in more detail in the next chapter, is the order in which the events occur. If the time of occurrence is fuzzy and the supports of the membership functions for the occurrence overlap, it is generally impossible to assert with certainty which of the events occurred earlier. It is possible, however, to determine the degree of possibility that a given event of the pair occurred earlier than the other.

Let e' and e'' be two events from $\mathscr{E}^*$, with the corresponding functions $g'(t)$ and $g''(t)$. Thus, $g'(t)$ is the degree of possibility that e' occurred prior to t, and similarly, $1 - g''(t)$ is the degree of possibility that e'' occurred after t. Consequently,

$$\min\{g'(t), 1 - g''(t)\} \tag{2.46}$$

is the degree of possibility that e' occurred before t and that e'' occurred after t.

It is therefore natural to define the possibility that e' occurred before e'' as

$$p(e', e'') = \sup_t \{\min[g'(t), 1 - g''(t)]\}. \tag{2.47}$$

We may then prove the next theorem.

THEOREM 2.10 *For any events* e', $e'' \in \mathscr{E}^*$ *we have*

$$p(e', e'') + p(e'', e') = 1. \tag{2.48}$$

For the proof see the Appendix at the end of this chapter.

Consider now three events, say, e, e' and e'', and the possibility that they occur in a specified order, say, e is first, then e', and last e''. If their membership functions are g, g', and g'', then we have, for the possibility that times t and t' will separate the events,

$$\min\{g(t), g'(t') - g'(t), 1 - g''(t')\}. \tag{2.49}$$

Consequently, we have

Poss (e precedes e' which precedes e'')

$$= \sup_t \sup_{t'} \min\{g(t), g'(t') - g'(t), 1 - g''(t')\}. \tag{2.50}$$

As before one can show that the above definition is consistent in the following sense.

THEOREM 2.11 *For any events,* e, e', *and* e'' *in* $\mathscr{E}^*$, *the sum of the possibilities of all six permutations of the events is* 1.

The above analysis did not account for the possibility of two events occurring simultaneously. If we interpret this term literally, then (for most events) the possibility of simultaneous occurrence may be taken as 0. However, one can interpret "simultaneously" as a fuzzy notion, meaning "both occurring within a short interval of time," the term "short" being fuzzy (relative to the context). In this case, the sum of possibilities that e' precedes e'', e'' precedes e', or both occur simultaneously is 1.

2.6 EVENTS IN PROBABILITY THEORY AND CAUSAL RELATIONS

The above interpretation of the notion of an event, even though quite general, is still a rather special case of the notion of an event in probability theory, where events are simply subsets of a certain set (called, usually, the "space of elementary events" or "sample space"). This set can be selected, in general, in various ways even for representation of the same phenomenon. Let us denote the sample space by Ω. The events then are interpreted as subsets of Ω, and it is assumed that the class of all events forms a σ field, that is, a class of sets containing Ω and closed under complementation and countable unions: denoting the set of events by $\mathscr{A}$, we have

(i) $\Omega \in \mathscr{A}$,
(ii) $A \in \mathscr{A} \Rightarrow \Omega - A \in \mathscr{A}$,
(iii) $A_1, A_2, \ldots \in \mathscr{A} \Rightarrow \bigcup_i A_i \in \mathscr{A}$.

The probability is now defined as a real-valued function defined on $\mathscr{A}$ satisfying the following axioms:

(a) $0 \leq P(A) \leq 1$ for all $A \in \mathscr{A}$,
(b) $P(\Omega) = 1$,
(c) If $A_1, A_2, \ldots \in \mathscr{A}$ and $A_i \cap A_j = \varnothing$ for $i \neq j$, then

$$P(\bigcup_j A_j) = \sum_j P(A_j).$$

The conditional probability of an event A given an event B with $P(B) > 0$ is defined as

$$P(A \mid B) = P(A \cap B)/P(B). \tag{2.51}$$

Two events A, B are said to be independent if

$$P(A \cap B) = P(A)P(B). \tag{2.52}$$

For the present purpose, we shall need the notion of conditional independence. Assume, for simplicity, that the space Ω is finite or countable, with elements denoted generally by ω, with or without subscripts. We say that events A and B are *conditionally independent*, given ω, if $P(\omega) > 0$ and

$$P(A \mid \omega)P(B \mid \omega) = P(A \cap B \mid \omega). \tag{2.53}$$

Our objective will be to explicate the concept of causal independence and causal dependence. For this purpose, it will be convenient to assume that events $A, B, C, \ldots$ are generated by some random variables. Thus, we consider three random variables X, Y, and Z and events of the form $[X = x], [Y = y]$, or $[X = z]$. We then say that X and Y are conditionally independent given Z if for all x, y, z with $P(Z = z) > 0$ we have

$$P(X = x, Y = y \mid Z = z) = P(X = x \mid Z = z)P(Y = y \mid Z = z). \tag{2.54}$$

It is worth observing that random variables X, Y, which are conditionally independent given Z, may be very strongly dependent, even deterministically. This may be illustrated by simple examples. Suppose that Z assumes only two values, say, 0 and 1, with probability $\frac{1}{2}$ each. Given the value z, let X and Y both be equal to z with probability 1. Then condition (2.54) holds, so that X and Y are conditionally independent (given Z). However, the joint probability distribution of X, Y is

$$P(X = Y = 0) = P(X = Y = 1) = \tfrac{1}{2}. \tag{2.55}$$

Thus, we always have $X = Y$, which means that X and Y are deterministically related (and their correlation is 1).

Similar examples may be constructed to show that, under conditional independence, X and Y can be statistically dependent in a nondeterministic way, with correlations assuming positive or negative values. This explains the fact that conditional independence is often called "symmetric dependence." In fact, conditional independence means simply that there is a common variable "influencing" both X and Y through formula (2.54). In the following it will be convenient to use both terms interchangably, thus making the explanations more intuitive.

The notion of conditional independence will now be used to explicate the notion of causal dependence or causal independence. Suppose we have a family of random variables $\{X_t\}$, indexed by the temporal index t. Let $t' < t''$, and let $X_{t'}$ and $X_{t''}$ be two random variables (e.g., representing two phenomena). We may say that the events generated by $X_{t''}$ are causally independent from the events generated by $X_{t'}$ if for all k and all $t_1, t_2, \ldots, t_k$ with $t_i < t''$, $t_i \neq t'$, $i = 1, \ldots, k$, the random variables $X_{t'}$ and $X_{t''}$ are conditionally independent, given any event generated by $X_{t_1}, \ldots, X_{t_k}$.

Let us give a justification of this explication. What this definition requires is that $X_{t'}$ and $X_{t''}$ be conditionally independent, given any event that occurred prior to t' (other than events generated by $X_{t'}$). Thus, whatever dependence exists between $X_{t'}$ and $X_{t''}$, it is all due to other variables that influenced both $X_{t'}$ and $X_{t''}$, still leaving them conditionally independent. In other words, two variables are causally independent if all their dependence is symmetric dependence and thus explicable in terms of dependence on some common factor.

2.7 FUZZY MARKOV CHAINS

In this section we shall consider a special case of fuzzy events, defined as fuzzy subsets of the set of nonfuzzy events. We shall use this construction to analyze the fuzzification of a Markov chain.

Let F be a fuzzy subset of the set of states of a Markov chain, say, $\{E_1, \ldots, E_N\}$. Thus, F is defined through its membership function, that is, the set of values $\mu_F(E_1), \mu_F(E_2), \ldots, \mu_F(E_N)$, where $\mu_F(E_i)$ is the degree to which the state E_i is F (as an example, one may think of $E_1, \ldots, E_N$ as some psychological states and F as the class of states that are "rather pleasant," etc.).

Let $P = [p_{ij}]$ be the transition matrix of the process. Then the probability of F in next step, given the state E_i at a given moment, is

$$P(F \mid E_i) = \sum_{j=1}^{N} \mu_F(E_j) p_{ij}, \qquad (2.56)$$

which corresponds simply to the expected value of membership in F at next step, given state E_i.

Similarly, one can define probabilities $P^{(2)}(F \mid E_i)$, $P^{(3)}(F \mid E_i), \ldots$ of F in 2, 3, $\ldots$ steps by

$$P^{(n)}(F \mid E_i) = \sum_{j=1}^{N} \mu_F(E_j) p_{ij}^{(n)}, \qquad (2.57)$$

where $p_{ij}^{(n)}$ is the n-step transition probability.

One may expect that, if the chain is ergodic, the influence of the initial state becomes gradually weaker, and the probability of F tends to a limit independent of the initial state. Indeed, we have the following.

THEOREM 2.12 *If the Markov chain is ergodic, then for every i we have*

$$\lim_{n \to \infty} P^{(n)}(F \mid E_i) = p(F). \qquad (2.58)$$

For the proof see the Appendix at the end of this chapter.

In a sense, the above introduction of fuzziness into Markov chains yields nothing new, except for interpretation; formally, the membership function is a certain valuation on states, and probabilities of fuzzy sets of states are formally analogous to payoffs, or rewards, connected with visits. The theory of such random variables connected with Markov chains, even with inclusion of control elements, has been extensively developed.

Let us now take another fuzzy set G, with membership function $\mu_G(E_i)$, $i = 1, \ldots, N$, and assume that this set is normal, that is, there is at least one index i_0 such that $\mu_G(E_{i_0}) = 1$. Assume that the chain is stationary, so that for every moment k the probability of state E_i at time k equals the ergodic probability $p(i)$. Moreover, assume that at some time (say, $t = 0$) the chain is in the set G in degree at least α. Then the expected degree of membership in the set F, denoted $P(F \mid G, \alpha)$, may be calculated as follows.

Let

$$S_{G,\alpha} = \{E_i : \mu_G(E_i) \geq \alpha\}. \qquad (2.59)$$

Since G is normal, we have $S_{G,\alpha} \neq \emptyset$ for every α. Denote

$$D = \sum_{i \in S_{G,\alpha}} p(i), \qquad (2.60)$$

where $p(i)$ are ergodic probabilities. Then the conditional probability that the chain is in state $E_i \in S_{G,\alpha}$ equals $p(i)/D$, and we may write

$$P(F \mid G, \alpha) = \sum_{i \in S_{G,\alpha}} \frac{p(i)}{D} \sum_{j=1}^{N} p_{ij} \mu_F(E_j). \qquad (2.61)$$

As an intuitive example, assume that we have some Markov chain and a certain number of fuzzy sets defined on its states. Thus, some states may be "very pleasant," "boring," "dangerous," and so on. Formula (2.61) allows us to calculate the expected membership value in a given set, say, "very pleasant," on the next step if it is known that at present the degree of membership in some other set is at least α, without specifying the state at present.

2.8 OBSERVABILITY CONSTRAINTS

Thus far we considered the case of one (possibly composite) attribute and its changes in time. Consequently, the analysis concerned one selected aspect of the object under study.

Generally, a description of an object is terms of one attribute is seldom sufficient, especially if this description is to serve for a number of goals, which are not specified in advance. This point is perhaps best explained by the following example. Suppose that one wants to study a random object, such as "epidemic," "inflation." Such objects may be characterized by a (perhaps fuzzy) set of states of a certain system, such as society described in terms of a specific disease through contacts between infectives and susceptibles, or economy, described in terms of supplies of various goods, prices, demands. It will be convenient to refer to the "system" under consideration as a *carrier*.

Thus, a specific carrier may be in a state of "epidemic," or in a state of "no epidemic"; another specific carrier may be in a state of "inflation"; and so on. The set of states of the carrier that are characteristic for an epidemic may be fuzzy or not; we shall return to this point in the subsequent parts of this section.

The main issue now is simply that in describing the state of the carrier at any given time, one has to make a decision as to which attributes are needed for the description of the state and which are not. To continue with the example of epidemic, the state description should be sufficiently rich to enable one to study a wide class of phenomena covered by "epidemic theory," yet sufficiently parsimonious to be practically usable.

For instance, if we restrict the analysis to one particular disease, say, D, the state description might involve

(a) the specification of the state of health (regarding the disease D) of all members of the society. This information has the form of a subset $S' \subset S$, where S is the set of all members of a given society and S' is the class of all members who have the disease D;

(b) the specification of all contacts between members of S' and members of $S - S'$, or, more generally, between members of S within some period of time, for example, the last 14 days. This information has the form of a relation $C \subset S \times S$, where sCs' means that s and s' contacted each other in the period of time under consideration;

(c) the location of each member of the society at a given time. This information has the form of a function, say, F, which assigns locations to elements of S.

Clearly, such a state description may be too rich for some purposes, and not rich enough for some other purposes. This example illustrates the fact that "completeness" of the state description is a concept relative to the given goal of analysis.

2.8.1 Observability Networks

Suppose that the decision about the choice of state description was made. Regardless of the particular form of this description (e.g., specification of the set S', relation $C \subset S \times S$, and function F, as in the case of epidemic), it may always be assumed that the state description is reducible to the form of a vector $(x_1, \ldots, x_n)$ of attribute values. Here

$$N = \{1, 2, \ldots, n\} \tag{2.62}$$

is the set of labels of attributes, and for each $i \in N$, we have $X_i \in V_i \cup \{*\}$, where V_i is the set of possible values of ith attribute, with $*$ denoting the fact that ith attribute is "not applicable" in a given situation.

The constraints of observability consist of the fact that not all attribute values may be observed *jointly*: it may happen that by observing a value x_i of the ith attribute in a given instance it may be impossible to observe the value x_j assumed by jth attribute.

Such observability constraints may be related to various causes. Sometimes observation of one variable (attribute) may make it physically impossible to observe some other variable or variables; sometimes the constraints may be due to economical reasons (e.g., limitations of costs), and so on.

Generally, the observability constraints may be characterized by specifying a family, say, $\mathcal{G}$, of subsets of N. The interpretation here is simply that, if $A \in \mathcal{G}$, then it is possible to observe all values of attributes from A in a given instance (in another instance one may select some other attributes to observe).

Naturally, the family $\mathscr{G}$ may be time-dependent; for simplicity, however, we assume that $\mathscr{G}$ is time-invariant.

We assume that $\mathscr{G}$ satisfies the following.

HYPOTHESIS 2.1   *If $A \in \mathscr{G}$ and $B \subset A$, then $B \in \mathscr{G}$.*

This hypothesis states that, if a certain set of attributes permits joint observability, then the same is true for every subset of this set. To justify this assumption on intuitive grounds, it suffices to rephrase it by saying that one can always not observe some attributes.

DEFINITION 2.9   We shall say that the attribute $i \in N$ is *observable* if

$$(\exists A): i \in A \text{ and } A \in \mathscr{G}. \tag{2.63}$$

Let N^* denote the class of all observable attributes. Hypothesis 2.1 allows us to define a natural concept, namely, that of maximally observable sets.

DEFINITION 2.10   A set $A \in \mathscr{G}$ will be called *maximally observable* if the conditions $A \subset B$ and $A \neq B$ imply $B \notin \mathscr{G}$.

Thus, a set is maximally observable if its attributes are observable jointly, but addition of one more attribute to this set makes it not in $\mathscr{G}$.

Clearly, the maximally observable sets are not unique; there may exist several of them. Generally, let $\mathscr{G}^*$ be the class of all maximal sets. We have then the next theorem.

THEOREM 2.13   *If $A, B \in \mathscr{G}^*$, then $A \subset B$ implies $A = B$.*

For the proof see the Appendix at the end of the chapter.

This theorem asserts that maximally observable sets are not comparable with respect to the relation of inclusion.

It turns out that the class $\mathscr{G}^*$ of maximally observable sets uniquely determines the class $\mathscr{G}$ of observable sets; we then have the following theorem.

THEOREM 2.14   *We have the identity*

$$\mathscr{G} = \{A : \exists B \in \mathscr{G}^* \text{ with } A \subset B\}. \tag{2.64}$$

For the proof see the Appendix at the end of this chapter.

We may now describe some of the most important contingencies that may occur.

DEFINITION 2.11   If $i \in \bigcap_{A \in \mathscr{G}^*} A$, we say that the ith attribute is *universally observable* and the set

$$C = \bigcap_{A \in \mathscr{G}^*} A \tag{2.65}$$

will be called the *core* of observability.

Each maximally observable set is therefore representable as a union $C \cup B$, where C is the core and B may be assumed disjoint with C.

Let $\mathscr{B}$ be the class of sets obtained in this way, so that

$$\mathscr{G}^* = \{C \cup B : B \in \mathscr{B}\}. \tag{2.66}$$

DEFINITION 2.12 We say that a set of attributes A' with $A' \cap C = \varnothing$ is *uniformly constrained*, if

(a) A' contains at least two elements;
(b) $C \cup A' \in \mathscr{G}$;
(c) $B \in \mathscr{B} \Rightarrow A' \subset B$ or $A' \cap B = \varnothing$.

DEFINITION 2.13 We say that sets A' and A'' constitute a *mutual trade-off* if they are uniformly constrained and for every $B \in \mathscr{B}$

$$[A' \subset B \Rightarrow A'' \cap B = \varnothing \ \& \ A'' \subset B \Rightarrow A' \cap B = \varnothing]. \tag{2.67}$$

To explain the concepts introduced, it is best to use an example. Let $a, b, c, \ldots$ denote the labels of attributes, and suppose that the class $\mathscr{G}^*$ of maximally observable sets contains the following sets:

$$\{a, b, c, d, e\}; \quad \{a, b, e, f, g, h\}; \quad \{a, b, f, g, h, i\}; \quad \{a, b, f, g, h, j\}.$$

Then a and b belong to every set in $\mathscr{G}^*$; in fact,

$$C = \bigcap_{A \in \mathscr{G}^*} A = \{a, b\}, \tag{2.68}$$

so that a and b are universally observable, and $C = \{a, b\}$ is the core.

Next, $\{c, d\}$ and $\{f, g, h\}$ appear always together: either all of these elements or none of them belong to every element of $\mathscr{G}^*$. This means that $\{c, d\}$ and $\{f, g, h\}$ are uniformly constrained. Moreover, if c and d belong to the observable set, then f, g, and h do not belong to it, and conversely, $\{c, d\}$ *and* $\{f, g, h\}$ constitute an observability trade-off.

In practice, this means that, if one decides to observe both c and d then one cannot observe any of the attributes f, g, and h.

The remaining elements, e, i, and j do not belong to any constrained set.

An example of observability constraints in the social sciences may be provided by the well-known experiment of Asch concerning the resistance to social pressure. There are eight subjects in the experiment, but only one of them is being tested, while the remaining seven are specially instructed to give deliberately false answers (e.g., to some question about length discrimination). The person tested replies as the last, and he may or may not "give up" under social pressure, replying as the others, or he may follow his convictions. Now, before the experiment starts, the resistance to social pressure may be tested for each of the eight subjects. However, the decision to observe it for one person makes it impossible to observe it for any of the remaining seven, since they must be instructed in a special way, preventing their measurement at any time later. Thus, the maximal observable sets here are singletons, or sets consisting of one person only.

The consequences of observability constraints are best seen when one considers their effect on the collection of statistical data. Suppose that the values of attributes $(x_1, \ldots, x_n)$ characterize the objects from some population. The elements of the population are sampled, and therefore the attribute values may be treated as random variables, say, $(X_1, \ldots, X_n)$, with some joint probability distribution

$$F(y_1, \ldots, y_n) = P(X_1 \leq y_1, \ldots, X_n \leq y_n). \tag{2.69}$$

This probability distribution represents, in a sense, the complete knowledge about the laws governing the attributes, their statistical interrelationships, etc.

Now, observability constraints, as specified by the class $\mathcal{G}$ of subsets of N, make it impossible to estimate certain joint distributions. For example assume for simplicity that x_1 and x_2 are observable separately but not jointly, so that

$$(\forall A \in \mathcal{G}): 1 \in A \Rightarrow 2 \notin A. \tag{2.70}$$

Consequently, for each sampled element we must make the decision whether to record the value of x_1 or x_2 (or perhaps none of them); one cannot observe both of them for the same element of the sample. This means simply that there is no access to the joint distribution of (X_1, X_2), even though we may estimate their marginal distributions.

A similar situation occurs for joint distributions of more than two random variables: the observability network $\mathcal{G}$, and in particular the class $\mathcal{G}^*$ of maximally observable sets, determines for which sets of random variables we may estimate their joint probability distributions.

In subsequent sections the concept of observability network will be combined with the notion of a *mask*, which specifies (within the observability constraints) the temporal pattern of collecting information in cases when we deal with a dynamically changing random object.

2.8.2　Further Constraints on Observability

This section will concern some additional constraints on observability, which operate, so to speak, within the observability networks. Suppose that the observer decides, in a given instance, to observe all attributes with indices in a set A, that is, all attributes x_i with $i \in A$. Naturally, we must have $A \in \mathcal{G}$, that is, all attributes that the experimenter intends to observe must be jointly observable.

Let $A = \{i_i, i_2, \ldots, i_k\} \subset N$, and let

$$X_A = (x_{i_1}, \ldots, x_{i_k}). \tag{2.71}$$

We may regard x_A as a realization of a vector-valued random variable X_A.

The constraints on observability that we shall consider in this section consist simply of the fact that the experimenter observes not the value of X_A but some (possibly random) function of X_A, say,

$$y = h(x_A, \xi). \tag{2.72}$$

Here h is some function, not necessarily numerical, and ξ is a random distortion of observation (with ξ and x_A not observable separately).

The above scheme is sufficiently general and rich to cover most cases that may occur in real life.

One typical case occurs when x_A represents a numerical value of an attribute, which one tries to measure by means of a certain instrument (e.g., a physical measurement tool, a psychological test). In this case, ξ is a random error, and

$$y = h(x_A, \xi) = x_A + \xi. \tag{2.73}$$

This simple additive model, according to which the observed value y is the sum of the (unobservable) true value of the attribute x_A and the (unobservable) error ξ, serves as a basis for a large number of statistical techniques of estimation.

Note that in the above setup x_A may be one-dimensional or multidimensional; the random disturbance ξ has as many components as x_A and addition in (2.73) is interpreted as addition of vectors.

Another fairly typical example is simply the grouping of the data. To illustrate the point, assume that ξ is absent and that the observations are grouped (i.e., assigned to classes of some classification). In this case we have

$$y = h(x_A) = \text{label of the class to which } x_A \text{ belongs.} \tag{2.74}$$

Typically, instead of learning (say) a person's age, one obtains the information that he belongs to the class labeled "between 25 and 30," and so on. In this case, denoting

$$h^{-1}(y) = \{x_A : h(x_A) = y\}, \tag{2.75}$$

we know, after observing y, that the attribute value x_A belongs to set (2.75).

A very common situation occurs when h assumes linguistic values and the set $h^{-1}(y)$ is fuzzy. Returning again to the example with x_A being the person's age, the observer learns, instead of the value x_A, only the value $h(x_A) = \text{OLD}$, and so on. Here $h^{-1}(\text{OLD})$ is a fuzzy subset of the real axis, with the membership function as discussed extensively by Zadeh, starting with his earliest papers on fuzzy set theory.

Generally, when the observations are disturbed by the function $h(x_A, \xi)$, the situation may be described as follows. In all cases of practical importance, one is either after some "truth" or one is trying to make a decision that is to be optimal from the point of view of some criterion. The truth may be identified here with the (unobservable) value x_A of the attribute or attributes or, alternatively, with the probability distribution of x_A. The function $h(x_A, \xi)$, then represents the restrictions concerning the access to the truth: the effects of random deviations from the truth and the effects of destroying information by grouping, classification, usage of fuzzy terms, and so on.

If one uses the knowledge of x_A for making the decision, the situation may be described as follows. Suppose that, if x_A were known, then the optimal decision (from the point of view of a given criterion) would also be known. Since x_A is unknowwn and only $y = h(x_A, \xi)$ is observed, one cannot, in general, expect to do as well as if x_A were known.

Suppose for simplicity that function h does not involve random component, so that $y = h(x_A)$ and sets $h^{-1}(y)$ defined by (2.75) are not fuzzy. Numerous ways have been suggested for measuring the loss of information due to the use of function h. To present one of them, based on the principle of "regret" from decision theory, assume that the available decisions form a set D and that with each decision $d \in D$ and attribute value x_A one may associate the "loss" $L(d, x_A)$ suffered if one makes the decision d under the "true state" x_A.

In the following we assume that function L is nonnegative. Moreover, assume that for each x_A there exists the "appropriate" decision $d(x_A)$ with $L(d(x_A), x_A) = 0$. Thus, if x_A were known, we would be able to find the decision that yields no loss (hence is optimal, since L is assumed to be non-negative).

Now, because of the constraints of observability, decision d has to be based on the observed value $y = h(x_A)$. Let us denote this decision by $d(y)$, so that the *decision procedure* is a function that maps the set of values of h into D. In other words, the decision procedure must be defined on the class of all sets of the form $h^{-1}(y)$ or, still differently, must be a function of x_A that is constant on the sets of partition generated by h.

Now, if we make decision $d(y)$, with the value of the attribute being x_A [and such that $y = h(x_A)$], then the loss is $L(d(y), x_A)$ and the maximal loss that may occur is

$$R(y) = \sup_{x_A \in h^{-1}(y)} L(d(y), x_A). \tag{2.76}$$

One may then take as a measure of the loss of information due to the use of function h the value

$$R = \sup_y R(y). \tag{2.77}$$

The measure above is somewhat pessimistic, in the sense that it assigns the same weights to all $x_A \in h^{-1}(y)$. In reality, one can usually consider the conditional probability distribution of x_A given y and then take the expected value of $L(d(y), x_A)$ instead of the supremum.

2.8.3 Observability Constraints and Poisson Processes

Let us now return to the analysis presented in Section 1.6 and consider the problem from a somewhat different point of view, treating it mostly as an example of observability constraints. To recall briefly, we consider a family of independent Poisson processes, indexed by some index z ("type" of events) and such that the parameter in the process of type z is λ_z. For any fixed t, we define $Y_z(t)$ as the waiting time, counting from t, for the first event of type z, that is, first event in process $\Pi(z)$ following the time t.

Formula (1.94) gives the expression for the probability that an event in process $\Pi(z_1)$ will occur earlier than an event from process $\Pi(z_2)$. This formula is

$$p(z_1, z_2) = P[Y_{z_1}(t) < Y_{z_2}(t)]$$

$$= \left[1 + \frac{1/\lambda_{z_1}}{1/\lambda_{z_2}} \right]^{-1}. \tag{2.78}$$

We may regard this situation as an observation made under the following observability constraint. At time t the observations begin, and they last only until the first event occurs, in either process $\pi(z_1)$ or process $\pi(z_2)$. No subsequent events are observable.

The object of inference, that is, the "truth," is the ratio of intensities of the two processes $\lambda_{z_1}/\lambda_{z_2}$.

In real life, such a situation occurs in assessing the effects of some methods of elimination of various diseases, social pathologies, inflation (in the social contexts), causes of failure of some equipment.

Omitting the assumption of exponential distribution of waiting times (characteristic for Poisson processes), we may consider the waiting times (counting from birth) for death due to cancer (say) as a random variable and waiting time (again counting from birth) for death due to any of the remaining possible causes, as another random variable. This simply means that, if a person is known to have died of cancer at age x, then it is not known at which age he would have died, if he had not died of cancer.

This scheme may, of course, be generalized to many other causes of death by separating "death due to reasons other than cancer" into various causes.

Given the statistical data concerning the times of (observable) ages at death due to various causes, one may answer different questions, for example, about the age distribution that would result if one of the "risks" (causes of death) were eliminated or modified in some given way.

Let us try to present the problem of two Poisson processes in terms of function h introduced previously. The attribute x_A may be the pair

$$x_A = (Y_{z_1}(t), Y_{z_2}(t)) \tag{2.79}$$

of waiting times. Define the random variable ξ as

$$\xi = \begin{cases} 1 & \text{if} \quad Y_{z_1}(t) < Y_{z_2}(t), \\ 0 & \text{if} \quad Y_{z_1}(t) \geq Y_{z_2}(t). \end{cases} \tag{2.80}$$

Then we may take $h(x_A, \xi)$ to be two-dimensional, specifically,

$$h(x_A, \xi) = (\xi, \xi Y_{z_1}(t) + (1 - \xi) Y_{z_2}(t)). \tag{2.81}$$

Indeed, if $Y_{z_1}(t) < Y_{z_2}(t)$, we are to observe $Y_{z_1}(t)$ and learn that this is an event from the first process. In fact, we have here $\xi = 1$, and the second component in (2.81) equals $Y_{z_1}(t)$.

On the other hand, if $Y_{z_1}(t) \geq Y_{z_2}(t)$, then $\xi = 0$ and the second component in (2.81) equals $Y_{z_2}(t)$.

We shall now extend the above scheme by imposing still other observability constraints. Again, the observations start at t and last until the occurrence of the first event in either of the two processes, with the second event already unobservable, with the additional provision that there is only a limited time for observation, say, T. In picturesque language, we set a "trap" of length T at time t and observe only the first event (if any) "caught" in the trap. This is illustrated on Fig. 2.6. Here the downward (upward) arrows indicate the times of occurrences of the events from the first (second) process. The solid arrows indicate the observed time, and the dotted ones indicate times that are not observable.

In case (a), an event from the second process occurs first after t and is

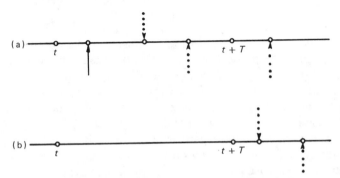

Fig. 2.6. (a) Observable and (b) unobservable events.

observed; subsequent events are not observable. In case (b), there are no events from either process that would occur until $t + T$, and therefore none of the events is observable.

To express these constraints in terms of the function h, we define $\xi = (\xi_1, \xi_2)$ as

$$\xi_1 = \begin{cases} 1 & \text{if} \quad \min[Y_{z_1}(t), Y_{z_2}(t)] < T, \\ 0 & \text{otherwise;} \end{cases} \tag{2.82}$$

$$\xi_2 = \begin{cases} 1 & \text{if} \quad Y_{z_1}(t) < Y_{z_2}(t), \\ 0 & \text{otherwise.} \end{cases} \tag{2.83}$$

For the value $h(x_A, \xi)$ for $x_A = (Y_{z_1}(t), Y_{z_2}(t))$, we take the pair

$$h(x_A, \xi) = (\xi_1 \xi_2, \xi_1[\xi_2 Y_{z_1}(t) + (1 - \xi_2) Y_{z_2}(t)]). \tag{2.84}$$

As one could expect, the effect of the "trap" diminishes as T (the length of the trap) increases. This is intuitively obvious since the trap distracts the observation only if nothing is "caught" in the trap (one trial is then lost, as it provides no information relevant to estimation of the ratios of the intensities). In fact, the probability that nothing is caught in the trap equals

$$\exp[-(\lambda_{z_1} + \lambda_{z_2})T, \tag{2.85}$$

which means that the fraction of "lost" experiments quickly decreases with the increase of the length of the trap T. In consequence, the ratio $\lambda_{z_1}/\lambda_{z_2}$ may still be estimated by using formula (2.78), given the data on frequency of cases when $\xi_2 = 1$, restricted to cases when $\xi_1 = 1$. In fact, we have the following theorem.

THEOREM 2.15   *The probability that* $Y_{z_1}(t) < Y_{z_2}(t)$ *given that* $\min[Y_{z_1}(t), Y_{z_2}(t)] \leq T$ *is*

$$P(\xi_2 = 1 \mid \xi_1 = 1) = \lambda_{z_1}/(\lambda_{z_1} + \lambda_{z_2}), \tag{2.86}$$

that is, it equals $p(z_1, z_2)$ *given by* (2.76).

For the proof see the Appendix at the end of this chapter.

Finally, let us consider still another modification of the distortion scheme for Poisson processes. Assume, namely, that we continue the observations until we record the first event from either of the processes, except that now each of the events in process $\pi(z_1)$ may be "missed" (impossible to record, "invisible," etc.) with probability a, and similarly, each of the events in the process $\pi(z_2)$ may be "missed" with probability b. Whether or not a given event is "visible" is independent of the visibility of other events.

Let now $Y_{z_1}^*(t)$ and $Y_{z_2}^*(t)$ be the waiting times for the first event that is "visible" in processes $\pi(z_1)$ and $\pi(z_2)$, respectively, counting from t. Then let

$\xi = (m, n, \xi_1)$ be defined as

$$m = \text{the index of the first visible event after } t \text{ in } \pi(z_1), \qquad (2.87)$$

$$n = \text{the index of the first visible event after } t \text{ in } \pi(z_2), \qquad (2.88)$$

$$\xi_1 = \begin{cases} 1 & \text{if } Y_{z_1}^*(t) < Y_{z_2}^*(t), \\ 0 & \text{otherwise.} \end{cases} \qquad (2.89)$$

As x_A we now take the sequences of interarrival times counted from t, say, $X_1^{z_1}, X_2^{z_1}, \ldots$ and $X_1^{z_2}, X_2^{z_2}, \ldots$ in the $\pi(z_1)$ and $\pi(z_2)$ so that

$$Y_{z_1}^*(t) = X_1^{z_1} + \cdots + X_m^{z_1}, \qquad (2.90)$$

$$Y_{z_2}^*(t) = X_1^{z_2} + \cdots + X_n^{z_2}. \qquad (2.91)$$

We then have

$$h(x_A, \xi) = (\xi_1, \xi_1 Y_{z_1}^*(t) + (1 - \xi_1) Y_{z_2}^*(t)). \qquad (2.92)$$

To calculate $P(Y_{z_1}^*(t) < Y_{z_2}^*(t))$, we start by finding the distribution of the random variables in question. To calculate $P(Y_{z_1}^*(t) \geq x + t)$ we may argue as follows. The moment $Y_{z_1}^*(t)$ of the first visible event from $\pi(z_1)$ falls after $x + t$ if all events (if any) that occurred between t and $x + t$ are not visible. Now, the number of such events equals m with probability

$$[(\lambda_{z_1} x)^m / m!] \exp(-\lambda_{z_1} x) \qquad (2.93)$$

and all are invisible with probability a^m. Summing over all possible m we obtain

$$P(Y_{z_1}^*(t) > x + t) = \sum_{m=0}^{\infty} \frac{(\lambda_{z_1} x)^m}{m!} a^m \exp(-\lambda_{z_1} x)$$

$$= \exp(-\lambda_{z_1} x) \sum_{m=0}^{\infty} \frac{(a\lambda_{z_1} x)^m}{m!} = \exp(-\lambda_{z_1} x) \exp(a\lambda_{z_1} x)$$

$$= \exp[-(1 - a)\lambda_{z_1} x], \qquad (2.94)$$

which is the exponential distribution with parameter $(1 - a)\lambda_{z_1}$. It follows that the visible events also form a Poisson process, only "thinned" by the factor $1 - a$. The same holds for the second process, with the factor $1 - b$, and we have

$$p^*(z_1, z_2) = P[Y_{z_1}^*(t) < Y_{z_2}^*(t)]$$

$$= \left[1 + \frac{1/(1 - a)\lambda_{z_1}}{1/(1 - b)\lambda_{z_2}} \right]^{-1} = \frac{(1 - a)\lambda_{z_1}}{(1 - a)\lambda_{z_1} + (1 - b)\lambda_{z_2}}. \qquad (2.95)$$

Consequently, it is possible to estimate the ratio of the intensities of the two processes. If they are both distorted in the same way $(a = b)$, then the formula is the same as for undistorted processes.

2.9 FILTERS AND MASKS

In the above context of two types of events, the distortion of observability (filter) was characterized by two numbers, representing, respectively, the probability of nonobserving of an event of each of the two types. Let us now generalize this scheme and consider the structure of the family of filters of the above type.

The phenomenon in question is a family of Poisson processes $\pi(q)$, where q runs through a certain parameter set Q. The experimenter's choice concerns the processes that he wishes to observe; this choice may be called a *mask* of the phenomenon, so that there may be different masks, not restricted to pairs of processes.

The following are some of the relevant definitions.

1. By a *filter* we shall understand a pair (U, f), where $U \subset Q$ is called a *base* and $f: U \to [0, 1]$ is a *selector*. To simplify the notations, such a filter will be denoted $F(U, f)$. The effect of $F(U, f)$ is as described above: it causes unobservability of each of the events in process $\pi(q)$ with probability $f(q)$. Speaking picturesquely, a filter causes "random thinning" of processes with parameter $q \in U$.

2. By an *atomic*, or *elementary*, *filter* we mean a filter with $U = \{q\}$, consisting of one element only, hence distorting just one process.

3. Given two filters $F(U, f)$ and $F(V, g)$ we say that they are *concordant*, if $x \in U \cap V$ implies $f(x) = g(x)$. In particular, any two filters with disjoint bases are automatically concordant.

4. A filter $F(U, f)$ is an *extension* of filter $F(V, g)$, if $V \subset U$ and the filters are concordant.

5. Given two filters $F(U, f)$ and $F(V, g)$, concordant or not, we define their *transparent superposition* $F(U, f) \wedge F(V, g)$ as filter $F(U \cup V, h)$ with function h defined by $h(x) = f(x)$ for $x \in U - V$, $h(x) = g(x)$ for $x \in V - U$, and

$$h(x) = \min[f(x), g(x)]$$

for $x \in U \cap V$. Similarly, the *opaque superposition* of filters is defined as $F(U \cup V, h)$, with h defined as above, except that min is replaced by max.

Thus, the transparent superposition of two filters is a filter that operates as $F(U, f)$ on $U - V$, as filter $F(V, g)$ on $V - U$, and on $U \cap V$ it operates as the "weaker" of the two filters; that is, it makes the events unobservable with the smaller of the two probabilities. The interpretation of the opaque superposition is similar.

From the above definitions it follows at once that we have the following theorem.

THEOREM 2.16 *If filters $F(U, f)$ and $F(V, g)$ are concordant, then their opaque and transparent superpositions coincide.*

Given two filters, $F_1 = F(U, f)$ and $F_2 = F(U, g)$, hence with $U = V$, we say that F_1 *dominates* F_2, to be denoted $F_1 \succcurlyeq F_2$, if $f(x) \geq g(x)$ for all $x \in U$. We then have the following theorem.

THEOREM 2.17 *For any two filters, their opaque superposition dominates the transparent superposition.*

Let $\Phi: Q \to [0, 1]$. We say that a family of filters is Φ-generated if for any filter $F(U, f)$ from this family the function f is a restriction of Φ to the set U. Obviously, if a family of filters is Φ-generated, then any two of them are concordant.

The above notions were expressed only through the base of the filter and the selector f, which maps the base into the interval $[0, 1]$. Technically, therefore, a filter is simply a fuzzy set in the parameter space Q. Phrased in these terms, the theory of filters acquires a degree of conceptual unification, due to the use of fuzzy set theory.

We shall now pass to the problems of constraints on observability connected with the observer's choice of the variables that he wishes to observe and the times of observation. Such constraints will be referred to as masks.

Generally, when studying a certain phenomenon, the observer faces the following situation. The phenomenon may be represented by a family of interrelated random variables, say, $\{X_w, w \in W\}$, where W is some parameter set. The elements of W are labels of observable random variables and the values of these random variables represent the results of experiments or observations. Sometimes the observed value is regarded as a "distorted," or biased, observation of some underlying "true" value.

As a rule, one of the components of W is time, so that the same random variable may be observed several times at various moments. Thus, it might be convenient to represent W as a Cartesian product $W = V \times T$, where V is the class of "generic labels" of random variables and T the time axis. Thus, $w = (v, t)$, and instead of writing $X_w = X_{(v,t)}$ it is more convenient to write $X_v(t)$, representing the value of the random variable X_v at time t.

The observer's first choice is to define operationally the phenomenon that he studies. This choice depends on the goal of research, and even for the same goal the choice need not be unique. This choice consists of selecting a finite number of elements of V, say, $v_1, \ldots, v_N$, that he intends to observe and that (in his opinion) "cover" the phenomenon. To give an example, suppose that the phenomenon in question is generally termed "measles." Various variables that one might wish to observe concern the individual course of illness, dynamics of appearance of symptoms, various facts pertaining to immunity, epidemiological properties, like spread of measles in a given community, and so on. The choice of variables depends on the goal of study, and for the same goal, two researchers are likely to choose different variables. Whether the selected variables "cover" the phenomenon, in the sense that they provide information sufficient to attain the goal, is usually impossible to determine a priori with full certainty.

Suppose now that the researcher made his decision, say, $v_1, \ldots, v_N$, of labels of variables to observe so that his objects of interest are variables $[X_{v_1}(t), \ldots, X_{v_N}(t)]$. This set of variables then provides a *state description* of the phenomenon. As a rule, these variables are interrelated, that is, they constitute a *system*. To collect information about the interrelations, one needs a sample of data about the values of these variables for a given set of moments. The temporal pattern of a sample point is a *mask*, as defined by Klir (1972). Thus, assuming for simplicity that time is discrete, a mask is a set of pairs of the form (v_i, k_{ij}), where k_{ij} are some nonnegative integers.

The intended interpretation is such that the variable with label v_i is to be observed at each of the times k_{ij}. For example, if the mask consists of pairs $(v_1, 2), (v_1, 3), (v_1, 5), (v_3, 0), (v_4, 0), (v_4, 1)$, and $(v_4, 5)$, then the random variable X_{v_1} is to be observed at times $t = 2, t = 3$, and $t = 5$, the random variable X_{v_3} is to be observed at $t = 0$, and the random variable X_{v_4} is to be observed at times $t = 0, t = 1$, and $t = 5$. Other random variables are not observed under this mask.

Denote now, for a given mask M

$$t_M = \min_{i,j} k_{ij} \tag{2.96}$$

and

$$h_M = \max_{i,j}(k_{ij} - t_M). \tag{2.97}$$

The moment t_M will be called the *anchoring time* of the mask M, and h_M will be called the *horizon* of mask M.

We shall say that mask M *strictly precedes* mask M' if

$$t_M + h_M < t_{M'}. \tag{2.98}$$

This condition means that the collection of data according to mask M' begins after the collection of data according to mask M is terminated. It follows in particular that if M strictly precedes M', then the sets of pairs in masks M and M' are disjoint.

Formally, a mask is simply a finite subset of the Cartesian product $V \times T$, where T is the time axis. Let F_M be the class of all masks M such that the set of variables $\{X_v(t), (v, t) \in M\}$ is jointly observable; the elements of F_M will be called *feasible masks*. In the following all considerations will be restricted to feasible masks.

If M is a mask, let

$$V(M) = \{v \in V : (v, t) \in M \text{ for some } t\}, \tag{2.99}$$

so that $V(M)$ is simply the class of all variables that are to be observed under mask M. Furthermore, for $v \in V(M)$ let

$$T_v(M) = \{t \in T : (v, t) \in M\} \qquad (2.100)$$

be the *temporal trace* of the variable with label v.

Finally, we introduce the following definition. Two masks, M and M' are said to be *temporally equivalent, $M \sim M'$*, if

$$(\exists t^*) : (v, t) \in M \qquad \text{iff} \qquad (v, t + t^*) \in M'. \qquad (2.101)$$

Obviously, the temporal equivalence is an equivalence relation, that is, it is reflexive, symmetric, and transitive, so that the class of all masks may be partitioned into subclasses of temporally equivalent masks.

We have the following theorem.

THEOREM 2.18 *If $M \sim M'$, then $V(M) = V(M')$, and the temporal traces of each variable $v \in V(M)$ are translations of one another by the amount t^*.*

We also have the next theorem.

THEOREM 2.19 *If $M \sim M'$ and $t^* > h_M$, then M strictly precedes M', and if $t^* < -h_M$, then M' strictly precedes M.*

To appreciate the variety of situation in which different types of masks are applied, it is best to consider some typical examples.

SYSTEMS WITH RESET POSSIBILITY

Consider a simple system with two components, labeled v_1 and v_2, and a control variable labeled v_3. In the deterministic case, the state of the system at t, that is, the triplet $[X_{v_1}(t), X_{v_2}(t), X_{v_3}(t)]$, uniquely determines the values $X_{v_1}(t + 1)$ and $X_{v_2}(t + 1)$, so that

$$X_{v_1}(t + 1) = f_1[t, X_{v_1}(t), X_{v_2}(t), X_{v_3}(t)] \qquad (2.102)$$

and

$$X_{v_2}(t + 1) = f_2[t, X_{v_1}(t), X_{v_2}(t), X_{v_3}(t)]. \qquad (2.103)$$

Typically, functions f_1 and f_2 are not known, and one of the main issues is to determine such properties of f_1 and f_2 that would enable one to optimally control the system, that is, to find a rule $d = d(t, X_{v_1}, X_{v_2})$ for setting the control variable at time $t + 1$ to optimize the performance of the system, the latter being measured by some known function of the sequence $\{X_{v_1}(t), X_{v_2}(t), t = 1, 2, \ldots\}$. By stating the problem in such a way we immediately generalize it to the case of more than two variables and more than one control variable.

Obviously, if the unknown functions f_1 and f_2 depend on t, there is not much that can be done. However, one may often assume stationarity, in which case they do not depend on time. Then functions f_1 and f_2 may be determined, at least partially, if one may reset arguments X_{v_1} and X_{v_2} (inputs) and X_{v_3} (control) at some values of interest and observe the subsequent values $X_{v_1}(t + s)$ and $X_{v_2}(t + s)$ for a given control sequence. The mask tells us which values to record.

In the case of a deterministic system, one such observed pattern may be sufficient to determine the values of functions f_1 and f_2 for given inputs. In the case of nondeterministic systems, one may need a series of "identical" observations, that is, each time one must apply a mask that is equivalent to the original one in the sense of time translation. For such observations one needs to be able to "reset" the system at will for some desired set of initial variables.

Often the system studied may appear in a number of independent "copies," in which case one may think of each copy as being "reset," but without the possibility of controlling the input variables. For instance, in assessing the long-term effects of some medical treatments, patients are asked to report to the hospital for a follow-up study. A mask may require that they report for a checkup (and measurement of some variables of interest) at specific times, such as every 2 weeks during the first 3 months, then one a month for a year, then every 6 months, and so on. Here the masks for each patient are the same up to the choice of the initial moment, so that they are equivalent. In this case, the masks do not have to precede one another, as in the case of a system that must be reset when new observations start.

STATIONARY PROCESSES

Resetting the system may be possible in cases of some instrument of device that may be "stopped" and observed, so to say, "from the beginning." Often this is not possible. Imagine, for instance, a system of price changes of some commodities, or weather characteristics in several localities. Here we deal with a process (which may or may not be under partial control) that occurs only once and cannot be repeated. In such a case, a reasonable sampling scheme would call for masks $M_1, M_2, \ldots$, with $M_1 \sim M_{i+1}$ for each $i = 1, 2, \ldots$ and such that t^* appearing in definition (2.101) is positive. Whether or not each mask M_i ought to be strictly preceding M_{i+1} depends on the statistical procedure employed. In the case of strict precedence, the sample points do not overlap. In the opposite case, it may happen that $M_i \cap M_{i+1} \neq \varnothing$, and the sample points may be linked into a chain.

RANDOM MASKS

Often the mask becomes changed in the process of taking the observations, that is, one may decide to take some additional observations of new variables or of the variables observed until a given time. Such a situation may occur, for example, in the case of follow-up medical studies mentioned above. Thus, one may decide to increase the frequency of checkups or take some additional measurements when observing some abnormal or otherwise interesting results. In this case, the plan calls for amending the mask, depending on the results of observations.

To describe it formally, such a random mask may be characterized inductively by a function K, whose arguments are sets of values observed up to time t (including the empty set), and its values are pairs (V', t') with $V' \subset V$ and $t' > t$ or with value $\emptyset$.

The rule K is to be interpreted as follows. Let $K(\emptyset) = (V', t')$, which means that we are to take the observations of variables $X_v(t')$, $v \in V'$. Given these values, let $K[(X_v(t'), v \in V')] = (V'', t'')$. This means that, having observed the values at t', we should now proceed to observe values $X_v(t'')$, $v \in V''$, and so forth. Eventually, when the value of K at some set of arguments is $\emptyset$, we stop taking the observations. The resulting mask, that is, the set of values to be observed and the times of taking these observations, is random and depends on the actually observed values. A typical example of such a mask is the process of sequential testing of hypotheses, where the mask is simply (assuming one observation per unit time) $t = \{1, 2, \ldots, N\}$, where N is the random number of observations.

The following are relevant definitions.

1.   The collection of data observed through a mask or a set of masks is the *database* for the study of the phenomenon in question.

2.   The variables observed through a mask are on various levels of generality. Given a mask M and the set $V(M)$ of observed variables, the latter partitions among various generality levels. If $V(M)$ is contained in one level of generality, the mask may be called *homogeneous*; in the opposite case, it may be called *heterogeneous* (with respect to generality levels). Since masks are sets in $W = V \times T$, one may consider various set-theoretical operations, so that one can speak of intersections, unions, and so on, of masks. In particular, if one chooses a subset of a mask on a given level of generality, one obtains a homogeneous mask.

3.   A mask may be called *faithful* if set $V(M)$ contains all variables relevant to a given phenomenon or to a given goal of study. In this sense, faithfulness is a goal-dependent concept.

4.   Given a class of semantically interrelated goals and a class of faithful masks, one may consider their intersection and call it the *base of faithfulness*. In this set, each variable belongs to each goal, hence one may call such a mask *invariant* with respect to the change of goals. If the estimated value (on the basis of a mask) is close to the true value, we say that the mask is *statistically faithful*, or *a posteriori faithful*, as opposed to the prior faithfulness discussed above.

5. Still another type of faithfulness may be identified with the *robustness* of the used method of estimation, that is, the sensitivity to the deviations from the true value of the parameters of the phenomenon.

All these concepts are fuzzy, because of the fuzziness of the underlying notion of relevance for a given goal (this is not to be confused with the possible fuzziness of a mask: the latter, being a subset of the set $V \times T$, may be in an obvious way generalized to the notion of a fuzzy mask, being a fuzzy subset of $V \times T$; all set-theoretical operations on masks carry over in an obvious way to the fuzzy case).

The relevance function may change in time and also as the result of experiments, so that the concept of faithfulness also changes: the mask that was faithful at a given time need not have this property at some other time.

Finally, let us mention that since the masks are used sequentially, they form strings of masks (for the same phenomenon). The class of all finite strings of masks that are admissible for a given phenomenon constitute the language of masks, in the sense to be found in Nowakowska (1973). In fact, we have here a fuzzy language of masks, if one considers grades of admissibility. One may also, using the criteria of admissibility, select subclasses that satisfy to a given degree the criteria of faithfulness and exactness. One could imagine further restrictions of these languages, by ethical or deontic valuations.

It is important to mention that in this case one can carry over some of the ideas of formal action theory (Nowakowska, 1973), especially in its fuzzy version, for example, the concepts of decisive moments, praxiological sets of masks, complete possibility, periodicity, and, in particular, the analysis of homonymity and synonymity.

One could hope that the outlined theory of masks and observability may turn out to be fruitful in the foundations of statistics, where the notions of observability and theory of experiments are still not uniformly developed, and there is a lack of unified formal foundations of the theory of observations. Also, the above concepts may prove useful in the theory of mathematical modeling.

APPENDIX

PROOF OF THEOREM 2.2

If $\varphi'(t) < 1$, then $t \notin V(w')$. On the other hand, condition $\varphi(t) = 0$ means that $t \notin V^+(w)$. Consequently, (2.20) asserts that

$$V(w')^c \subset V^+(w)^c,$$

which is the same as the first part of the assertion of the theorem. The second part is proved in the same way.

PROOF OF THEOREM 2.5

Suppose that w is a part of itself. Then we have $V^+(w) \subset V(w)$ and $U_t^+(w) \subset U_t(w)$ for all t. Since the opposite inclusions are always true, we obtain $V(w) = V^+(w)$ and $U_t(w) = U_t^+(w)$ for all t, which proves the theorem.

PROOF OF THEOREM 2.6

The proof is analogous to that of Theorem 1.16.

PROOF OF THEOREM 2.9

If g_1, g_2, and g_3 are nondecreasing, so are their maxima and minima. Since g_e is built only out of the operations of maximum and minimum, the function g_e is nondecreasing. The second assertion follows from the fact that function f assumes the value 1 when all arguments are 1 and that g_e is a continuous function of its arguments.

PROOF OF THEOREM 2.10

To prove this theorem, consider the function $\min[g'(t), 1 - g''(t)]$. Since $g'(t)$ increases and $1 - g''(t)$ decreases, for sufficiently small t we have $g'(t) \leq 1 - g''(t)$ and consequently, $\min[g'(t), 1 - g''(t)] = g'(t)$, which increases with t. Starting from some point t_0 at which $g'(t_0) = 1 - g''(t_0)$, the situation is reversed, and we have $\min[g'(t), 1 - g''(t)] = 1 - g''(t)$, which decreases with t. Consequently, $p(e', e'') = g'(t_0)$, where t_0 is a point at which $g'(t_0) + g''(t_0) = 1$. By symmetry, we have $p(e'', e') = g''(t_0)$, which shows that $p(e', e'') + p(e'', e') = g'(t_0) + g''(t_0) = 1$, which proves the assertion.

PROOF OF THEOREM 2.12

If the chain is ergodic, then $P_{ij}^{(n)} \to p(j)$, independently of i as $n \to \infty$. Let us write

$$P^{(n)}(F \mid E_i) = \sum_j \mu_F(E_j) p_{ij}^{(n)}.$$

Passing to the limit with $n \to \infty$, we obtain

$$\lim_n P^{(n)}(F \mid E_i) = \lim_n \sum_j \mu_F(E_j) p_{ij}^{(n)}$$

$$= \sum_j \mu_F(E_j) \lim_n p_{ij}^{(n)} = \sum_j \mu_F(E_j) p(j),$$

and the last term does not depend on i, which proves the theorem.

PROOF OF THEOREM 2.13

If $A \in \mathcal{G}^*$, then $B \supset A$ implies $B \notin \mathcal{G}^*$ unless $A = B$, by Definition 2.10. In words, if A and B are maximally observable and distinct, then neither of them may be contained in the other.

PROOF OF THEOREM 2.14

Denote the right-hand side of (2.64) by $\mathscr{B}$. Suppose that $A \in \mathscr{B}$. Then $A \subset B$ for some $B \in \mathscr{G}^* \subset \mathscr{G}$. Thus, A is a subset of an observable set and must itself be observable by Hypothesis 2.1, so that $A \in \mathscr{G}$. This shows that $\mathscr{B} \subset \mathscr{G}$.

For the inclusion $\mathscr{G} \subset \mathscr{B}$, let $A \in \mathscr{G}$. If A is maximal, that is, $A \in \mathscr{G}^*$, then we may take $B = A$ in the definition of $\mathscr{B}$, obtaining $A \in \mathscr{B}$. If A is not maximally observable, then we may find $B_1 \supset A, B_1 \neq A$, with $B_1 \in \mathscr{G}$. Again, if $B_1 \in \mathscr{G}^*$, we obtain $A \in \mathscr{B}$. If B_1 is not maximal, we choose $B_2 \supset B_1$ with $B_2 \in \mathscr{G}$, and so on.

This procedure must eventually lead to a set B_k in $\mathscr{G}^*$, since otherwise we could construct an infinite strictly increasing sequence $A \subset B_1 \subset B_2 \subset \cdots$ of sets in $\mathscr{G}$, which is impossible in view of finiteness of N.

PROOF OF THEOREM 2.15

We have

$$P[Y_{z_1}(t) < Y_{z_2}(t) \mid \min(Y_{z_1}(t), Y_{z_2}(t)) \leq T]$$

$$= \frac{P[Y_{z_1}(t) < Y_{z_2}(t) \,\&\, \min(Y_{z_1}(t), Y_{z_2}(t)) \leq T]}{1 - P[\min(Y_{z_1}(t), Y_{z_2}(t)) > T]}$$

$$= \frac{P[Y_{z_1}(t) \leq T \,\&\, Y_{z_2}(t) > Y_{z_1}(t)]}{1 - \exp[-(\lambda_{z_1} + \lambda_{z_2})T]}.$$

The numerator of the last formula may be written as

$$\int_0^T \lambda_{z_1} \exp(-\lambda_{z_1}x) \exp(-\lambda_{z_2}x)\, dx = \frac{\lambda_{z_1}}{\lambda_{z_1} + \lambda_{z_2}} \{1 - \exp[-(\lambda_{z_1} + \lambda_{z_2})T]\},$$

which completes the proof.

3 MULTIMEDIAL UNITS AND LANGUAGES: VERBAL AND NONVERBAL COMMUNICATION*

3.1 INTRODUCTION

This chapter shows how one can incorporate into one system a formal description of simultaneous communication events and actions occurring in everyday life. It is worth stressing at the beginning that the theory introduced is of a wider importance and applies to phenomena other than verbal and nonverbal communication; in particular, it may be used for descriptions of perceptual phenomena, as well as for a certain class of neurobiological phenomena observed in perceptual areas of the brain [see, e.g., Hubel and Wiesel (1981)].

This theory is an extension of the formal theory of actions (see Nowakowska, 1973); its outline was first presented, among others, at a semiotic colloquim in Vienna in 1975, as well as at a conference on cognition in Madrid and an open lecture at Harvard in 1977.

The analysis in this chapter will concern the communication carried out simultaneously on several media, such as verbal medium (utterances), accompanied by gestures or other body movements, facial expressions, and so on.

One of the main concepts of the suggested system is that of a *multimedial unit* of communication. It plays the same role as a unit used for formal analysis of languages (e.g., a word) except that it has a number of components corresponding to actions on various media. The concept of such a unit is fuzzy, for obvious reasons connected with the difficulty of identifying actions on media such as facial expressions. Nevertheless, it is worthwhile to begin the

*From Nowakowska (1985). Reprinted with permission from *Mathematical Social Sciences,* 10, 1985, copyright by North-Holland Publishing Company, Amsterdam, 1985.

analysis with the simplest (and admittedly idealized) case, assuming that one can unambiguously specify "vocabulary" of actions on each medium, and define a multimedial unit as a vector of actions on various media, each taking up the same amount of time and occurring simultaneously. Such a definition, owing to the idealization involved, allows us to concatenate the units and consider strings of units. Consequently, in Sections 3.2 and 3.3, the analysis concerns languages regarded as classes of admissible strings of multimedial units. Section 3.2 deals with syntactic aspects of such multidimensional languages. It is clear that such a language also determines languages (i.e., classes of admissible strings) on each medium separately and that the actions on various media are interrelated (e.g., a specific action on a give medium may exclude or enforce another action on a different medium).

In Section 3.3 the considerations concern the semantics of multimedial languages of communication. Here the main point is that the meanings of units are fuzzy (as opposed to purely verbal communication, where the meanings of words or sentences are much less ambiguous). The situation is such that an action on a nonverbal medium tends to support or inhibit a given meaning expressed on verbal medium (e.g., a smile tends to enhance a friendly verbal expression).

Section 3.4 is devoted to some "global" properties of semantics of multimedial languages, in particular to problems of expressibility of certain meanings in situations where some of the media are excluded from use (e.g., ballet, communication between deaf and mute).

Sections 3.5 and 3.6 return to the main issue, namely, defining a multimedial unit. Here the idealized assumption that all actions take up the same amount of time is abandoned. As a result, there is no precise "boundary" at which a unit starts or terminates. These conceptual difficulties are overcome by reference to semantics: a unit is the smallest set of actions on various media, performed at more or less the same time and expressing a given meaning in full degree.

The above-outlined considerations concern the properties of the analyzed multimedial language irrespective of the intentions of the sender or the possibilities of the receiver. Looking at communication from the point of view of the latter, it is clear that to extract the meaning from an unit the receiver has to perceive the actions on different media. Here the situation is not much different from that of perceiving a composite picture and assigning to it a meaning.

Looking at the situation from the viewpoint of both the sender and the perceiver, one can consider the goals of the former and the means of attaining them. This leads to an algebraic approach to these goals [similar to that suggested by Nowakowska (1976a)] except that the considerations (Section 3.7) include the role of context.

On the other hand, the receiver may pay more attention to some media or have some preferences among them which may lead to biases in the perceived meanings. Also, various media (or, more precisely, actions on these media) have various degrees of importance for recognizing a given meaning. Section 3.7 presents a possible approach to defining "weights" of actions for a given meaning and their possible empirical determinations.

Also, a given unit may have several meanings that "compete" one with another. The decision about the meaning may depend, among others, on the order of inspection. A model of this phenomenon is suggested in Section 3.7.

Finally, Section 3.8 contains the application of the concepts introduced to the analysis of dialogues.

3.2 THE BASIC CONCEPTUAL SCHEME

The analysis will start from the conceptually and formally simplest case, when all actions on every medium take up a unit time. After such a system is developed, both the motivation and the formal development of the more complex setup will become much easier to appreciate.

The considered system will be based on the following quintuplet of primitive concepts:

$$\langle M, V, L, S, f \rangle, \tag{3.1}$$

where $M = \{m_1, m_2, \ldots, m_r\}$ is the set of media, V the vocabulary (or alphabet) of actions, L the set of all admissible strings of units called language of communication actions, S the set of meanings, and f the function describing fuzzy semantics.

At first, only the three concepts M, V, and L will be discussed. It will be shown how they allow the expression of various notions relevant to the analysis of syntactic constraints in communication.

3.2.1 The Concept of Unit of Communication

Owing to the special convention accepted here, namely that each action in V takes up a unit of time, it is possible to construct a purely formal definition of a communication unit. This will simply be a specification of all actions that occur at particular media at a given time.

Now, to describe what happens on each medium is equivalent to describing a function $h: M \to V$, that is, a function that assigns an action to each medium. If $M = \{m_1, \ldots, m_r\}$ is the set of all media and the elements of V are denoted by letters $v, w, \ldots$ with or without subscripts, then a unit h is a set of actions $v_1 = h(m_1), \ldots, v_r = h(m_r)$, interpreted as simultaneous performances of these actions. The class of all such units will be denoted H.

For subsequent considerations, it will be necessary to introduce a special way of describing the fact that a given medium remains "neutral" or "inactive." Such a "neutral action," or "pause," will be denoted $\#$ regardless of the medium.

In the case of medium m_1 (verbal), "remaining inactive" means simply silence. For other media, the concept of neutrality is fuzzier. Thus, in the case of the medium of facial expressions, $\#$ may stand for some neutral expression; in the case of body movements $\#$ stands for lack of movements, and so on.

The second comment here is that it ought to be clear that the set H is very large and comprises the admissible units, together with the inadmissible. To see why it is so, it is perhaps best to consider some examples of units, both admissible and inadmissible.

Medium	Admissible h	Inadmissible h
m_1 = verbal	$h(m_1)$ = "Hello!"	$h(m_1)$ = bow
m_2 = facial expressions	$h(m_2)$ = smile	$h(m_2)$ = tipping the hat
m_3 = body movements	$h(m_3)$ = bow	$h(m_3)$ = bow
m_4 = right hand	$h(m_4)$ = tipping the hat	$h(m_4)$ = smile
$\vdots$	$\vdots$	$\vdots$

In the accompanying tabulation the admissible unit, in the middle column, represents something like "greeting." The inadmissible unit, given in the right column, is plainly nonsensical: it assigns, for instance, the action "smile" to the medium of movements of the right hand, and so forth.

Thus, it becomes necessary to eliminate from H the units that are not admissible and also define the sets of actions that are appropriate for each of the media. These sets of actions will be appropriate subsets of V. The definitions here will be based on the third primitive notion of system (3.1), namely the language of communication L.

The formal construction is exactly the same as in mathematical linguistics. One considers the class of all finite strings of elements of H (technically; the *monoid* over H), denoted H^*, and then one identifies the language of actions L with a subset of H^*. The only difference is that in this case the "strings" are composed of multimedial units. Therefore a string is really a matrix, or a "bundle" of parallel strings, one on each medium. Thus justifies the term "multidimensional" in referring to the language of actions L.

Thus each string of units has the form

$$u = h_1 h_2 \cdots h_n = \begin{bmatrix} v_{11} & v_{12} & \cdots & v_{1n} \\ v_{21} & v_{22} & \cdots & v_{2n} \\ \vdots & \vdots & \cdots & \vdots \\ v_{r1} & v_{r2} & \cdots & v_{rn} \end{bmatrix}, \tag{3.2}$$

where v_{ij} is the action on medium m_i in the jth unit; that is, we have $v_{ij} = h_j(m_i)$.

3.2.2 Multidimensional Language of Communication Actions

Formally, L will be a subset of H^*, that is, a set of matrices of actions of the form of (3.1). Elements of L will be interpreted as admissible strings of units. Naturally, since subset L of admissible strings of units is a primitive concept, one cannot say explicitly which strings are in L and which are not. That is, one cannot describe a *formal procedure* that could distinguish admissible strings from inadmissible ones.

It should be quite obvious why such a procedure is impossible to give: it is impossible, despite numerous attempts, even for a much simpler structure, namely, for the natural language.

Thus, the program here is more or less similar to that in analytical models in linguistics: to take the concept of language, that is, the set of admissible strings, as a primitive one, and rely on common intuition in distinguishing admissible strings from nonadmissible ones, perhaps agreeing that L is a fuzzy subset of H^*. Then, instead of trying to find a grammar that would generate L, one might try to find useful methods of analysis of L.

In the case under consideration, each "string"—being in fact a matrix of actions—describes a fragment of communication behavior, taking into account all that is happening on all media during the considered time interval.

The intuition of the language of communication L, or equivalently of admissibility of a given string of communication actions, is such that a given string (matrix) is admissible if it is physically performable and also if it represents a fragment of behavior that is meaningful, socially acceptable, and so on.

It is not necessary to give more exact interpretations, mainly because the flexibility of this interpretation gives the model more applicability. For instance, if one wants to describe and analyze some communication actions of a special type, such as royal court protocol or a Japanese tea ceremony, the set L (or admissibility) has to be appropriately defined in each context (conforming to court protocol, etc.).

3.2.3 Admissibility of a Unit and Language of a Given Medium

The preliminary formal definitions expressed in terms of L are the following.

DEFINITION 3.1 The set H_A of admissible units, sets V_i and L_i (*vocabulary*), and *language of medium* m_i are defined in the following way:

$$H_A = \{h \in H : \exists u = h_1 h_2 \cdots h_n \in L \text{ such that } h = h_i \text{ for some } i\}; \quad (3.3)$$

$$V_i = \{v \in V : \exists u = h_1 h_2 \cdots h_n \in L \text{ such that } h_j(m_i) = v \text{ for some } j\}; \quad (3.4)$$

$$L_i = \{v_1 v_2 \cdots v_n : \exists u = h_1 h_2 \cdots h_n \in L \text{ such that}$$
$$h_1(m_i) = v_1, h_2(m_i) = v_2, \ldots, h_n(m_i) = v_n\}. \quad (3.5)$$

Here H_A is the class of all admissible units, that is, all units that may appear in matrices belonging to L. Similarly, V_i is the class of all actions that may appear in medium m_i in strings from L, and L_i is the class of all ith rows of matrices from L. Thus, L_i is the class of all strings of actions that may appear in medium m_i, and it is justified to refer to L_i as the *language of the ith medium.* The two immediate consequences of the above definitions may be formulated as follows.

THEOREM 3.1 *If* $u = h_1 h_2 \cdots h_n \in L$, *then* $h_i \in H_A$ *for* $i = 1, 2, \ldots, n$.

THEOREM 3.2 *If* $h \in H_A$ *and* $h(m_i) = v$, *then* $v \in V_i$.

These are, of course, very tautological consequences, asserting that an admissible string of units must consist of admissible units only and that an admissible unit must consist only of actions that are admissible for their media. What is of some interest and importance, however, is the realization that the converse implications need not hold.

In the first case, even though each unit may be admissible, that is, possible in some context, the string of such units need not be admissible. For example, greeting of a person in a certain way, such as shaking his hand or saying "Hello!", is admissible, but doing it twice in succession usually is not admissible.

Similarly, the converse to the second implication need not be true, that is, a unit may consist of such actions that each of them is admissible in some context, but it is impossible to perform them simultaneously. For instance, such a combination is an utterance in a verbal medium and sticking out the tongue in a medium of facial expressions.

3.2.4 Equivalence and Parasiticity

Individual languages L_i, as well as the whole language L of communication actions, may be analyzed by means of some linguistic concepts such as L-equivalence and L-parasiticity (resp. L_i-equivalence and L_i-parasiticity).

Generally, we may introduce the following definitions.

DEFINITION 3.2 Let $A \subset L$. We say that two multimedial strings x, y are *A-equivalent*, written $x \sim_A y$, if for all $u, v \in H^*$ we have $uxv \in A$ if and only if $uyv \in A$.

DEFINITION 3.3 A string $x \in H^*$ is said to be *A-parasitic* if for all $u, v \in H^*$ we have $uxv \notin A$.

Taking $A \subset L_i$ and replacing H^* by V_i^* (the class of all strings formed out of elements of V_i), one obtains the definitions of A-equivalence and A-parasiticity for strings in L_i.

The most important case occurs when one takes $A = L$ (resp. $A = L_i$). Then two strings are equivalent if they play the same role in forming strings in L, in the sense that embedding them into any context (preceding and subsequent string) leads to strings that have the same status with respect to L: either they are both in L or both outside of L.

The class of L-parasitic strings reflects, in a sense, *negative constraints* in formation of language L: it is the class of strings that are neither in L nor form any parts of strings in L.

To use a linguistic example in which L is the class of all sentences, L-equivalence yields the so-called distributive partition. For instance, *dog* and *cat* belong to the same class (are L-equivalent), since any string of words containing the word *dog* does not change its status (being a sentence or not being a sentence) if *dog* is replaced by *cat*. On the other hand, *dog* and *dogs* are not in the same class: replacing in the sentence *The dog chases a rabbit* the word *dog* by the word *dogs* leads to a nonsentence *The dogs chases a rabbit*.

Naturally, we have the following.

THEOREM 3.3   *Any two L-parasitic strings are L-equivalent.*

3.2.5   Enforcing and Exclusion

The definitions of the preceding section are standard in linguistic contexts. However, one can define some other concepts that utilize the fact that we deal now with units ("words") that have their own multidimensional structure. These concepts (still obtained without any reference to semantics) will describe the "intermedial" constraints between actions.

The general idea is to analyze those actions that on a given medium are implied and those that are eliminated by the fact that a certain action is performed on some other medium. Let us put

$$B_i(v) = \{h \in H : h(m_i) = v\}; \qquad (3.6)$$

thus $B_i(v)$ is the set of all admissible units that have action v on medium m_i.

One can now define the relation of enforcing and excluding as follows.

DEFINITION 3.4   The relation of *enforcing* is defined as

$$uF_{ij}v \quad \text{iff} \quad h \in B_i(v) \Rightarrow h(m_j) = u \qquad (3.7)$$

(i.e., any unit with action v on medium m_i must have action u on medium m_j).

DEFINITION 3.5   The relation of *excluding* is defined as

$$uE_{ij}v \quad \text{iff} \quad h \in B_i(v) \Rightarrow h(m_j) \neq u \qquad (3.8)$$

(i.e., no unit with action v on medium m_i can have action u on medium m_j).

It ought to be mentioned that these definitions are of a syntactic nature: both enforcing and excluding mean that, if any unit h has some property, then it must or cannot have some other property. Breaking any of these rules would result in a unit that is outside the class H of admissible units.

From these definitions it follows at once that the relation of enforcing is *transitive*: if action *u* enforces action *v* and action *v* enforces action *w*, then action *u* also enforces action *w*. However, this relation need not be symmetric: one can show examples of actions *u* and *v* such that one of them must be accompanied by the other (that is, enforces it), but the latter may be also performed alone.

On the other hand, the relation of excluding is *symmetric* but need not be transitive. Indeed, *u* may exclude *v* and *v* may exclude *w*, but it does not follow that *u* excludes *w*: these two actions may be performed simultaneously.

In general, the knowledge of relations of enforcing and excluding may provide information about the structure of the communication units in a given situation that one wants to analyze.

3.3 SEMANTICS

Let us now turn to the last two primitive concepts of the system, namely the set S of meanings (sememes) and the function f describing the (fuzzy) meanings of strings of actions. Formally, the function f maps the set $L \times S$ into the interval $[0, 1]$; that is, it assigns to every pair (u, s) consisting of a string u of communication actions and a meaning s, the number $f(u, s)$, which represents the *degree to which u means s*.

Since the language L of communication actions contains, among others, the utterances, the set S must contain all possible meanings of sentences. In the present section, however, the main object of interest will be those meanings that are carried mostly by nonverbal media; examples of such meanings are "friendliness," "annoyance," "contempt," "dislike." Most of these meanings have the property that they may appear in modalities; thus, the set S will contain meanings such as "mild annoyance" or "extreme annoyance."

A group of meanings (sememes) representing various degrees of a meaning s will be considered as forming a scale; that is, they will be assumed to be ordered along a certain continuum specific for the given semem s.

Let us now turn to the interpretation of function f. As already mentioned, the value of $f(u, s)$ is to be treated as the degree to which the string of communication units u expresses the meaning s. The meaning of the string u need not be unique: there may be more than one element s such that $f(u, s) > 0$.

3.3.1 Meanings of Units and Empirical Interpretation of f

The assumption of the existence of function f imposes certain restrictions on the possible interpretation of elements of S and L. It ought to be clear that such a broad concept as a function assigning meanings to the whole strings (in a fuzzy or nonfuzzy way) would be of a limited value if it were not accompanied by the assumption that meanings are also assigned to particular units in the string. Indeed, having only the meanings of separate units and also the meanings of strings of those units, one may express various ways in which a particular medium contributes to the meaning of a unit and in which a given unit contributes to the meaning of a string.

Thus, it will be assumed that function f assigns meanings also to admissible units (equivalently, it suffices to assume that all one-element strings are in L).

The assumption of existence of fuzzy membership function f (for single units, as well as for the strings) requires the clarification of the following points: (i) to which extent, and how, does it narrows down the possible choices of units? (ii) how does one interpret the concept of fuzziness in the context of present considerations?

Regarding the first question, the answer is that, to obtain the proper interpretation, one cannot distinguish units that are too small: each unit must be sufficiently large to carry *some* meaning. The problem of choice of units will be discussed in some detail in subsequent sections, where we abandon the simplifying assumption that all actions take up the same length of time.

Regarding the second question, namely, the interpretation of fuzzy membership function f, there are several alternative ways in which one can interpret the fact that $f(h, s) = p$, that is, "the degree to which the meaning of unit h is s, equals p." First, it may mean that p is the fraction of persons who, when confronted with unit h, will claim that its meaning is s. Second, s may be one of the possible meaning of h, and p is the frequency of occasions in which it is used to denote s. Third, p may be the degree of certainty (of a given person) that the unit h was used, on a particular occasion, in meaning s. Finally, there is a fourth interpretation possible connected with the following conceptualization of unit h.

Generally, h consists of some utterance, that is, action on verbal medium, and a number of actions on other media. Now, these media concern gestures, facial expressions, body movements, and so on, and there is a certain degree of arbitrariness of performing a gesture, within the limits imposed by the constraints of the human body and the surrounding space. Formally, it could perhaps be described by an appropriate parametrization of h, that is, by treating h as a family of units, say, h_z, where z runs through a parameter set. Different h_z differ in the degree to which some gestures, expressions, and so on, are performed. As z changes, units h_z change their meanings somewhat. A typical example is when a gesture loses its meaning when it is exaggerated, that is, when the parameter z assumes some extreme value. In this interpretation, function f would represent the fraction of cases (values of z) for which a given meaning s is associated with h_z.

Regardless of the interpretation of the value of the function f, one can use it to express the role played by various media (or actions on particular media) in contributing to a given meaning of a unit, as well as the role played in the given string of units by a particular unit.

The first of these problems will be discussed in some detail in the next section, and the second problem will be sketched in subsequent sections.

3.3.2   The Role of Actions for Meaning of a Unit

In general, the definitions below will be based on the comparison of meanings of two units, which differ only on one medium.

Let h be a fixed unit, with action v on medium m_i, that is, such that $h(m_i) = v$. Furthermore, let $h_i(u)$ be the unit h with action v replaced by action u, that is, such that $h(m_i) = u$ and $h(m_j)$ is unchanged for $j \neq i$. In this notation, we have $h_i(v) = h$.

All definitions below will be relative to a fixed meaning s. They will be based, as mentioned, on the comparison of values $f(h_i(v), s)$ and $f(h_i(u), s)$, where s is the selected meaning. In particular, some definitions will concern the unit $h_i(\#)$, that is, a unit with action v replaced by pause $\#$.

Generally, we say that in context h, the action v expresses meaning s stronger than action u if

$$f(h_i(v), s) > f(h_i(u), s).$$ (3.9)

We may now formulate the following definitions.

DEFINITION 3.6   The action v, in context h

(a)   *supports* meaning s if

$$f(h_i(v), s) > f(h_i(\#), s);$$ (3.10)

(b)   *generates* meaning s if

$$f(h_i(v), s) > f(h_i(\#), s) = 0;$$ (3.11)

(c)   *inhibits* meaning s if

$$f(h_i(v), s) < f(h_i(\#), s);$$ (3.12)

(d)   *cancels* meaning s if

$$0 = f(h_i(v), s) < f(h_i(\#), s);$$ (3.13)

(e)   is *neutral* for meaning s if

$$f(h_i(v), s) = f(h_i(\#), s).$$ (3.14)

These definitions are context-dependent in the sense that whether v supports, inhibits, and so on, meaning s depends on the context h (actions on other media) in which v is embedded. To make these definitions context-independent, one has to relativize with respect to classes of contexts.

Let Q be the class of all multimedial units that satisfy the condition $h(m_i) = v$. We may then define the following sets:

$$Q_s^+ = \{h \in Q : f(h, s) > f(h_i(\#), s)\}; \tag{3.15}$$

$$\bar{Q}_s^+ = \{h \in Q : f(h, s) > f(h_i(\#), s) = 0\}; \tag{3.16}$$

$$Q_s^- = \{h \in Q : f(h, s) < f(h_i(\#), s)\}; \tag{3.17}$$

$$\bar{Q}_s^- = \{h \in Q : 0 = f(h, s) < f(h_i(\#), s)\}; \tag{3.18}$$

$$Q_s^0 = \{h \in Q : f(h, s) = f(h_i(\#), s)\}. \tag{3.19}$$

Clearly, we have the following relations:

$$Q = Q_s^+ \cup Q_s^- \cup Q_s^0 \tag{3.20}$$

and
$$\bar{Q}_s^+ \subset Q_s^+, \qquad \bar{Q}_s^- \subset Q_s^- \tag{3.21}$$

We may now introduce the following definition.

DEFINITION 3.7   Action v *supports* meaning s if $Q_s^+ = Q$; it *inhibits* s if $Q_s^- = Q$ and is *neutral* with respect to s if $Q_s^0 = Q$. Furthermore, if $Q_s^+ \cup Q_s^0 = Q$ (so that $Q_s^- = \varnothing$), we say that v is *positively associated* with s; and if $Q_s^- \cup Q_s^0 = Q$ (so that $Q_s^+ = \varnothing$), we say that v is *negatively* associated with s. Finally, if both Q_s^+ and Q_s^- are nonempty, we say that v is *heterogeneous* with respect to s.

Thus, supporting of a meaning occurs if adding action v increases the degree of expression of meaning s above the level that would have occurred if action $\#$ were placed in medium m_i in place of v. In particular, in the latter case, if meaning s would not be present at all, one could say that v generates s.

Other definitions are based on a similar principle: *inhibition* occurs if replacing pause by v decreases the degree of expression of meaning s, and so forth.

The second definition, that of positive and negative association, concerns the case of support and inhibition (with possible neutrality) regardless of the context. A typical example of support, for the meaning such as "friendliness," might be an accompanying smile.

To obtain an example of generation of meaning by an action, one can take some religious or magic ceremonies, where lack of a certain action—other conditions being equal—makes the meaning totally absent. Such "magic ingredients" occur outside religion also. For instance, in some countries, a person may be taken by the police, handcuffed, and so on, but all those actions do not signify the meaning "lawful arrest" unless the policeman also utters the formula telling a person about some specific rights that he has, warning him that whatever he says may be used against him, and so on.

In a similar way, one may find examples of other concepts concerning the influence of specific actions on the meaning of a unit of actions.

The definitions above concerned the case of one action on one medium only. This situation is, of course, more complex, in the sense that the same meaning is often carried by the simultaneous performance of several actions on appropriate media. To express some of the concepts describing this case, let $h_{ij}(u, w)$ denote the unit h, with actions u and w placed at media m_i and m_j. Thus, $h_{ij}(\#, \#)$ is the unit h with pauses in media m_i and m_j, and so on.

One may now formulate the following definition.

DEFINITION 3.8   In context h, for meaning s, we say that u and v are *positively associated in supporting s* if

$$f(h_{ij}(\#, \#), s) < \min[f(h_{ij}(u, \#), s), f(h_{ij}(\#, v), s)] \qquad (3.22)$$

and

$$\max[f(h_{ij}(\#, \#), s), f(h_{ij}(\#, v), s)] < f(h_{ij}(u, v), s); \qquad (3.23)$$

moreover, *u catalyzes v* if

$$0 = f(h_{ij}(\#, \#), s) = f(h_{ij}(\#, v), s) < f(h_{ij}(u, v), s). \qquad (3.24)$$

Those are only some of the possible combinations. The positive association in supporting s occurs if each of the actions u and v separately supports s, but in combination their effect is greater than the effect of each of them separately. In a similar way, one may define the concept of negative association.

The second notion, that of catalyzing, occurs if one action alone does not have any effect, unless it is accompanied by the other.

Examples for the first concept are quite obvious and may be omitted. As regards the second concept, that of catalyzing, one can think again of some magic actions, religious ceremonies, and so on, where the whole string of actions has no meaning unless one adds some crucial action, such as some gesture or expression; when this magic action is performed, the ceremony becomes "valid," that is, it acquires the intended meaning. The example here is the same as for the case of generation of the meaning, because when u catalyzes v, it also generates the meaning.

3.3.3   The Role of a Unit in a String; Standard Units

The concepts that pertain to the role of an action in a unit for expression of some meaning may be transported to the case of the role of a unit in a string of units. The general idea is, of course, the same: to compare two strings that differ only by one unit.

Let u be a fixed string involving unit h at the ith place, and let $u_i(g)$ denote the same string u with h replaced by g. As before, we say that, in context u, the unit h expresses the meaning s *stronger* than unit g if

$$f(u_i(h), s) > f(u_i(g), s). \tag{3.25}$$

However, for defining analogues of other concepts, it is necessary to have something that would play the role of pause $\#$. Here the situation is somewhat complicated. The idea is to use as a standard for comparison the notion of a "standard" unit.

The definition of the standard unit is as follows. First, one considers a fixed meaning and its modifications, both in positive and negative directions. One may visualize it in the form of a scale, with the meaning s located somewhere on it.

Conceptually, one can represent such a scale as

| | non-s | somewhat non-s | s | very s | extremely s |

(e.g., for s = "polite," one may have, from left to right, meanings such as "rude," "impolite," "somewhat impolite," "polite," "very polite," "extremely polite").

A standard unit for expressing the meaning s is defined as a unit that satisfies two conditions: first, it does not express negative modifications of the meaning at all, and, second, among all units that meet this condition, it expresses the given meaning in the highest degree.

Formally, h is a *standard unit* for s if

$$f(h, -s) = 0 \tag{3.26}$$

$$f(h, s) = \max\{f(h', s) : f(h, -s) = 0\}. \tag{3.27}$$

It is important to stress that a standard unit does not express the highest degree of meaning s. Thus, for instance, for meanings such as "politeness," a standard unit is not an extremely polite behavior, but a behavior that is simply "polite," but in the highest degree of expressing simple politeness.

Clearly, the concept of standard unit is somewhat fuzzy, and standard units are not unique. Intuitively, a standard unit is a completely "normal and average" way of doing things.

The definitions of concepts that may be expressed in terms of standard units will not be given here: they are, to a large extent, analogous to the concepts expressed by means of comparison of units with and without a given action.

3.4   PRAGMATIC SEMANTICS

Let us now present one more conceptual construction, provisionally called "pragmatic semantics." Intuitively, the problem may be described as follows. Imagine that one is restricted in his expressions to only some medium or media, such as in ballet or for deaf and mute persons, where the medium of utterances is not allowed; in silent films, where one has only the medium of facial expressions to his disposal (at least in some scenes); in programs on the radio, where one has only the verbal medium, without facial expressions. The problem is then to determine the possibilities of expressing some meanings, of differentiating between meanings, and so on, with the use of only certain permitted media of expression.

Thus, we distinguish in the language L of communication some subset $L' \subset L$, such as "ballet language." For a given meaning s, we can then define two subsets of L':

$$L^+(s) = \{u \in L' : f(u, s) > 0\} \tag{3.28}$$

and

$$L^0(s) = \{u \in L' : f(u, s) = 0\}. \tag{3.29}$$

Thus, $L^+(s)$ is the subset of L' consisting of those strings that express s in some positive degree, and $L^0(s)$ is that class of strings that does not express the meaning s at all.

Using these sets, one can define the following concepts of "pragmatic semantics." Naturally, all these concepts are relative to the selected language L', that is, to the selected constraints on the means of communication.

DEFINITION 3.9 Given two meanings, $s, t \in S$, we say that s is *embedded* in t if

$$L^+(s) \subset L^+(t); \tag{3.30}$$

furthermore, s and t are *inseparable* if $L^+(s) = L^+(t)$.

DEFINITION 3.10 The meanings $s, t \in S$ are *incompatible* if

$$L^+(s) \subset L^0(t) \qquad [\text{hence also } L^+(t) \subset L^0(s)], \tag{3.31}$$

and s, t are *orthogonal* if

$$L^+(s) \cap L^+(t) \neq \varnothing \neq L^+(s) \cap L^0(t). \tag{3.32}$$

The first concept, of embedding, corresponds to the usual concept of inclusion of meanings in semantics. Here, however, the inclusion is due not to the content of s and t but rather to the limitations of using only certain media, but not the others.

As regards the second concept, inseparability, it corresponds in semantics to the concept of partial synonymy: when two meanings are overlapping, expressing one of them means that automatically the other one is also expressed, at least partially.

The third concept, of inseparability, is perhaps closest to the concept of negation or, more precisely, to the entailment of negation of one meaning by the other.

Finally, the last concept, of orthogonality, corresponds to logical independence.

These concepts utilize only part of the information contained in function $f(u, s)$, namely the fact that its value is zero or is positive. This is why these concepts may be termed "presence–absence" concepts. It is also possible to express some concepts that utilize the full information contained in these functions. They may therefore be termed "degree-of-expression" concepts. For that purpose, denote

$$L_b(s) = \{u \in L' : f(u, s) \geq b\} \tag{3.33}$$

that is, the class of all strings that express the meaning s in the degree at least b. One can now define *synonymity* by the requirement that

$$L_b(s) = L_b(t) \qquad \text{for all } b, \tag{3.34}$$

so that s and t are synonymous if $f(u, s) = f(u, t)$ for all u, which is equivalent to equality of all sets $L_b(s)$ and $L_b(t)$.

Another notion is that of *b-supporting*: t is *b*-supporting s if

$$(\exists b_0)(\forall b \geq b_0) : L_b(s) \subset L^+(t). \tag{3.35}$$

This concept is related specifically to fuzzy meanings and has no direct counterpart in the usual semantics. It is especially connected with two facts:

1.   Meanings may be expressed in varying degrees, which, as should again be stressed, is not the same as expression of a higher degree of the meaning.

2.   An expression—unit or string of communication units—may express several meanings at once.

The concept of *b*-supporting describes the situation when an expression of a given meaning, if it is sufficiently clear or unambiguous (i.e., if the meaning is expressed in sufficiently high degree), must also involve the expression of some other meaning. It is therefore close to the notion of enforcing actions on some media by other actions, except that now the notion concerns semantics, not syntax.

Supporting of a meaning is quite an interesting phenomenon: it shows the interrelations between meanings imposed by the restrictions due to certain media. The meanings as such may be conceptually distinct, but because of limitations on the media, one cannot be expressed without the other. This set of relations between meanings shows therefore the extent of "blurring" due to various media.

To use some examples, consider the difficulties encountered by actors in silent films who had to convey meanings by facial expressions only and had to differentiate (say) among surprise, fear or hate, jealousy and anger.

Finally, the last problem to be mentioned here is that of interchangeability of media, that is, expression of the same meaning in one medium instead of the other. Here the definitions are as follows. First, one has to consider strings of units involving actions on one medium only (or on a fixed set of media), that is, to consider situations when some media are "banned." Generally, let $u(i)$ stand for a string that involves only medium m_i, that is, strings containing only actions on medium m_i, and all other media contain pauses $\#$.

One may now say that meaning s is *expressible* in medium m_i if

$$\exists u(i): f(u(i), s) = 1, \tag{3.36}$$

that is, if one can express s in full degree by using medium m_i only.

Let $Q_i(s)$ be the shortest length of a string $u(i)$ that expresses s in full if s is expressible on medium m_i. Given two media, the ratio $Q_i(s)/Q_j(s)$ measures the relative "dilution" or "contraction," relative to media m_i and m_j, of meaning s.

To use an example, a dialogue in which the man says "Let's go for a walk," and the woman replies "Oh, leave me alone" may take several seconds if verbal medium is allowed. The same meanings expressed in a ballet scene may take some minutes; and in a medium of facial expressions only, it is not expressible at all, at least the man's part, since no facial expression can convey with any reasonable lack of ambiguity a suggestion of a walk.

3.5 DEFINITION OF A UNIT IN THE GENERAL CASE

Let us now outline the theory for the case when we abandon the simplifying assumption that all actions take up the same amount of time. One could then proceed as follows. Let $g_i(t)$ denote the action performed in medium m_i at time t. Let us for the moment assume that $g_i(t)$ is defined without any fuzziness; in other words, let us assume that there is exactly one action from the alphabet (or "vocabulary" V_i of the ith medium) performed at any given time t. This is an idealization of reality, since it implies that for any action on a given medium one can always identify its beginning and its end. Such an assumption is perhaps justifiable in case of utterances; however, it may not be so in the case of a smile, for example.

Nevertheless, as a first approximation we can idealize the situation and assume that we have functions $g_i(t)$ defined for each medium separately. The values of the ith function $g_i(t)$ are simply actions from the vocabulary V_i of medium m_i. Thus, at the time t, we simultaneously have actions $g_1(t)$, $g_2(t), \ldots, g_r(t)$; as already mentioned, $g_1(t)$ is the utterance at time t, that is, the action of verbal medium m_1.

The vector of actions at t will be denoted $G(t)$, so that

$$G(t) = (g_1(t), \ldots, g_r(t)). \tag{3.37}$$

Now, each of the actions performed at t lasts for some time (possibly 0, if the action just starts at t) and will last for some time (again, possibly 0 if the action is just to be terminated).

Generally, we shall denote these times for medium m_i by $T_i^-(t)$ and $T_i^+(t)$. Formally, for $i = 1, \ldots, r$ we have

$$T_t^-(t) = \min\{t^* < t : g_i(\tau) = g_i(t) \text{ for all } \tau \text{ with } t^* \leq \tau \leq t\}, \quad (3.38)$$

and

$$T_i^+(t) = \max\{t^* > t : g_i(\tau) = g_i(t) \text{ for all } \tau \text{ with } t \leq \tau \leq t^*\}. \quad (3.39)$$

The meaning of the times $T_i^-(t)$ are as follows: $T_i^-(t)$ is simply the time when the action in the ith medium, which is performed at time t, originated. Thus $t - T_i^-(t)$ is the length of time this action is performed at t. Similarly, $T_i^+(t)$ is the time of termination of the action on medium m_i, which is being performed at t.

Thus, $T_i^+(t) - t$ may be called the *residual* time at t for the action in ith medium, and $T_i^+(t) - T_i^-(t)$ the total duration of the action performed at t.

Now define

$$T^-(t) = \max_i T_i^-(t), \qquad T^+(t) = \min_i T_i^+(t). \quad (3.40)$$

Then $T^-(t)$ and $T^+(t)$ are, respectively, the times of the last change (start of a new action) prior to time t and of the first change (end of action performed at t) after t.

We therefore have the following.

THEOREM 3.4 *For all τ such that $T^-(t) \leq \tau \leq T^+(t)$ we have $G(\tau) = G(t)$, where $G(t)$ is the vector of actions performed at time t.*

This proposition simply asserts that between times $T^-(t)$ and $T^+(t)$ all actions are the same as at time t.

To define the unit of communication action, it is necessary to use the notions of meaning and of fuzzy relation between meanings and multimedial actions introduced earlier. Denote, as before, the set of meanings as S, and let $G(t_1, t_2)$ denote the fragment of $G(t)$ consisting of all actions with $t_1 \leq t \leq t_2$. Thus, $G(t_1, t_2)$ is the string of simultaneous actions on all media, truncated at t_1 and t_2. Let $\mathscr{G}$ denote the class of all such strings, for different t_1 and t_2. Finally, as before, f will stand for the relation of "expressibility," or "fuzzy meaning," so that f is a function

$$f : \mathscr{G} \times S \to [0, 1]. \quad (3.41)$$

For $G(t_1, t_2) \in \mathscr{G}$ and $s \in S$, the value $f[G(t_1, t_2), s]$ is the degree to which the string of actions $G(t_1, t_2)$ expresses the meaning s. In particular, if

$f[G(t_1, t_2), s] = 1$, then the string in question expresses s in full degree, and if $f[G(t_1, t_2), s] = 0$, then it does not express it at all. The intermediate values represent partial expressions.

The idea of a unit in multimedial communication will be based on the above notion of expressibility of meanings. Roughly speaking, a unit will be defined as the shortest string that expresses some "atomic" meaning.

Thus, the last notion to be needed to define the concept of a unit will be that of a *reduction* of a string of multimedial actions. For given $G(t_1, t_2)$, we define reduction $\bar{G}(t_1, t_2)$ as any string obtained from $G(t_1, t_2)$ by replacing one or more actions performed either at t_1 or t_2 (but not continuously between t_1 and t_2) by the neutral action $\#$.

Formally, consider $G(t) = (g_1(t), \ldots, g_r(t))$, and consider the state at t_1, together with the values $T_i^-(t)$, that is, the moments of terminations of actions performed at t_1. For all media m_i for which the following holds:

$$T_i^+(t_1) < t_2, \qquad T_i^-(t_1) < t_1, \qquad g_i(t_1) \neq \#, \qquad (3.42)$$

we put $g_i(t) = \#$ for all t with $t_1 < t < T_i^+(t_1)$.

Condition (3.42) means that the replacement concerns only the media for which the action performed at t_1 will last to some time earlier than t_2, originated strictly before t_1, and is not an "idle" action $\#$.

Next, we perform analogous reduction on the other side. Consider, therefore, time t_2 and times $T_i^-(t_2)$. The replacement concerns only the media m_i for which

$$T_i^-(t_2) > t_1, \qquad T_i^+(t_2) > t_2, \qquad g_i(t_2) \neq \#. \qquad (3.43)$$

For media satisfying (3.43) we replace $g_i(t)$ by $\#$ for all t such that $T_i^-(t_2) < t < t_2$.

Let us denote by $\bar{G}(t_1, t_2)$ the string of multimedial actions performed simultaneously on various media obtained from $G(t_1, t_2)$ by the operations of reductions described above. Given $\bar{G}(t_1, t_2)$ we may perform other reductions, namely by abbreviating or removing other actions that occur between t_1 and t_2. In general denote such reductions by $R\bar{G}(t_1, t_2)$, and finally define the notion of unit as follows.

Let $s \in S$ and let $G(t_1, t_2)$ be such that $f[G(t_1, t_2), s] = 1$. Then a string of multimedial actions, say, G, will be called a *unit* contained in $G(t_1, t_2)$ if the following conditions hold:

$$f(G, s) = 1; \qquad (3.44)$$

$$G = R\bar{G}(t_1, t_2); \qquad (3.45)$$

there exists no substring G' of G such that G' is a proper reduction of G and $f(G', s) = 1$. $\qquad (3.46)$

Thus, in a sense, a *unit* is the smallest string of actions in all media that carries a given meaning to the full degree.

Naturally, for given s and $G(t_1, t_2)$ with $f[G(t_1, t_2), s] = 1$, the units that may be obtained from $G(t_1, t_2)$ may not be unique: the same string may be reduced in several ways, leading to different units. Thus, as opposed to the previous definition, where the units of multimedial actions were defined on syntactic grounds (as any vector of actions lasting for the same duration of time), the present definition is of a predominantly semantic character, being based on function f.

3.6 LANGUAGES OF PARTICULAR MEDIA

Let us now consider the function

$$G(t) = (g_1(t), \dots, g_r(t)) \tag{3.47}$$

on some interval, say, $(0, T)$.

Each function $g_i(t)$ assigns to $t \in (0, T)$ an action from the vocabulary V_i. Consequently, it determines a string of consecutive actions (including the neutral action $\#$) on m_i, say, $v_1, v_2, \dots$ defined as follows.

First, we put

$$v_1 = g_i(0) \tag{3.48}$$

and consider $T_i^+(0)$ defined in the preceding section. By definition, we have $g_i(t) = v_1$ for all t with $0 \le t \le T_i^+(0)$.

Consequently, at $t_1 = T_i^+(0)$ action v_1 changes into some other action v_2. We consider now $t_2 = T_i^+(T_i^+(0)) = T_i^+(t_1)$, and by definition, $g_i(t) = v_2$ for all t with $t_1 < t < t_2$. In a similar way, we define $t_3 = T_i^+(t_2)$, and so forth.

In this manner, for each medium m_i we define a double sequence

$$(v_1, t_1), (v_2, t_2), \dots \tag{3.49}$$

such that action v_j lasts between t_{j-1} and t_j. Naturally, such a sequence concerns the ith medium, and therefore the full notation would require adding an index i to all v_j's and t_j's.

Now, it is clear that not all functions $G(t)$ of form (3.47) are admissible. If we agree to regard admissibility as a fuzzy notion, described by a membership function A, then $A(G)$ is the degree to which the string of actions G is admissible.

The admissibility function A is therefore defined on the classes of all vector-valued functions defined on some interval of time. It cannot be entirely arbitrary; rather, it must satisfy appropriate internal constraints, obtained as follows.

Let $G(0, T)$ be the string of multimedial actions performed between 0 and T, and let $0 < s < T$. Denote by $G(0, s)$ and $G(s, T)$ the functions g_i restricted to sets of arguments $(0, s)$ and (s, T). Then the admissibility function A must satisfy the condition

$$A(G(0, T)) = \min A(G(0, s)), A(G(s, T)). \tag{3.50}$$

It follows from the above condition that we have the following.

THEOREM 3.5   *For any* t_1, t_2 *with* $0 \le t_1 \le t_2 \le T$ *we have*

$$A(G(0, T)) \ge A(G(t_1, t_2)). \tag{3.51}$$

Given the admissibility function A, we may define languages of multimedial actions [for a given interval of time, say, $(0, T)$] by putting, for any b with $0 \le b \le 1$,

$$L_b = L_b(0, T) = \{G(0, T): A(G(0, T)) \ge b\}. \tag{3.52}$$

In particular, for $b = 1$ we obtain the smallest language, consisting of all strings $G(0, T)$ admissible in degree 1. For lower b, the languages become gradually less restrictive as regards the admissibility of their strings. In particular, if $a \le b$, then $L_b \subset L_a$.

Our next objective is to define admissibility for separate strings on particular media using the admissibility of multimedial strings. The main source of difficulty here lies in the fact that the same string g_i on medium m_i may appear in various contexts, each of them having different admissibilities.

Consequently, let $\mathscr{G}_i = \mathscr{G}_i(0, T)$ denote the class of all strings of actions during $(0, T)$ in medium m_i, and let $\mathscr{G} = \mathscr{G}(0, T) = \mathscr{G}_1 \times \cdots \times \mathscr{G}_r$. Let g_i^* be a particular string of actions on medium m_i. Then its admissibility $A(g_i^*)$ may be defined as

$$A(g_i^*) = \sup_{g_1, \ldots, g_{i-1}, g_{i+1}, \ldots, g_r} A((g_1, \ldots, g_{i-1}, g_i^*, g_{i+1}, \ldots, g_r)). \tag{3.53}$$

Verbally, admissibility $A(g_1^*)$ is the supremum of admissibilities of all multimedial strings that have g_i^* as the substring on medium m_i.

Let us now decompose g_i^* into two parts, one on $(0, s)$ and the other on (s, T), to be denoted by g_i' and g_i''. Let us also introduce the symbol $\oplus$ denoting the operation of composing two functions on contiguous intervals into one function, so that we have $g_i^* = g_i' \oplus g_i''$.

We then have the following.

THEOREM 3.6 *The admissibility function satisfies the relation*

$$A(g_i) \leq \min[A(g_i'), A(g_i'')]. \tag{3.54}$$

Proof We have

$$A(g_i) = A(g_i' \oplus g_i'')$$

$$= \sup_{g_1, \ldots, g_{i-1}, g_{i+1}, \ldots, g_r} A((g_1, \ldots, g_{i-1}, g_i, g_{i+1}, \ldots, g_r))$$

$$= \sup_{g_1', g_1'', \ldots, g_r', g_r''} \min[A(g_1', \ldots, g_r'), A(g_1'', \ldots, g_r'')]$$

$$\leq \min \left\{ \sup_{g_1', \ldots, g_r'} A(g_1', \ldots, g_r'), \sup_{g_1'', \ldots, g_r''} A(g_1'', \ldots, g_r'') \right\}$$

$$= \min[A(g_i'), A(g_i'')].$$

In the way described above we obtained medial languages $L_1, \ldots, L_r$, where the ith medial language L_i is defined as the class of all strings g_i with admissibility $A(g_i)$ exceeding a certain threshold.

In a similar way we may define the language for a fixed set of media. To take the case of a pair of media m_1 and m_j the admissibility of a pair of strings (g_i, g_j) is defined as the supremum of admissibilities of all strings containing g_i and g_j. Clearly, if $A(g_i, g_j) \geq b$, then also $A(g_i) \geq b$ and $A(g_j) \geq b$, which means that we have the following.

THEOREM 3.7 *For all $i_1, \ldots, i_k$ and b, if*

$$A(g_{i_1}, \ldots, g_{i_k}) \geq b,$$

then

$$\min_{1 \leq j \leq k} A(g_{i_j}) \geq b.$$

In particular, if strings $(g_{i_1}, \ldots, g_{i_k})$ are jointly admissible in degree 1, then each of them is also admissible in degree 1. The converse need not be true. Consequently, we may introduce the following definition.

DEFINITION 3.11 A set $(g_{i_1}, \ldots, g_{i_k})$ of strings on media $m_{i_1}, \ldots, m_{i_k}$ is called *jointly compatible* if $A(g_{i_j}) = 1$ for all $j = 1, \ldots, k$ and $A(g_{i_1}, \ldots, g_{i_k}) = 1$.

3.7 FUZZY UNIT AND PERCEPTION

We shall now consider the setup from the preceding sections enriched by the inclusion of a context and also considered separately from the point of view of the sender and from the point of view of the receiver of the fuzzy unit.

3.7.1 The Sender: Planning of a Unit in a Context

Assume that the sender wants to send a message with meaning s, and he wants it to be expressed with sufficient clarity (lack of ambiguity), as specified by level p. He must then choose a string of multimedial units that carries meaning s in degree at least p.

For simplicity, assume that we deal here with simple, relatively easily separable units, like greetings, congratulations, consolations. We shall assume that the set

$$A_{s,p} = \{G : f(G,s) \geq p\} \tag{3.55}$$

is not empty.

As far as expressing s in degree at least p is concerned, any element from the set $A_{s,p}$ is equally well serving the purpose. For the description of the action of the sender, it is necessary to formulate some conditions that characterize the process of choice of an element from $A_{s,p}$.

Here one may distinguish several factors that influence this choice. First, it is clear that the sender may want not only to convey the meaning s but also some other meanings s', s'', ... and avoid expressing some other meanings.

Again, for simplicity, suppose that the sender wants to express s and s' and not s''. Here the situation is describable in terms of the algebra of goals and means, as introduced by Nowakowska (1975, 1976a). Indeed, the composite meaning that the sender wants to convey is simply s & s' & $-s''$, in some appropriate degree. Thus, he must choose a unit (a string) from the set

$$A_{s,p_1} \cap A_{s',p_2} \cap A_{-s'',p_3}. \tag{3.56}$$

It is clear that to any composite meaning there corresponds an appropriate set of units (or strings) to express that meaning. Thus, we may assume at once that the sender wants to send some meaning denoted by s, composite or not, and that no considerations of any other meaning would influence his choice from the appropriate set $A_{s,p}$.

Another factor that may influence the choice is the context, that is, the situation in which the multimedial unit is to be performed. In general let C stand for the class of all possible contexts. With each $c \in C$ and $G \in A_{s,p}$ one may associate the value $R_c(G)$, representing the degree to which the unit G is "appropriate" for context c. Naturally, it is assumed that

$$0 \leq R_c(G) \leq 1. \tag{3.57}$$

Moreover, we assume that

$$(\exists c \in C)(\exists G \in A_{s,p}): R_c(G) = 1. \tag{3.58}$$

Thus, $R_c(\cdot)$ may be regarded as a fuzzy subset of $A_{s,p}$ of those units G that are appropriate for context c. Condition (3.58) asserts that for some c the corresponding subset is normal; that is, the membership value 1 is actually attained.

We may now introduce the following definition.

DEFINITION 3.12 Any elements (c, G) with $R_c(G) = 1$ will be called *standard units*.

Thus a standard unit is actually a pair, consisting of a context c and a unit G which is appropriate for this context in full degree and also expresses the intended meaning s in the degree at least p.

Given the function R_c one may define two possibility distributions, in a sense dual one to another. Thus, for $D \subset A_{s,p}$ we put

$$\text{Poss}(D \,|\, c) = \sup_{G \in D} R_c(G), \qquad (3.59)$$

and for $E \subset C$ we put

$$\text{Poss}(E \,|\, G) = \sup_{c \in E} R_c(G). \qquad (3.60)$$

Formula (3.59) gives the possibility that a unit is in set D of units, given context c, whereas formula (3.60) gives the possibility of the context being in the set E of contexts given that the unit performed was G.

Thus we have the following theorem.

THEOREM 3.8 *If (c, G) is a standard unit and $c \in E$, then $\text{Poss}(E \,|\, G) = 1$.*

Returning now to the problem of choice of the sender, the units in $A_{s,p}$ may be arranged into a sequence according to the values of $R_c(\cdot)$ for each context c separately, that is, ranked according to their appropriateness as regards context c.

However, context c is often not known completely; for instance, it may change fast (e.g., during social encounters) and the sender may be overlooking some relevant clues, or simply some important information may be unknown to the sender. As a result, at the time of choice, the sender may know only that context c belongs to a class $C^* \subset C$ of contexts.

To exhibit the choice situation structure, let us neglect all other factors that might influence the choice (e.g., the preference of the sender to some types of units) and assume that the only criterion is the sender's desire to produce the most appropriate unit (from $A_{s,p}$, i.e., conveying the intended meaning s in degree at least p). The problem is that for various elements of C^* we may have various orderings of $A_{s,p}$ according to the degree of appropriateness.

To consider an example, imagine an envoy arriving at the court of the king of another country, planning the ceremony of greeting the monarch, presenting gifts, pleading for his cause, and so on. The context about which he is uncertain pertains to the king's attitude toward his country and the issue in question, and the units under consideration may differ by components such as depth of the bow or ways of addressing the monarch.

It may be worth while to analyze in some detail the structural aspects of the choice situation here. Formally, we have choice set $A_{s,p}$, set C^* of contexts, and a set of functions R_c, $c \in C^*$, each mapping $A_{s,p}$ into $[0, 1]$. In addition, we may sometimes have a measure that allows us to rank contexts in C^* according to how feasible or probable they are. Typically, we might have a prior probability distribution on C^*, say, P, with $P(c)$ being the probability that the true context is (or will be) c.

The choice function must assign to a system

$$\langle A_{s,p}, C^*, \{R_c, c \in C^*\}, P \rangle \tag{3.61}$$

a nonempty subset $A_{s,p}^*$ of $A_{s,p}$ of "optimal" elements (possibly consisting of just one element). Here the choice situation falls under the general scheme of decision making under uncertainty, and one can apply various existing criteria [see, e.g., the classical book of Luce and Raiffa (1957)]. In particular, an important class of choice functions may be built using the numerical information contained in function R_c. Thus, one may assign to each $G \in A_{s,p}$ the value

$$R_1(G) = \sum_{c \in C^*} R_c(G)P(c), \tag{3.62}$$

rank elements of $A_{s,p}$ according to the values of R_1, and take as the choice set $A_{s,p}^*$ the set of those G yielding the highest values of R_1. This is, in essence, Bayes's rule, where the choice is based on the maximal expected utility evaluated according to the prior distribution P.

As another rule, which does not utilize the prior distribution, one may use the value function

$$R_2(G) = \min_{c \in C^*} R_c(G), \tag{3.63}$$

leading to the minimax choice.

It is of more interest, however, to explore the rules that utilize only the ordinal information contained in functions R_c. Thus, we may consider orderings of $A_{s,p}$ induced by each R_c and try to build a rule that assigns the choice set $A_{s,p}^*$ to the resulting set of orderings of $A_{s,p}$. In this way we obtain the situation of choice analyzed in detail by Arrow (1963).

The Impossibility Theorem of Arrow asserts that there exists no decision rule that would satisfy certain "natural" postulates formulated by Arrow. Consequently, each decision rule must break at least one of these requirements [for some consequences of a similar interpretation of individual decisions as group decisions and the use of Arrow's theorem to derive certain psychological consequences, see Nowakowska (1973)].

In the present case, the situation is still more complex; this is connected with the fact that R_c not only provides an ordering of units according to their appropriateness in context c but also may single out some units as totally unappropriate in c such that $R_c(G) = 0$. Naturally, all G satisfying the above condition are at the end of the ordering induced by R_c.

Denote

$$U_c = \{G : R_c(G) = 0\}, \tag{3.64}$$

and put $V_c = A_{s,p} - U_c$. One may then impose the condition that if

$$V = \bigcap_{c \in C^*} V_c \neq \varnothing, \tag{3.65}$$

then $A_{s,p}^* \subset V$. This condition means that the decision rule must select only those units that are admissible in some positive degree regardless of the context c if only such units exist.

If $V = \varnothing$, that is, for each unit there exists at least one context c for which this unit is totally inappropriate, then one may try to proceed as follows. The inclusion relation among sets

$$H(G) = \{c \in C^* : R_c(G) = 0\} \tag{3.66}$$

induces a partial order among units G. If this partial order has the unique smallest element, then it may be taken as choice $A_{s,p}^*$; otherwise, one may require that the choice set be a subset of the class of all least elements in the above ordering. Formally, the last condition states that

$$\text{if } H(G_1) \subset H(G_2) \text{ with } H(G_1) \neq H(G_2), \text{ then } G_2 \notin A_{s,p}^*. \tag{3.67}$$

It does not seem possible to specify the actual decision rules that govern the choice of a unit, that is, the human behavior in the analyzed social contexts. One may, however, describe this process as follows. To specify how the sender is choosing the optimal unit (optimality being assessed from the point of view of a given goal, i.e., meaning s), one may try to use dynamic programming. This approach presupposes that the unit is selected sequentially, in the sense that the actions on various media start at different times. It also presupposes that a partially performed unit may be associated with a degree to which it satisfies a given goal (or the degree to which it is possible to complete it so as to satisfy the goal). For instance, the goal may be to make the receiver trusting, win his confidence, make him friendly, make him scared, and so on.

To describe the situation formally, we visualize the unit as "sliced" into narrow parts of length τ (say), where τ is the length of some short time interval. Let K be the class of all such small slices, so that $G = v_1 \cdots v_N$, where $v_i \in K$.

Naturally, each v_i is a vector of actions, or parts of actions, that is, it has the same nature as a unit, except that no meaning needs to be attached to it, even in a fuzzy sense.

Then, assuming the total length of a unit to be $N\tau$ and denoting by Q the degree of attainment of the goal, we have the following conditions:

(a) The choice of v_N, given $v_1, \ldots, v_{N-1}$, is determined by the formula $Q(v_1, \ldots, v_{N-1}, v_N^*) = \max_{v_N} Q(v_1, \ldots, v_{N-1}, v_N)$.

(b) If $v_{j+1}^*, \ldots, v_N^*$ are already selected for each $v_1, \ldots, v_j$, then v_j^* is determined from $Q(v_1, \ldots, v_{j-1}, v_j^*, \ldots, v_N^*) = \max_{v_j} Q(v_1, \ldots, v_{j-1}, v_j, v_{j+1}^*, \ldots, v_N^*)$.

In this way we may determine the sequence $v_1^*, \ldots, v_N^*$ that gives the optimal (in the sense of maximizing the function Q) unit of actions.

If one interprets v_i as a unit of actions (and not as a "slice" of a unit), one obtains the principle of choosing the optimal string of actions (for a given goal, whose degree of attainment is measured by Q).

The above considerations concern the "ideal" case, when one may assess without ambiguity the degree to which a goal has been attained at each stage before the "message" is completed for any sequence of hypothetically completing units (the still unperformed part of the unit or sequence of units).

Second, these formulas concern the deterministic situation. In reality, one usually deals with some level of "noise," which makes it impossible to associate the value $Q(v_1, \ldots, v_j)$ with an "incomplete" unit $v_1 \cdots v_j$. The best one may hope is to be able to determine the expected degree of attainment of the goal, given the partial sequence $v_1 \cdots v_j$. In this case the optimization process is the same, except that Q is to be interpreted as expected goal attainment.

In the above general description of preferential ordering of units with respect to contexts (which may also be described in terms of contextual utility of units), each subject may also have his "context-free" ordering of units, by taking into account only those actions that he prefers deontically, aesthetically, motivationally, and so on. These context-free and context-dependent orderings need not coincide, and this may lead to some form of an internal conflict.

Let us consider the situation of sender in more detail. Before the actual choice of the unit is made, the sender has some expectations regarding the context (at least in some cases important to him) that he takes into account in designing a unit. What is meant here is that the sender chooses a unit for a hypothetical context. The actual unit performed may differ from the planned unit, among other reasons because the actual context may differ from the expected one (as well as because of some other random effects).

To the concept of design of a unit there corresponds a concept of generative verbal structure (GVS), which will be discussed later. Here it suffices to say that

GVS is, most generally, a set of propositions describing the planned unit. On the other hand, the realized unit in a given context is in fact a praxical, or actual copy of GVS, which may or may not be in discrepancy with it. In other words, linguistic expressions describing multimedial units are mapped into an organized set of actions, which are called *praxical copies*.

From the point of view of psychological problems of communication, the most interesting are the deviations between planned and actual units, how they are explained, justified, and so on.

When the sender simultaneously performs a set of actions (multimedial unit), the perceiver deals with the praxical copy of the sender's intentions. The receiver may also form a verbal copy of the perceived message, for himself or for someone else, which may differ from the sender's verbal copy of the performed unit. Depending on the interpretation, the receiver is designing his response set and chooses a response unit, thus completing a cycle.

3.7.2   The Receiver: Some Problems of Perception of Units

Perception is an active, dynamic process in which the eye "touches" and "jumps" over different fragments of the object (in this case: a multimedial unit), visiting some parts more often than others. In this way, the eye maps the unit into its frequential image, generated by the path of the eye. The perceptual work of the receiver is connected with testing the hypotheses about the meaning.

Metaphorically speaking, the eye builds a whole sequence of incomplete or complete units, amplifying the stimulating role of the actual unit. In this way, memory is supplied with a sequence of stimuli. An essential element of perception for recognition of the meaning is the order of exhaustion of media of actions. This order is important, especially in the case of short-term expositions, which do not permit a complete inspection of the whole unit. As a consequence, there is higher probability of misperception, that is, accepting the wrong hypothesis about the meaning intended by the sender. The "walk" over the set of media by the eye of the receiver is determined by his preferences, context, and the strategies of inspection used by the receiver.

Formally, the receiver performs a random walk on the set of media of the sender's unit. When a medium is visited for a limited time, it may not be sufficient to identify the action on this medium. This necessitates a return to the same medium several times, until the action is identified.

The crucial point in the perception of a message is the receiver's expectation concerning the unit and its context and receiver's preferences toward certain media, connected with such factors as his knowledge about the importance of various media for understanding the message, his knowledge concerning the properties of the sender's choices of media, his standards, that is, his personal preferences connected with using some actions and contexts and avoiding some others, constraints on the time of exposition, or the necessity of attention shifts to other messages or situations. Some of these factors will be discussed in subsequent sections. Here we shall present a general scheme of the process, emphasizing the receiver's expectations.

The latter may be represented as a meaning s^*, and associated with it a set $A_{s,p}^*$ for some p close to 1. In other words, the receiver expects a unit from the set $A_{s,p}^*$.

As regards preferences, they determine the order of inspection of media. More precisely, the preferences are representable in the form of probabilities of inspection of the next medium, that is,

$$P(x_{j+1} = m_i \,|\, B_j), \tag{3.68}$$

where B_j denotes, in general, all factors that may influence the probability that the next medium inspected, x_{j+1}, is equal to m_i.

In particular, the two main components of B_j are the preferences toward certain media and the knowledge about the unit accumulated until jth inspection. Calling the first factor u and the second v_j, we may symbolically write $B_j = u + v_j$. It may be conjectured that, initially, when knowledge v_j is still scarce, u is the main factor that determines the choice of the next unit to be inspected. Later, when knowledge v_j becomes more substantial, the influence of preferences u diminish.

Thus, at every stage we have an ordering of media induced by probabilities (3.68), as well as an initial ordering obtained when $v_j = \varnothing$. These two orderings of media may agree or not. The latter case is of great interest and would usually indicate that a significant contribution to the meaning is carried by an "unexpected" medium.

Generally, the perceiver may have a number of hypotheses about the meaning of the unit, say, $H_1, \ldots, H_N$, some of them more likely than others. Let the subjective probabilities of these hypotheses be $p_1, \ldots, p_N$, with $p_1 + \cdots + p_N = 1$ (which means that the hypotheses exclude one another and exhaust the set of all possibilities).

The nature of these hypotheses may be different in various applications. For instance, the hypotheses may assert something about the values of the sender's attributes (e.g., his attitude).

For every hypothesis H_i and unit G, one has the probability $P(G \,|\, H_i)$ that unit G will be performed if hypothesis H_i is true. In other words, with each H_i we have associated a probability distribution on the class of all units (some of the probabilities may be zero). Then if G^* is the actually observed unit, the posterior probability of hypothesis H_i is given by Bayes's formula

$$P(H_i \mid G^*) = \frac{p_i P(G^* \mid H_i)}{\sum\limits_{j=1}^{N} p_j P(G^* \mid H_j)}. \tag{3.69}$$

3.7.3 Perception of Units under Temporal Constraints

The concepts introduced in the preceding section are closely related to the problems of perception. Consider a short, multimedial string $G = G(t_1, t_2)$. The word "short" is naturally fuzzy. What is meant here is that the action string G is so short that a person perceiving it may have some troubles in perceiving all actions or all the details of actions in G.

It is not necessary that G be a unit of actions in the technical sense, as defined in the preceding section, but it will be convenient to refer to it as a unit of action, even though there may be no s with $f(G, s) = 1$.

What will be essential is that G may be modified in various ways, without losing its "principal characteristic" (this notion will be made precise below). Let G^* denote the class of modifications of G; it will be convenient to index the elements of G^*, writing g_v for modifications of G. Here v runs through some parameter set V. We may now consider the membership function f as a function of two variables, meaning s and modification g_v, or equivalently, parameter v. Thus, we let

$$f(v, s) = f(G_v, s), \tag{3.70}$$

the value $f(v, s)$ representing the degree to which G_v expresses the meaning s.

Thus, for any s we may define a weak order in the set V simply by putting $v_1 \leq_s v_2$ iff $f(v_1, s) \leq f(v_2, s)$. Clearly, each relation $\leq_s$ is reflexive, transitive, and connected. Relations $<_s$ and $\sim_s$ are now defined in the usual way. These relations allow us, in turn, to define various relations between the meanings s.

DEFINITION 3.13   The meanings s_1 and s_2 are said to be positively associated if

$$\forall v_1, v_2 : v_1 \leq_{s_1} v_2 \quad \text{iff} \quad v_1 \leq_{s_2} v_2. \tag{3.71}$$

DEFINITION 3.14   Meanings v_1 and v_2 are said to be negatively associated if

$$\forall v_1, v_2 : v_1 \leq_{s_1} v_2 \quad \text{iff} \quad v_2 \leq_{s_2} v_1. \tag{3.72}$$

DEFINITION 3.15   Meanings s_1, s_2 are said to be *independent* if they are neither positively nor negatively associated.

Thus, for independent meanings s_1, s_2 we must have the following property:

$$\exists v_1, v_2, v_3, v_4 : v_1 \leq_{s_1} v_2 \ \& \ v_1 \leq_{s_2} v_2 \ \& \ v_3 \leq_{s_1} v_4 \ \& \ v_4 \leq_{s_2} v_3. \tag{3.73}$$

In other words, there must exist a pair of units v_1, v_2 such that G_{v_2} expresses more strongly both s_1 and s_2 than G_{v_1} and also units v_3, v_4 such that G_{v_4} expresses s_1 stronger than G_{v_3}, while G_{v_3} expresses s_2 stronger than G_{v_4}.

Various relations between meanings may be illustrated geometrically as follows. Let us fix an arbitrary meaning s_0 and order parameters v according to the relation $\leq_{s_0}$. Then the values of $f(v, s_0)$ will yield a nondecreasing function of v.

If s_1 is positively associated with s_0, then $f(v, s_1)$ is also a nondecreasing function of v. If s_2 is negatively associated with s_0, then $f(v, s_2)$ is nonincreasing. If s_1 is independent of s_0, then $f(v, s_1)$ is neither increasing nor decreasing.

The mutual relations between s_1 and s_2 may also be expressed by using the ordering according to s_0: indeed, s_1 and s_2 are positively associated if $f(v, s_1)$ and $f(v, s_2)$ are "parallel" in the sense that whenever one of the functions increases so does the other. The relations of negative association and independence are interpreted in a similar way.

3.7.4 Importance of Particular Media for a Given Meaning

Using the ideas introduced by Nowakowska (1967) one may define the importance of actions on particular media for recognition of a given meaning. Intuitively, these degrees of importance vary: for instance, in many cases, the utterance (verbal action) will be of primary importance. This means that to determine the meaning of a unit of multimedial actions it is necessary to hear the utterance in the verbal medium. In some other cases, action in certain nonverbal medium may be of high importance, for example, gestures accompanying the utterance.

The general definition of the weight of an action for a given meaning will be based on the theory of voting coalitions. Consider a multimedial action $G = (g_1, \ldots, g_r)$ and a given meaning s, satisfying the condition $f(G, s) = 1$. The object will be to assign the weights, say, $w_s(g_i)$, representing the importance of g_i in recognizing the meaning of the unit as s.

The definition is based on the fact that one may often assign meaning s to an "incomplete" unit, in which some of the actions are missing, that is, replaced by the neutral action #.

Let $I = (i_1, \ldots, i_r)$ be a permutation of numbers $1, \ldots, r$, interpreted as a permutation of media $m_1, \ldots, m_r$. With each permutation I one may associate a sequence of $r + 1$ "incomplete" units in the following way. The first unit $G_1(I)$ has neutral action # on all media except m_{i_1} and on m_{i_1} it has action g_{i_1}. The next unit $G_2(I)$ has actions g_{i_1} and g_{i_2} on media m_{i_1} and m_{i_2} and neutral actions # on all other media. Proceeding in a similar way, we define the sequence of less and less incomplete units $G_1(I), G_2(I), \ldots, G_r(I)$; each sequence is connected with one permutation I.

Now, suppose that each such sequence is observed sequentially, until the observer establishes that the meaning is s. Naturally, each permutation must involve a different observer. As a rule, recognition of the meaning would usually occur before the last unit; that is, recognition is possible on the basis of an incomplete unit.

If in the permutation I the recognition occurs at term $G_j(I)$, then actions $g_{i_1}, \ldots, g_{i_{j-1}}$ are not enough to recognize the meaning as s, whereas actions $g_{i_1}, \ldots, g_{i_{j-1}}, g_{i_j}$ are already sufficient for the recognition. We then say that action g_{i_j} is *pivotal* in permutation I. This establishes a function, say, p, that maps the class of all permutations of $g_1, \ldots, g_r$ into the same set $\{g_1, \ldots, g_r\}$. Let $p(I) = g_k$ mean that the pivotal element in permutation I is g_k, and let J_r be the class of all permutations of $g_1, \ldots, g_r$.

We may now introduce the following definition.

DEFINITION 3.16   The *weight* $w_s(g_i)$ of action g_i in unit G is defined as

$$w_s(g_i) = \frac{\text{number of permutations } I \in J_r \text{ with } p(I) = g_i}{r!} \tag{3.74}$$

Obviously, we have

$$w_s(g_1) + \cdots + w_s(g_r) = 1. \tag{3.75}$$

This definition of weights is based on the voting power index of Shapley and Shubik (1954).

3.7.5 Some Empirical Problems Connected with the Determination of Weights

The idea of defining weights of recognition using the theory of voting coalitions has much wider applicability than using multimedial signs. It was applied, among others [see Nowakowska (1979c)], in the foundations of semiotics.

In the present context, there are several sources of difficulty. First, there is the question of construction of elements of the sequence $G_i(I)$ for various permutations I. Presumably, each unit could be recorded in the form of a brief film scene. Next, with # on verbal medium there is not much of a problem: one may always remove the sound. It may take some inventiveness, however, to remove body movements (say) or some gestures.

Even if one succeeds in the construction of all the necessary combinations of units with "incomplete actions," there remains the problem of empirical access to the weights, that is, determination of numbers of permutations with a given action being pivotal.

Clearly, one subject may test at most one permutation. Since the number of permutations increases rapidly with the number of media under consideration, it appears that the size of the sample of persons increases beyond feasible bounds if the number of media exceeds four. Indeed, for five media there are already 120 permutations, and each of them needs to be tested on several subjects.

Alternatively, one could think of sampling permutations at random and determining their pivotal elements. The difficulty with such an approach lies in the high chance of omitting the permutations in which elements of low weights are pivotal.

In practice, the determination of pivotal elements in permutations is often fuzzy, since it involves subjective decisions about recognition of the meaning as s, which may occur with varying degree of certainty. Thus, suppose that the experiment is performed until the recognition of the meaning as s occurs with subjective certainty at least until b. This leads to a b-pivotal element in each permutation, and the b-weight of g_i, to be denoted $w_{s,b}(g_i)$, is defined as

$$w_{s,b}(g_i) = \frac{\text{number of permutations in which } g_i \text{ is } b\text{-pivotal}}{r!} \tag{3.76}$$

We have naturally

$$w_{s,b}(g_1) + w_{s,b}(g_2) + \cdots + w_{s,b}(g_r) = 1. \tag{3.77}$$

It is of considerable interest to study the changes of the vector of weights as s and b change. Intuitively, for $b \leq 1$, many elements will be taken as pivotal earlier than for $b = 1$, that is, before attaining complete certainty. This might yield the allocation of elements as pivotal to be less concentrated, and as a consequence, the weight distribution will be closer to uniform. If this conjecture is true, then the entropy

$$H(b) = \sum_{j=1}^{r} w_{s,b}(g_i) \log \frac{1}{w_{s,b}(g_i)} \tag{3.78}$$

should be a decreasing function of b; in other words, we may formulate the following conjecture.

Conjecture A   If $a \leq b \leq 1$, then

$$H(a) \geq H(b). \tag{3.79}$$

3.7.6   Some Problems of Simultaneous Recognition and Discrimination

Consider a unit $G = (g_1, \ldots, g_r)$, which may be inspected and perceived for a limited period of time only and is assumed to be short enough to prevent a person from systematic inspection of all elements of G. The constraints on time may be due to a control by the perceiver, a goal of the person (target perception), or an imposition by the experimenter or external circumstances. The function $f(G, s)$ describes, as before, the degree to which the meaning of G is s. Thus, G may have several meanings, $s, s', \ldots$, all in sufficiently high degree. Alternatively, G may be unambiguous, if there is a unique s with $f(G, s)$ close to 1 and $f(G, s')$ close to 0 for all other s'.

Next, for all meanings s with $f(G, s)$ sufficiently close to 1, we may consider weights $w_{s,b}(g_i)$, expressing the importance of g_i for recognition (with certainty at least b) of G as s.

Now, when G is inspected only for a limited period of time, one cannot inspect all g_i's. In such cases, one can reasonably assume that perception is sequential, stopped either by the decision about meaning (or meanings) or by the end of the exposition, whichever comes earlier.

It would appear reasonable to expect that the order of inspection is somewhat related to the weights $w_{s,b}(g_i)$ of actions on various media. However, such an assumption should not be made for the obvious reasons that there may be several alternative meanings, and each of them may induce different weights. Thus, we assume that the unit is characterized by some intrinsic laws that determine (perhaps only in a probabilistic sense) the order of inspection.

Generally, we shall assume the following model of perception. The whole structure G, to be assigned a meaning or meanings, consists of n elements, $g_1, \ldots, g_n$, also abbreviated simply as $1, 2, \ldots, n$. Denote $N = \{1, 2, \ldots, n\}$. (The g_i's are actions, but there may be more than one action on one medium, so that n is the total number of actions rather than the number of media.)

We assume that the next element to be inspected is sampled from noninspected elements, with probability distribution depending on the last element inspected. Thus, for any subset $A \subset N$ and $j \in A$ (interpreted as the set already inspected and the element inspected most recently), we have a probability distribution on $N - A$, to be denoted by $p(\cdot \,|\, A, j)$. In addition, we have a probability distribution $\pi(\cdot)$ on N, regarded as the initial distribution. Consequently, the probability of the inspection following the permutation $I = (i_1, i_2, \ldots, i_n)$ is

$$p(I) = \pi(i_1)p(i_2 \,|\, \{i_1\}, i_1)p(i_3 \,|\, \{i_1, i_2\}, i_2) \ldots p(i_{n-1} \,|\, \{i_1, \ldots, i_{n-2}\}, i_{n-2}). \quad (3.80)$$

[The last term omitted here equals $p(i_n \,|\, \{i_1, \ldots, i_{n-1}\}, i_{n-1}) = 1$, since the distribution $p(\cdot \,|\, \{i_1, \ldots, i_{n-1}\}, i_{n-1})$ must be concentrated on just one point.]

As a consequence, we have defined a probability distribution on the class of all permutations I. We shall now assume the following recognition model. The meanings under consideration will be denoted $s_1, \ldots, s_m$. A person samples permutation I according to the probability distribution $p(I)$ described above. He is allowed to inspect at most $k < n$ elements of the permutation, because of the time limitations. He inspects these elements sequentially, according to permutation I until he either finds an element pivotal for some of the $s_1, \ldots, s_m$ or until he reaches kth element, in which case he is forced to stop. He may then announce one or more among the meanings $s_1, \ldots, s_m$ as possibilities, adding perhaps modal frames expressing his degree of certainty, for example, "it might be..." or "perhaps...."

At the same time, during the process of inspection of the first k elements, some meanings may become eliminated, if a negative s-pivotal element is encountered (where negative pivotal element is defined in the same way as positive pivotal elements, except that one considers blocking coalitions instead of winning ones). In general, such negative conclusions ("This is not x") are not uttered (though, of course, they may be uttered spontaneously or elicited by questioning).

The probability of decision s_j about the meaning being reached with certainty, say, $D(s_j, 1)$, may be expressed as follows. Let $j(s, I)$ denote the index of the s-pivotal element in permutation I. We have then

$$D(s, 1) = \sum_{I \in A(s,r)} p(I), \qquad (3.81)$$

where

$$A(s, r) = \{I = (i_1, \ldots, i_n) : j(s, I) = \min_{1 \leq i \leq m} j(s_i, I) \text{ and } j(s, I) \leq r\}. \qquad (3.82)$$

Thus, $A(s, r)$ is the class of all permutations for which the pivotal element for s occurs earlier (not later) than the pivotal elements for other meanings; moreover, this pivotal element occurs not later than at the alotted time, that is, not later than the rth inspected element.

3.7.7 Strings of Units

Let us now consider strings of units $G_1, G_2, \ldots$ and their meanings. The situation here, considered from a rather general viewpoint, is similar to that of sequential hypothesis testing, applied to several hypotheses at once.

Let us consider a fixed meaning s. In the simplest situation each of the units G_i may be classified into three categories with respect to s: positive, negative, and neutral. Let us define

$$e_i(s) = \begin{cases} +1 & \text{if} \quad G_i \text{ is positive for meaning } s, \\ 0 & \text{if} \quad G_i \text{ is neutral for meaning } s, \\ -1 & \text{if} \quad G_i \text{ is negative for meaning } s. \end{cases} \qquad (3.83)$$

Thus, $e_i(s)$ is the "contribution" of G_i toward or against the meaning s.

We may now define the process $S_n(s) = S_n$, where S_n will express, in some simplification, the degree to which the initial part of the string, consisting of n elements $G_1, \ldots, G_n$, expresses the meaning s.

Let us fix some value $K > 0$, and define the process S_n inductively by

$$S_n = \begin{cases} \min\left\{1, S_{n-1} + \dfrac{1}{K}e_n(s)\right\} & \text{if } e_n(s) \geq 0, \\[2ex] \max\left\{0, S_{n-1} + \dfrac{1}{K}e_n(s)\right\} & \text{if } e_n(s) \leq 0. \end{cases} \tag{3.84}$$

Thus process $\{S_n\}$ is restricted to the interval $[0, 1]$, with parameter K representing the scaling constant that determines how many "positive" units must occur before meaning s reaches a "saturation level." Naturally, the value S_0 must be given *a priori* as the initial value (e.g., representing the prior conviction about the meaning s).

Such a model of "pseudoadditive" construction of meaning has the following important property: in a string of a finite length, the terminal part has, relatively speaking, more influence than other parts. To see why it is so, observe that the total support for s depends on the location of positive and negative terms, not merely on their total numbers. This is due to the fact that a run of consecutive positive units, applied in the situation when S_n is 1, has no influence, whereas in the same situation a run of consecutive negative units will lead to a decrease of S_n. A similar situation occurs if $S_n = 0$. Thus the character of the terminal part of the string determines the "total effect" of the whole string.

3.7.8 Meaning of a Unit

One could try to proceed differently and assume that each action g_i in a unit $G = (g_1, \ldots, g_r)$ carries some specific meaning or meanings, and the meaning of G is a result of the meanings carried by actions on particular media. This requires introducing an appropriate algebra of meanings.

Thus, assume at first that each medium carries just one meaning in full degree; let these meanings be s_1 on m_1, s_2 on m_2, and so on. The meaning s of the whole unit is some function $R(s_1, \ldots, s_r)$ of meanings $s_1, \ldots, s_r$. The problem lies in determining the form of function R, which formally maps the set $S_1 \times \cdots \times S_r$ into the set S_R of the resultant meanings.

In general, action on each medium carries various meanings to various degree; let these meanings be s_1 on m_1, s_2 on m_2, and so on. The meaning s of medium m_i expresses meaning s in degree $f(g_i, s)$, where some $f(g_i, s)$ may be zero. Therefore the resultant meaning is expressed as a function $f(G, s)$. Thus, f is a function that assigns to each vector $F = (f_1, \ldots, f_r)$ and s a number $f(G, s) \in [0, 1]$, which depends on values of the functions $f_i(g_i, s)$, $i = 1, \ldots, r$.

The unit as a whole, $G = (g_1, \ldots, g_r)$, expresses various meanings s in varying degrees, depending on the meanings expressed in particular media and the degree of expression of these meanings. Thus, degree $f(G, s)$ to which G expresses s, depends also on values $f_i(g_i, s')$ for various f_i and various s'. Consequently, f must be a function whose arguments are meaning s and functions $f_1(g_1, \cdot), \ldots, f_r(g_r, \cdot)$ and whose values are numbers in $[0, 1]$.

To define various relevant concepts, let us simplify the notations and agree to write $f_i(\cdot) = f_i(g_i, \cdot)$. Here the dot signifies the fact that we consider the function as a whole, not its value at one point.

Now, as a rule, the function

$$F(f_1(\cdot), f_2(\cdot), \ldots, f_r(\cdot); s) \tag{3.85}$$

does not depend on all values of the functions f_i but only on some selected values $f_i(s_1), \ldots, f_i(s_k)$.

In general, let $B_i \subset S$, and let $f_i(\cdot) \sim_{B_i} f'_i(\cdot)$ if $f_i(s) = f'_i(s)$ for all $s \in B_i$. Thus, two functions are B_i-equivalent if they are identical on the set B_i.

We say that the value $f(G, s)$ is $(B_1, \ldots, B_r)$-*determined* if

$$F(f_1(\cdot), \ldots, f_r(\cdot); s) = F(f'_1(\cdot), \ldots, f'_r(\cdot); s)$$

for all $f'_1, \ldots, f'_r$ with $f'_i \sim_{B_i} f_i$, $i = 1, \ldots, r$. This condition means essentially that the value $F(f_1(\cdot), \ldots, f_r(\cdot); s)$, namely, the degree to which G expresses s, depends only on the values $f_i(s)$ for $s \in B_i$, $i = 1, \ldots, r$.

DEFINITION 3.17   For given $G = (g_1, \ldots, g_r)$ and $s \in S$, the sets $(B_1, \ldots, B_r)$ for which $F(f_1, \ldots, f_r; s)$ is $(B_1, \ldots, B_r)$-determined is called the *base* of s.

The smallest sets $(B_1, \ldots, B_r)$ that form a base will be called the *minimal base*.

Thus, if $(B_1, \ldots, B_r)$ is the minimal base, then the meaning s (and its degree) depends only on the values $f_1(s), s \in B_1, \ldots, f_r(s), s \in B_r$. In particular, if sets B_i are finite, then the value $F(G, s)$ depends only on a finite number of meanings and their degrees. If $B_i = \varnothing$ for some i, then the meanings expressed on ith medium m_i do not contribute to the meaning s.

3.7.9 An Automaton Interpretation

Let us assume again that each action takes up a unit of time and that all actions on various media are synchronized. Thus a unit action is a vector $v = (v_1, v_2, \ldots, v_k)$, where v_i is the action performed on medium m_i.

As already outlined, the multimedial action language L determines languages $L_1, L_2, \ldots, L_k$ on various media. These languages may be represented by an automaton. To describe such an automaton, let V_i be the vocabulary on medium m_i.

Intuitively, the automaton will have some set of internal states, an input consisting of actions on all media, and an output (nondeterministic) in the form of the next multimedial unit.

Formally, let Q describe the set of states, and let $h, h', \ldots$ denote multimedial units.

Then the operation of the automaton may be described by the transition function

$$T: Q \times H^* \to Q \times (2^H - \{\varnothing\}), \tag{3.86}$$

where H^* is the monoid over H, that is, the class of all finite strings of elements of H, including the empty string.

Thus, to every $q \in Q$ and $u = u_1 \cdots u_n \in H^*$, the function T assigns the value $T(q, u)$, equal to the pair (q', A), where $q' \in Q$ (next state), while A is a nonempty subset of H. Elements of A are interpreted as units allowed in state q and input u.

Given an automaton, one can define the multimedial action language L in the following way. Suppose q_0 is the initial state of the automaton. We say that the string $u = h_1 h_2 \cdots h_m$ is admissible (is in L) if it meets the following conditions:

$$h_1 \in A(q_0, \varepsilon), \quad \text{where} \quad \varepsilon \text{ is the empty string;} \tag{3.87}$$

Let q_k and $h_1, \ldots, h_k$ be already defined, and let $T(q_k, h_1 \cdots h_k) = (q, A)$. Then

$$q_{k+1} = q \quad \text{and} \quad h_{k+1} \in A. \tag{3.88}$$

Thus q_{k+1} is the state of the automaton, as determined by the transitions up to the kth moment, while unit h_{k+1} is chosen (in an arbitrary way) from the set A, depending on the previous choices and state. This gives the class of all strings that one may generate with the use of the automaton. For an interesting application of automata theory to action languages, see Skvoretz and Fararo (1980).

3.8 A FORMAL APPROACH TO DIALOGUES

From the very rich range of topics of formal theory of dialogues [see Nowakowska (1976b, 1979c,d, 1980a,c,d, 1981a)] only a small fragment will be shown here, which will nevertheless allow us to analyze the interchanging actions of sender and receiver. The dialogue will be analyzed through the multidimensional or multimedial communication discussed earlier, that is, by taking into account the nonverbal media also. In addition, this approach will take into consideration the role of context.

3.8.1 Units in Dialogue Actions

It is quite clear that the two most important actions in every dialogue are uttering sentences and listening. However, it is also clear that the information in a dialogue may be conveyed by means of such actions as facial expressions, gestures, and body movements. As in Section 3.2, we shall refer to these as media of expression (including verbal medium), and denote them as m_1, $m_2, \ldots, m_r$. For the formal theory it is not essential to specify what these media are; the actual list of all media may vary depending on the goal of the analysis. However, in the following, m_1 will always stand for the verbal medium.

With each medium we associate its "vocabulary," that is, the class of all actions that are appropriate for it. Let V_i be the vocabulary of medium m_i. Thus, V_1 is the vocabulary of the verbal medium, so that its elements are words. In addition, V_1 will be assumed to contain also the action denoted by $\#$ to represent silence (no utterance).

We shall idealize the situation (as in the initial sections of this chapter) by assuming that each action on each medium takes one unit of time to perform. Moreover, let us for simplicity restrict the analysis to dialogues of two persons only, denoted A and B. A dialogue unit may now be defined as follows. Let

$$Q = V_1 \times V_2 \times \cdots \times V_r \tag{3.89}$$

be the class of all vectors $(v_1, v_2, \ldots, v_r)$ with $v_i \in V_i$, $i = 1, \ldots, r$. Furthermore, define the partition of Q into Q^+ and Q^- as

$$Q^+ = \{(v_1, \ldots, v_r) : v_1 \neq \#\} \tag{3.90}$$

and

$$Q^- = \{(v_1, \ldots, v_r) : v_1 = \#\}. \tag{3.91}$$

We may interpret the elements of Q as multidimensional units of actions of one participant in the dialogue, in the sense discussed earlier. Set Q^+ consists then of those units that involve the utterance of some word, and elements of Q^- are multimedial units that involve no utterance on the verbal medium.

Now let

$$D = (Q^+ \times Q^-) \cup (Q^- \times Q^+) \cup (Q^- \times Q^-). \tag{3.92}$$

The elements of D will be denoted generally by

$$(v_1^A, \ldots, v_r^A; v_1^B, \ldots, v_r^B), \tag{3.93}$$

with superscripts A and B corresponding to the speakers in the dialogue. We have, therefore, from definition (3.92) of Q, the following implications:

$$v_1^A \neq \# \Rightarrow v_1^B = \# \tag{3.94}$$

(hence also $v_1^B \neq \# \Rightarrow v_1^A = \#$).

Thus a dialogue unit is a vector, which provides information about actions of both speakers on all media, with the only restriction (thus far) being that it is not admissible for both v_1^A and v_1^B to be different than $\#$ (i.e., are both utterances). In other words, this condition excludes simultaneous speaking.

Set D is the basic set of "dialogue units." It differs from the set of multimedial units considered in Chapter 3 by the fact that we are now considering *pairs* of multimedial units, representing simultaneous actions of both participants.

Given class D, it is natural to consider monoid D^* over D, that is, the class of all finite strings of elements of D. The class of all those strings that represent the dialogues is now a subset D' of D^*.

One may proceed in several ways. One of them is to explore the ideas of formal linguistics: assume that D' is given and study its structure by introducing various notions (e.g., distributive classes, parasitic strings, as was done for multimedial languages of communication). In this section we shall adopt a somewhat different approach, aimed at explicating the role of nonverbal actions in a dialogue. Thus we shall assume that class D' of strings that form admissible dialogues is given. After presenting some necessary conditions for the strings in D', the analysis will be directed at a formal characterization of the role of nonverbal actions in a dialogue.

Let $u \in D'$ be a dialogue, that is, $u = d_1 d_2 \cdots d_n$, where each d_i is an element of D, so that

$$d_i = (v_{1i}^A, v_{2i}^A, \ldots, v_{ri}^A; v_{1i}^B, v_{2i}^B, \ldots, v_{ri}^B). \tag{3.95}$$

A necessary (but by no means sufficient) condition for admissibility of string u (i.e., for the condition $u \in D'$) may now be formulated in terms of the strings $v_{11}^A, \ldots, v_{1n}^A$ and $v_{11}^B, \ldots, v_{1n}^B$, which represent the verbal actions of persons A and B. Clearly, each of these strings is an element of V_1^*, that is, monoid over the vocabulary V_1 of verbal actions, plus the "silence" $\#$.

Roughly speaking, both these strings combined should represent a string of sentences. To put it formally, for a given $u = d_1 \cdots d_n \in D^*$ first define strings $q^A(u)$ and $q^B(u)$ as follows: $q^A(u)$ equals string $v_{11}^A \cdots v_{1n}^A$ with elements $\#$ deleted. String $q^B(u)$ is defined similarly. Thus, $q^A(u)$ and $q^B(u)$ are simply the strings of words uttered by A and B, respectively.

Now let $V_1^+ = V_1 - \{\#\}$, and let $L \subset (V_1^+)^*$ be the natural language of dialogue, so that strings in L are sentences. The last concept needed for formulating the necessary conditions mentioned before for admissibility of strings in D^* is the class

$$L' = \{a \in (V_1^+)^* : \exists b \in (V_1^+)^* \text{ such that } ab \in L\}. \tag{3.96}$$

Thus L' is the class of all strings that are either sentences (elements of L) or may be completed to sentences in L.

Let

$$L^\infty = L' \cup (L \times L') \cup (L \times L \times L') \cup \cdots = \bigcup_n (L^{(n)} \times L'), \tag{3.97}$$

where $L^{(n)} = L \times \cdots \times L$ (n times). We then have the following criterion.

Criterion A   If $u \in D^*$ and either $q^A(u)$ or $q^B(u)$ is not in L^∞, then u is not admissible as a dialogue.

3.8.2   Meaning

Thus far the dialogue was consider from a purely syntactic viewpoint, without reference to the meanings of utterances and units. Now let S be the set of possible meanings, and let us distinguish a subclass of D^*, say, D^{**}, consisting of elements u such that $q^A(u)$ and $q^B(u)$ belong to $L^{(1)} \cup L^{(2)} \cup \cdots$ (i.e., each sentence is complete).

With each $u \in D^{**}$ and $s \in S$ one may associate a value $f(u, s)$ representing the degree to which u carries the meaning s. This amounts to postulating the existence of a function

$$f : D^{**} \times S \to [0, 1] \tag{3.98}$$

representing the semantics of dialogues.

For $u \in D^{**}$ let

$$S(u) = \{s \in S : f(u, s) = 1\} \tag{3.99}$$

and

$$S'(u) = \{s \in S : f(u, s) > 0\}. \tag{3.100}$$

Then $S(u)$ is the class of all meanings that string u represents in full degree, and $S'(u)$ is the set of all meanings that u expresses in some positive degree. A string u is then said to be *strongly admissible* as a fragment of a dialogue if $S(u) \neq \varnothing$, that is, if it carries at least one meaning in full degree, and is said to be *weakly admissible*, if $S'(u) \neq \varnothing$.

To express other notions, one may impose some structure on the set S. Through simplification, one may treat the elements of S as built out of elementary meanings by means of negation, conjunction, and disjunction. In other words, we postulate that S contains a class, say, S', of simple (indecomposable) meanings and is closed under conjunction, disjunction, and negation.

Clearly, S cannot be consistent, since with each meaning s it also contains its negation. Thus, to exhibit further the structure of S, let $A \subset S$ and let $C(A)$ be the class of all consequences of elements of A.

Thus $p \in C(A)$ if and only if there exist $p_1, \ldots, p_n \in A$ such that $p_1 \& \cdots \& p_n \to p$. We may say that A is consistent, if $C(A)$ does not contain any pair of the form $(p, -p)$.

For a given $u \in D^{**}$, let $q^A(u)$ and $q^B(u)$ be defined as before, as strings of utterances of A and B. We define the sets $S[q^A(u)]$, $S'[q^A(u)]$, $S[q^B(u)]$, and

$S'[q^B(u)]$ of meanings of $q^A(u)$ and $q^B(u)$ expressed in full or in some positive degree.

Suppose that $u \in D^{**}$ is a dialogue; let u_n denote its initial fragment consisting of n units.

DEFINITION 3.18   We say that dialogue u is a *controversy* if there exists n such that $u_n \in D^{**}$, the sets $C(S[q^A(u_n)])$ and $C(S[q^B(u_n)])$ are consistent, and the set $C[S(u_n)]$ is not consistent.

This means that in some initial stage of the dialogue there is a difference of opinions: each of the speakers asserts his views, and they are consistent, but their views jointly are not consistent.

Suppose that u is a controversy. If it is resolved, that is, if the speakers reach an agreement, then at least one of them must have changed his opinion. Thus, a *necessary* condition for the resolution of a controversy in a dialogue is that one or both of the sets $C(S[q^A(u)])$ and $C(S[q^B(u)])$ be inconsistent.

Clearly, this is only a necessary condition, since a dialogue may remain totally unresolved, yet one (or both) speakers may change their opinion, so that the totality of the sentences uttered by one speaker is inconsistent.

3.8.3   Meaning of a Unit

Let us now consider the role of nonverbal strings of units in a dialogue. For this purpose, let us separate the string $u \in D^{**}$ into four substrings, $q^A(u)$, $q^B(u)$, defined as before, and $n^A(u)$, $n^B(u)$, being the strings of nonverbal units [vectors $(v_2, \ldots, v_r)$] accompanying the verbal utterances or listening.

What we want to describe formally is the fact that the primary meaning is carried by the verbal strings $q^A(u)$ and $q^B(u)$, and the accompanying nonverbal strings $n^A(u)$ and $n^B(u)$ may (but need not) add some "special" meanings, such as emphasis or irony, to the verbal ones. The crucial aspect here is that the nonverbal actions *always* accompany the verbal ones in one form or another but only in special cases do they modify the meanings of verbal utterances.

Thus, we introduce first the notion of standard meanings of verbal utterances. These will be defined as sets $S[q^A(u)]$ and $S[q^B(u)]$, that is, sets of meanings of $q^A(u)$ and $q^B(u)$, respectively, expressed in full degree. Roughly, these are the meanings of utterances in a dialogue, as if they were written and not accompanied by nonverbal actions.

We may now say that $n^A(u)$ is *weakly* standard for $g^A(u)$ if

$$S[q^A(u)] = S[(q^A(u), n^A(u))], \tag{3.101}$$

and $n^A(u)$ is *strongly* standard for $q^A(u)$ if

$$S'[q^A(u)] = S'[(q^A(u), n^A(u))]. \tag{3.102}$$

Thus a standard string $n^A(u)$ is such that it does not alter the meaning of the verbal string (i.e., either it does not change the meanings expressed in full degree, in the case of weakly standard strings, or it does not alter any of the meanings expressed in some positive degree, in the case of strongly standard strings).

Suppose now that the string $n^A(u)$ is not weakly standard for $q^A(u)$. Then

$$S[q^A(u)] \neq S[(q^A(u), n^A(u))]. \tag{3.103}$$

If $s \in S[q^A(u)] - S[(q^A(u), n^A(u))]$, then $f(q^A(u), s) = 1$ and $f[(q^A(u), n^A(u)), s] < 1$, so that the words alone express s in full degree, while if accompanied by $n^A(u)$, the string expresses s in lesser degree. As an example, one may take verbally warm greetings, but without the usual accompanying smile.

On the other hand, if $s \in S[(q^A(u), n^A(u))] - S[q^A(u)]$, then $f[(q^A(u), n^A(u))] = 1$ and $f[q^A(u)] < 1$. Thus, the words alone do not fully express s, and the accompanying nonverbal string $n^A(u)$, jointly with words, expresses s in full degree.

4 JUDGMENT FORMATION AND PROBLEMS OF DESCRIPTION*

4.1 INTRODUCTION

This chapter will be devoted to the problems of the mechanisms underlying the formation of judgments, as well as the problems of expression of these judgments in forms ranging from simple answers to binary questions to generation of texts or discourses. In other words, this chapter will deal with psychological, logical, and linguistic aspects of judgment. Particular emphasis will be put on the role of ambiguity and its unavoidability, connected with such properties of perception as the abilities of discrimination and identification. It will also be shown how these properties of perception constrain the logical values, such as truth, leading to its uncertainty and vagueness.

The analysis begins with the problems of judgment formation (Section 4.2), relevant not only for the social sciences and linguistics but especially for the foundations of fuzzy set theory.

The latter theory acquired considerable popularity in the cognitive sciences, in particular in modeling information processing, artificial intelligence, and such diverse fields as psychology, sociology, medicine, management sciences, operations research, pattern identification, and systems analysis, for representation and manipulation of their soft data, that are nonstatistical in nature "in the sense that they relate, in the main, to the presence of fuzzy sets rather than to random measurement errors or data variability" (Zadeh, 1981).

Thus far fuzzy set theory has been concerned mainly with designing and analyzing ways of constructing membership functions of composite fuzzy sets, given membership functions of elementary fuzzy sets (similar to probability theory, which deals with methods of calculating probabilities of composite events given the probabilities of some simpler events). However, unlike

*From Nowakowska (1985). Reprinted with permission from *Mathematical Social Sciences,* 9, 1985, copyright by North-Holland Publishing Company, Amsterdam, 1985.

probability theory, fuzzy set theory does not provide the means of assigning fuzzy membership functions to elementary fuzzy subsets; this is done purely subjectively.

In Section 4.2 it is shown how one can measure (using some concepts of psychological test theory) the degree of membership in certain fuzzy sets. Such a possibility, despite its limitations to some special fuzzy sets, is therefore a breakthrough in the foundations of fuzzy set theory.

The subsequent parts of Section 4.2 concern the basic issue involved in such a measurement, namely the process of question answering (hence the underlying process of arriving at the judgment and deciding whether or not to disclose it). It is shown that the clue to such mechanisms lies in the statistical variability of answers to questions. Accordingly, certain models of statistical estimation and also simulation models of question answering are suggested.

By introducing the concept of ambiguity area, these models show the role of ambiguity and the difficulty of discrimination in the formation of the judgment, and they also (especially the simulation models MASIA) capture certain psychological mechanisms that interfere in judgment disclosure (verbal expression).

The latter models allow, among others, the reconstruction of the statistical characteristics of the answers in a population, thus determining the type and estimating the magnitude of the bias. The models have been successfully validated empirically [see van der Zouwen *et al.* (1979)] and are the first of the type in the psychological and sociological literature.

These results are of special significance for the foundations of fuzzy set theory, since they bring to the attention of all those who develop and apply the theory certain inherent important cognitive problems that restrain to some extent the development of the theory and its applications. They show, therefore, the necessity of concentrating efforts not so much on more sophisticated technical development of the theory but rather on its foundations.

One should mention here that other important problems in the foundations of fuzzy set theory have been discussed, for example, by Schefe (1980) and Yager (1979a–c).

Specifically, in Section 4.2 attention will be devoted to the questions of existence and the properties of uncertainty and/or vagueness areas on the continuum of the modal concept (trait) that underlie the fuzzy membership function of a fuzzy set under consideration. Very roughly, the vagueness area may be compared with the support of the fuzzy membership function or with its level sets. The essential point here is that—as opposed to the standard situations in fuzzy set theory—the argument in the fuzzy membership function is either not given explicitly or is itself fuzzy.

As is well known, the motivation for introduction of fuzzy set theory by Zadeh was the need for precision in speaking about vagueness and imprecision. But, as will be shown, even the sophisticated and intuitively acceptable tools for dealing with vagueness cannot avoid their own uncertainty and/or vagueness area, varying in size and location. This is due to some specific psychological mechanisms intervening in judgment formation. This looks quite paradoxical and has some surprising philosophical consequences concerning negative bounds in the possibility of removing uncertainty and vagueness.

The problem of the degree to which one can reduce uncertainty has been studied in probability theory, statistics, and information theory. These studies concerned the uncertainty of probabilistic nature. However, the degree to which one could remove fuzziness has not received as much attention as it should. It has been recognized that the degree of fuzziness may itself be fuzzy. This led to the introduction of various versions of higher-order fuzzy sets. Surprisingly little research was done, however, on the assignment of the degree of membership in a fuzzy set, and especially the stability of this assignment [for a notable exception, see Zimmermann and Zysno (1980)].

The phenomenon of the existence of cognitive bounds in removing fuzziness was hardly noticed, let alone investigated, since no one was interested in the stability or instability of membership function value assignments. This is quite odd in view of the importance of the applications of fuzzy set theory, especially in decision making, optimization problems in information processing and operations research, and so on.

Section 4.3 deals with a theory of descriptions, referred to as "verbal copies." Here the subject evaluates an object on its various semantic dimensions or, equivalently, classifies it according to various categories or, still in other words, performs a multiple linguistic measurement [for the latter concept, see Nowakowska (1979a). This notion is an extension and an alternative approach to Zadeh's fuzzy set theory].

These are simple judgments whose normal form is "x is w in degree p." The analysis of such judgments leads to important problems connected with observability, as well as validity and reliability of observations. The basic concepts here are faithfulness and exactness.

It is assumed that each object of a given set has a specific value (possibly fuzzy) of every attribute (from a given set of attributes). The whole description may then be identified with a vector of fuzzy sets, each concerning one attribute, where the sets are obtained by algebraic operations on fuzzy sets of attribute values. The main problems analyzed concern exhibiting the structural aspects of such descriptions and their relation to reality, especially truth (referred to as faithfulness, in the fuzzy case), and precision.

The section explores the limitations imposed on the descriptions by the choice of the language of descriptors, that is, the vocabulary of permitted terms (linguistic or numerical) for the given set of attributes. These cognitive limitations are perhaps best visible for theories, that always carry their own cognitive upper bounds. Overcoming such a bound involves the necessity of a new theory, allowing more faithful and more exact description of the phenomenon under study. In Nowakowska (1979a) it was shown that the limitation imposed by the accepted language of description may be partially overcome by construction of *ad hoc* categories resulting from operations on the existing ones or by invention of new concepts.

Another bound on descriptions is connected with the degree of fuzziness of the truth. It may seem paradoxical, but crisp truth imposes more constraints on description than fuzzy truth. The reason is simply that to describe in a faithful way a crisp truth one may use both crisp and fuzzy descriptors, but for fuzzy truth one may use only fuzzy descriptors.

If a verbal copy is understood as a sequence of classificatory statements, then one can assign to it a sequence of attributes and/or their values mentioned in the copy. The class of all sequences so obtained may be regarded as an abstract classificatory (attributional) language.

For the analysis of problems of description dynamics, the notion of verbal copy is enriched by temporal variables. This allows the introduction of the concept of generative verbal structure, which describes dynamically changing objects or their future states. The essential notion for this analysis is the concept of history, understood as a sequence of events or sequence of states of some fragment of reality. A special class of histories, corresponding to backward and forward branching, is considered. (These notions refer to finding possible continuations or possible previous parts of history.)

To study generative verbal structures, an algebra of goals and means [introduced by Nowakowska (1975, 1976a)] was used. This algebra is based on an isomorphism between composite goals and sets of means of attaining them. A composite goal is obtained by substitution of elementary goals in some propositional function. The basic notions for the algebra of goals and means is that of complete possibility, which allows in turn the introduction of a formal theory of conflicts, understood as joint unattainability of some goals, and the devising of a very rich taxonomy of these conflicts. [For the theory of conflicts, see Nowakowska (1973).]

This algebra of goals and means is a highly flexible tool, which can be used for describing various situations of attainability of composite goals. It is used again in the last section of this chapter for a dynamic study of discourses.

For the study of generative verbal structures and their faithfulness and exactness, it is essential to define the notion of a true state of history and to determine the provisions for satisfiability with respect to temporal constants. In other words, one needs to determine conditions under which a proposition is true in a given history. These considerations of histories and generative verbal structures lead to the notion of fuzzy stochastic processes.

The remainder of the chapter deals with theories of texts, understood as composite descriptions in the system whose rules and logic of relations between objects are defined by the author of the text. On the other hand, the theory of texts is also regarded as a certain theory of knowledge.

As opposed to Section 4.3, where the considerations concerned an idealized description reduced to a conjunction of some statements, in Section 4.4 the analysis concerns texts as they are expressed linguistically. Some models are suggested for a statistical analysis of semantic connections that exist between various parts of the text, as well as stochastic models of changes of topics.

Section 4.5 gives a formalization of the idea that a text may be regarded as a sequence of responses to a (hypothetical) sequence of questions, and Section 4.6 concerns the structural aspects of the knowledge expressed by a text. The special topic here is the overall valuation of this knowledge, in terms of its possibility, credibility, believability, and so on, given the values of the same attribute for the constituents of the knowledge. Here the theory suggested treats all suitable functions generally and introduces the concept of α-bility of a set (of propositions).

Finally, Section 4.7 concerns still another aspect of the generation of a text (or, generally, a discourse), regarding it from the viewpoint of its goal or goals. Here one may distinguish some basic types of goals and explore the structural constraints on the discourse imposed by goals of each type and, in general, by a composite goal built out of partial goals.

An important complementation of all considerations of judgments, their variability, relation to events and sequences, and so on, is the notion of a cognitive space underlying the linguistic representation of motivation. Here we refer to the model suggested by Nowakowska (1973), which shows a general scheme of internal decisions interpreted as group decisions. The model uses Arrow's Impossibility Theorem [see Arrow (1963)]. The deductive consequences of this theorem lead to distinguishing important mechanisms and thus to overall decisions, given the partial decisions and judgments.

This chapter connects the topics of subjective and objective time (Chapter 1) with the topics of random objects (Chapter 2) and ordering events in time (histories). Whereas in Chapter 1 simple judgments about orders of events (and misperception of these orders) were considered, this chapter treats the topics of judgments more generally, allowing all subjective judgments. It considers the general models of distortions of judgments connected with difficulties of discrimination and identification.

Inclusion into this chapter of theories of texts and knowledge, as an extension of judgment formation underlying simple and composite statements, is a certain methodological novelty leading to connecting the topics that are usually treated separately.

Finally, let us mention that this chapter is devoted to the analysis of the role of one medium (verbal), and in this sense it deepens the analysis of Chapter 3 on multimedial communication languages.

4.2 MODELS OF ANSWERING QUESTIONS

4.2.1 Measurement of Fuzziness

The problems considered in this section will constitute, in a sense, a continuation of the earlier work on empirical access to the values of membership function [see Nowakowska (1977)]. The main issue there was the connection of the concept structure with a measurement tool in the form of a questionnaire, that is, a compound classificatory device. The basic assumptions underlying this kind of measurement are (1) modality of the construct, that is, the possibility, at least theoretical, of its modal representation and (2) monotonicity of questions with respect to the measured construct.

To be able to apply the suggested method, the elements of the basic underlying set were people, and the considered concepts were only those that could be expressed as (fuzzy) sets of people.

To define a concept and explicate its structure, let $\mathscr{G}$ denote the class of "elementary" fuzzy subsets of X, where X is the set of persons under consideration. The term "elementary" is taken here as a primitive notion. The intended interpretation is such that a set $\mathscr{G}$ (of persons) is regarded as elementary if the question "Do you belong to the set G?" may be expressed in simple, everyday terms.

We may postulate accordingly that the class $\mathscr{G}$ is closed under complementation: if $G \in \mathscr{G}$, then $-G$ (not G) is also in $\mathscr{G}$.

Now let $\mathscr{G}''$ be the class of sets formed of elements of $\mathscr{G}$, using only the operations of conjunction and disjunction, and let $\mathscr{G}'$ be a (fuzzy) subset of $\mathscr{G}''$ consisting of sets built out of large numbers of elementary sets.

At this point it is worthwhile to point out the essential difference between the present approach and that of the authors dealing with an empirical approach to fuzziness, notably Sambuc (1975). In his paper, he analyzes fuzzy sets (concepts) from G'' (but not from G'). To use his example, he defines such notion as hyperthyroidism as (tachycardia OR weight loss) AND (thermophobia OR increased thirst) AND (increased seric T4 values OR increased seric T3 values). His objective is to assign meaningful and useful representations of doctor's assessments of various symptoms to be able to assess finally the degree of membership of the patient in a given disease. This is achieved by introducing the concept of Φ fuzzy sets, where membership values are intervals (representing indeterminacy) instead of points.

As opposed to that, in this section the analysis concerns the problem of an empirical access to membership functions in its "classical" sense, as defined originally by Zadeh. To be more precise, it will be shown that, in certain cases (of some concepts from G', hence involving large numbers of "elementary" sets), one may assess the L_2 distance between two concepts. A typical case of applicability of this result would be as follows: imagine two scientists who introduce two concepts bearing the same name (e.g., concept such as "democrat"). As a rule, definitions of such concepts differ to some extent, and to determine the degree of difference (as expressed by expected squared difference between membership functions) is of considerable theoretical interest and practical importance.

Given $G' \in \mathcal{G}'$, one may construct a classificatory device (test) for measurement of the fuzzy concept G'. To this end, each of the elementary sets G that enter in $\mathcal{G}'$ is converted into a question, such as "Do you belong to the set of persons who usually feel tired in the morning?" (i.e., "Do you usually feel tired in the morning?").

For a test composed of such questions to constitute a coherent measure of the concept, one needs the following condition: to represent the concept in the form of a classificatory device (test), for every $G \in \mathcal{G}$, either G or $-G$, or none of them, *but not both*, may appear in the representation. Also, the classification induced by the question must be monotone, in the sense that the probability of answer "yes" to the question about membership in the set G is an increasing function of $f_G(x)$, that is, the membership value of person x in the set G. Briefly, the higher is the degree of membership of person x in the set G, the more likely is it that he will answer "yes" to the question "Do you belong to G?"

As is usually the case, it is easier to explain the importance of the above assumptions by a negative example. Thus, a nonmonotone (hence not suitable for a test) question might be "Do you occasionally feel awkward because of your height?". If the underlying concept is height, then both very tall and very short persons might tend to reply "yes," while persons of intermediate heights will tend to answer "no."

As regards coherence, the condition prevents simply obtaining positive scores for both membership in G and its complement.

Given two tests measuring the concepts G^* and G^{**} from $\mathcal{G}'$, one may evaluate the distance between them, defined as

$$d(G^*, G^{**}) = \int [f_{G^*}(x) - f_{G^{**}}(x)]^2 p(x)\,dx, \tag{4.1}$$

where $p(x)$ is a sampling scheme.

Remembering that x is in the present context a tested person, one usually assumes that $p(x)$ is uniform distribution on some subpopulation (of persons to whom the test is applicable and about whom the inference is being made).

One can prove the following formula [see Nowakowska (1979a)]:

$$d(G^*, G^{**}) = \sigma^2(T^*)\rho(T_1^*, T_2^*) + \sigma^2(T^{**})\rho(T_1^{**}, T_2^{**})$$
$$- 2\sigma(T^*)\sigma(T^{**})\rho(T^*, T^{**}) + [E(T^*) - E(T^{**})]^2, \qquad (4.2)$$

where T^*, T^{**} are the test scores corresponding to G^* and G^{**}, E, σ, and ρ stand, respectively, for expectation, standard deviation, and correlation coefficient, and T_1^*, T_2^* (similarly T_1^{**}, T_2^{**}) denote the results in two parallel applications of the test T^*.

All quantities on the right-hand side of the formula are empirically accessible from the results of two measurements of the same group of persons twice by means of tests T^* and T^{**}.

Two concepts may be called *synonymous* (more precisely L_2-synonymous) if $d(G^*, G^{**}) = 0$ (or is sufficiently small); this formula therefore provides the means to assess the degree of synonymity.

Let us observe that formula (4.2) gives the distance in L_2-metric, not in uniform metric $d_1(G^*, G^{**}) = \sup_x |f_{G^*}(x) - f_{G^{**}}(x)|$. The problem of estimating the uniform distance appears difficult. To point out the difference between uniform distance and L_2-distance, it is enough to observe that (qualitatively speaking) uniform distance is small if the membership functions are close to each other at each point (person), and L_2-distance is small if large differences occur seldom.

4.2.2 General Assumptions about the Mechanism of Question Answering

The previous analysis was based on the idea of representing "elementary" fuzzy sets by questions. This necessitates a more detailed analysis of the mechanisms involved in question answering, especially the mechanisms related to uncertainty and vagueness. As an empirical clue providing access to such mechanisms we shall take the variability of answers upon repetition of the question.

To define the uncertainty and/or vagueness area (in short, the UC/V area), let us introduce the following assumption. The subject has some knowledge concerning the evaluated concept (attribute or trait, as the case may be) in the sense that he knows his own value of the trait, at least approximately; this value will be denoted by x_S. The subject perceives also the cutoff point of the question on the continuum of the trait, say, x_E. This point has the property that for all persons whose value x_S lies to the right of x_E the answer is "yes," and for all other persons, the answer is "no."

The mechanism of answer is then such that the subject "perceives internally" the values x_E and x_S, and if $x_S > x_E$, he gives the answer "yes," and in the opposite case, he gives the answer "no." Of course, the internal perception may differ if the question is repeated.

To use an example, imagine a person replying to a question such as "Are you rich?". One can visualize the mechanism of answering so that the person (a) chooses a certain level x_E (of salary, assets, etc.) above which he would classify the person as rich. He then perceives x_S, the level of his own assets and replies "yes" or "no" depending on mutual relation between x_E and x_S.

For some questions, the underlying axis with points x_E and x_S is harder to conceptualize (e.g., "Do you consider yourself to be a liberal?").

Suppose now that the same question is asked twice of each of n subjects. They will then split into three categories: those who gave answer "yes" twice, those who gave answer "no" twice, and finally, those who changed their answer. Denote the numbers of subjects in the above categories by Y, N, and C.

A question will be called *stable* if C is small in comparison with $Y + N$; otherwise, it is called *variable*. On the other hand, the question is called *balanced* if $Y \approx N$; otherwise it is called *extremal*.

It appears that these categories are closely related one to another. One can formulate the following empirical laws, generalizing the findings of numerous empirical studies on psychological tests and properties of their items:

LAW 4.1   The more extremal is the question, the more stable it is.

One could also interpret the question for which $x_S \approx x_E$ as *difficult* and/or *unclear*, and questions for which $x_S \gg x_E$ or $x_E \gg x_S$ as *easy* and/or *unambiguous*. We may then formulate the following laws:

LAW 4.2   If the question is easy, then variability is low, and conversely, if the question is difficult, then variability is high.

LAW 4.3   If the question is unambiguous, then variability is low, and conversely, if the question is vague, the variability is high.

It is important to realize that these laws connect properties of questions from various generality levels. Thus, stability and extremeness are global properties, characterized by statistical features of answers (under repetition). On the other hand, difficulty and ambiguity and their opposites are "local" properties, related to both the question and the respondent (i.e., the same question may be easy for one person and difficult for another). Thus, in the last two laws, variability should be understood as high probability that the answer may be changed when the question is repeated.

4.2.3   Discriminability

Let us now consider questions from the point of view of the goal of asking them. Imagine that the population is ranked according to some criterion (it may be either an external criterion, for example, physical, or results of some test). Here one of the crucial concepts is that of discriminability. Imagine that the question has two categories of answer, "yes" and "no." In the ideal case, in the partition of population into categories whose sizes were denoted by Y, N, and C (answer changed), the first two categories should occupy the initial and end fragments of the ordering of the population.

For example, imagine that the ordering of population is according to height. A "good" (in the sense of discrimination) question might be "Do you wear shoes (shirt, etc.) of the size larger than so and so?".

In general, denoting $x_1, x_2, \ldots$ as the elements of the population according to rank, one can take as a measure of the quality of discrimination supplied by the question the number

$$Q = \sum_{x_j \in U_Y} 1 - \sum_{x_j \in U_N} 1, \tag{4.3}$$

where U_Y and U_N are sets of persons who twice gave the same answers "yes" and "no." (This, naturally, is not the only measure of discrimination. Another commonly applied measure is the correlation coefficient.)

The above cases, however, concerned discriminability with respect to some external criterion. It is of considerable interest to see what happens if one omits the assumption about the existence of the external criterion (ordering of the population). In such a case, one may ask for the internal discrimation index, which shows the potential discriminating possibilities contained in the statistical properties of the question.

One of the obvious choices for such an index of discriminability is the entropy of the response distribution. Another interesting choice is based on the ratio of the number of pairs that are actually discriminated to the number of all possible pairs.

Generally, imagine that the population consists of N members, and let us agree to say that two members are discriminated (by the given question) if they belong to different categories of answers; otherwise they are not distinguished. Suppose now that the question has $r \geq 2$ categories of answer, and let m_1, $m_2, \ldots, m_r$ be the actual numbers of members of the population in these categories. The number of all pairs equals $\binom{N}{2} = N(N-1)/2$. To calculate the number of pairs that are actually discriminated, let us calculate the number of pairs that are not discriminated. Clearly, these will be all pairs formed of groups classified in the same way. Thus, the jth class gives $m_j(m_j - 1)/2$ nondiscriminated pairs, and the total number of nondiscriminated pairs is

$\sum_{j=1}^{r} m_j(m_j - 1)/2$. The total number of discriminated pairs is therefore

$$N(N - 1)/2 - \sum_{j=1}^{r} m_j(m_j - 1)/2 \qquad (4.4)$$

and the index of internal discriminability is

$$D = 1 - \sum_{j=1}^{r} \frac{m_j(m_j - 1)}{N(N - 1)}. \qquad (4.5)$$

Denoting $z_j = m_j/N$, the last quantity may be written approximately as

$$D \approx 1 - \sum_{j=1}^{r} z_j^2, \qquad (4.6)$$

where values $z_1, \ldots, z_r$ are constrained, in view of the condition $m_1 + \cdots + m_r = N$, by $z_1 + \cdots + z_r = 1$. It is easy to see that the maximal value of D is attained when all z_j are equal. This means that the uniform distribution gives the best internal discrimination: there are more pairs distinguished than under any other distribution. Consequently, a balanced question will have the highest internal discrimination index.

Laws 4.1–4.3, combined with the knowledge about the discrimination indices, provide the means for using the parameters of the question for prediction of the stability of the answers.

4.2.4   Models of Answering Questions

Let us now return to the problem of answering questions, and assume at the beginning the following simple model. Suppose that the subjects may be partitioned (with respect to a given question) into three categories: those who always answer "yes," those who always answer "no," and those who are undecided and give answer "yes" or "no" independently from trial to trial with probability $\frac{1}{2}$ each. Let p, q, and z denote the proportions of subjects in each of these three categories so that (in view of $p + q + z = 1$) two of these numbers may be taken as parameters of the question. The object is to estimate these parameters from the statistical data on answers, collected from a double trial on the same question. Thus, the data have the form of a triplet of numbers (Y, N, C), where Y, N, and C denote, respectively, the numbers of persons in the sample who answered "yes" on both times, "no" on both times, and those who changed the answer. Furthermore, let $n = Y + N + C$, and assume that

$$C \leq \min(2N, 2Y). \qquad (4.7)$$

This assumption is justifiable in view of the assumed model of random answers of persons from category U_C. On average, one-quarter of them will give answer "yes" twice, one-quarter will give answer "no" twice, and half will change their answer.

Let us now try to find the maximum likelihood estimators of probabilities p, q, and z. The probability of answer "yes" is $p + \frac{1}{4}z$; the probability of answer "no" is $q + \frac{1}{4}z = 1 - p - \frac{3}{4}z$, and the probability of change of the answer is $\frac{1}{2}z$. Consequently, the likelihood function is

$$L = (p + \tfrac{1}{4}z)^Y(1 - p - \tfrac{3}{4}z)^N(\tfrac{1}{2}z)^C, \tag{4.8}$$

which gives

$$\log L = Y\log(p + \tfrac{1}{4}z) + N\log(1 - p - \tfrac{3}{4}z) + C\log z - C\log 2. \tag{4.9}$$

Differentiating with respect to p and z yields, after some simplifications, the equations

$$(N + Y)p + \tfrac{1}{4}z(N + 3Y) = Y$$
$$Cp + \tfrac{1}{4}z(2N + 3C) = C. \tag{4.10}$$

Solving, we finally obtain for p, q, and z

$$p = (2Y - C)/2n, \qquad q = (2N - C)/2n, \qquad z = 2C/n, \tag{4.11}$$

where $n = Y + N + C$.

If one now adds some distributional assumptions, one may use these formulas to obtain information about the location of certain points on the continuum of the trait.

Suppose that the distribution of values of the trait in the population is normal, with some known mean m and known standard deviation σ. Further, suppose that the persons who will answer "yes" are characterized by their values x_S being less than some threshold a. Similarly, those who will answer "no" satisfy the condition $b < x_S$, and those who are undecided and answer randomly satisfy the condition $a \le x_S \le b$.

Then the values a and b may be determined from

$$\Phi\left(\frac{a - m}{\sigma}\right) = \frac{2Y - C}{2n}, \qquad \Phi\left(\frac{b - m}{\sigma}\right) = \frac{2Y + 3C}{2n}, \tag{4.12}$$

where $\Phi(x)$ is the standard normal distribution.

The difference $b - a$ may be called the width of the UC/V area (expressed in units equal to σ, with zero at m). If we return to the interpretation according to which each person is characterized by a value x_S, then the UC/V area will consist of those values of the trait x_S for which $a \le x_S \le b$.

The fraction of changes of answers C depends not only on the width of the UC/V area but also on the density of normal distribution over this area; it depends on the integral

$$\frac{1}{\sigma\sqrt{2\pi}} \int_a^b \exp\left[-\frac{(t - m)^2}{2\sigma^2} \right] dt. \tag{4.13}$$

One may therefore formulate the following hypothesis relating the width of the UC/V area $b - a$ and its position on the axis (central, i.e., close to m, versus extremal, i.e., on the tail of the distribution).

1. If width $b - a$ is small, then the variability of answers is low, regardless of the location of the UC/V area. The question is balanced or not depending on the location of the UC/V area. If the question is balanced, it has high internal discrimination index.

2. If the width $b - a$ of the UC/V area is large, the variability is large in the case of central position and small in case of extreme position of the UC/V area. The question has high internal discriminatory index in the case of the central position of the UC/V area.

4.2.5   A Fuzzification of the Model

The above model needs to be fuzzified, since in the present form it postulates discontinuities at points a and b in the sense that all subjects with values of trait x_S lying to the left from a behave in a different way from those subjects with x_S with $a \le x_S \le b$, and these in turn behave differently than subjects with $x_S > b$.

A more realistic model would assume that values a and b (equivalently, the UC/V area) are fuzzy. To construct its membership function, say, $v(x)$, choose a number $\varepsilon < (b - a)/2$, and assume that $v(x) = 1$ for $a + \varepsilon < x < b - \varepsilon$, $v(x) = 0$ for $x < a - \varepsilon$ and $x > b + \varepsilon$, and on the intervals $(a - \varepsilon, a + \varepsilon)$ and $(b - \varepsilon, b + \varepsilon)$ the membership function $v(x)$ is given by formulas

$$v(x) = \frac{1}{2} + \frac{1}{\pi} \arctan \frac{a - x}{(x - a + \varepsilon)(x - a - \varepsilon)}$$

$$= \frac{1}{2} + \frac{1}{\pi} \arctan \frac{a - x}{(x - a)^2 - \varepsilon^2} \qquad \text{for} \quad a - \varepsilon < x < a + \varepsilon, \tag{4.14}$$

and

$$v(x) = \frac{1}{2} + \frac{1}{\pi} \arctan \frac{x - b}{(x - b)^2 - \varepsilon^2} \qquad \text{for} \quad b - \varepsilon < x < b + \varepsilon. \tag{4.15}$$

Here ε is a number indicating, in a sense, the degree of fuzziness: the smaller the value ε, the steeper is the increase and decrease of the membership function $v(x)$ in the neighborhoods of the points a and b (see Fig. 4.1).

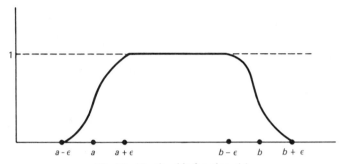

Fig. 4.1. Membership function $v(x)$.

Another way of avoiding the assumption of discontinuities consists of assuming that answer "yes" is not determined in a deterministic way by values x_S and x_E but depends on these values in a stochastic manner. To be more specific, let us assume the following answer model: the subject first visualizes values x_S and x_E on the continuum of the trait; the rule for answering is the same as before, but now we assume that x_S and x_E are random variables.

Let us take as distribution for x_S and x_E the independent random variables with normal distribution. If x_S has normal distribution $N(m_S, \sigma_S)$ and x_E has normal distribution $N(m_E, \sigma_E)$, then to calculate the desired probabilities it is, of course, necessary to postulate how the probability of answer "yes" depends on the mutual position of points x_S and x_E. Let us assume that this probability is given by some function f, depending on the difference $x_E - x_S$; naturally, positive values should give high probability of answer "yes," and negative values tend rather to give the "no" answer. Then the probability of answer "yes" will be

$$P(Y) = \frac{1}{\sigma_E \sigma_S 2\pi} \iint f(x - y) \exp\left[-\frac{(x - m_E)^2}{2\sigma_E^2} - \frac{(y - m_S)^2}{2\sigma_S^2}\right] dx\, dy. \quad (4.16)$$

This approach, although probably the most adequate to reflect the conditions of answering, involves the unknown function f, which must be postulated, and four constants m_S, σ_S, m_E, and σ_E. The estimation requires using the computer optimization routines.

4.2.6   MASIA: An Alternative Model

Let us observe that the model of answering from the preceding section did not allow for the possibility that the answer given is "I don't know": a person in the UC/V area produced a random answer, and the width or location of this area was assessed on the basis of statistics of replies to repeated questions.

One can introduce another model in which the problem of the "I don't know" answer is analyzed as follows. The basic assumptions about answering resemble the ones from the preceding sections. Thus, there is the cutoff point for the question x_E, and the answer is determined by comparison of "answer values" with x_E.

The difference between the present and the preceding models lies in the assumption that the subject samples several (in the present version: two) "trial values" for each answer, for example, x_S' and x_S'', and determines first two trial answers, say, t' and t''. These trial answers are determined according to the following general rule:

$$t' = \begin{cases} \text{yes} & \text{if} \quad x_S' < x_E, \\ \text{no} & \text{if} \quad x_S' \geq x_E, \end{cases} \qquad t'' = \begin{cases} \text{yes} & \text{if} \quad x_S'' < x_E, \\ \text{no} & \text{if} \quad x_S'' \geq x_E. \end{cases} \tag{4.17}$$

In addition, the true answer t is determined according to the rule

$$t = \begin{cases} \text{yes} & \text{if} \quad x_S < x_E, \\ \text{no} & \text{if} \quad x_S \geq x_E. \end{cases} \tag{4.18}$$

Trial values x_S' and x_S'' are simply the value x_S with some distortions to be described later; thus,

$$x_S' = x_S + \xi_1, \qquad x_S'' = x_S + \xi_2, \tag{4.19}$$

where ξ_1 and ξ_2 are the distortions.

The trial answers, or the true answer, are not disclosed: they determine the final answer, say, t^*, according to one of the number of rules. Thus, we have in effect a family of models named MASIA, depending on the choice of the answering rule. The simplest rule is as follows:

If $t' = t''$, then $t^* = t'$.
If $t' \neq t''$, then $t^* =$ "I don't know" (DK).

This version, therefore, is characterized by the property that the final answer agrees with the trial answers if the latter coincide; otherwise, it is "I don't know."

It remains to describe the nature of distortions ξ_1 and ξ_2. It is assumed that they result from the interplay among three factors: the tendency to answer "yes," the tendency to answer "no," and the importance of the question. To describe formally the nature of these tendencies, let

$$I_r(x) = \begin{cases} 0 & \text{if} \quad x < r, \\ x & \text{if} \quad x \geq r. \end{cases} \tag{4.20}$$

Let y_1, y_2, y_3, y_4 be four independent random variables, say, with uniform distribution on $(0, 1)$, and let $a > 0$ and $b > 0$ be two thresholds for "yes" and for "no," respectively. Then distortions ξ_1 and ξ_2 are

$$\xi_1 = u[I_b(y_2) - I_a(y_1)],$$
$$\xi_2 = u[I_b(y_4) - I_a(y_3)],$$

(4.21)

where u (random or not) is the importance of the question.

Thus, the tendency to answer "yes" or "no" begins to act only if it exceeds its threshold (a or b); the importance of the question acts multiplicatively. (Actually, u is a measure of the unimportance of the question: the higher the value of u, the higher tend to be the distortions of the true value of the trait x_S, hence more likely it is that the true and trial answers will differ.)

4.2.7 Comparison of Treatment of Vagueness in the Models Discussed

Let us try to compare the UC/V areas in the MASIA models, and in other models discussed in this section. Let us observe, first of all, that in the considered models the approach to the problems of vagueness and uncertainty (expressed in terms of the variability of answers, in terms of the probability of answer "yes," or in terms of the probability of the DK answer) was varying from model to model, and only in one case did the model postulate localization of UC/V areas on the continuum of the trait. In all other cases, the degree of vagueness or uncertainty depended on the *mutual* position of points x_S and x_E, not on their location on the continuum. Such an approach appears more adequate and intuitively plausible, since vagueness or uncertainty, as might be argued, is associated with difficulty in self-assessment before answering the question, and (in terms of the models) self-assessment becomes more difficult when the values that are to be compared are close one to another.

In the case of MASIA models, vagueness and uncertainty are expressed by the probability of the answer coded as "I don't know" (DK).

The rule that determines the type of answer, given the trial answers t' and t'' and the true answer t, depends on the particular MASIA model; in each case, the rule may be represented as an area in the (x_S', x_S'') plane. For instance, for the case presented in this section the rule is as shown on Fig. 4.2.

In other MASIA models, the shape of the DK area is different. For instance, one could argue that uncertainty occurs only if the trial values x_S' and x_S'' are close one to another. This gives the DK area shown in Fig. 4.3.

Some DK areas lead to easier estimation of the parameters of the model on the basis of empirical data. In particular, for the model named MASIA 7, when the DK area was as shown in Fig. 4.4, it was possible to derive explicit formulas for the probabilities of various combinations of answers and thus to create the basis for maximum likelihood estimation of parameters.

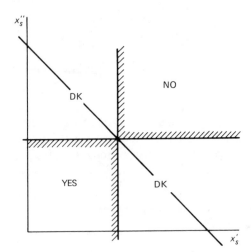

Fig. 4.2. A typical decision value in MASIA modeling.

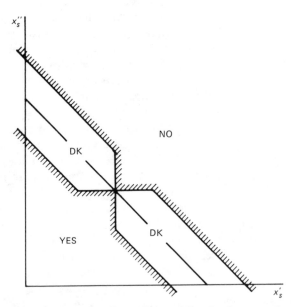

Fig. 4.3. A decision value in MASIA modeling showing uncertainty.

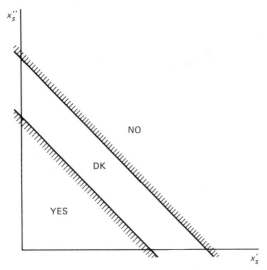

Fig. 4.4. A decision value in MASIA 7.

Generally, in this model, the given answer t^* is DK if $x'_S + x''_S$ is sufficiently close to $2x_E$ (see Fig. 4.4). Thus, MASIA 7 operates according to the rule

$$t^* = \begin{array}{lll} \text{yes} & \text{if} & x'_S + x''_S \le 2x_E - k, \\ \text{DK} & \text{if} & 2x_E - k < x'_S + x''_S < 2x_E + k, \\ \text{no} & \text{if} & 2x_E + k \le x'_S + x''_S. \end{array} \qquad (4.22)$$

Here k is a parameter representing the (un)importance of appearing decisive: if k is small, then $x'_S + x''_S$ must lie very close to $2x_E$ to elicit reply DK.

What is needed are the theoretical formulas determining the probabilities of six possible combinations of true and given answers, that is, for t being "yes" or "no," and t^* being "yes," "no," or "I don't know." Given such probabilities and given the empirical data in the form of a table of six frequencies corresponding to the above-mentioned six probabilities, one could try to find the "best" values of parameters to fit the data. Such a trial-and-error method was used [for a somewhat different version of MASIA] by van der Zouwen *et al.* (1979).

In the case of MASIA 7 one could, however, use the maximum likelihood method as follows.

First, let us make the following assumption.

ASSUMPTION 4.1   *Values x_S, y_1, y_2, y_3, y_4 are independent random variables, distributed uniformly on* $(0, 1)$.

Denote by $F(z) = F_{ab}(z)$ the distribution of random variable η_i $(i = 1, 2)$ defined as $\eta_1 = I_b(y_2) - I_a(y_1)$ and $\eta_2 = I_b(y_4) - I_a(y_3)$, with the function I defined in Section 4.2.6.

One can then determine the six probabilities obtained by combining true answers t and given answers t^*. For instance,

$$P_1 = P(t = t^* = \text{yes}) = P(x_S < x_E \ \& \ x_S' + x_S'' < 2x_E - k)$$

$$= P(x_S < x_E \ \& \ \eta_1 + \eta_2 < (2x_E - k - 2x_S)/u)$$

$$= \int_0^{x_E} P(\eta_1 + \eta_2 < (2x_E - k - 2x_S)/u) \, dx_S, \qquad (4.23)$$

where η_1 and η_2 are independent random variables with distribution F.

Substituting $(2x_E - k - 2x_S)/u = t$, we obtain $dx_S = -\frac{1}{2}u \, dt$, hence

$$P_1 = \frac{1}{2}u \int_{-k/u}^{(2x_E - k)/u} G(t) \, dt, \qquad (4.24)$$

where $G(t) = P(\eta_1 + \eta_2 < t)$ is the distribution function of the sum $\eta_1 + \eta_2$.

In a similar way one can write expressions for the remaining probabilities, such as $P(t = \text{yes}, t^* = \text{DK})$, etc. The problem remains only to determine the distribution function $F(t)$ of the random variable η_1; function $G(t)$ will then be the convolution of F with itself.

To determine F one has to distinguish among four cases, depending on whether $a + b < 1$ or $a + b \geq 1$ and whether $a < b$ or $a \geq b$. The full results may be found in Nowakowska (1981c); here we give only the final result for the case $a + b < 1$, $a < b$. We then have

$$F(t) = \begin{cases} 0 & \text{for} \quad t \leq -1, \\ b(1 + t) & \text{for} \quad -1 < t \leq -(1 - b), \\ b(1 + t) + (1 - b + t)^2/2 & \text{for} \quad -(1 - b) < t \leq -a, \\ b(1 - a) + (1 - b + t)^2/2 & \text{for} \quad -a < t \leq 0, \\ \text{mass } ab & \text{for} \quad t = 0, \\ 1 - (1 - b)(1 + b - 2t)/2 & \text{for} \quad 0 < t \leq b - a, \\ 1 - a(1 - b) - (1 - a - t)^2/2 & \text{for} \quad b - a < t \leq b, \\ 1 - a(1 - t) - (1 - a - t)^2/2 & \text{for} \quad b < t \leq 1 - a, \\ 1 - a(1 - t) & \text{for} \quad 1 - a < t \leq 1, \\ 1 & \text{for} \quad t > 1. \end{cases} \qquad (4.25)$$

4.2.8 Vagueness, Uncertainty, and Discriminability

Let us now try to combine the considerations of discriminativeness with the problems of vagueness and uncertainty of questions. At first sight, it would appear that high discriminativeness, which amounts to the property that the question is a good measure of the concept, should imply stability (hence lack of vagueness and uncertainty): intuitively, if the question supplies good information, the answer should not be variable. It might seem paradoxical, but this expectation cannot be satisfied, because of the almost nonexistence in the social sciences of questions that are at the same time stable and well discriminating. This shows some interesting cognitive *lower* bounds on vagueness and uncertainty, which must be met to have an adequate measurement. In other words, we have the following.

Proposition   In order for a question to be discriminating, its variability (which is a measure of vagueness and/or uncertainty) must exceed some threshold: the questions that are very stable are not discriminating.

To prove this, we may proceed as follows. Let $q_1, q_2, \ldots$ be the questions (assumed binary, or essentially binary, i.e., with allowed DK reply), and let T be the total score equal to the number of questions answered "yes." The value of T is the required measure of the concept (trait).

Suppose now that the classificatory system (test) is applied to a large group of persons, and suppose that they are ordered with respect to the T scores.

Consider a fixed question, say, q_1, and treat the ordering of population according to T scores as the criterial ordering, which should be discriminated by question q_1. Intuitively, this would mean that there exists some relation between the answer ("yes" or "no") and the location in the ordering according to T scores. Such a relation may be measured in a number of ways, of which some have already been sketched in Section 4.2.3.

One of the reasonable methods consists of choosing some fraction, say, a, and then taking into account only the first $m = Na$ and the last m persons in the ordering, where N is the size of the population. If the discrimination is good, then, ideally, one of these groups should contain only those who replied "yes" and the second, only those who replied "no."

More exactly, let L_Y, L_N, U_Y, U_N denote the numbers of answers "yes" and "no" in the lower and upper groups (so that $L_Y + L_N = m = U_Y + U_N$). Then the index of discriminativeness may be built from two values, say, L_Y and U_Y (the other two are determined). The index should be zero if $L_Y = U_Y$ and attain its maximal value (e.g., 1) if one of the numbers is 0 and the other is m.

Naturally, the quality of discrimination depends on the cutoff point m; if m is too small, there is the risk of taking too small a sample. If m is too large, then the sample also includes parts of the group of persons who tend to change their answers, and one cannot expect such a mixture to give the same answer. This will generally tend to lower the index of discriminativeness.

Let us now try to combine the above measure of discriminativeness and stability of the question, measured by the number of changes of answers under repetition. First, let us observe that we may consider the following two dichotomous categorizations of questions: a question may be stable or not (variable), and also, it may be balanced or extremal. Out of the four combinations, the case (variable, extremal) is not possible: indeed, variability implies that on at least one of the trials there are many answers "yes" and also many answers "no." This excludes the possibility of a question being extremal.

There remain three combinations: (variable, balanced), (stable, extremal), and (stable, balanced). Denoting C as the change of answer and remembering that in any one trial about half of the C's equal "yes" (Y) and half equal "no" (N), the above three types of questions may be represented as follows (the axis representing the ordering of the population according to T scores):

(variable, balanced)

YYYYYYY|YYYCCCCCCCCCCCCCCCCCCCCCCCCCCCCCCCCCCCCNNN|NNNNNNN

(stable, extremal)

YYYCCCC|CCNNNNNNNNNNNNNNNNNNNNNNNNNNNNNNNNN|NNNNNNN

(stable, balanced)

YYYYYYY|YYYYYYYYYYYYYCCCCCCNNNNNNNNNNNNNNNNNNN|NNNNNNN

Out of these three types, the last one, as already mentioned, is very rare in the social sciences, practically nonexistent. Consequently, the most common types of questions are the first two: (variable, balanced) and (stable, extremal). It appears that these are responsible for the assertion in the theorem on cognitive bounds of vagueness and uncertainty.

Indeed, if the question is variable and balanced, then most of the "yes" and "no" answers must come from persons who did change their answers (see the first graph of answers above), and these persons must occupy the central position on the continuum. It follows that the remaining persons (those who always answer "yes" and those who always answer "no") will occupy the opposite ends of the scale. Consequently, if we cut m members of the population from each of the ends of the scale, then the discrimination index may be high, because the two cutoff groups may well be such that $L_Y = m$, $U_Y = 0$, or vice versa, hence giving the highest possible discrimination index. We therefore have a phenomenon of high discriminability combined with high variability (low stability).

On the other hand, consider a question of the type (stable, extremal). This means that there are few persons who change their answer. Since the question is extremal, one type of answer must dominate the other. As a result, (see second model above) one of the cutoff ends is likely to be mixed, that is, to contain both "yes" and "no" answers, and the other may be not mixed, that is, $L_Y = m$, $0 < U_Y < m$, or vice versa. This gives a low index of discriminativeness, and we have a phenomenon of stable, but poorly discriminating questions. This completes the proof.

These considerations show, in a sense, the necessity or unavoidability of vagueness and uncertainty, and their role in defining and measurement of concepts in the social sciences.

The proved theorem also shows the negative relation between stability and discriminability. The latter may be understood as semantic validity of the question with respect to the criterion (modal concept). On the other hand, stability may be understood as precision, or reliability of measurement.

The theorem shows, therefore, that two highly desirable properties, namely semantic validity and precision, bound one another, leading to the existence of a cognitive upper limit, which does not allow access beyond a certain value of semantic validity under the required precision.

A freer and looser interpretation of this theorem may be that a certain amount of vagueness helps the precision, but there exist some limits of tolerance to vagueness and also the need and necessity of controlling it.

4.3   VERBAL COPIES AND CLASSIFICATION THEORY

We start from a general theory of descriptions, referred to as "verbal copies." The particular topic analyzed here will be the limitations on the precision of description imposed by the language used.

By a *description* we shall mean a specification of the values of the relevant attributes of the object described, sufficient to identify the object, or at least a reasonably narrow class to which it belongs. This specification may be fuzzy.

When the description of the object, however, has to be expressed linguistically, there arises the problem of the possible loss of precision. To use an oversimplified example, a full description may involve specification of the numerical values of the dimensions of the object. However, linguistic limitations may require using only expressions such as "long," "short," or "rather short."

4.3.1   General Scheme: A Formal System for Verbal Copies

We introduce now a formal system in terms of which we shall express the relevant notions. This system will constitute a quintuplet

$$\langle W, R, X, T, L \rangle, \tag{4.26}$$

where W is the set of all attribute values, R a binary relation in W, and X the class of objects under consideration. The primitive concepts T and L will represent, respectively, the truth system and the linguistic constraints. The specific assumptions and conceptual constructions will be introduced step by step, by imposing some assumptions on the primitive concepts, and new notions will be defined in terms of the system.

4.3.2 Algebra of Descriptions (Classifications)

The first concept in system (4.26), namely W, will be interpreted as the set of all values of the attributes under consideration. Next, R will be a binary relation in W, assumed to satisfy the following.

POSTULATE 4.1 Relation R is reflexive, symmetric, and transitive, that is, for all $u, v, w \in W$ we have

$$uRu; \tag{4.27}$$

$$\text{if } uRv, \text{ then } vRu; \tag{4.28}$$

$$\text{if } uRv \text{ and } vRw, \text{ then } uRw. \tag{4.29}$$

Consequently, R is an equivalence relation in W and, hence, partitions W into disjoint classes, say, $W_1, \ldots, W_n$, where $W = W_1 \cup \cdots \cup W_n$.

The intended interpretation is such that classes $W_1, W_2, \ldots$ correspond to attributes, and their elements, to values of these attributes. For example, if W_i is the attribute "color," then we may have $w_1 = $ "white," $w_2 = $ "red," $\ldots$, where $w_1, w_2, \ldots \in W_i$.

We start by developing an algebra of descriptions, at first without reference to the objects being described.

DEFINITION 4.1 By a *description* we mean a vector

$$V = (V_1, \ldots, V_n), \tag{4.30}$$

such that $V_i \subset W_i$ for $i = 1, \ldots, n$.

The intended interpretation is such that vectors of form (4.30) will serve as descriptions of elements of X by specifying that the value on attribute W_1 lies in the set V_1, the value of attribute W_2 lies in the set V_2, and so forth. In particular, if $V_i = \{v\}$, then the description is exact on attribute W_i: it specifies completely the value of this attribute. On the other hand, if $V_i = W_i$, then description (4.30) provides no information about attribute W_i. Finally, if $V_i = \varnothing$, we shall say that the description is inconsistent on attribute W_i.

It will be convenient to allow the possibility that sets V_i appearing in the descriptions are fuzzy; in such a case, the symbol V_i will be interpreted as a membership function, defined on W_i, so that

$$V_i: W_i \to [0, 1], \tag{4.31}$$

with $V_i(w)$ being the degree to which value w of attribute W_i belongs to the description of the object.

As mentioned, vectors V will serve as descriptions of objects or situations (elements of the set X). When necessary, elements of X will be assumed to possess a certain structure, that is, constitute relational systems of some sort, consisting of some parts connected by relation "being a part of" (this relation may also be a fuzzy one, leading to a fuzzy tree of an object).

At any rate, attributes $W_1, \ldots, W_n$ are assumed to exhaust all information needed about the object, from the point of view of the goal of description. For instance, if the objects are books, the attributes may be W_1 = name of author, W_2 = title, W_3 = publisher, and so forth.

Suppose now that $V' = (V'_1, \ldots, V'_n)$ and $V'' = (V''_1, \ldots, V''_n)$ are two description; the components may be fuzzy or not. We shall define their union and intersection as

$$V' + V'' = (V'_1 \cup V''_1, \ldots, V'_n \cup V''_n) \tag{4.32}$$

and

$$V' \cdot V'' = (V'_1 \cap V''_1, \ldots, V'_n \cap V''_n). \tag{4.33}$$

The union and intersection of descriptions is therefore the set-theoretical sum and set-theoretical intersection of the corresponding components.

Naturally, when sets V'_i and V''_i are fuzzy, the union and intersection ought to be interpreted as fuzzy sets with membership functions.

$$[V'_i + V''_i](w) = \max[V'_i(w), V''_i(w)], \tag{4.34}$$

$$[V'_i \cdot V''_i](w) = \min[V'_i(w), V''_i(w)]. \tag{4.35}$$

Now define the inclusion of two descriptions as follows.

DEFINITION 4.2   We say that description V' is *contained* in description V'' if for every $i = 1, \ldots, n$ we have

$$V'_i \cap V''_i = V'_i. \tag{4.36}$$

Thus the inclusion between descriptions is defined as an inclusion between all corresponding components.

To appreciate the meaning of the notions introduced thus far, consider a simple example. Suppose that an object x is being described, and one of the attributes is color. One description specifies the color to be "blue or purple" so that the corresponding set V_i is the set {blue, purple}. Suppose that another description gives the color of x as "red or purple," so that $V'_i = \{\text{red, purple}\}$. The intersection of these two sets contains just one element "purple," but the union contains all three colors—red, purple, and blue.

In case of fuzzy sets, the situation is very similar, except that in addition to elements like "blue," and "red," descriptions V' and V'' specify their degrees of membership in V'_i and V''_i. (A somewhat more general approach, involving α-bility functions will be given in later parts of this chapter.)

The addition and multiplication of descriptions satisfies the usual laws of set-theoretical operations, such as associativity, idempotence and distributivity. Thus, if V, V', and V'' denote arbitrary descriptions, and $\varnothing = (\varnothing, \dots, \varnothing)$, $1 = (W_1, \dots, W_n)$, then we have

$$V + V = V \cdot V = V, \tag{4.37}$$

$$V + \varnothing = V, \quad V \cdot \varnothing = \varnothing, \quad V + 1 = 1, \quad V \cdot 1 = V, \tag{4.38}$$

$$V + V' = V' + V, \quad V \cdot V' = V' \cdot V, \tag{4.39}$$

$$(V + V') + V'' = V + (V' + V''), \tag{4.40}$$

$$(V \cdot V') \cdot V'' = V \cdot (V' \cdot V''), \tag{4.41}$$

$$(V + V') \cdot V'' = V \cdot V'' + V' \cdot V'', \tag{4.42}$$

$$V \cdot V' + V'' = (V + V'') \cdot (V' + V''). \tag{4.43}$$

The inclusion gives a partial order in the class of all descriptions, with

$$V \cdot V' \subset V \subset V + V' \tag{4.44}$$

for all V, V'. Consequently, the class of all descriptions, with the operations of union and intersection, forms a lattice, the minimal element being $\varnothing$ and the maximal element being 1.

4.3.3   Descriptions of Objects

Let us now impose some conditions on the next two primitive concepts of system (4.26), namely X and T.

As already mentioned, X is the class of objects under consideration. The elements of X will be denoted x, y, z, ..., with or without subscripts. The primitive concept T will be interpreted as the "truth system." To explicate its formal nature, let W^* denote the class of all descriptions, fuzzy or not, so that the elements of W^* are vectors $(V_1, \dots, V_n)$, where each V_i is a subset of W_i.

We shall now assume that T is a function

$$T : X \to 2^{W^*} \tag{4.45}$$

that assigns to each $x \in X$ a class, say, $T(x)$, being the class of all descriptions applicable for x.

The main property of every set $T(x)$ is that, if two descriptions are appropriate for x, so must be their intersection. Also, the "noninformative" description $1 = (W_1, \dots, W_n)$ is appropriate for every object. Finally, it is assumed that every object has some value on every attribute, so that a description that has at least one coordinate $\varnothing$ is not appropriate for x.

Accordingly, we shall assume the following postulate.

POSTULATE 4.2   *For any $x \in X$, the class $T(x)$ is closed under intersection, that is, whenever $V, V' \in T(x)$, then $V \cdot V' \in T(x)$. Moreover, it is assumed that $1 \in T(x)$ and that no description $V = (V_1, \ldots, V_n)$ with $V_i = \varnothing$ for some i is in $T(x)$.*

This postulate asserts that an intersection of two descriptions of the same object x is again a description of x. Also, this postulate eliminates "false" descriptions: the last condition states that the descriptor V_i on every attribute must be nonempty.

To better appreciate how this postulate eliminates false descriptions, consider an example. Suppose that the elements of X are persons and that the attributes of the system are $W_1 = $ age, $W_2 = $ number of children, (and some other attributes as well).

Suppose that the description V of some specific person x_0 gives $V_1 = $ in the thirties, $V_2 = $ two, while another description V' (of the same person, at the same time) gives $V_1' = $ about thirty-five, $V_2' = $ three. These descriptions more or less agree as to the attribute "age" and disagree completely as regards the attribute "number of children," so that $V_2 \cap V_2' = \varnothing$.

It follows from Postulate 4.2 that V and V' cannot both be descriptions of the same person: indeed, if they were, so would their intersection (by Postulate 4.2); but this intersection has the empty set on attribute W_2, which violates the last requirement of Postulate 4.2.

Observe that in the above example some of the descriptions concerning age (attribute W_1) are fuzzy, but the "true value" of this attribute, whether known or not, are not fuzzy. It is important to realize that there are objects (situations) in which the truth itself is fuzzy.

To give an example, suppose that the described object x is a traffic jam on some specific intersection. The attributes of x may be $W_1 = $ time of occurrence, $W_2 = $ number of cars involved, and so forth. Here none of the two attributes allows a crisp description, while there is a variety of fuzzy descriptions. For instance, as regards W_1 we may have descriptors such as "yesterday afternoon," "about 4 p.m. yesterday," or "sometime between 3 and 5 p.m. last night." The point is that even the best description will have to be fuzzy because of the inherent fuzziness of the concept of *traffic jam* and the time of its occurrence.

Define now

$$T^*(x) = \bigcap_{V \in T(x)} V. \tag{4.46}$$

Thus $T^*(x) = (V_1^*(x), \ldots, V_n^*(x))$ with $V_i^*(x)$ being the intersection of all sets V_i that appear as ith coordinates in vectors V from $T(x)$.

From Postulate 4.2 the next theorem follows.

THEOREM 4.1   For every x, description $T^*(x)$ satisfies condition $V_i^*(x) \neq \emptyset$, $i = 1, \ldots, n$.

For the proof see the Appendix at the end of this chapter.

The interpretation of intersection $T^*(x)$ of all descriptions in class $T(x)$ is simply that $T^*(x)$ is the best available (in the system) description of "truth" about object x. If x is interpreted as a situation, then $T^*(x)$ represents the best available description of what really takes place if x occurs.

Let $W^{**} \subset W^*$ be the subset of all descriptions, consisting of all descriptions that have all coordinates nonempty, so that $V = (V_1, \ldots, V_n) \in W^{**}$ if and only if $V_i \neq \emptyset$ for all i.

As a result of (4.46) and Theorem 4.1, we obtained a mapping

$$T^*: X \to W^{**}, \tag{4.47}$$

which assigns to every x the description $T^*(x)$.

DEFINITION 4.3   We shall say that system (4.26) is *adequate* if for every element $V \in W^{**}$ there exists an $x \in X$ such that $T^*(x) = V$.

Thus, a system is adequate if for any description there exists an object described by it.

We may also require that descriptions be exact, in the following sense. Let $\sim$ be an equivalence relation in X, with the interpretation that $x \sim x'$ if objects x and x' are regarded as identical from the point of view of the analysis. We then say that x and x' are copies of one another.

We may now introduce the following definition.

DEFINITION 4.4   The description system (4.26) is called *strongly exact* if the condition $x \sim x'$ implies $T(x) = T(x')$ and *weakly exact* if $x \sim x'$ implies $T^*(x) = T^*(x')$.

Thus, a description system is strongly exact if any two elements that are copies of one another are assigned the same sets of appropriate descriptions. Equivalently, if x and x' are not copies of one another, then $T(x) \neq T(x')$. Now, $T(x) \neq T(x')$ means that there exists a description $V = (V_1, \ldots, V_n)$ that belongs to $T(x)$ but not to $T(x')$, that is, a description appropriate for x and not appropriate for x'.

On the other hand, for weak exactness, one requires only that $T^*(x) = T^*(x')$ whenever x and x' are copies of one another. Thus, the sets $T(x)$ and $T(x')$ may differ, and the condition of weak exactness specifies that intersections of these classes be equal.

4.3.4   Verbal Copies

Let us now formulate assumptions about the last primitive concept of system (4.26), namely L. Generally, L will represent the linguistic constraints on descriptions.

The fact that $V = (V_1, \ldots, V_n) \in T(x)$, that is, that V is an appropriate description of x, coincides with the truth of the conjunction of propositions "x is V_i" for $i = 1, \ldots, n$.

Now, since V_i is a subset of W_i, the proposition "x is V_i" should be interpreted as "The value of ith attribute of x belongs to the set V_i." In the case of nonfuzzy sets $V_i = \{v_1, \ldots, v_k\}$, this in turn means the disjunction "x is v_1 or x is v_2, or $\cdots$ or x is v_k."

In the case of fuzzy sets V_i, the sentence "x is V_i" should be interpreted as "The degree to which the value of the ith attribute of x belongs to V_i is $V_i(w)$, if this value is w."

Now, the point is that not every statement of the form "x is V_i" is expressible in linguistic terms. For such a statement to be expressible, V_i itself must be expressible. Consequently, the last primitive concept of system (4.26), namely L, will be a pair (Q, f), where Q is some set of linguistic expressions, simple or composite; it will also be assumed that Q contains a special symbol, say, @, that signifies "no name." Finally, f will be a function

$$f: \bigcup_{i=1}^{n} F(W_i) \to Q, \tag{4.48}$$

where $F(W_i)$ is the class of all fuzzy subsets of W_i (of course, $F(W_i)$ also contains nonfuzzy sets, being a special case of fuzzy sets).

Let $A \in \bigcup F(W_i)$. Then A is a fuzzy or crips subset of some set W_i, that is, a set of values of attribute W_i. The value $f(A)$ will be interpreted as follows. If $f(A) \neq @$, then $f(A)$ is the name (or label) of the set A. If $f(A) = @$, then set A has no name.

Generally, Q contains names of sets of values of the attributes. Thus, in the case of an attribute such as *length*, Q will contain names like "between 5 and 7 inches," "long," "very long," and "shorter than a pencil."

We shall assume that, if $q \in Q$ and $q \neq @$, then also $-q \in Q$; that is, Q is closed under negation.

We shall now assume the following.

POSTULATE 4.3   *If* $A \subset W_i$ *and* $f(A) = q$ *with* $q \neq @$, *then* $f(W_i - A) = -q$.

We shall now define the verbal copy as follows.

DEFINITION 4.5   By *verbal copy* we shall mean a description $V = (V_1, \ldots, V_n)$ such that $f(V_i) \neq @$ for $i = 1, \ldots, n$.

Thus a verbal copy is a description, interpreted as a conjunction of statements "the value of the ith attribute of x is in the set V_i," except that they should to be expressed in linguistic terms; that is, set V_i must belong to the class of sets that have the name. In other words, a verbal copy is a conjunction of sentences "x is $f(V_i)$," where $f(V_i) \neq @$.

Clearly, within the constraints of language, as imposed by Q, one may not be able to describe object x in full; that is, the description $T^*(x)$ defined by (4.21) may not be expressible in linguistic terms. To use an example, imagine that the attribute of interest is length and that the linguistic restrictions in Q are such that one is allowed to use only the expressions derived from comparisons with some fixed set of objects $O_1, O_2, \ldots$. Thus Q will contain expressions of the form "longer than O_i," "shorter than O_i," "equal in length to O_i," and their fuzzifications, such as "about the same length as O_i."

Now, how exactly the length of x may be expressed within the constraints of such "language of comparisons" depends on the properties of the set of objects $O_1, O_2, \ldots$. For instance, if O_1 is "matchbox" and O_2 is "pencil" and there are no other objects allowed, then the length of x may be described in terms of five main categories:

(1) shorter than matchbox,
(2) equal in length to matchbox,
(3) longer than matchbox, but shorter than pencil,
(4) equal in length to pencil,
(5) longer than pencil.

In addition, we may have the fuzzifications of the above categories.

Observe here that one obtain much richer possibilities if one is allowed to concatenate the objects and use the concatenations for comparisons. In other words, the possibilities increase if one is allowed comparisons of the form "longer than six matchboxes put end to end, but shorter than two pencils put end to end."

4.3.5 Faithfulness

The two properties of verbal copies (and descriptions in general) are related to the questions: "Is the verbal copy of x truthful?" and "Is the verbal copy of x exact?" In this section, the discussion will concentrate on the first of these question.

Now, since the description contains fuzzy terms, it will be more adequate to use the term "faithfulness" instead of "truth" (in the case of nonfuzzy descriptions, these two concepts will coincide).

A description of an object may be faithful with regard to some attributes and not faithful with regard to other attributes. In particular, an object may possess a hierarchical structure of some sort, that is, may consist of parts that in turn consist of some other parts, and so on. Each of these parts may have its own attributes and also be connected with other parts by some relations (other than the relation "to be a part of"). Consequently, a verbal copy may be faithful as regards some level of the hierarchy and not faithful as regards some other levels.

These intuitions suggest introducing the concept of faithfulness relative to some subsets of the class of all attributes. Depending on the location of this subset in the hierarchy of the object, one may then distinguish the highest and/or lowest level at which the verbal copy is faithful, and so forth.

It follows from this discussion that the basic, elementary concept that needs to be explicated is that of faithfulness with respect to *one* attribute. Then the notions of faithfulness with respect to a set of attributes, total faithfulness, or faithfulness with respect to a given level of hierarchy will be obtainable by standard extensions of the basic definition of faithfulness with respect to a given attribute.

Thus, let W_i be the set of values of the ith attribute, and let

$$F^*(W_i) = \{A \in F(W_i) : f(A) \neq @\}, \tag{4.49}$$

where, as before, $F(W_i)$ is the class of all subsets of W_i, fuzzy and crisp. Thus $F^*(W_i)$ is the class of subsets of W_i that have their own name, that is, that are expressible.

Let $V(x)$ be a fixed verbal copy of x, and let $V_i(x)$ be the descriptor used in $V(x)$ for the ith attribute. By assumption, we have $V_i(x) \in F^*(W_i)$; that is, $V_i(x)$ is a subset of W_i that has its own name $f(V_i(x))$. To put it differently, a verbal copy is simply a description in which all descriptors are linguistically expressible.

Naturally, faithfulness of a verbal copy of x with respect to W_i, to be called i-faithfulness, will be defined in terms of relations between the set $V_i(x)$ and the set $V_i^*(x)$, that is, the ith component of the "truth" vector $T^*(x)$ defined by (4.46).

DEFINITION 4.6 Verbal copy $V(x)$ will be called *i-faithful* if

$$V_i^*(x) \subset V_i(x). \tag{4.50}$$

In the case of nonfuzzy sets $V_i^*(x)$ and $V_i(x)$, the interpretation of i-faithfulness is simple: the set of values that are in fact the values of the ith attribute of x is contained in the set of values asserted in the verbal copy. In particular, suppose that object x has value w_i on the ith attribute, so that $V_i^*(x) = \{w_i\}$. In terms of membership functions, $V_i^*(x)$ is a function of w given by

$$[V_i^*(x)](w) = \begin{cases} 1 & \text{if } w = w_i, \\ 0 & \text{otherwise.} \end{cases} \tag{4.51}$$

In this case, a verbal copy is i-faithful if the set $V_i(x)$ is *normal* and its membership function $[V_i(x)](w)$ satisfies the condition $[V_i(x)](w_i) \geq [V_i(x)](w)$ for all w. (This automatically implies that $[V_i(x)](w_i) = 1$ in view of the assumed normality.)

In other words, if an object has a nonfuzzy value w_i on the ith attribute and is described faithfully on this attribute, then the descriptor that used V_i must contain w_i in full degree.

Observe that, if $V_i(x) = 1$, then the verbal copy $V(x)$ is automatically i-faithful. This means that if attribute i is not mentioned in $V(x)$, that is, the copy is noninformative as regards W_i, then it is also i-faithful.

Thus, if some attributes are omitted (not mentioned) in the description, the verbal copy is automatically faithful with respect to these attributes: if there is no description, there cannot be a false or unfaithful description.

Observe that condition (4.50) asserts the inequality between the "truth" membership function and that of a faithful description. Consequently, the "true state" of the object provides a lower bound for faithful descriptions.

This, of course, imposes no constraints in the case of a crisp true state. However, in the case of fuzzy truth (e.g., in the example of time of occurrence of a traffic jam), one cannot discover more truth about the object than the object contains. In other words, one cannot give a more faithful description than that allowed by the truth about the object.

Now let

$$B(x) = \{i : V(x) \text{ is } i\text{-faithful}\} \tag{4.52}$$

be the *base* of faithfulness of $V(x)$, that is, the set of all attributes with respect to which the verbal copy $V(x)$ is faithful. Given two verbal copies of x, say, $V'(x)$ and $V''(x)$, one may consider a combined copy (the conjunction or intersection of them) $V(x) = V'(x) \cdot V''(x)$, with

$$V_i(x) = \min[V_i'(x), V_i''(x)]. \tag{4.53}$$

Consequently, if both copies V' and V'' are i-faithful, so is their conjunction. In other words, we have the following.

THEOREM 4.2   *The basis of faithfulness of the conjunction of two verbal copies equals the intersection of their bases of faithfulness, that is,*

$$B_{V' \cdot V''}(x) = B_{V'}(x) \cap B_{V''}(x). \tag{4.54}$$

It may be worthwhile to carry over the analysis from Section 4.2 (concerning the degree of vagueness and/or uncertainty) to the present case of verbal copies. This may be achieved by observing successive classifications of the form "x is V_i in degree p," that is, classifications of object x with respect to the attribute W_i ($i = 1, \ldots, n$). This is equivalent to observing the variability of linguistic measurements of an object and, hence, will allow us to determine the degree of parallelism, or semantic homogeneity, of two verbal copies.

Assuming for simplicity that the bases of both verbal copies are the same, the variability of the copies may be measured by the distance between the fuzzy sets V_{i1} and V_{i2}, $i = 1, \ldots, n$, where the second index refers to the number of trial (first or second copy).

Now, the distance between two fuzzy sets may be measured in a number of ways (see Section 4.2), especially by their L_1-metric or L_2-metric. Thus, we have

$$d_1(V_{i1}, V_{i2}) = \sup_{w_i \in W_i} |V_{i1}(w) - V_{i2}(w)|, \tag{4.55}$$

and

$$d_2(V_{i1}, V_{i2}) = \int [V_{i1}(w) - V_{i2}(w)]^2 p(w)\, dw \tag{4.56}$$

where p is some probability distribution on the set of values of the ith attribute.

It appears, in view of the results of Section 4.2.1, that metric (4.56) may be more suitable for analysis because of its empirical accessibility. Then the overall distance between verbal copies of the same object x might be

$$d(V, V') = \sum_{i=1}^{n} c_i d_2(V_{i1}, V_{i2}), \tag{4.57}$$

where the c_i are weights of attributes.

The question now is to what extent a verbal copy determines the object x that it describes. This may be expressed by the possibility distribution on the set X of objects, given verbal copy V. Suppose, for simplicity, that we have only one attribute W, and let $T^*(x)$ be the true value of x on this attribute. Thus, $T^*(x)$ is the membership function of some fuzzy set, and it will be convenient to denote it by $T^*(x, w)$, $w \in W$. Now let V be a verbal copy of some (unknown) object, and assume that V is faithful. Then $T^*(x, w)$ may be interpreted as the possibility that the object is x, if the attribute were w. Consequently, $\sup_{w \in W} \min[V(w), T^*(x, w)]$ is the possibility that the object is x given its verbal copy V, and

$$\text{Poss}(x \in A \mid V) = \sup_{x \in A} \sup_{w \in W} \min[V(w), T^*(x, w)] \tag{4.58}$$

is the possibility distribution (defined on subsets A of X) given the verbal copy V.

If one studies the variability of assignments of verbal copies across a population, one obtains information about the degree of ambiguity or uncertainty/vagueness of the truth. This variability has three main sources: one is the differences between the objects being described (some may be "clearer" than others); the second source is the differences between perception in the population (subject-to-subject variations of judgments); and finally, the third source of variability is the intraindividual change in perception of the same truth after some time.

The information about variability of judgments often leads to a paradoxical conclusion about vagueness of truth—paradoxical because truth is usually associated with clarity (here the truth may be clear for each subject separately at any given time, but the overall picture will be that of vagueness of judgments). However, the most important fact is that vagueness of truth tends to increase the validity of vague statements. Indeed, this was the reason why Pythias in ancient Greece were so successful in their predictions.

4.3.6 Exactness

Suppose now that we have a verbal copy $V(x) = (V_1(x), \ldots, V_n(x))$. By exactness of verbal copy $V(x)$ we shall mean, intuitively speaking, the relative lack of ambiguity contained in description $V(x)$. This lack of ambiguity is the property of (possibly fuzzy) sets $V_i(x)$.

Again, as in the case of faithfulness, the "elementary" notion will be that of i-exactness, that is, exactness with respect to the ith attribute.

Generally, for a fuzzy set $V_i(x)$, with membership function $[V_i(x)](w)$, $w \in W_i$, we may associate two nonfuzzy sets, namely,

$$V_i^+(x) = \{w \in W_i : [V_i(x)](w) = 1\} \tag{4.59}$$

and

$$V_i^-(x) = \{w \in W_i : [V_i(x)](w) = 0\}. \tag{4.60}$$

The first of these sets, $V_i^+(x)$, consists of all those attribute values that are possible (as values of the ith attribute of object x) in degree 1. On the other hand, set $V_i^-(x)$ consists of all those values that are impossible.

Obviously, the description becomes more exact when $V_i^+(x)$ becomes smaller, and also when $V_i^-(x)$ becomes larger. This suggests introducing a partial order among the descriptions induced by the relations of inclusions of the corresponding sets.

Naturally, one or both of the sets $V_i^+(x)$ and $V_i^-(x)$ may be empty. Indeed, $V_i^+(x)$ is empty if set $V_i(x)$ is not normal, and $V_i^-(x)$ is empty if $V_i(x)$ has the whole set W_i as its support.

Consequently, we restrict our attention to the class of descriptions (verbal copies) for which both sets $V_i^+(x)$ and $V_i^-(x)$ are nonempty; let this class be denoted by $E_i(x)$. Let $V'(x)$ and $V''(x) \subset E_i(x)$, and for simplicity, denote (A_1, B_1) and (A_2, B_2) as sets $V_i^+(x)$ and $V_i^-(x)$ for $V'(x)$ and $V'''(x)$, respectively. We may now introduce the following definition.

DEFINITION 4.7   We say that verbal copy $V'(x)$ is *more i-exact* than verbal copy $V''(x)$ if

$$A_1 \subset A_2 \quad \text{and} \quad B_1 \supset B_2. \tag{4.61}$$

Obviously, the relation of being more *i*-exact is a partial order in the class $E_i(x)$: it is reflexive, antisymmetric, and transitive.

The extreme points in this ordering are crisp singleton sets $V_i(x)$. Indeed, if $V_i(x) = \{w_i\}$, then $V_i^+(x) = \{w_i\}$ and $V_i^-(x) = W_i - \{w_i\}$. A verbal copy with the above property may be called *most i-exact*.

As in the case of faithfulness, one may extend the relation "being more *i*-exact than" to the relation of being more exact with respect to a set of attributes or to attributes on some level of hierarchy of the object. We shall omit the details of these definitions, as they are quite standard.

Observe that the properties of faithfulness and exactness are, in a sense, negatively related. Indeed, suppose that component $V_i^*(x)$ of set $T^*(x)$ given by (4.21) is not a singleton (either it involves fuzziness or it is a crisp set containing more than one element). Then a faithful verbal copy of x cannot be most exact. In fact, a *necessary* condition for existence of a most *i*-exact verbal copy of x is that $V_i^*(x) = \{w_i\}$. This condition, however, is not sufficient, since it may still not be possible to express set $\{w_i\}$ as an intersection of linguistically expressible sets.

We have then the following.

THEOREM 4.3   *For the existence of an i-faithful and most i-exact verbal copy of x, it is necessary and sufficient that $V_i^*(x) = \{w_i\}$ and that there exists a sequence $A_1, \dots, A_m$ of elements of $F^*(W_i)$ with $A_1 \cap A_2 \cap \cdots \cap A_m = \{w_i\}$.*

This theorem simply asserts that every value of an attribute must be expressible as an intersection of some "permissible" fuzzy sets, that is, as sets that are expressible in the language.

Now, given the above notions of faithfulness and exactness, it is easy to explain why the vagueness of Pythia's predictions increased their validity. First of all, by giving too few divergent and fuzzy attributes, it was possible to find many objects that somehow satisfied the predictions. The additional effect of an increase of validity was due to vagueness. By giving too few (or no) fuzzy values of attributes, it was possible to increase it still further.

The importance of exactness lies in the fact that it allows one to better identify the objects, that is, to improve possibility distribution (4.58). One can speak of inexactness of exactness, in the sense of variability of judgments in time (under the assumption of invariance of the true state of the object in time).

There is a sort of negative relation between faithfulness and exactness. To satisfy the first, the assertion about a given attribute of x must be representable as a membership function that dominates the true membership function. For the second, it must be equal to it. Consequently, in attempting to provide more exact descriptions, one risks making them not faithful. Conversely, to be more certain of faithfulness, one has to resign from exactness.

To explore the problem somewhat deeper, observe that in forming a verbal copy one is allowed to use only some fuzzy sets (those that are linguistically expressible). On the other hand, the truth (fuzzy or crisp) may have any membership function. The problem of a mutual relation between faithfulness and exactness becomes a constrained approximation problem, formally expressible as follows.

Reducing the issue to one attribute only (the generalization to the case of n attributes is obvious), we are given a set W (of attribute values) and a class H of some fuzzy subsets of W. Thus, each element of H is a membership function defined on W.

The elements of H are "elementary" fuzzy sets, which are permissible in verbal copy. The class H is then used to generate the class H^*, which is the smallest class containing H and closed under all set-theoretical operations. Thus, $H \subset H^*$, and whenever $f_1, f_2 \in H^*$, then $f_1 \vee f_2 = \max(f_1, f_2)$, $f_1 \wedge f_2 = \min(f_1, f_2)$, and $1 - f_1$ are also in H^*.

Now let g be any membership function on W, not necessarily in H^*. The problem is to find an element of H^* that dominates g (which will ensure faithfulness) and also approximates g as well as possible.

What is left is a specification of the metric in the class of all fuzzy membership functions, i.e., explicating in which sense the elements of H^* are to approximate "truth" g. Here one can use the L_2-metric (as in Section 4.2, by choosing some suitable distribution p), or the L_1-metric. In the latter case (which in this instance appears more natural, since it does not involve arbitrary assumptions about the sampling scheme expressed by p), the problem may be formulated as follows: for a given g, find functions $f_1, \ldots, f_r \in H$ and a propositional function F involving only the functors of negation, conjunction, and disjunction such that

$$F [f_1(w), \ldots, f_r(w)] \geq g(w) \qquad \text{for all } w \in W; \qquad (4.62)$$

$$\text{the quantity } \max_{w \in W} \{F [f_1(w), \ldots, f_r(w)] - g(w)\} \text{ is minimal.} \qquad (4.63)$$

If $f_1, \ldots, f_r$ and F are solutions of such an optimization problem, then the composite expression $F(f_1, \ldots, f_r)$ is a faithful and most exact representation of the truth g allowed in vocabulary H. Indeed, condition (4.62) ensures faithfulness of the expression, and condition (4.63) ensures that by using expressions from H it is not possible to find any better representation of truth g that would also be faithful.

4.3.7   Language of Classification and Verbal Copies

Before reduction to the form of a vector $V = (V_1, \ldots, V_n)$, a verbal copy of an object is represented as a string of propositions of the form "x is V_{ij}." Each such proposition involves the choice of an attribute i and then a (fuzzy or not) descriptor on this attribute, denoted V_{ij}. Here i refers to the attribute and j to the number of successive propositions concerning this attribute. We have here $V_i = \bigcap_j V_{ij}$ if the verbal copy is represented as the vector V. However, if the order of production of the verbal copy is to be taken into account, one can consider the bivariate sequence

$$(r_j, s_j), \qquad j = 1, 2, \ldots, \tag{4.64}$$

where r_j is the index of the attribute in the jth proposition (so that $r_j \in I = \{1, \ldots, n\}$) and s_j is a fuzzy subset of W_{r_j}, which has its own name (is expressible).

We may now introduce the monoid I^* over I, that is, the class of all finite strings of elements of I, and a monoid, say, C^*, of all finite strings of (labels) of fuzzy sets of attributes. Then a verbal copy is an element of $I^* \times C^*$, that is, a pair of strings $r_1 \cdots r_m \in I^*$ and $s_1 \cdots s_m \in C^*$ (of equal length) such that s_j is a fuzzy subset of W_{r_j}.

As the described objects x (or subjects who describe them) change, we obtain a certain class of strings in $I^* \times C^*$. This class, say, C, may be called the *f-language of classification* (with f standing for the adjective *formal*) to stress the fact that we consider here, not the natural language, but a class of strings of elements other than words, namely classificatory statements.

The f-language C determines the classes of languages (admissible sets of strings) in I^* and also in each of the sets W_i. Thus C_I would be defined as

$$C_I = \{u \in I^* : (u, v) \in C \text{ for some } v\} \tag{4.65}$$

with languages in W_i defined similarly.

One could expect that the structural properties of these languages will provide some information about the process of generation of verbal copies. For instance, one may conjecture that whenever a string $V_{i1} \cdots V_{ik}$ belongs to the language corresponding to the ith attribute, then we cannot have $V_{it} \subset V_{it'}$ for $t < t'$. In other words, a more general descriptor should not follow a more specific one.

4.3.8 Generation of Stochastic Structures

In this section we shall consider some interrelations between temporal and probabilistic structures by using the idea of realization of propositional structures.

Suppose that we have a formula involving temporal variables, say, $F(x, y, z, ...)$. Such a formula describes a local structure of some process, for example, a possible configuration of events. If we now superimpose an appropriate stochastic structure on it, we obtain a stochastic process in which various events occur at times x, y, z, ... Similarly, imposing a probabilistic structure one obtains a temporal probabilistic process.

This rather general scheme will now be illustrated by some examples. Consider, for instance, the formula

$$(\exists x)(\forall y) : (x < y \Rightarrow Q_y) \ \& \ (x \geq y \Rightarrow -Q_y), \tag{4.66}$$

where Q stands for a certain property and Q_y means that this property holds at time y.

Let us now add the probabilistic structure. In this case, it requires a specification of the distribution of the appearance of the point x. Thus, suppose that $P(x \leq t) = F(t)$. The types of questions one may wish to ask concern the probability that at some time t we shall have property Q, that is, that we shall have Q_t. In this case, the answer is simple and is given by

$$P(Q_t) = F(t). \tag{4.67}$$

Indeed, from (4.66) it is clear that Q_t will hold for all times after x, so that Q will hold at t if x occurs before t, which has probability $F(t)$.

Given two points t_1 and t_2 one could ask for the probability that Q_{t_1} and not Q_{t_2}. We have here

$$P(Q_{t_1} \ \& \ -Q_{t_2}) = F(t_2) - F(t_1). \tag{4.68}$$

In the case of possibilistic structures, the crucial moment is also x, and the whole process depends on the moment of its occurrence. If for some reasons it is not possible to specify the probability distribution of x, then one may sometimes specify subjectively its possibility distribution, by assigning to sets A the possibility that x is in A.

4.3.9 Histories

In this section we shall formally introduce and analyze the notion of a history, understood as a sequence of events or, alternatively, a sequence of states of some fragment of the reality of interest. The issues involved here are related to the notion of time discussed in Chapter 1, especially subjective time, which allows the subject to order the events in the past according to the times of their occurrence.

From the formal points of view, it is convenient to consider the class of all histories that could conceivably occur, so that this class contains the "true" history, and to analyze the ways of singling out the true history, or at least assigning possibility degrees to particular histories.

It is worthwhile to mention here that the notion of history is the basic concept in the theory of stochastic processes: the latter are simply the probability measures on classes of histories.

In the following T will denote the time axis. Since T is a linearly ordered set, we may define the notion of history up to the time t^* as a function

$$h_{t^*}: T \cap (-\infty, t^*) \to Z^*, \tag{4.69}$$

where Z^* is defined as

$$Z^* = \varnothing \cup \bigcup_{n=1}^{\infty} Z^n \tag{4.70}$$

and Z^n is the Cartesian product $Z \times \cdots \times Z$ (n times), with Z being a set of events.

The interpretation of history h_{t^*} is as follows. Let $t < t^*$; if $h_{t^*}(t) = \varnothing$, then no event from Z occurs at time t. If $h_{t^*}(t) = (A_1, \ldots, A_n) \in Z^n$, then at t there occurs the combination of events $A_1, \ldots, A_n$.

Let us observe that the notion of a history is relative to the class of events Z; we are interested in the occurrence of events from Z and their combinations. Observe that it is tacitly assumed that all events in Z are "crisp" in the sense that the time of their occurrence is well defined.

As an example of a history, consider a fixed patient: then Z would usually comprise the events pertaining to his illness, such as occurrence of symptoms and visits to a doctor. Here the subjective sequencing of events may be fuzzy, due to memory lapses or other causes.

Let us observe that the notion of history allows for a multiple occurrence of elements from Z.

Let H_{t^*} denote the class of all histories up to time t^*. We then have, for $t_1 < t_2$, the following theorem.

THEOREM 4.4   *For every $h_{t_2} \in H_{t_2}$ there exists $h_{t_1} \in H_{t_1}$ such that*

$$(\forall t \le t_1): h_{t_1}(t) = h_{t_2}(t). \tag{4.71}$$

Equivalently, one may say that for any element h_{t_1} there exists h_{t_2} such that h_{t_1} is embedded in it.

This theorem simply asserts that a fragment of a history covering the period until t_1 is itself a history (from the class of all histories lasting until t_1).

In the case when T is discrete (e.g., integer-valued), both definitions may be formulated in a simpler way, since then it is easier to deal with sequences of events than with event-valued functions of continuous time.

Generally, Theorem 4.4 allows us to replace the notion of history up to time t by the notion of history defined as a function $h: T \to Z^*$. Denote the class of all such histories by H. Theorem 4.4 allows us then to define in a natural way classes H_{t*} introduced earlier, namely, as restrictions of elements of H to the set $T \cap (-\infty, t^*)$. For simplicity, as well as for the uniformity of notations, it is more convenient to operate with one class H.

Class H may appear to be a somewhat artificial construct, introduced to achieve unity and simplicity of notations. An element of H is a history extended indefinitely into the future, hence comprising also the events that did not yet occur. A restriction of such a sequence of events to those occurring up to time t^* is, by definition, a history up to t^*. By changing t^* we obtain histories with various terminal points. The advantage of such an approach lies in the fact that we start from one class H and generate from it various classes of histories, instead of starting from a family of classes, indexed by terminal points, which would have to meet various consistency conditions imposed *a priori*.

For the subsequent considerations we shall need some special types of classes of histories, corresponding to backward and forward branching.

The intuitive background here is such that if some fragment of a history is not known, one has to consider various sets of events occurring in that fragment, in a sense considering all possibilities. If the unknown portion comprises events that occurred after some moment t (while the preceding part is known), we have a set of histories with forward branching: they all have common beginning, up to t, and then "branch off" into various possible continuations. When only the last portion is known, we consider various beginnings and a common ending: we then have "backward branching."

As an example, consider the history (sequence of events in life) of a friend. If he is one's friend from childhood and school (say) and then the contact is lost, the initial fragment (life until finishing school) is the known beginning, which must be somehow complemented with various more or less plausible continuations.

For backward branching, consider a friend one knows well for (say) the last 5 years but whose previous life is unknown. Here one has various conceivable life histories, perhaps ranked with respect to their degree of plausibility, all ending with the same known terminal stretch of 5 years.

Each history is, in effect, an ordering of events, with some events occurring simultaneously. Consequently, the class of all histories gives the class of all possible orderings, the true one as well as all the others.

Since the orderings are not known exactly, and are given only in terms of fuzzy relations $W_i(A, B)$ from Chapter 1, the histories are not known explicitly either. One could, however, order histories according to their degree of possibility. To present it formally, with each t one may connect a mapping $r_t: H \rightarrow [0, 1]$, where $r_t(h)$ is the possibility, evaluated at t, of history h. Given function r_t, one may extend it to some classes of subsets of H. Consider first the class, say, A, of all histories h such that

$$(\exists t' < t): [h_1, h_2 \in A \Rightarrow (\forall \tau \le t')h_1(\tau) = h_2(\tau)]. \tag{4.72}$$

Thus, set A consists of all histories that have the same beginning up to time t'. It is therefore clear that every set A determines a history $h_{t'}$, so that we may write $A(h_{t'})$ to denote the class with common beginning $h_{t'}$.

One may then extend function r_t, defining it on the class $A(h_{t'})$, by putting

$$r_t[A(h_{t'})] = \sup_{h \in A(h_{t'})} r_t(h). \tag{4.73}$$

In a sense, set $A(h_{t'})$ comprises all histories that coincide with $h_{t'}$ until time t' and then "branch off" in various directions. We therefore have forward branching.

One can define also another type of sets of histories. Consider a set $B \subset H$ such that

$$(\exists t' < t): h_1, h_2 \in B \Rightarrow [(\forall \tau): t' \le \tau \le t \Rightarrow h_1(\tau) = h_2(\tau)]. \tag{4.74}$$

Thus, every set B consists of all histories whose "slice" between t' and t is the same; we may therefore write $B(h_{t',t})$.

One can now extend function r_t by defining it on sets $B(h_{t',t})$ as

$$r_t[B(h_{t',t})] = \sup_{h \in B(h_{t',t})} r_t(h). \tag{4.75}$$

We have here a sort of "backward branching" of histories: they all converge to the same function $h_{t',t}$, so that one could speak of branching if one moved backward in time.

Extension of the possibility function r_t from individual histories to sets of histories, as given above, is the possibility extension suggested by Zadeh, according to which the possibility of a set is the supremum of possibilities of its elements. For some alternative extensions, see Section 4.6.

It is of some interest to observe that one could take the notion of history as primitive and define the concepts of an event and its occurrence, eliciting these from the postulated properties of histories. To sketch this approach, let H be the class of all functions $h: T \rightarrow E$, where E is some set (of states of the considered fragment of reality).

Next, for any $t^* \in T$ define the relation $\sim_{t^*}$ in H as

$$h_1 \sim_{t^*} h_1 \qquad \text{iff} \quad (\forall t): t \le t^* \Rightarrow h_1(t) = h_2(t). \tag{4.76}$$

Obviously, this relation is an equivalence in H, and it partitions H into equivalence classes. These classes are characterized by the "forward branching" property: the elements of one equivalence class all have a common beginning up to t^*.

Let $H_{t'}$ and $H_{t''}$ be sets of equivalence classes of $\sim_{t'}$ and $\sim_{t''}$. We then have the following.

THEOREM 4.5   *If $t' < t''$, then for every $A \in H_{t''}$ there exists $B \in H_{t'}$ with $B \supset A$.*

In other words, the partition into equivalence classes of $\sim_{t''}$ is finer than the partition into equivalence classes of $\sim_{t'}$. Moreover, to every equivalance class A of $\sim_{t'}$ one can assign a function on $T \cap (-\infty, t')$, being the common beginning of elements of A. This defines the class, say, $J_{t'}$, of functions on $T \cap (-\infty, t')$, and we have the next theorem.

THEOREM 4.6   *Classes $J_{t'}$ satisfy the assertion of Theorem 4.4.*

Let us now return to sets $A(h_{t'})$ of histories with common beginning h_t, and let G be the class of all functions that appear in $A(h_{t'})$ as continuations of $h_{t'}$. Let us introduce a special symbol to denote the fact that one function is a continuation of another; thus, $f * g$ will denote the function composed out of two parts, defined on two contiguous intervals.

Formally, let f be defined on (t_1, t_2) and let g be defined on $[t_2, t_3)$. Then $(f * g)(t)$ for $t \in (t_1, t_3)$ is defined as $f(t)$ on (t_1, t_2), and as $g(t)$ on $[t_2, t_3)$.

In this notations we may write

$$A(h_t) = \{h : h = h_t * g \text{ for some } g \in G\}. \tag{4.77}$$

Suppose now that part g of the history is known; one may refer to it as to the *slice* of history extending onto the past up to time t.

If r_t is, as before, the possibility function on the class of histories (as judged at t), then the possibility assigned to the initial fragment may be defined as the possibility of the whole history, with the given fragment as initial, that is,

$$\text{Poss}(h_t \,|\, g) = r_t(h_t * g). \tag{4.78}$$

The left-hand side gives the conditional possibility of past history h_t, given its "slice" g. The justification of this formula lies in the fact that g, as a part that is known to have happened, must have possibility 1.

Sometimes it happens that the histories are selected randomly, according to some probability distribution; in other words, the generation of a history is a stochastic process. In such cases one may, of course, ask for the conditional probability of a given history given its slice, that is, for the probability

$$P(h_{t'} \,|\, g_{t',t}) = \frac{P(h_{t'} * g_{t',t})}{P(g_{t',t}),} \tag{4.79}$$

which may serve as a measure of doubt, uncertainty, and so on, depending on its value.

4.3.10   Generative Verbal Structures and Histories

Let us now consider verbal paralleling of sequences of events (histories). As may be seen, there appears here a new aspect of interrelations between descriptions and objects. First, rather than a verbal copy of some existing object, we take instead a look at the dynamic description of the process, which parallels it and is (or may be) continuously satisfied in a dynamic object.

By a *generative verbal structure* we shall mean now a conjunction of some sentences.

As distinct from a verbal copy, we allow at present not only the propositions of the form "x is V_i", but also the temporal variables such as "x is V_i at time t." Naturally, a conjunction of such sentences may be reduced by the use of quantifiers, for example, instead of saying "x is V_i at t_1 and x is V_i at t_2...," we may say "x is always V_i." Similarly, instead of "x is V_i at t, y is V_i at t, and...," we may say "all x's are V_i at t."

The normal form, that is, the conjunction of sentences of the form "x is V_i at t_i," also comprises the inferential forms, such as "If ..., then ...."

The essence of generative verbal structures is the knowledge of forming composite structures out of normal forms, that is, forming higher-order normal structures, which allow inferential schemes.

Both the premise and conclusion of such a scheme have a form reducible to propositional functions f and g, where f and g are functions involving only operations of negation, conjunction, and disjunction [see Nowakowska (1976a, 1979b)]. Thus, the general scheme of inference is "If $f(x_1,...,x_n)$, then $g(y_1,...,y_m)$," where $x_1,...,x_n$, $y_1,...,y_m$ are propositions (not necessarily distinct). For instance, in a special case when $f(x_1,...,x_n) = x_1 \& \cdots \& x_n$ and $g(y_1,...,y_m) = y_1 \vee \cdots \vee y_m$, we obtain "If $x_1 \& \cdots \& x_n$, then $y_1 \vee \cdots \vee y_m$" or "If all x_i, then at least one y_j." Naturally, if x_i and y_j refer to temporal variables, then the formulation might be different, for example, "If always x, then sometimes y."

Other quantifiers, in particular temporal, are obtained in a similar way. For instance, for large m the function

$$g(y_1,...,y_m) = \bigvee_{i=1}^{m} \left(y_1 \wedge \bigwedge_{j \neq i} y_j \right) \vee \bigvee_{i=1}^{m} \bigvee_{j \neq i} \left(y_i \wedge y_j \wedge \bigwedge_{k \neq i, k \neq j} - y_k \right) \quad (4.80)$$

may correspond to "seldom y." The quantifier "often y" may be defined as symmetric to "seldom y"; alternatively, both of them may be defined as fuzzy subsets of $[0, 1]$, that is, of the set of limiting frequencies, "often" being close to 1 and "seldom" being close to 0.

It is obvious that arguments x_i and y_j may be fuzzy; this will simply involve interpreting them as membership functions and replacing operations $\wedge$ and $\vee$ with minimum and maximum. Thus, conjunction $x_1 \& \cdots \& x_n$ will have membership function $\min_i x_i$, and similarly for the disjunction. For instance, $g(y_1,\ldots,y_m) = \bigvee_{i=1}^m (y_i \wedge \bigwedge_{j \neq i} - y_j)$ will be transformed to

$$\max_i \left\{ \min \left[y_i, \min_j (1 - y_j) \right] \right\}, \tag{4.81}$$

which for large m may be interpreted as "very seldom." Thus, in each case, functions f and g will be built from arguments x_i and y_j by operations of maxima, minima, and subtracting from 1. One may also take the possibility distribution, namely, if f is a membership function, then

$$\text{Poss } f(A) = \sup_{x \in A} f(x), \tag{4.82}$$

where $x = (x_1,\ldots,x_n)$.

Now let us consider function g appearing in the conclusion of the inferential proposition and assume that all arguments y_j are propositions concerning the occurrence of some event at specific times, so that each y_j is of the form "E occurs at t" (or "the possibility that E occurs at T is such and such," in case of a fuzzy interpretation of y_j).

Let L be the class of all strings of actions of the person in question, and let R be the relation connecting actions and their outcomes (events); relation R may be fuzzy. In particular, denoting by (E, t) the occurrence of E at t, let $K_a(E, t)$ be the set of all strings of actions that cause the occurrence of E at t in degree at least a. Thus, we have in effect a fuzzy set $K(E, t)$, defined by the membership function $K(E, t)(u)$, $u \in L$, with

$$K_a(E, t) = \{u \in L : K(E, t)(u) \geq a\}. \tag{4.83}$$

Now, if $g(y_1,\ldots,y_m)$ is a function involving only the functors of negation, conjunction, and disjunction and the y_j are "E_j occurs at t_j" for some E_j and t_j, then g may be interpreted as a composite goal, say, $g(C)$. For instance, in the simplest case—when g is the conjunction of its arguments—the goal is "occurrence of E_1 at t_1, occurrence of E_2 at t_2, and ...." In the case of more complex functions g, the verbal expression of the goal might be more complex.

Now, as shown by Nowakowska (1976a), there exists an isomorphism between goals and means of attaining them, so that the class of all strings of actions leading to goal $g(C)$ in degree at least a is obtained by the following procedure:

(a) for $i = 1,\ldots,m$, substitute set $K_a(E_i, t_i)$ in place of variable x_i;

(b) replace negation, disjunction, and conjunction by complement to 1, set-theoretical union, and set-theoretical intersection.

This will yield set $K_a[g(C)]$, that is, the set of all strings of actions that give goal $g(C)$ with degree at least a.

If $K_a(E_1, t_1) \subset K_a(E_2, t_2)$, then each string causing the occurrence of E_1 at t_1 (in degree at least a) also causes the occurrence of E_2 at t_2 in the same degree. Similarly, if $K_a(E_1, t_1) \subset -K_a(E_2, t_2)$, then the occurrence of E_1 at t_1 causes the nonoccurrence (i.e., prevents the occurrence) of E_2 at t_2. This illustrates the interrelations that may hold between particular occurrences of events. A special case, when there are no such relations, is called *complete* possibility. In the nonfuzzy case, it means attainability of all goals of the form

$$\bigcap_{i \in A} K_a(E_i, t_i) \cap \bigcap_{j \in M-A} -K_a(E_j, t_j), \tag{4.84}$$

where $M = \{1, 2, \ldots, m\}$. Thus, complete possibility means the attainability of any combination of events and the avoidability of all others. The notion of complete possibility allowed, among others, the introduction of a formal theory of conflicts [see Nowakowska (1973)], represented by a number of jointly unattainable events, and the obtaining of a rich taxonomy of such conflicts.

4.3.11 Generative Verbal Structures and True States in Histories

We shall now carry over to the present case the considerations of faithfulness and exactness of generative verbal structures. As in the preceding sections, we shall consider a propositional function $g(x_1, \ldots, x_m)$ with variables of form (E_i, t_i) substituted for x_i. We assume that events $E_1, \ldots, E_m$ are fixed. In this case, g becomes a function of temporal variables t_i. It becomes in turn a proposition when these variables are fixed or quantified.

To use an example, let $g(x_1, x_2) = x_1 \& x_2$, so that for fixed events $A = E_1$ and $B = E_2$ we obtain the propositional function "A occurs at t_1 and B occurs at t_2." By putting some special values, fuzzy or not, on t_1 and t_2, we obtain propositions such as "A occurred at 3 p.m. and B occurred much later in the evening." Adding the quantifier ($\exists t_1, t_2$ with $t_1 < t_2$), we obtain the proposition "A occurred earlier than B."

Now let D denote the class of all propositional functions described above, and for each d in D, let Q_d be the class of propositions obtained by specifying or quantifying the temporal variables. The problem is to determine the conditions for truth (or faithfulness, in the fuzzy case) of a proposition $p \in Q_d$ given history h, which is known (partially) up to time t.

To illustrate the difficulties, consider a simple case, when the histories concern weather in some fixed locality. Suppose that p states "rain today and tomorrow." Assume that time t is today's evening. Now, if it has not rained today, statement p cannot be faithful, regardless of the weather tomorrow. On the other hand, if it has rained today, then p cannot be decided to be faithful at present, since its faithfulness depends on the weather tomorrow.

Now, a history h describes the past, present, and future, so that for each p one can determine to which extent p is faithful in h; let this degree be $u(p, h)$. If $p \in Q_d$, let us write $p = p_t \& q_t$, where p_t is the conjunction of all propositions in the generative verbal structure p concerning the events prior to t, with q_t being the analogous conjunction concerning the events that occurred later than t and their relations to the events prior to t. Roughly, p_t comprises those propositions whose truth may be ascertained on the basis of the knowledge of history prior to t and q_t those whose truth may be ascertained only if one knows some occurrences after t.

Denote

$$H_a(p) = \{h : u(p, h) \geq a\}, \tag{4.85}$$

so that $H_a(p)$ is the class of all histories for which p is a description faithful in degree at least a. The generative verbal structure p will be said to be a-satisfiable if $H_a(p)$ is not empty.

Suppose now that the evaluation is made at time t. Set $H_a(p_t)$ consists of all histories that satisfy part p_t of the generative verbal structure. Let $H_a(q_t)$ be defined similarly. We then say that generative verbal structure $p = p_t \& q_t$ is *potentially a-faithful* if

$$H_a(p_t) \cap H_a(q_t) \neq 0. \tag{4.86}$$

Let us observe that it may happen that both $H_a(p_t)$ and $H_a(q_t)$ are nonempty, while the intersection on the left-hand side of (4.86) is empty. This means that the assertions made in p about the past from t are incompatible with those made about the times after t, even though they may be separately satisfiable.

One may obtain a systematic categorization of the concepts and entities introduced thus far (or those that may be constructed in terms of the present system) as follows. Let θ be a certain set; the nature of elements of θ has to be specified in each instance. One of the main such specifications is when $\theta = \{\theta_1, \theta_2\}$, interpreted as "true" and "false," or when $\theta = [0, 1]$, interpreted as values of an appropriate membership function.

Now let Δ be a class of some entities from the model, primitive or defined (e.g., the class of all histories, class of all elementary events, class of all composite events, class of all sentences.) We may now consider two types of formal objects, to be referred to as "valuations" and "chronologies."

By a *valuation*, or more precisely, a θ-valuation, we mean a function $f : \Delta \to \theta$. In a particular case, when Δ may be represented as $\Delta = \Delta_1 \times H$, we say that θ-valuation is relative to histories. To give an example, let $\Delta = \Delta_1 \times H$, with Δ_1 being a class of propositions, and let $\theta = \{\theta_1, \theta_2\}$, with θ_1 interpreted as "true" and θ_2 as "false." Then one can consider, for

$h \in H$, the set $Z_1(h) = \{\delta \in \Delta_1 : f(\delta, h) = \theta_1\}$, being the class of all sentences in Δ_1 that are true in history h.

To define chronology, one needs certain auxiliary constructions. Thus, let $\Delta^n = \Delta \times \cdots \times \Delta$ (n times), and let $\Delta^* = \bigcup_n \Delta^n$, so that Δ^* is the class of all vectors with components from Δ. Next, let π_n be a permutation of numbers $1, 2, \ldots, n$, that is, a 1–1 mapping $\pi_n : \{1, \ldots, n\} \to \{1, \ldots, n\}$. We may define $\Phi_{\pi_n} : \Delta^n \to \Delta^n$ by putting $\Phi_{\pi_n}(x_1, \ldots, x_n) = (x_{\pi_n(1)}, \ldots, x_{\pi_n(n)})$.

Now let us define the relation $\sim$ in Δ^* as $x \sim y$ iff $(\exists n)(\exists \pi_n) : \Phi_{\pi_n}(x) = y$, where x and y are n-dimensional vectors of elements of Δ. We then have the following.

THEOREM 4.7   *If $x \sim y$, then x and y belong to the same component Δ^n in Δ^*.*

Moreover, we have also the next theorem.

THEOREM 4.8   *Relation $\sim$ is an equivalence in Δ^*.*

Consequently, one may introduce the quotient set $\Delta^*/\sim$ of equivalence classes of the relation $\sim$.

Obviously the partition into equivalence classes concerns each component of Δ^*, that is, each Δ^n separately. Moreover, we have the following.

THEOREM 4.9   *Let $x = (x_1, \ldots, x_n) \in \Delta^N$. The class of abstraction of x consists of exactly one element x if, and only if, the components of x are all distinct.*

Let Δ^{**} be the set $\Delta^*/\sim \cup \{\varnothing\}$. By a *chronology* of Δ we mean a mapping $f : T \to \Delta^{**}$; the condition $f(t) = \varnothing$ means that the moment t is not occupied by elements from Δ. On the other hand, the condition $f(t) = \delta \in \Delta^*$ describes the occupancy of the moment t by elements from Δ.

A chronology of a class of events, fuzzy or not, is a substring of a certain history h. How big this subhistory is depends on the choice of the class Δ of events.

In short, we have here the following inclusions. A history is complete as regards time and the class of events (or, equivalently, states); a chronology is complete as regards time but concerns only a selected class of events. Finally, the mapping defined for generative verbal structures is restricted as regards both time and events (only those mentioned in the generative verbal structure).

The conceptual constructions of the present section lead in a natural way to definitions of fuzzy stochastic processes. To sketch this construction, let us briefly analyze various ways of defining stochastic processes.

Thus, a stochastic process may be regarded as a mapping that to every t assigns a random variable X_t. This way of defining is probably closest to the phrase that stochastic processes are "descriptions of random phenomena varying in time."

Second, a stochastic process may be defined by specifying all finite-dimensional distributions, that is, joint distributions of values of the process at various sets of moments. Such a definition is concordant with the idea that in probability theory one should use only those concepts and constructions that have observable counterparts.

Finally, one can define stochastic process as a probability measure over an appropriately defined space of functions, called variously "realizations," "histories," and so on.

All these approaches lead to equivalent definitions.

For fuzzification, it seems most appropriate to use the third approach, and the definition of a fuzzy stochastic process is, in a sense, an extension of the very natural definition of probability of a fuzzy event.

Thus, let H be the (nonfuzzy) set of all histories. A subset (fuzzy or not) of H, say, B, is described in terms of its membership function $\mu_B(h)$, $h \in H$, with values in $[0, 1]$.

If we have now a probability distribution P on H, that is, a nonfuzzy stochastic process, we may fuzzify it by putting, for a fuzzy subset B of H,

$$P(B) = \int \mu_B(h)\, dP(h). \qquad (4.87)$$

This gives the definition of fuzzy events, understood as subsets of H. One would like to apply this definition to obtain probabilities of events corresponding to cylinder sets, in particular to fuzzy events pertaining to one moment of time. Let $t_0 \in T$ be fixed, and let B be a fuzzy subset of H specified by membership function $\mu_B(h)$.

Out of two possible interpretations of history, namely $h: T \to S$ and $h: T \to E^* \cup \{\varnothing\}$, the first may be somewhat more convenient here. Thus, $h(t_0)$ is the state at time t_0, and if D is a (nonfuzzy) subset of S, one can determine the probability of state in D at t_0, that is, $h(t_0) \in D$, from the relation

$$P_{t_0}(D) = \int I_D[h(t_0)]\mu_B(h)\, dP(h) = \int_D \mu_B(h)\, dP(h), \qquad (4.88)$$

where I_D is the characteristic function of the set D.

In the case when D is a fuzzy subset of the set of all states, with membership function μ_D, we may write

$$P_{t_0}(D) = \int \mu_D[h(t_0)]\mu_B(h)\, dP(h). \qquad (4.89)$$

The definition of joint distributions, in both fuzzy and nonfuzzy case, is based on the same principle, and there is no need to present it here.

The above is a general definition of a stochastic process in the fuzzy case. Naturally, in the case of some special processes, such as Markov chains (see

Chapter 1), or random walks, one can find it more convenient to build the process from the beginning, instead of applying the general definition.

4.4   COMPLEX DESCRIPTIONS: A THEORY OF TEXTS

As opposed to the preceding sections, which dealt with texts as descriptions of some specific objects (sets of objects, perhaps changing), the theory of texts presented here will approach the problem from a different angle, not related to any specific semantic features, even though semantics of texts will play a prominent role in the theory.

Roughly, the approach will be similar to that used in formal linguistics, where language is taken as a primitive notion to be characterized by a set of postulates. Similarly, here the texts will be characterized by formal means, that is, by attempts to specifying the constraints that a string of words must meet to qualify as a text.

Intuitively, a "text" is a coherent string of speech units. The concept of "coherence" may be explicated intuitively by the requirement of the existence of one or more topics to which the particular speech units are related and by the requirement of appropriate interrelations between speech units of the string. That is to say, the speech units must be related among themselves, and they must also be related to some "world."

A traditional approach to text theory consists of specifying these relations. Instead, in this section, the notion of a text will be taken as a primitive (fuzzy) concept. The theory will then consist of formal explication of various concepts related specifically to texts (as opposed to sentences) and to the relation between texts and the "worlds" they describe. In addition, an empirical approach to texts will be outlined that will allow a statistical characterization of texts, again as opposed to sentences, and will provide certain measurable parameters of topics.

4.4.1   The Basic Formal Scheme

Let L denote the natural language in question, regarded as the class of all admissible sentences or, more generally, speech units formed from a certain vocabulary V. The set L will be assumed fuzzy; that is, we assume that L is characterized by a pair

$$\langle V, f_L \rangle, \tag{4.90}$$

where V is the vocabulary and

$$f_L : V^* \to [0, 1]; \tag{4.91}$$

here V^* is the monoid of all finite strings of elements of V.

If $u \in V^*$, then relation $f_L(u) = 1$ is interpreted so that string u belongs to the language in full degree, that is, it is a proper sentence. Relation $f_L(u) = 0$ means that u does not belong to the language, hence it is not a sentence (generally, a unit of speech). Intermediate cases $f_L(u) = a$ with $0 < a < 1$ indicate partial membership of u in L, that is, "admissibility in degree a."

Naturally, one could take an ordered class of linguistic variables representing membership degree, instead of the interval $[0, 1]$, to serve as the values of f_L, such as "fully," "almost," "to a large degree," "not at all." Since the values of membership degrees are not accessible empirically [for some rare exceptions, see Nowakowska (1977, 1979a)], such an approach might well replace deceptively more exact numerical approach.

As usual, with the fuzzy set (4.91) one may associate the family of a-level (nonfuzzy) sets defined by

$$L_a = \{u \in V^* : f_L(u) \geq a\}, \tag{4.92}$$

so that L_a consists of all strings whose degree of membership in L, that is, degree of acceptability, is at least a. In particular, L_1 is the set of all strings that are fully acceptable.

The intuition that one wants to capture here is that L is the set of all sentences (speech units). Thus, in most cases the value of the function f_L will be 0 or 1; that is, a string of words will be either a sentence or not a sentence, and only seldom will there occur intermediate cases, with strings of words that are "acceptable, but not fully."

Now, a concatenation of two or more sentences is *not* a sentence. Consequently, it appears reasonable to accept the following postulate.

POSTULATE 4.4   For any $n = 2, 3, \ldots$, if $f_L(u_1) = \cdots = f_L(u_n) = 1$, then $f_L(u_1 u_2 \cdots u_n) = 0$.

Let us now consider the case of texts. Intuitively, texts are strings of speech units, that is, strings of elements of language L. Since L is assumed to be fuzzy, it is not possible to define texts directly as concatenations of elements of L (because the notion "element of L" is not well defined). Thus, we shall again characterize the class of texts by a pair

$$\langle V, f_T \rangle, \tag{4.93}$$

where, as before,

$$f_T : V^* \to [0, 1] \tag{4.94}$$

is a function that maps the monoid V^* of all finite strings of words from vocabulary V into the interval $[0, 1]$. The interpretation is as before: relation $f_T(u) = 1$ means that u is a text, $f_T(u) = 0$ means that u is not a text, and the intermediate clases are interpreted as for the case of language L.

We define the a-level texts as

$$T_a = \{u \in V^* : f_T(u) \geq a\}, \tag{4.95}$$

and again, T_1 is the class of strings of words that are texts in full degree.

It is now necessary to impose some conditions on f_L and f_T, expressing the fact that, although elements of L and elements of T are both strings of words, the latter are also strings of sentences. This intuitive requirement may be expressed by the following postulate.

POSTULATE 4.5   *Let $u \in V^*$ be such that $f_T(u) = 1$, so that u is a text. Then*

$$(\exists k)(\exists w_1, \ldots, w_k \in V^*) : u = w_1 \cdots w_k \ \& \ (\forall i = 1, \ldots, k) : f_L(u_i) = 1. \tag{4.96}$$

The meaning of this postulate is as follows. If a string u is a text in full degree, then it may be decomposed into strings of words, each being a sentence in full degree. Consequently, this postulate rules out strings in which one or more speech units are not fully acceptable. In other words, texts consist only of acceptable sentences.

This is a fairly strong idealizing assumption. To make a somewhat more realistic assumption, one may proceed as follows. Let $u \in V^*$ and let $Q(u)$ denote the class of all decompositions of u, that is, class of all sets $(w_1, \ldots, w_k)$ such that $u = w_1 \cdots w_k$, where k may be equal $1, 2, \ldots$. It is not necessary that w_i be sentences.

DEFINITION 4.8   *By degree of decomposability of $u \in V^*$ we shall mean the number*

$$d(u) = \max_{(w_1, \ldots, w_k) \in Q(u)} \ \min_{1 \leq i \leq k} f_L(w_i). \tag{4.97}$$

Using this definition, Postulate 4.5 may be expressed as an implication

$$f_T(u) = 1 \Rightarrow d(u) = 1, \tag{4.98}$$

that is,

$$T_1 \subset \{u : d(u) = 1\}. \tag{4.99}$$

A weaker and more realistic version of Postulate 4.5 may now be formulated as follows.

POSTULATE 4.5′   *There exists a function $h : [0, 1] \to [0, 1]$ that is strictly increasing and such that $h(1) < 1$, for which the following implication holds for all u:*

$$f_T(u) = a \Rightarrow d(u) \geq h(a). \tag{4.100}$$

This implication expresses the requirement that if u is a text admissible in degree at least a, then it may be decomposed into substrings such that each of them belongs to language L in degree at least $h(a)$.

In particular, for $a = 1$, the last condition requires that the degree of decomposition of a string in T_1 be at least equal $h(1)$, which is less than 1. Thus, Postulate 4.5′ is, indeed, weaker than Postulate 4.5.

Clearly, the converse to implication (4.98) need not hold and is, in fact, false in general: there exist strings with $d(u) = 1$, hence consisting of sentences, but are not acceptable as texts.

For subsequent considerations, it will be convenient to assume that Postulate 4.5 holds.

The following considerations are aimed at explicating the idea that a text must show some form of cohesiveness; that is, its sentences must be related one to another in some way.

Before presenting the definition, it is worthwhile to explain the main idea behind it. Now, what is attempted, is a definition of a relation between two sentences in a text that does not refer to the meanings of these sentences. Intuitively, this may be accomplished by using the idea of replacement: two sentences are related, if replacing one of them by some other sentence makes the string not acceptable. More precisely, two sentences are related, if both must be suitably modified, or replaced, if the whole string is to be acceptable as a text.

To proceed formally, let u be a fixed text, that is, $f_T(u) = 1$, and let $u = w_1 \cdots w_k$ be its decomposition as specified in Postulate 4.5, that is, $f_L(w_i) = 1$ for all i.

DEFINITION 4.9 For $i = 1, \ldots, k$ let

$$Z(w_i) = \{w'_j : f_L(w'_j) = 1, f_T(w_1 \cdots w_{j-1} w'_j w_{j+1} \cdots w_k) = 1\}. \quad (4.101)$$

It follows that $Z(w_i)$ is the class of all sentences that may be put in place of w_i in text u without making the resulting string inadmissible.

To give an example, suppose that some text contains a certain assertion $w = $ "It was very hot in the afternoon." Suppose that this assertion may be replaced by $w' = $ "It was rather cool in the afternoon" without making the text inadmissible (i.e., the subsequent parts of the text do not rely too much on the assertion w). Then w' is an element of $Z(w)$. Similarly, if the assertion "It was very hot in the afternoon" may be dropped altogether and the text would still make sense, then the empty string would belong to $Z(w)$.

It is now possible to express the internal relations between two sentences w_i and w_j in the text; here we assume that $i < j$, so that w_i precedes w_j in the text.

DEFINITION 4.10 Sentences w_i and w_j in text $u = w_1 \cdots w_i \cdots w_j \cdots w_k$ are said to be *related* if

$$(\exists w'' \notin Z(w_j))(\exists v): f_T(w_1 \cdots w_{i-1} v w_{i+1} \cdots w_{j-1} w'' w_{j+1} \cdots w_k) = 1. \quad (4.102)$$

Thus two sentences are related if one can find the sentences w'' and v with the following properties:

(a) if w'' were used instead of w_j, the resulting string of sentences would not be a text;

(b) if, in addition, sentence w_i were replaced by v, then the resulting string would again be a text.

Naturally, a given sentence w_j may be related to more than one w_i with $i < j$; that is, it may be related to several of the preceding sentences. Thus we may define

$$a_u^-(j) = \text{number of } w_i \text{ to which } w_j \text{ is related with } i < j \qquad (4.103)$$

and

$$b_u^-(j) = \min[i : i < j, w_j \text{ is related to } w_i]. \qquad (4.104)$$

Similarly,

$$a_u^+(j) = \text{number of } w_i \text{ that are related to } w_j \text{ with } i > j \qquad (4.105)$$

and

$$b_u^+(j) = \max[i : i > j, w_i \text{ is related to } w_j]. \qquad (4.106)$$

Then $a_u^-(j)$ and $a_u^+(j)$ are measures that reflect, for a given text u, how strongly the jth sentence w_j is related to the preceding and following parts of the text. Consequently, the importance of w_j may be measured by the sum $a_u^-(j) + a_u^+(j)$.

Similarly, $b_u^-(j)$ and $b_u^+(j)$ measure how deeply backward and forward reach the influence of w_j in the text u. Consequently, the difference $b_u^+(j) - b_u^-(j)$ measures the "range" of influence of the sentence w_j.

Typically, a text would contain statement of its topic, questions raised, and so on, shortly after the beginning, in the initial sentences or paragraphs. If this topic is then developed, many sentences in subsequent parts of the text would be related to the initial parts. This means that $a_u^+(j)$ would typically be large for small j (i.e., for initial sentences w_j, which will be related to many subsequent sentences). Consequently, the number $b_u^+(j)$ would be large for small j; that is, the influence of the initial statement of the topic would reach into the subsequent parts of the text, even distant ones.

The numbers $a_u^-(j)$ for large j, that is, for later sentences, may or may not be large, depending on whether the text covers the topic by splitting it into a number of separately discussed subtopics (in this case, the values $a_u^-(j)$ need not be large) or whether the discussion is "homogeneous." As regards $b_u^-(j)$ for j corresponding to later sentences, it would typically be large, since more sentences would be related to the statement of the topic at the beginning of the text.

As opposed to that, a loose text, representing chatter, would have relatively weak relationships between sentences, and these relationships might not reach too far backward or forward, since chatter is characterized by the fact that the sentences are most often responses to some "local" stimuli in the form of other sentences.

4.4.2   Statistical Measures of a Text

In this section the considerations will be aimed at an anaysis of certain statistical counterparts of the notion of dependence between sentences in the text. Consider a fixed, sufficiently long text u. According to Postulate 4.5, u may be decomposed into a string of sentences, so that $u = w_1 w_2 \cdots w_k$. One can now treat this text as a realization of a certain stochastic process with values in L; that is, one may treat consecutive sentences as sampled from "universe" L of sentences (for simplicity, we assume here that L is not fuzzy; in fact, elements of the string u belong to L_1).

Naturally, the laws of sampling, that is, the laws that determine the probability of the next sentence given the preceding parts of the text, are not known. Thus, the idea will be to compare text u with some artificially produced sequence whose laws are known. Specifically, we shall try to capture the overall characteristics of text u, such as its "tightness" and "changes of topic," by comparing the behavior of process $w_1, w_2, \ldots$ with another process, say $v_1, v_2, \ldots$, where the v_i's are sampled independently from the same universe.

Empirically, one may think here of comparing text u consisting of several pages (say) of a given book with the "text" formed as follows: one samples first the page number from the book in question and then a sentence from this page.

Obviously, the latter text, $v_1, v_2, \ldots$, will be a meaningless string of sentences, sampled from the same basic universe, namely, the set of sentences of a given author.

Intuitively, the difference between text $u = w_1 w_2 \cdots$ and $v = v_1 v_2 \cdots$ will consist of a higher proportion of repeated words in u than in v. This is due to the fact that, in u, the consecutive sentences are likely to deal with the same topic, and hence some words are likely to be repeated. This is not the case for text v.

Now, to determine the "tightness" of u, one may proceed as follows. First, let us represent the true text u and random text v as strings of words:

$$u = x_1 x_2 \cdots, \tag{4.107}$$

$$v = y_1 y_2 \cdots, \tag{4.108}$$

where x_i and y_i are consecutive words.

Since we are interested in the repetitions of words, we may assign to each word in sequences (4.107) and (4.108) an index, say, 0 or 1, depending on whether this word has already appeared in the text or not. Formally, we define

$$z_i' = \begin{cases} 1 & \text{if } x_i \neq x_j \quad \text{for } j = 1, 2, \ldots, i-1, \\ 0 & \text{otherwise} \end{cases} \qquad (4.109)$$

$$z_i'' = \begin{cases} 1 & \text{if } y_i \neq y_j \quad \text{for } j = 1, 2, \ldots, i-1, \\ 0 & \text{otherwise.} \end{cases} \qquad (4.110)$$

For example, the values of z_i in the diagram below are marked over the words:

1   1   1   1   1   1   0   1   1   1   1   0   1   0
The day was very hot and very humid. In fact, it was so hot...

Here 1 indicates a new word, which has not appeared before in the text, and 0 indicates a word that is a repetition of a previously appearing word (thus 0 was assigned to *very*, *was*, and *hot* on their second appearence).

Now put

$$Z_n' = \sum_{i=1}^{n} z_i', \qquad Z_n'' = \sum_{i=1}^{n} z_i'', \qquad (4.111)$$

so that Z_n' is simply the number of distinct words among the first n words of the text u (and, similarly, Z_n'' is the number of distinct words among the first n words in the random text v). Obviously, the processes Z_1', Z_2', ... and Z_1'', Z_2'', ... are nondecreasing: two consecutive values are either the same or differ by 1.

Since one may expect that the words repeat more often in u than in v, this property should be reflected in the rates of increase of processes Z_n' and Z_n'', the second increasing faster than the first. To develop some theoretical background for comparison, one needs to derive the theoretical properties of process Z_n''.

For large n, we may assume that it is not sentences, but words, that are sampled independently from some basic vocabulary V of the given author and topic. Clearly, in each text u and v there will be some group of words, such as linguistic connectives or articles, that will become exhausted rather soon. We may simplify the problem by disregarding these words and restricting our attention to the vocabulary, say, V', with all such words removed. Assume, therefore, that Z_n'' is defined as above but after deleting from text v all words from the group of linguistic connectives, and so on.

Let V' be the basic vocabulary after such a deletion. As a first approximation, one may then assume that the words are sampled independently, with equal probability for each word. We have therefore

$$P(Z''_{n+1} = k + 1 \mid Z''_n = k) = 1 - k/N \qquad (4.112)$$

and

$$P(Z''_{n+1} = k \mid Z''_n = k) = k/N, \qquad (4.113)$$

where N is the size of vocabulary V'.

Indeed, if $Z''_n = k$, then k out of N words have already appeared in the text. The probability of a new word being sampled equals $(N - k)/N$, and the probability of sampling a word that has previously appeared is k/N. In the first case, Z''_{n+1} equals $k + 1$, and in the second, it equals k, which proves formulas (4.112) and (4.113).

From formulas (4.112) and (4.113) we obtain

$$E[Z''_{n+1} \mid Z''_n = k] = \left(k + 1 \right)\left(1 - \frac{k}{N} \right) + k \cdot \frac{k}{N}$$

$$= 1 + \frac{N - 1}{N} k = 1 + \frac{N - 1}{N} Z''_n. \qquad (4.114)$$

One may prove the following theorem.

THEOREM 4.10   *For process* Z''_n *we have*

$$E(Z''_n) = N\left[1 - \left(\frac{N - 1}{N} \right)^n \right], \qquad n = 1, 2, \ldots. \qquad (4.115)$$

For the proof see the Appendix at the end of this chapter.

The behavior of process Z'_n was used to estimate the size N of the vocabulary of a given author on the basis of a sample path of the process obtained from a text. In analyzing texts one may also proceed somewhat differently, using Theorem 4.10. Assume that processes Z'_n and Z''_n may be approximated by exponential functions

$$Z'_n \sim N(1 - e^{-an}), \qquad Z''_n \sim N'(1 - e^{-bn}). \qquad (4.116)$$

Such an approximation is clearly suggested by Theorem 4.10 for the process Z''_n.

By using methods of least squares (say), one may estimate parameters N, N', a, and b for true text u and random text v. We may then define

$$S = N/N', \qquad t = a/b, \qquad (4.117)$$

called, respectively, the *scope* of the text u and its relative *tightness*. Intuitively, values of S close to 1 indicate that the vocabulary of text u is close to the vocabulary of the universe of discouse of the given author, whereas small values of S indicate that text u is confined to a narrow topic, with limited vocabulary.

On the other hand, large values of t indicate that the text covers its domain quickly (both processes Z'_n and Z''_n grow at approximately the same rate), and exhaustion is more rapid when a/b is small.

The above considerations concern the comparison of process Z'_n with "reference" process Z''_n, constructed on the basis of artificial text v. In much the same way one may define other processes on the basis of u, describing the "inner dynamics" of text u as follows. Let $A \subset V$ be a subset of the vocabulary, and let

$$Z_n(A) = \text{number of distinct words from } A \text{ among } x_1, \ldots, x_n. \quad (4.118)$$

Obviously, $Z_n(A)$ is again a nondecreasing process; however, it may start with the value 0 and remain 0 for some time.

In a similar way one may define processes $Z_n(B), Z_n(C), \ldots$ for other subsets of V (not necessarily disjoint). If, for instance, $A, B, \ldots$ are vocabularies specific for some topics, then the graphs of $Z_n(A), Z_n(B), \ldots$ would indicate how the text moves from one topic to another; for example, the value n at which a given process, say, $Z_n(A)$, increases most steeply indicates those sentences that begin to cover the topic with vocabulary A.

4.4.3 A Statistical Approach to Semantic Constraints in a Text

The preceding section was devoted to exploring the idea that semantic constraints in a text should reveal themselves (among others) in the rate of word repetitions and in the relative size of the vocabulary used. The main problems lie in the construction of a "reference process" with which one could compare the obtained measures.

In this section, the statistical methods will be designed to analyze the depth and strength of the relation between sentences. In a sense, these will be statistical counterparts of the concepts of $a_u^-(j)$, $a_u^+(j)$, $b_u^-(j)$, and $b_u^+(j)$ defined in Section 4.4.2.

For statistical analysis one may take a simple operational definition of semantic relations between sentences based on repetition of words. One may select some suitable set A contained in vocabulary V and define, for sentences w_i and w_j of a text u $(i < j)$,

$$w_i T(v) w_j \quad \text{if} \quad w_i \text{ and } w_j \text{ both contain the word } v. \quad (4.119)$$

Next, define relation $T(A)$ as the union of all relations $T(v)$ for v ranging through A, that is,

$$w_i T(A) w_j \quad \text{iff} \quad (\exists v \in A): w_i T(v) w_j. \quad (4.120)$$

Now we may define inductively

$$w_i T^1(A) w_j \qquad \text{iff} \qquad w_i T(A) w_j, \qquad (4.121)$$

and for $n = 2, 3, \ldots$

$$w_i T^n(A) w_j \qquad \text{if} \quad (\exists w_r): w_i T^{n-1}(A) w_r \text{ and } w_r T^1(A) w_j \text{ for } i < r < j. \quad (4.122)$$

Naturally, it may happen that $w_i T^n(A) w_j$ and $w_i T^m(A) w_j$ for some n and m. In particular, the graph of the relation $T(A)$ may look like that in Fig. 4.5. Here $w_1 T(A) w_3$ and also $w_1 T^2(A) w_3$, since $w_1 T(A) w_2$ and $w_2 T(A) w_3$. One may now define the index of strength of the semantic relation between two sentences w_i and w_j ($i < j$) as the probability that, starting from w_i, a random walk on the graph of relation $T(A)$ moving only to the right, will reach the sentence w_j. For example, in Fig. 4.5, this index, for the relation between w_1 and w_6 equals

$$\tfrac{1}{3} + \tfrac{1}{3}(\tfrac{1}{4} + \tfrac{1}{4} \cdot \tfrac{1}{2}) = \tfrac{11}{24}. \qquad (4.123)$$

Indeed, there is one path leading directly to w_6, which occurs with probability $\tfrac{1}{3}$ (as there are three paths leading from w_1). With probability $\tfrac{1}{3}$ we select the path to w_2 from which the probability of reaching w_6 is $\tfrac{1}{4}$ via the direct path, and $\tfrac{1}{4} \cdot \tfrac{1}{2}$ for the path via w_5.

The crucial issue in such an analysis lies, of course, in the proper choice of set A. It is easy to give negative recommendations, that is, to indicate sets A that do not serve the purpose well. For instance, such words as linguistic connectives, personal pronouns, and modal frames should not be included in set A. The reason is simply that the appearance of such words in two sentences does not indicate any semantic relation between them.

Clearly, the more words in set A, the more sentences will become related. Of course, A need not contain only words; it may also contain such element as phrases.

An interesting prospect might be to analyze a given text with respect to several relations, specified by sets $A_1, A_2, \ldots$. These sets may correspond to various topics discussed in the text. Naturally, when such a program is

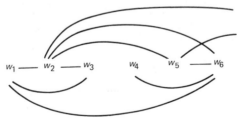

Fig. 4.5. A graph of relation $T(A)$.

implemented on a computer, some errors are bound to occur. These errors will be in both directions, that is, missing a semantic relation when it in fact exists (these errors occur therefore when the two sentences in question are related semantically but contain no words in common). Another type of error occurs when there appears a spurious relation, that is, two sentences have some words in common but are semantically unrelated.

Despite such possibilities of errors, one could hope that, with a sufficiently large text and the proper choice of set A, one would obtain a relation matrix that would exhibit certain characteristics of interest.

4.4.4 Changes of Topic

This section will be devoted to a brief outline of the possibility of construction of a dynamic model of text generation. The model will be similar, in its basic ideas, to the model of perception discussed in Chapter 5, concerning shifts in the eye focus, such as locations of consecutive glances and their duration.

Suppose that one distinguishes a certain number of topics, say, $C_1, C_2, \ldots,$ and assume that in analyzing a text it is possible to identify a topic to which a given fragment (sentence) belongs.

To present the model, let us start from some informal intuitions. First, we restrict our attention to "loose" texts, for example, records of conversations, as opposed to (say) philosophical essays, in which the changes of topics are well planned in advance. The reason for such a restriction is simply that the model will attempt to describe stochastic mechanisms of changes of topics; thus, the model will pertain to such texts as may be reasonably regarded as selected by some random mechanisms from the universe of all texts.

We shall assume the following mechanism: with each topic there is associated its "attraction," which varies in time. This attraction function decreases when the topic is being discussed ("exhaustion" of the topic). When a given topic is discussed, the attraction values for other topics remain constant for most of the time; however, occasionally there occur "impulses," which give an increase of attractiveness of other topics. Consequently, the attractiveness function for a topic that is *not* discussed in some time interval increases by jumps and remains constant between jumps.

Finally, a change of topic is a result of interplay of attraction functions: generally, termination of discussion of a topic (shift) occurs when the attraction of a given topic becomes sufficiently small (topic becomes exhausted). The discussion then shifts to the topic with highest attractiveness.

Now these intuitions have to be represented in the form of specific assumptions, which will enable us to derive some theoretical consequences.

These consequences, in turn, might serve as a basis for testing or estimation procedures using the data on various texts.

Formally, we describe the model in the form of the following series of postulates. To simplify the formalism, we shall treat time as continuous, rather than measuring it in discrete units, such as sentences.

Let $U = \{C_1, C_2, \ldots\}$ denote the universe of topics (which may, but need not, be discussed in the text).

POSTULATE 4.6   *With each $C_i \in U$ there is associated a nonnegative function $f_i(t)$ that represents the "attractiveness" of topic C_i at time t.*

The next postulates describe the mechanisms of growth and decline of attraction functions.

POSTULATE 4.7   *At each time t, the text deals with exactly one of the topics in U. If between t_1 and t_2 the topic discussed is C_i, then for all $t \in [t_1, t_2]$ we have*

$$f_i(t) = f_i(t_1)e^{-c_i(t-t_1)}, \tag{4.124}$$

where c_i is some positive constant (rate of decay of topic C_i).

POSTULATE 4.8   *Suppose that between t_1 and t_2 the topic discussed is C_i. Then for any topic $C_j \neq C_i$ and any $t \in [t_1, t_2]$ we have*

$$f_j(t) = f_j(t_1) + X_{ij}(t_1, t), \tag{4.125}$$

where $X_{ij}(t_1, t)$ is a Poisson random variable with

$$P[X_{ij}(t_1, t) = k] = [b_{ij}(t - t_1)]^k e^{-b_{ij}(t-t_1)}/k!. \tag{4.126}$$

POSTULATE 4.9   *If at time t the discussion concerns topic C_i, then the probability that the topic will become changed before time $t + \Delta t$ equals $\Delta t / f_i(t) + o(\Delta t)$; the discussion then shifts to that among those remaining topics with the highest attractiveness.*

Thus, the model depends on the vector of decay constants $[c_1, c_2, \ldots]$ and the matrix of parameters $[b_{ij}]$. The decay constants determine the "exhaustion rate": generally, the higher the value of c_i, the shorter will be the discussion of topic C_i.

Constants b_{ij} may be interpreted as measures of interrelations between the topics: b_{ij} is the intensity of "impulses" for topic C_j arising from the discussion of topic C_i. In particular, if $b_{ij} = 0$, then discussion of C_i does not give any impulses for C_j; one may say then that C_j is independent of C_i. On the other hand, in the case of a close relationship between C_i and C_j, the discussion of C_i may provide many impulses toward discussing the topic C_j.

Observe that b_{ij} need not be the same as b_{ji}. Indeed, the discussion of C_i may give many impulses toward discussing C_j, but it may be that discussion of C_j

provides no incentive toward discussing C_i. In still other words, the relation of independence expressed through vanishing of coefficient b_{ij} is not symmetric.

Let us start by deriving some conclusions about the probability distribution of the length of an uninterrupted discussion of a given topic. We have then the following theorem.

THEOREM 4.11 *Assume that the discussion of topic C_i starts at some time t_0, and let $f_i = f_i(t_0)$ be the attraction of C_i at that time. Further, let T_i be the time, counted from t_0, of the discussion of C_i. Then T_i has density*

$$h_i(t) = \frac{1}{f_i} \exp(c_i t) \exp\left\{ -\frac{1}{f_i c_i} \left[\exp(c_i t) - 1 \right] \right\}. \tag{4.127}$$

For the proof see the Appendix at the end of this chapter.

Suppose now that at some time t_0 the attractiveness values of various topics are $f_1, f_2, \ldots$. Without loss of generality we may put $t_0 = 0$. Assume that the discussion starts with topic C_i. We then have the following theorem.

THEOREM 4.12 *The probability that the next topic discussed will be C_j ($j \neq i$) equals*

$$P_{ij}(f_1, f_2, \ldots) = \int_0^\infty \sum_{r=0}^\infty \frac{(b_{ij}t)^r}{r!} e^{-b_{ij}t}$$

$$\times \prod_{k:k \neq j, k \neq i} \sum_{n=0}^{r+f_j-f_i} \frac{(b_{ik}t)^n}{n!} e^{-b_{ik}t} h_i(t)\, dt, \tag{4.128}$$

where $h_i(t)$ is given by (4.127).

For the proof see the Appendix at the end of this chapter.

Formula (4.128) allows us, at least in theory, to obtain the transition probabilities for the process of changes of topics in a text.

4.5 GENERATION OF A TEXT

We shall now regard a text as a series of responses to a string of hypothetical questions. In other words, we shall consider a certain "question space" and the process of sampling questions from this set, according to some rules; this process will be called *generation of a q-string*. The successive questions and answers to them determine (in a probabilistic sense) the next question to be asked, and the answer to it constitutes the successive fragment of the text. We shall start by outlining a theory of questions, that is, the nature of the Q-space.

Let U denote the universe of discourse, that is, a set of all objects that may be mentioned in the text, as the set of possible attributes of these objects, as well as the sets of possible binary, ternary,... relations between the objects. Formally, U will be represented as a system

$$U = \langle A, R^{(1)}, R^{(2)}, \ldots \rangle, \tag{4.129}$$

where A is the set of objects under considerations and $R^{(n)}, n = 1, 2, \ldots$, is a set of n-ary relations in A. The elements of $R^{(n)}$ will be generally denoted by R^n, with the superscript n omitted if there is no danger of confusion, that is, when it is clear from the context what the number of arguments in relation $R^{(n)}$ is. The letters $a, b, c, \ldots$ will be used for individual names of elements of A, and $x, y, \ldots$ will denote free variables with values in A.

The elements of $R^{(1)}$ are simply subsets of A, to be called *attributes* of elements of A. If $R^1 \in R^{(1)}$, then the symbol $R^1(a)$ means that a has attribute R^1; we shall also use the standard notation $a \in R^1$. Similarly, $R^1(x)$ will denote the propositional function, to be read "x has attribute R^1," also to be written as $x \in R^1$.

Now, with elements of $R^{(2)}$, that is, binary relations, we shall use the same notation. Thus, $R^2 \in R^{(2)}$ will stand generally for a binary relation in A, and $R^2(a, b)$ will denote the fact that elements ab are in relation R^2. Again $R^2(x, y)$ will be the corresponding propositional function.

Let now $R^n \in R^{(n)}$, and let $a_{i_1}, \ldots, a_{i_k}, k < n$ be fixed elements of A. We shall then denote by $R^n_{a_{i_1}, \ldots, a_{i_k}}$ the $(n - k)$-ary relation obtained from R^n by fixing specific k of its arguments.

For example, let R^2 be the relation "is younger than" (assuming elements of A are people). Thus, R^2(Mary, John) stands for "Mary is younger than John."

Suppose that we fix $a_2 = $ John, leaving the first argument free, and consider the relation $R^2_{\text{John}} = R^2(\cdot, \text{John})$. This becomes then a one-argument relation, leading to the one-place predicate "younger than John."

We shall now impose the following assumption on the system of relations (4.129).

ASSUMPTION 4.2 *For any n, any $R^n \in R^{(n)}$, and arbitrary $a_{i_1}, \ldots, a_{i_k} \in A$, $k < n$, relation $R^n_{a_{i_1}, \ldots, a_{i_k}}$ belongs the class $R^{(n-k)}$.*

We shall now distinguish three types of elementary questions concerning the elements of set A. These three types will be referred to as *specific* questions, or *S*-questions, *enumerative* questions, or *E*-questions, and *general* questions, of *G*-questions. Each of these questions will be connected with one of the relations in $R^{(1)} \cup R^{(2)} \cup \cdots$, that is, with a relation $R^{(n)}$ for some n.

It will be convenient to use the notation $a^{(n)}$ for an element of A^n, that is, for an n-tuple of elements of A, and $x^{(n)}$ for a variable with range in A^n.

An S-question will be characterized by a pair $(a^{(n)}, R^n)$, with $a^{(n)} \in A^n$ and $R^n \in R^{(n)}$ and will be denoted by

$$R^n[a^{(n)}]?. \tag{4.130}$$

This will be interpreted as "Is it true that the n-tuple $a^{(n)}$ is in the relation R^n?". In particular, if $n = 1$, the question $R^1[a^{(1)}]?$, or simply $R[a]?$, is "Does a belong to R?" or "Does element a have the attribute R?", and so on.

In case $n = 2$, the question $R^2[a^{(2)}]?$ may be written as $R[a, b]?$, and it reads "Are objects a and b in relation R?".

The S-questions are specific in the sense that they concern a concrete object, or n-tuple of objects, and a specific attribute (or n-ary relation). The answer to a question $R^n[a^{(n)}]?$ is "yes" if $R^n(a^{(n)})$ and "no" otherwise.

Next, an E-question will characterized by a single element R^n and will be denoted by

$$R^n[x^{(n)}]?. \tag{4.131}$$

This will be interpreted as "Which n-tuples $x^{(n)}$ are in relation R^n?". In particular, for $n = 1$, the E-question becomes $R[x]?$ or simply $R(x)?$. It will be interpreted as the question "Which elements of A have attribute R?".

Similarly, for $n = 2$, the question becomes $R^2[x^{(2)}]?$, that is, $R(x, y)?$, which reads: "Which pairs (x, y) of elements of A are in relation R?".

Putting $y = $ John and interpreting R as "is younger than," the question $R^2_{\text{John}}[x]?$ becomes "Who is younger than John?".

The complete answer to the E-question $R^n[x^{(n)}]?$ is the set of all n-tuples $x^{(n)}$ for which $R^n(x^{(n)})$ is true. An incomplete answer may consist of giving a subset of this set, perhaps even consisting of a single element. Thus, the full answer to the above question $R^2_{\text{John}}[x]?$ consists of listing all persons in A who are younger than John, while an incomplete answer may simply be "Mary and Bill." The latter answer is correct if $R^2_{\text{John}}(\text{Mary})$ and $R^2_{\text{John}}(\text{Bill})$.

Finally, the G-questions will concern the properties of set A (or A^n) as a whole. We have here two questions, corresponding to the existential and general quantifier. Thus, if $R^n \in R^{(n)}$, then the two questions will be

$$(\exists x^{(n)}): R^n[x^{(n)}]? \tag{4.132}$$

and

$$(\forall x^{(n)}): R^n[x^{(n)}]?, \tag{4.133}$$

to be interpreted, respectively, as "Does there exist an n-tuple $x^{(n)}$ that satisfies R^n?", and "Is it so that R^n holds for all n-tuples $x^{(n)}$?".

The complete answer to either (4.132) or (4.133) is either "yes" or "no." Moreover, a positive answer to (4.132) and a negative answer to (4.133) is *supercomplete* if it provides an *n*-tuple that satisfies R^n in the case of (4.132) or does not satisfy R^n in the case of (4.133).

For example, in the case $n = 1$, we may ask

$$(\exists x): R[x]?, \tag{4.134}$$

that is, "Does there exist an element of A that has attribute R?". The answer may be "yes" or "no." A supercomplete answer would have the form "Yes, element a has attribute R." Similarly, in the case of the question

$$(\forall x): R[x]?, \tag{4.135}$$

that is, "Do all elements of A have attribute R," the answer may be "yes" or "no." A supercomplete answer would then be "No, element a does not have attribute R."

The above-outlined question theory is sufficiently general to enable one to incorporate the basic questions "What?", "Which?", "When?", "Where?", and "Why?". Indeed, each of the questions of the above categories may be obtained by appropriate specification of relation R^n.

For instance, the question "When?" will typically concern events. We may then include in A both events and time moments, and take relation $R^2(a, t)$ to hold if and only if the event a occurred at time t.

Now, fixing event a_0, we obtain attribute $R^2_{a_0}(\cdot)$, namely, the times of occurrence of a_0. The question "When did a_0 occur?" will now become an E-question of the form $R^2_{a_0}[t]?$, with the full answer being the set of all times of occurrence of a_0.

Similarly, the question "Where?", such as "Where was a at time t?", requires introducing a ternary relation $R^3(a, t, z)$, where a is an object, t a moment of time, and z a location. Fixing a_0 and t_0, we obtain a one-place attribute $R^3_{a_0, t_0}(\cdot)$ of locations of a_0 at t_0. The question is again of an E-type, written as $R^3_{a_0, t_0}[z]?$. The same question may be phrased as an S-question if we specify the location z_0, and ask $R^3_{a_0, t_0}[z_0]?$, that is, "Was a_0 at z_0 at time t_0?".

The question space, by generating the answers, supplies in fact a classification of objects, events, and relations from system (4.129). As shown by Nowakowska (1979a), the description, understood as a classification in the natural language, is the weakest form of measurement, called *linguistic measurement*. The mechanisms of decision making based on such classifications were shown in Nowakowska (1973), in which the individual decision was interpreted as a group decision and use was made of Arrow's Impossibility Theorem. The situation (external or internal) of the observer was assumed to be based on classification (linguistic measurement) on some set of scales, forming a representation of the underlying cognitive psychological scales.

On the basis of linguistic measurement in decisional situations, when the results do not lead to unambiguous preferential ordering, it was shown how people achieve a compromise decision by resigning from some "democratic" choice mechanisms. In other words, in decisionally ambiguous situations, the man imposes less weight to some measurements or classifications than to others, attaining a preferential ordering. [For a thorough model analysis of mechanisms of enforcing the decisions in such cases, see Nowakowska (1973).]

It is worth stressing that the above is one of the basic mechanisms of perception and action.

In further development, the concept of classification and linguistic measurement may be extended to the notion of dynamic classification, as shown by Nowakowska (1980a).

The generation of a text by questions must meet some additional constraints on composition. The point is that description has a linear character, whereas the described objects have, in general, a multimodal hierarchical structure. This implies the necessity of a certain order of description meeting certain construction constraints and allowing for differentiation between, for example, literary and scientific texts.

To enable an analysis of such constraints, one may introduce the notion of a multimedial conceptual unit of text, call it MCUT, which may be compact or distributive. This unit is a certain idealized structure, which in its canonical form may be described as follows. For a given level of generality of description, MCUT is a full information unit supplied by a complete set of questions from the question space. This assumes that at a given time the object is classified, or linguistically measured, on all dimensions, leading thus to an exhaustive description, determining who, where, when, why, and how something was done. Such a complete multimedial measurement of an object, event, relation, or set of objects, events, or relations, with respect to all independent dimensions of the question space, is understood as an idealized conceptual unit of text.

Such units appear in three basic forms: compact, distributive, and degenerate. In this interpretation, the text is a concatenation of such units. One of the parameters is the interaction and distribution of such units with respect to one another.

In other words, MCUT is a certain finite portion of information about the object supplied by linguistic measurement for a given level of generality and at a given time.

Naturally, the producer of a text may return to a given object for the same moment of time, producing a description on a different level of generality, following the possible strategies of inspection of hierarchical topic structure and various strategies of exhausting it.

Since the world that is linguistically measured and over which a given text is generated through the question space is changing, the description mostly parallels and comments on the changing attributes and relations. The proportion of loops, that is, returns to measurement (description) of the same objects on different levels of generality, is one of the important parameters of the text. Another parameter is the degree of dispersion of atomic information from a conceptual unit. The atomicity is understood here as one of the sentences of a MCUT, which is generated by one of the independent dimensions of question space and concerning one object on a given level of generality at a given time.

Still another parameter is the presence of degenerate units, having the form of composite sentences, which usually do not exhaust all dimensions of the question space. The proportion of degenerate units to full and distributed ones is a parameter of the text.

One could think of a typology of texts, based on these parameters, an on various (e.g., aesthetic) effects connected with various values of text parameters.

The importance of the analysis of texts as a complex description (or complex dynamic measurement) of real or imagined objects is obvious. What makes it even more important is the realization that text theory should be regarded, in effect, as a part of a theory of knowledge. Understanding the problems of the structure of texts leads to a construction of some aspects of the theory of knowledge.

4.6 TEXTS AND A THEORY OF KNOWLEDGE

In this section we shall assume that a text provides a description of some reality. The main issue will be that this description may be (and usually is) incomplete and also not quite reliable. In other words, not all facts about the described world are represented in the text, and also the propositions pertaining to some other facts may be imprecise and have only limited credibility.

4.6.1 α-bility

Before introducing the conceptual scheme of the suggested theory of knowledge, it is worthwhile to introduce some auxiliary notions, especially that of α-bility [see Nowakowska (1982b)].

Let

$$\alpha: [0, 1] \times [0, 1] \to [0, 1] \qquad (4.136)$$

be a function satisfying the following.

Condition A *Symmetry*   For all x, y we have

$$\alpha(x, y) = \alpha(y, x). \qquad (4.137)$$

Condition B *Monotonicity*   The function $\alpha(x, y)$ increases in y for every x (hence, by symmetry, it also increases in x for every y).

Condition C *Boundary Conditions*

$$\alpha(x, 1) = 1, \qquad \alpha(0, 0) = 0. \qquad (4.138)$$

Condition D *Transitivity*   For all x, y, z we have

$$\alpha[x, \alpha(y, z)] = \alpha[\alpha(x, y), z]. \qquad (4.139)$$

Generally, such functions α will be used to obtain extensions of point functions to set functions, such as possibility, credibility, believability, to be called, in general, α-bility. For example, if

$$\alpha(x, y) = \min(x, y), \qquad (4.140)$$

we obtain Zadeh's possibility measure. As other examples, one may take

$$\alpha(x, y) = x + y - xy, \qquad (4.141)$$

which gives probabilistic summation, or Yager's (1980) function

$$\alpha(x, y) = \min[1, x^p + y^p]^{1/p}. \qquad (4.142)$$

For a thorough discussion of such functions and their properties, see Dubois and Prade (1982).

Now let

$$g: U \to [0, 1] \qquad (4.143)$$

be a function, defined on an arbitrary set U, with values in $[0, 1]$. By an α-*extension* of g, to be denoted g_α, we shall mean a function defined on the class 2^U of all subsets of U as

$$g_\alpha(\varnothing) = 0, \qquad (4.144)$$

$$g_\alpha(\{u\}) = g(u) \qquad \text{for all } u \in U, \qquad (4.145)$$

if $S = \{u_0, u_1, \ldots, u_n\}$ is a finite subset of U, then $g_\alpha(S) = c_n$, where the sequence $c_0, c_1, \ldots$ is defined recursively by

$$c_0 = g(u_0),$$

$$c_{k+1} = \alpha[c_k, g(u_{k+1})], \qquad k = 0, 1, \ldots; \tag{4.146}$$

for an arbitrary subset S of U, we put

$$g_\alpha(S) = \sup\{g_\alpha(S') : S' \subset S, S' \text{ finite}\}. \tag{4.147}$$

It is easy to verify that the value $g_\alpha(S)$ defined in (6.11) does not depend on the particular ordering of the set S. This follows from symmetry and transitivity of the function α. Indeed, we have the following theorem.

THEOREM 4.13 *Conditions (4.144)–(4.147) determine the function $g_\alpha : 2^U \to [0, 1]$ uniquely.*

Suppose, for example, that $U = \{a, b, c, d\}$ and that the values of the function g are

$$g(a) = 0.1, \qquad g(b) = 0.2, \qquad g(c) = 0.6, \qquad g(d) = 0.9. \tag{4.148}$$

Table I gives the values of $g_\alpha(S)$ for selected functions α, namely,

$$\alpha_1(x, y) = \max(x, y), \qquad \alpha_2(x, y) = x + y - xy,$$

$$\alpha_3(x, y) = \min[1, x^2 + y^2]^{1/2}, \tag{4.149}$$

$$\alpha_4(x, y) = \min[1, x^{3/4} + y^{3/4}]^{4/3},$$

$$\alpha_{5,6}(x, y) = \frac{x + y - xy - \min(x, y, 1 - v)}{\max(1 - x, 1 - y, v)},$$

Table I

Extension g_α for Various Functions α

S	g_{α_1}	g_{α_2}	g_{α_3}	g_{α_4}	g_{α_5}	g_{α_6}
$\{a, b\}$	0.200	0.280	0.224	0.373	0.200	0.242
$\{a, c\}$	0.600	0.640	0.608	0.817	0.600	0.621
$\{a, d\}$	0.900	0.910	0.906	1.000	0.900	0.905
$\{b, c\}$	0.600	0.680	0.632	0.974	0.600	0.663
$\{b, d\}$	0.900	0.920	0.922	1.000	0.900	0.916
$\{c, d\}$	0.900	0.960	1.000	1.000	0.947	0.958
$\{a, b, c\}$	0.600	0.712	0.640	1.000	0.600	0.681
$\{a, b, d\}$	0.900	0.928	0.927	1.000	0.900	0.920
$\{a, c, d\}$	0.900	0.964	1.000	1.000	0.947	0.960
$\{b, c, d\}$	0.900	0.968	1.000	1.000	0.947	0.965
$\{a, b, c, d\}$	0.900	0.971	1.000	1.000	0.947	0.966

where $v = 0.75$ for α_5 and $v = 0.95$ for α_6 [for the latter function α, see Dubois and Prade (1980)].

4.6.2 Knowledge and Its Representation

As mentioned, the function g_α represents an extension of the basic valuation g on U to the set function g_α. Before utilizing this concept, and the associated notion of α-ability, let us describe the basic scheme of knowledge representation.

Let X be a certain set whose elements will be interpreted as *possible states* or possible *histories* of the world. The exact nature of the elements of X is not essential; the intended interpretation is such that we are interested in some specific fragment of reality about which we have only incomplete information. It is assumed that the "true state" or "true history" is adequately described by exactly one element of X, with other elements of X exhausting all theoretically possible states (histories). In other words, it is assumed that exactly one element of X (but unknown which) represents the "truth" about the fragment of the world in question.

A typical case might be when we are interested in some dynamically occurring phenomenon: the elements of X are then "histories," that is, functions describing the state of the phenomenon at each time. In this case, the elements of X are functions.

As other example, one may think of an object that is known to belong to a certain class of objects; it is described in terms of a number of attributes. In this case, the elements of X are possible vectors of attributes of the objects of the class under consideration, with one vector being "true" (describing the object in question). In the following discussion x_0 will denote the unknown true element of X.

Consider now an arbitrary proposition p. With each p we may associate a subset (in general fuzzy) of X, representing information about the truth x_0 given by proposition p. Let B_p denote this subset. It is given in the form of the membership function, to be denoted by the same symbol, so that we have

$$0 \le B_p(x) \le 1 \qquad \text{for all } x \in X. \tag{4.150}$$

We interpret B_p as the subset of X that is to contain x_0. Obviously, the "smaller" set B_p is, the more precise is the information about x_0 (provided this information is true).

It is worthwhile to consider some simple examples. Suppose that X consists of histories and p is the proposition "event E_1 occurred shortly before event E_2." Let $x = x(t)$ be a history from X. Now, an event E is defined in terms of a history, as it was done in Chapter 2. Moreover, we may associate with each history x which leads to an event E its time of occurrence in x, say, $T_x(E)$.

Let $u(t_1, t_2)$ be the membership function of the fuzzy set of pairs of times (t_1, t_2) such that moment t_1 occurs shortly before moment t_2. For instance, we may have here (on the time scale appropriate for the events in question) $u(3{:}15 \text{ p.m.}, 3{:}17 \text{ p.m.}) = 1$, whereas $u(3{:}15 \text{ p.m.}, 4{:}15 \text{ p.m.})$ assumes a smaller value. Also $u(t_1, t_2) = 0$ whenever $t_2 < t_1$, and so on.

The set B_p of histories associated with the proposition $p = \text{``}E_1$ occurred shortly before $E_2\text{''}$ then has membership function given by

$$B_p(x) = 0 \text{ if history } x \text{ is such that event } E_1 \text{ and/or } E_2 \text{ does not} \tag{4.151}$$
$$\text{occur in } x;$$

$$B_p(x) = u(T_x(E_1), T_x(E_2)) \text{ if both events } E_1 \text{ and } E_2 \text{ occur in } x. \tag{4.152}$$

The first condition asserts that proposition p excludes all histories x that do not lead to the occurrence of both E_1 and E_2. The second condition asserts that the degree of membership of a history x in the set B_p equals the value of the function u evaluated at times of occurrences of E_1 and E_2 in history x.

Let us now consider more complex statements about the "world," and the fuzzy sets B_p associated with them. The point is that a proposition p may be preceded by some modal frame, such as "I believe that p," "I am almost certain that p," and "It is possible that p." These modal frames pertain to the attitudes toward the truth of the propositions [for an analysis of the class of such modal frames, forming a motivational calculus, see Nowakowska (1973)]. Thus to each modal frame there corresponds a function α with the properties described in the preceding section. Let α_{MF} be such a function assigned to MF (where MF is a modal frame), and let $B_{\mathrm{MF}p}(x)$ be the membership function of the "constraint" on the knowledge imposed by the sentence MFp.

The latter function is obtained as follows. First, one may associate with MFp a class of disjoint subsets of X, say, $V = \{X_1, \ldots, X_n\}$, where $X_i \subset X$ for all $i = 1, \ldots, n$, and $X_i \cap X_j = \varnothing$ for all $i \neq j$, and there exists a function

$$g : V \to [0, 1]. \tag{4.153}$$

The pair (V, g) may be called the *skeleton* of the sentence MFp. Here the sets X_i represent various possibilities connected with proposition p, and the values $g(X_i)$ represent the α-bilities of X_i associated with the particular modal frame MF.

Now let V^* be the class of all subsets of V, that is, the smallest class containing all sets in V and closed under set theoretical operations. Further, we define the α-extension g_α of the function g to the class V^*. Finally, let G_α be the class of all functions $f : X \to [0, 1]$ such that

$$f(S) = g_\alpha(S) \qquad \text{for all } S \in V^* \tag{4.154}$$

and

$$B_{\mathrm{MF}p}(x) = \sup\{f(x) : f \in G_\alpha\}. \tag{4.155}$$

4.6.3 Adequacy of Knowledge

Suppose now that the knowledge about the world takes on the form of a set of propositions, with the modal frames. Let $B_1(x)$, $B_2(x),\ldots,B_N(x)$ be the corresponding fuzzy subsets of X. Then the knowledge, call it K, determines the fuzzy subset of X defined by

$$B_K(x) = \min_i B_i(x). \tag{4.156}$$

The internal properties of K, such as its consistency, may be expressed through the properties of B_K only. On the other hand, the properties related to truth, adequacy, precision, and so on, of knowledge K are those that may be expressed by relations between the function $B_K(x)$ given by (4.156) and the "true" element x_0.

DEFINITION 4.11 Knowledge K will be called *consistent* if

$$\sup_{x \in X} B_K(x) = 1, \tag{4.157}$$

that is, if the fuzzy set B_K is normal.

This means that for consistent knowledge K there exists at least one element x in X such that it belongs to the set B_K in full degree. In other words, there exists an element x that satisfies all the constraints imposed by the propositions forming knowledge K.

On the other hand, if $\sup_x B_K(x) = 0$, knowledge K is totally inconsistent: there is no element x that satisfies the constraints in K in any positive degree.

Weakening the above extremes, we may introduce the following definition.

DEFINITION 4.12 Knowledge K is said to be *ε-inconsistent* if

$$\sup_x B_K(x) = 1 - \varepsilon. \tag{4.158}$$

For $\varepsilon = 0$ we obtain consistency, and for $\varepsilon = 1$ we have total inconsistency.

Even though K may be inconsistent, partially or totally, some of the subsets of K may be consistent. If $K' \subset K$ is a subset of proposition forming K, then we may define

$$B_{K'}(x) = \min_{K'} B_i(x), \tag{4.159}$$

where minimum is extended over those indices i for which the corresponding proposition is in K'. We may then introduce the following.

DEFINITION 4.13 The set $K' \subset K$ is said to be *maximally consistent* if

$$\sup_{x \in X} B_{K'}(x) = 1 \tag{4.160}$$

and

$$\sup_{x \in X} B_{K''}(x) < 1 \qquad (4.161)$$

for any set K'' with $K' \subset K'' \subset K$ and $K' \neq K''$.

Denote

$$C_{K'} = \{x : B_{K'}(x) = 1\}, \qquad (4.162)$$

so that K' is consistent if $C_{K'}$ is nonempty.
We have the following.

THEOREM 4.14 *Assume that K' and K'' are two maximally consistent subsets of K. If $K' \neq K''$, then $C_{K'} \cap C_{K''} = \varnothing$.*

For the proof see the Appendix at the end of the chapter.

Let us now analyze the properties of knowledge as regards the truth x_0. We may introduce here the following definition.

DEFINITION 4.14   We say that knowledge K is *adequate* if

$$B_K(x_0) \geq B_K(x) \qquad \text{for all } x \in X \qquad (4.163)$$

and *strictly* adequate if

$$B_K(x_0) > B_K(x) \qquad \text{for all } x \neq x_0. \qquad (4.164)$$

Furthermore, we say that K is *truthful* if $B_K(x_0) = 1$, that is, if $x_0 \in C_K$. If K is truthful and strictly adequate, then it is called *precise*.

Thus precise knowledge allows us to identify the truth x_0 as that point that yields the unique maximum equal to 1 of the function $B_K(x)$.

In parallel with sets C_K given by (4.162), we may define the *exclusion* sets

$$D_K = \{x : B_K(x) = 0\}. \qquad (4.165)$$

Suppose now that knowledge is gained step by step, so that we have in effect a sequence $K_1 \subset K_2 \subset \cdots$ of sets of propositions. We then have $C_{K_1} \supset C_{K_2} \supset \cdots$ and $D_{K_1} \subset D_{K_2} \subset \cdots$. Intuitively, C_{K_i} expresses the uncertainty connected with K_i: it is the set of all those x that are "α-able" to degree 1. Similarly, D_{K_i} expresses "negative certainty" connected with K_i: it is the set of all those x that are α-excluded (hence have α-ability zero). We may then say that K_{i+1} decreases the uncertainty (relative to K_i) if $C_{K_{i+1}} \neq C_{k_i}$ and increases the certainty if $D_{k_{i+1}} \neq D_{k_i}$. Thus if K_{i+1} decreases the uncertainty, then some x which have α-ability 1 under K_i acquire α-bility less than 1. On the other hand, if K_{i+1} increases the certainty, then some x which have positive α-bility under K_i acquire α-bility 0 under K_{i+1}.

4.7   AN ALGEBRAIC APPROACH TO DISCOURSES AND THEIR GOALS

In this section we shall analyze texts, or, more generally, discourses, that is, strings of sentences that are either uttered or written, from the point of view of their goals. As in the preceding sections, $u = w_1 w_2 \cdots w_k$ will stand for a string of sentences and $f_T(u)$ will represent the degree to which u constitutes a discourse. In particular, if $f_T(u) = 1$, then we say that w_k is a possible termination sentence of discourse u.

Denote for simplicity

$$x_1 = w_1, \qquad x_{n+1} = x_n w_{n+1}, \qquad (4.166)$$

which means that x_{n+1} is obtained from x_n by concatenating it from the right with sentence w_{n+1}.

Consider now the sequence

$$d_n = f_T(x_n), \qquad n = 1, 2, \ldots, \qquad (4.167)$$

so that d_n represents the degree to which the string of initial n sentences represents a discourse. If $d_n = 1$, we shall also say that n is an admissible termination moment.

4.7.1   Goals of a Discourse

Every discourse has its goal or goals. These goals may either be quite specific or vague; they may be stated explicitly or be only inferred from the discourse. To give some examples, a person X may want to break some bad news to Y(goal 1) but avoid making him unnecessarily upset (goal 2); at the same time, he may want to explain something to Y(goal 3). These three goals will serve as typical examples of three large categories of goals in discourses.

The goals of the first category will be referred to as *positive* goals. They are characterized by the existence of an event or state that is to be attained, and once this occurs, the subsequent sentences cannot change this fact. The example here is "Breaking the bad news."

The situation may be formally characterized as follows. Let G be a given goal and let $r_G(x)$ be the degree to which the string x satisfies this goal. We assume that the function r_G is defined for all strings x with $f_T(x) \geq a$, that is, for all strings that constitute a discourse to the degree exceeding a certain threshold a.

DEFINITION 4.15   We say that the goal G is of *type* 1, or *positive*, if the following conditions hold:

(a)   If $r_G(x)$ is defined, then $r_G(x) = 0$ or 1.
(b)   If $r_G(x)$ and $r_G(xy)$ are defined, then $r_G(x) = 1$ implies that $r_G(xy) = 1$.

Condition (a) means that goals of type 1 are of nonfuzzy character: they are either completely fulfilled or not fulfilled at all. Condition (b) states that if at a certain stage x of the discourse the goal G, is satisfied, then the same is true regardless of any way y in which the discourse is continued. This is the same as stating that fulfillment of goal G is irreversible.

Returning to the example, suppose that goal G is "to break bad news to X." Condition (a) states that the news in question is such that it cannot be conveyed gradually: either the receiver is totally unaware of it or he knows it in full. Consequently, the degree of attainment of G can be only 0 or 1. Condition (b) means that once the news reaches X, it cannot be taken back, regardless of subsequent parts of the discourse. Naturally, this may be an idealization of the real situations. However, one can argue that (a) and (b) describe reasonably well a certain category of goals.

The second category of goals, referred to as negative, is exemplified by "To avoid frustrating or upsetting Y." Here the situation is, in a sense, opposite to the case of positive goals: there exists a state or event that must be avoided, otherwise the goal will never be reached. In other words, if the distinguished state is actually reached, then the possibility of attaining the goal is lost. Formally, we express it as follows.

DEFINITION 4.16 We say that goal G is of *type* 2, or *negative*, if its satisfies the following conditions:

(a)   If $r_G(x)$ is defined, then $r_G(x) = 0$ or 1.
(b)   If $r_G(x)$ and $r_G(xy)$ are defined, then $r_G(x) = 0$ implies $r_G(xy) = 0$.

The interpretation of conditions (a) and (b) is similar to the one in the case of positive goals. In particular, condition (b) asserts that if the string x is such that the goal G is "forfeited," then the same is true for any subsequent strings y. In other words, once the goal is forfeited, it remains such regardless of all subsequent actions.

Referring again to our main example, goal G may be "Not to upset X." Such a goal would usually be incompatible with the goal "Break bad news to X." The point is, however, that (again in some idealization) the goal may be attained in degrees 0 or 1 only, and in order to attain it, one should avoid certain actions that cause the attainment of the goal impossible.

Finally, we define the third category of goals as the remainder.

DEFINITION 4.17 A goal that is neither of type 1 nor of type 2 will be called of *Type* 3.

Thus, goals of Type 3 are those that do not satisfy either condition (a) of Definitions 4.15 and 4.16 or conditions (b) of both definitions. In other words, a goal will be of type 3 if the degree to which it is satisfied may be neither 0 nor 1 for some strings of sentences. Also, it is of type 3 if this degree is 0 or 1 but may fluctuate.

Goals of type 3 are exemplified by "To explain something to Y." Such goals may be satisfied to some degree that is neither 0 nor 1, and this degree may undergo some changes, both in the positive and in the negative direction (e.g., when a new convincing argument is added to the preceding parts of the discourse, one may expect the goal to be satisfied in a higher degree; when a confusing statement is made, the goal may be thought to be satisfied to a lesser degree).

It is clear that goals of types 1 and 2 impose more structure on the class of all strings that constitute a discourse than goals of type 3. The conditions for goals of types 1 and 2 are similar to those for breaking and fulfilling promises, analyzed by Nowakowska (1973). In particular, under some conditions, the classes of all strings that satisfy goals of types 1 and 2 form context-free languages [for the proof, see Nowakowska (1973); for the definition of the concept of a context-free language, see, e.g., Chomsky (1957) or Ginsburg (1968)].

4.7.2 Goals of Types 1 and 2

Let us start the analysis by discussing goals of type 1, that is, positive goals. Denote by D_G the class of all strings x that satisfy goal G, that is,

$$D_G = \{x : r_G(x) = 1\}. \tag{4.168}$$

Furthermore, let

$$D(a) = \{x : f_T(x) \geq a\}. \tag{4.169}$$

Thus, $D(1)$ is the class of all discourses, that is, the class of all strings such that their termination is an admissible termination moment for a discourse. On the other hand, $D(a)$ is the domain of definition of function r_G. We have therefore the inclusions

$$D_G \subset D(a), \qquad D(1) \subset D(a). \tag{4.170}$$

If the only objective of the discourse were to satisfy the goal G, then its attainability would depend on whether set $D_G \cap D(1)$ were empty. Indeed, any $x \in D_G \cap D(1)$ is an admissible discourse that satisfies G, and since G is of type 1, if it is satisfied at all, it must be satisfied in degree 1.

These considerations did not take into account the specific assumptions about goals of Type 1, in particular condition (b) of Definition 4.15. For any string $x = w_1 w_2 \cdots$ consider the sequence d_n defined by (4.167), and let n_1, $n_2, \ldots$ be successive indices with $d_{n_1} \geq a, d_{n_2} \geq a, \ldots$. Denote $v_1 = w_1 \cdots w_{n_1}$,

$v_2 = w_{n_1+1} \cdots w_{n_2}, \ldots$ so that $x = v_1 v_2 \cdots$. Intuitively, each v_j is a string of sentences such that, after k such strings, the resulting concatenation $v_1 \cdots v_k$ is a discourse admissible in degree at least a. The class of all discourses may now be represented in the form of a tree (see Fig. 4.6). Each branch of the tree represents a string of sentences of form v_i and each node represents a discourse in degree at least a, consisting of the branches leading from the top to this node.

We have here two types of nodal labeling. One labeling represents the degree to which goal G is satisfied, with $\bigcirc$ representing $r_G(x) = 0$ and $\bullet$ representing $r_G(x) = 1$. The second type of labeling corresponds to the degree to which a given branch is a discourse: here only those nodes that have degree equal to 1 are marked with asterisks (i.e., those are admissible termination points in the discourse).

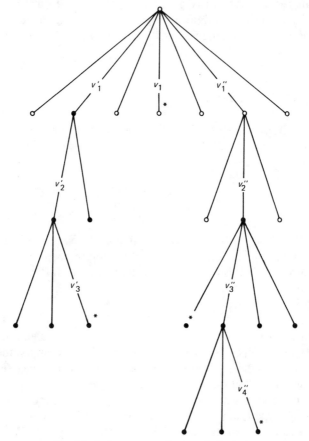

Fig. 4.6. A discourse tree for a goal of type 1.

Assumption (b) of Definition 4.15 means that if a node is labeled ●, then the same is true for all nodes of the subtree starting from this node. Thus, a discourse is a "walk" over a tree, such as is shown in Fig. 4.6, which starts from the top node and descends. At each node, a choice is made of the next sentence or string of sentences. The asterisks mark admissible termination points, that is, discourses that complete a thought, argument, and so on.

The object of the discourse, with G as its only goal, is to continue until reaching the first node, which is labeled ● and also * (i.e., the goal is satisfied, and the node represents an admissible termination of the discourse). Two of such discourses are marked in Fig. 4.6 as $x = v_1' v_2' v_3'$ and $x = v_1'' v_2'' v_3'' v_4''$ (observe that v_1 alone is an admissible discourse, but it does not satisfy the goal G). It is clear from the figure that each such discourse x [i.e., every element of $D_G \cap D(1)$] may be partitioned into three parts, $z_1(x)$, $z_2(x)$, and $z_3(x)$: the initial part $z_1(x)$ leading to the last node labeled ○, the middle part $z_2(x)$ leading from the last node marked ○ to the first node marked ●, and the remainder part $z_3(x)$. In the string $x = v_1'' v_2'' v_3'' v_4''$ we have $z_1(x) = v_1''$, $z_2(x) = v_2''$, and $z_3(x) = v_3'' v_4''$. In the string $x = v_1' v_2' v_3'$ we have $z_1(x) = \varepsilon$ (empty string), $z_2(x) = v_1'$, and $z_3(x) = v_2' v_3'$.

Let us denote

$$C = \{(u, v) : x \in D_G \cap D(1) \text{ with } z_1(x) = u, z_2(x) = v\}. \qquad (4.171)$$

We may now introduce the following.

DEFINITION 4.18   A goal G of type 1 will be called *context-free* if $C = A \times B$ for some sets A, B; otherwise, G will be called *context-dependent*.

Intuitively, C is the class of all pairs consisting of an initial part of the discourse and the part that is responsible for satisfying goal G. If the goal is context-free, then there exists a set A of initial parts and a set B of parts responsible for G such that any element of A may be combined with any element of B. In other words, if a goal is context-free, then in order to attain it, it suffices to add to the initial part of the discourse *any* string from B. The crucial point is that there are no semantic constraints joining elements from A and B in the sense that any combination of them is acceptable.

Goals of type 2 have a structure that is, in many respects, analogous to that of goals of type 1. To illustrate this, let us return to Fig. 4.6, interpreting ○ as the end of a string that satisfies G and ● as the end of a string that does not satisfy G. Condition (b) of Definition 4.16 asserts again that a subtree marked with a vertex ● must have all nodes marked ● (once the goal is forfeited, it remains forfeited forever). The object is now to reach a node that is marked ○ and also marked with an asterisk (e.g., string v_1 satisfies this condition).

For the analysis, consider the class

$$D_G' = \{x : r_G(x) = 0\}, \qquad (4.172)$$

that is, a class of all strings that do not satisfy goal G of type 2. In each string $x \in D'_G$ we distinguish its parts $z_1(x)$, $z_2(x)$, and $z_3(x)$ as before, where $z_1(x)$ is the longest initial part with $r_G[z_1(x)] = 1$, $z_2(x)$ is the shortest part such that $r_G[z_1(x)z_2(x)] = 0$, and $z_3(x)$ is the remainder. Let

$$B = \{u : \exists x \in D'_G \text{ with } z_2(x) = u\}. \tag{4.173}$$

Thus B is the class of all those strings that are responsible for the goal G to become forfeited, that is, impossible to attain.

DEFINITION 4.19   A goal G of type 2 is called *context-free* if whenever $x = v_1 u v_2$ for some v_1, v_2 and $u \in B$, then $r_G(x) = 0$.

This means that, if a discourse contains a fragment from set B, then it cannot satisfy the goal.

Again, this definition appears to capture the intuition carried by the term "context-free": it means that any element of B combined with any preceding string makes attainment of the goal impossible.

4.7.3   The Case of Multiple Goals

Typically, a discourse may have several goals. These goals may then be grouped into three classes, depending on their types. In this section, we shall consider the case of more than one goal of types 1 and 2. Without loss of generality, we restrict the analysis to such cases when there are two goals G_1 and G_2, both of type 1, both of type 2, or one of type 1 and one of type 2.

Assume first that G_1 and G_2 are both of type 1. Each of them is characterized by the set of pairs of form (4.171), say, C_1 and C_2. First, we introduce the following definition.

DEFINITION 4.20   We say that G_1 is a *prerequisite* for G_2, to be denoted $G_1 \prec G_2$, if whenever $(u, v) \in C_2$, then there exist $(u', v') \in C_1$ and w such that $u = u'v'w$.

This condition simply means that G_2 may be attained only in a situation when G_1 has already been attained. Obviously, if $G_1 \prec G_2$ and $G_2 \prec G_3$, then $G_1 \prec G_3$; that is, the relation $\prec$ is transitive.

DEFINITION 4.21   If neither $G_1 \prec G_2$ nor $G_2 \prec G_1$, we say that G_1 and G_2 are *independent*.

Thus, when two goals are independent, they may be attained simultaneously; also attaining one of them may precede attaining the other.

In the case when both G_1 and G_2 are context-free, with $C_1 = A_1 \times B_1$, $C_2 = A_2 \times B_2$, the attainment of both G_1 and G_2 requires one string from B_1 and one string from B_2. Let

$$Q = \{u : u = v_1 w v_2 w' \text{ with } v_1 \in B_1, v_2 \in B_2 \text{ or } v_1 \in B_2, v_2 \in B_1\}. \quad (4.174)$$

Then

$$D_{G_1 \& G_2} = \{x : x = yu \text{ with } u \in Q\}. \quad (4.175)$$

Consider now two goals of type 2, with sets B_1 and B_2 defined by (4.173). Then the joint goal $G_1 \& G_2$ is not attained if any string from $B_1 \cup B_2$ appears. It follows that to attain $G_1 \& G_2$ one must avoid strings from $B_1 \cup B_2$.

Similarly, if G_1 is a context-free goal of type 1 and G_2 is a context-free goal of type 2, then to attain $G_1 \& G_2$ one must have a string from B_1 and avoid all strings from B_2.

One may now suggest the following algebraic approach to the problem of composite goals. Suppose that $G_1, \ldots, G_n$ are some goals of type 1 and $G'_1, \ldots, G'_m$ are some goals of type 2. Let $f(x_1, \ldots, x_n, y_1, \ldots, y_m)$ be a propositional function of $n + m$ variables, involving only the functors of conjunction and disjunction. Then $G = f(G_1, \ldots, G_n, G'_1, \ldots, G'_m)$ may be regarded as a composite goal. For example, if $f(x_1, \ldots, x_n, y_1, \ldots, y_m) = (x_1 \vee \cdots \vee x_n) \& (y_1 \& \cdots \& y_m)$, then G is the goal "attain at least one among the goals G_i and avoid all goals G'_j." Clearly, the class of all composite goals that may be defined in this way by a suitable choice of function f is very large and covers most cases of interest.

Let $D_{G_i}, i = 1, \ldots, n, D_{G'_j}, j = 1, \ldots, m$ be the sets of all strings that constitute discourses and attain the respective goals. Then, to attain the composite goal $G = f(G_1, \ldots, G_n, G'_1, \ldots, G'_m)$ it is necessary and sufficient [see Nowakowska (1976b)] that the discourse x belongs to the set $f(D_{G_1}, \ldots, D_{G_n}, D_{G'_1}, \ldots, D_{G'_m})$, where the latter set is obtained by replacing in the function f the functors of conjunction and disjunction by the operations of intersection and union.

Since now we have some information about the form of the discourses that satisfy goals of types 1 and 2 (at least for context-free goals), we may express the above requirement for attaining the composite goals as follows. Let $I = \{1, \ldots, n\}$ and $J = \{1, \ldots, m\}$. The composite goal $G = f(G_1, \ldots, G_n, G'_1, \ldots, G'_m)$ may be expressed in the form of a disjunction of conjunctions of the form

$$\bigcap_{i \in I'} G_i \& \bigcap_{j \in J'} G'_j, \quad I' \subset I, \quad J' \subset J. \quad (4.176)$$

For instance, if $f(x_1, \ldots, x_n, y_1, \ldots, y_m) = (x_1 \vee \cdots \vee x_n) \& (y_1 \& \cdots \& y_m)$, then sets (4.176) are of the form $x_i \& y_1 \& \cdots \& y_m$, so that sets I' are singletons and $J = J$.

We have then the following theorem.

THEOREM 4.15 *Suppose that all goals G_i and G'_j are context-free, and let B_i, B'_j be the corresponding sets defined by (4.171) and (4.173). Let $G = f(G_1, \ldots, G_n, G'_1, \ldots, G'_m)$ be a composite goal representable as*

$$G = \bigcup_Q \left[\bigcap_{i \in I'} G_i \ \& \ \bigcap_{j \in J} G'_j \right], \tag{4.177}$$

where the union is extended over some class Q of pairs of subsets $I' \subset I$, $J' \subset J$. Then $x \in D(1)$ is discourse satisfying the composite goal G if and only if for some $(I', J') \in Q$ the following condition hold:

(a) $(\forall i \in I'): x = v_1 u v_2$ *for some v_1, v_2 and $u \in B_i$;*
(b) $(\forall j \in J')(\forall v_1, v_2): [x = v_1 u v_2 \Rightarrow u \notin B'_j]$.

To explain the intuitive meaning of this theorem, observe the following. A composite goal G of the form considered can be split into a disjunction of ways of attaining it. For example, if G is described as "Attain at least two among G_1, G_2, and G_3 and also avoid G_4," then it may be attained in ways such as $G_1 \ \& \ G_2 \ \& -G_4$ or $G_1 \ \& \ G_3 \ \& -G_4$.

Now, each of the terms of the disjunction is a conjunction of goals of types 1 and 2. If a string x is to attain such a conjunction, it must contain a substring which is in every set B_i corresponding to goals of type 1 (which will guarantee attaining G_i in the case of context-free goals) and should not contain any substring in set B'_I corresponding to goals of type 2 (so as not to forfeit the possibility of attaining goals of type 2).

4.7.4 Goals of Type 3

As opposed to goals of types 1 and 2, the goals of type 3 do not impose too much of a structure on the set of discourses satisfying these goals. This is quite clear, because the attainment of the goal may be graded. For instance, in spoken discourses, the degree to which the goal is attained depends not only on the string uttered but also on the reaction of the person who listens. Consequently, it may not be possible to characterize those strings of sentences that satisfy the goal in a given degree.

For example, consider a goal such as "Explain a certain phenomenon to X." Obviously, the same string of sequences may lead to attaining the goal (understanding of the issue by X) for some receivers X and may be futile in the case of other receivers.

Nevertheless, it is still possible to use some elements of the algebraic approach to composite goals. Thus, let $G''_1, \ldots, G''_k$ be a class of goals of type 3 and let as before, $f(x_1, \ldots, x_k)$ be a function of n variables involving only the functors of conjunction and disjunction used for generating a composite goal

$G = f(G_1'', \ldots, G_k'')$. Let us write

$$G = \bigcup_{I' \in Q} \bigcap_{i \in I'} G_i'', \qquad (4.178)$$

where Q is some class of subsets of $I = \{1, \ldots, k\}$. Then the degree to which a discourse x satisfies a particular term in G equals $\min_{i \in I'} r_{G_i''}(x)$.

Consequently, x satisfying goal G is the degree

$$\max_{I' \in Q} \min_{i \in I'} r_{G_i''}(x), \qquad (4.179)$$

and the problem lies in finding x to maximize expression (4.179) subject to the constraints that $x \in D(1)$, that is, that x is an admissible discourse and that x satisfies the goals of types 1 and 2.

Naturally, function $r_{G_i''}(x)$, and consequently criterion (4.179), is seldom defined with sufficient precision so as to enable one to use the analytical techniques of optimization. Nevertheless, once functions $r_G(x)$ are defined, one can attempt to maximize (4.179) numerically. Here we have a different situation for a written discourse and for a spoken discourse. Roughly, the difference lies in the fact that in the latter the parts that are already uttered cannot be altered, while a text can be altered at will with "returns" to the initial parts.

In fact, the process of writing and rewriting a text may be regarded as an attempt to maximize a criterion of form (4.179) with some intuitive feelings about the component functions r_G.

As opposed to that, in the case of spoken discourses, the decisions have to made sequentially. This involves considering "partial" situations, that is, when fragment of the discourse has already been uttered, and the optimum of (4.179) is to be found in the class of all discourses with a given beginning.

APPENDIX

PROOF OF THEOREM 4.1

First, observe that the vector $T^*(x)$ is well defined since class $T(x)$ is nonempty (as vector 1 belongs to it). Next, each description in $T(x)$ satisfies $V_i \neq \varnothing$ for every i, and the class is closed under intersections, so that $V_i' \cap V_i''$ is also nonempty.

PROOF OF THEOREM 4.10

Let us look for a martingale Y_n of the form

$$Y_n = a_n Z_n'' + b_n. \qquad (A.1)$$

Using formula (4.114) we obtain

$$E[Y_{n+1} \mid Y_n] = E[Y_{n+1} \mid Z_n''] = a_{n+1}\left(1 + \frac{N-1}{N}Z_n''\right) + b_{n+1}, \quad \text{(A.2)}$$

which must also be equal to $a_n Z_n'' + b_n$. Comparing the coefficients at Z_n'' we obtain

$$a_{n+1}\frac{N-1}{N} = a_n. \quad \text{(A.3)}$$

Putting $a_0 = 1$ we obtain, by simple induction,

$$a_n = \left(\frac{N}{N-1}\right)^n. \quad \text{(A.4)}$$

We must also have $a_{n+1} + b_{n+1} = b_n$, and putting $b_0 = 0$, we have

$$b_n = -(a_1 + \cdots + a_n), \quad \text{(A.5)}$$

which yields

$$b_n = -N\left[\left(\frac{N}{N-1}\right)^n - 1\right]. \quad \text{(A.6)}$$

Consequently, the martingale Y_n becomes

$$Y_n = \left(\frac{N}{N-1}\right)^n Z_n'' - N\left[\left(\frac{N}{N-1}\right)^n - 1\right]. \quad \text{(A.7)}$$

We check directly that $E(Y_1) = 0$, which yields $E(Y_n) = 0$, and using formula (A.7) we obtain the theorem.

PROOF OF THEOREM 4.11

According to Postulate 4.8 we have

$$P(T_i > t) = \exp\left[-\int_0^t du/f_i(u)\right]$$

$$= \exp\left[-\int_0^t \frac{1}{f_i}e^{c_i s}\,ds\right] = \exp\left[-\frac{1}{f_i c_i}(e^{c_i t} - 1)\right].$$

Differentiating, we obtain $h_i(t) = -(d/dt)P(T_i > t)$. $\qquad$ (A.8)

PROOF OF THEOREM 4.12

For given $T_i = t$, the transition from C_i to C_j occurs if at time t we have $f_j + X_{ij} > f_k + X_{ik}$ for every $k \neq i, j$, where $X_{ij} = X_{ij}(0, t)$ and $X_{ik} = X_{ik}(0, t)$.

We have $P(X_{ij} = r) = (b_{ij}t)^r e^{-b_{ij}t}/r!$, and given $X_{ij} = r$, the transition to C_j occurs if $X_{ik} < f_j + r - f_k$ for all $k \neq i,j$. The latter event has probability equal to the product of terms

$$P(X_{ik} < r + f_j - f_k) = \sum_{n=0}^{r+f_j-f_k} (b_{ik}t)^n e^{-b_{ik}t}/n!. \tag{A.9}$$

Integrating with respect to the density $h_i(t)$ of T_i we complete the proof of the theorem.

PROOF OF THEOREM 4.14

By maximality of K' and K'', the set $K' \cup K''$ is not consistent, so that $\min_{i \in K' \cup K''} B_i(x) < 1$ for all $x \in X$. If $x \in C_{K'}$, then $\min_{i \in K'} B_i(x) = 1$, so that we must have $\min_{i \in K''} B_i(x) < 1$, which means that $x \notin C_{K''}$. This completes the proof.

5 MEMORY AND PERCEPTION: SOME NEW MODELS

5.1 INTRODUCTION

It may be argued that there exists a tight interrelation between the mechanisms of memory and those of perception. This chapter presents some models (in addition to models treating separate aspects of these phenomena) that connect memory with perception, that is, they connect the character of memory processes with the way in which the information to be stored is perceived.

Section 5.2, however, starts with a "pure" memory model, that is, a model that does not utilize any assumptions about the structure of the stimulus. Here the main issue lies in an reconciling two facts:

1.   that the duration of memory storage (i.e., the process of forgetting) is to a large extent random and
2.   that the subject may control one's memory, at least to some degree.

The models suggested in Section 5.2 are based on the concept of metamemory, which controls memory by means of some internal stimulation, called internal recalls. The latter result in "copying" the information and, hence, increasing the probability of recall by simply increasing the number of copies.

Actually, two models are analyzed: one in which an internal recall causes an increase of one in the number of copies, and a second in which an internal recall causes a doubling of the number of copies. Earlier versions of these models were introduced for the first time at the Conference of Cognition and Memory in Berlin in 1978 [see Nowakowska (1980b, 1981b)].

The cognitive importance of this model lies in the fact that it analyzes the statistical interrelations between actions of various memory cells (the term "cell" need not be treated literally: it is meant here as a system of cells, interrelated in some specific way, designed to store some items of information). More precisely, it is assumed that the destruction (forgetting) of information stored in a given memory cell in a given unit of time depends on the state of some other memory cells in the sense that loss of information in one cell enhances the probability of loss in some other cells. In short, the process of forgetting is "self-accelerating."

In Section 5.3, the model of memory with internal recalls is applied to the process of remembering sentences. Here the internal recalls are not induced by conscious effort of recalling, with the intended purpose "to remember better at some later time," but by semantic interrelations between some words. This means that the stimulus, in the form of a consecutive word of a sentence (whether heard or read) may trigger recalling (hence "copying") some of the preceding words. In consequence, some words of the sentence are remembered better than others. The simulated data agree here with the observed phenomenon of a tendency to better recall the initial and terminal words of a sentence.

Section 5.4 concerns some elements of a new theory of perception, which assumes an event-representation of the perceived object, connected with the physiological properties of the eye, as well as the perceptual constructive work of the eye.

The model introduces a unit of conscious perception, called a glance. Roughly, a glance is a change of the focus of the eye, followed by a period of fine movements in the domain of the new focal point. A glance may be connected with the jumping movement of the eye or may be related, if necessary, with head and body movement.

A glance, naturally, is a fuzzy unit. It is distinguished from fine eye movements or saccadic eye movements by a conscious component: one knows that one glances at a particular point. In other words, the glance involves both the jumping and fine eye movements, as well as the awareness of a conscious inspection of the object. More precisely, in a glance one may distinguish the point at which the eye "touches" the object (focal point) and its fuzzy neighborhood. In addition, the head and body movements allow exploration of the spatial properties of the object.

This process of conscious exploration by glances should be distinguished from loose and spontaneous passive glances over the object. In the process of perception, the subject makes a sequence of glances, with various combinations of repetitions, thus forming some order of inspection. In other words, even for a stable configuration of objects, the subject generates a dynamic system of events, due to the process of cognition; he remembers what he saw earlier and what he saw later. Moreover, he has a feeling for the amount of perceptual work invested in the construction of knowledge about the object.

In the case of changing situations, the perceiver generates events on events. More precisely, for a changing object and various moments, the perceiver generates (by glancing) an event-representation of the object, retained for some time in memory. From these event copies of the object (the first-order representation, so to speak), the subject generates a second-order representation, so that the perception process generates events on events.

Also, one may distinguish another type of event generation, namely that which occurs through mental representations over mental events.

The suggested perception theory will consist of a series of interrelated models, each dealing with specific perceptual mechanisms involved, namely, the internal structure of a glance; the structure of the process of successive glances; and the structure of the process induced by successive glances.

As regards the internal structure of a glance, it is assumed that the eye performs some fine movements, centered as a focal point. These fine movements cause the corresponding fine movements of the image on the retina, thus leading to a sharpening of the contours.

Here the model will concern those aspects of the process that seem to be relevant for explanation of some visual illusions, namely the "return" process: the fine eye movements themselves are assumed to constitute the so-called Ornstein–Uhlenbeck process [see Feller (1968)].

During the fine eye movements centered at some point, the image of some figure on the retina performs a movement, consecutively covering and uncovering any fixed point close to the boundary of the figure, so that the figure "returns" to this point from time to time. Naturally, the frequency of returns and the other characteristics of this process depend on the location of the point under consideration with respect to the figure. In short, one has many interrelated processes, one for each of the points close to the boundary of the figure.

It turns out that the properties of these processes offer a possible explanation of the Müller–Lyer illusion. In explaining the mechanism of illusions, it will be assumed that on a relatively low level of cognition there appears some specific type of "modeling" by the organism. The illusion processes are proposed as examples of such modeling. The explanation of illusion will be based on the notion of competing perceptual systems (basic and contextual) giving different evaluations of some observed values of attributes. It is postulated that there exists a "constructivistic" resultant system that gives the optimal solution for diverging and conflicting values. [For a review of different approaches and explanations of visual illusions, see, e.g., Eijkman *et al.* (1981) and also Lee (1981), Caelli (1981), or Ullmann (1979)].

It should be clear that for objects of more complex nature than that considered in illusions the distortions of perception are more complex and more difficult to analyze. This, however, will not be considered here; instead, the main emphasis will be put on modeling the approaches to perceptual mechanisms.

Returning to the main issue of the suggested approach, namely partial controllability of the perception process, which is understood as the conscious component in the placement of glances, the jumping eye movements allow the economy of perceptual work. This economy may be achieved under some additional constraints; it should satisfy the criterion of semantic continuity. For instance, the eye and head movements cannot, in general, follow the path of a tennis ball. There exists, however, sufficient supplementary knowledge of the situation, providing semantic continuity and smoothness of the situation, and thus its understanding.

There are four, apparently most important, perceptual mechanisms involved here. First is the changes of pre-events into events, where an event is a result of a complex chain of neurological occurrences that originate with the image of the object falling on the retina and terminate with some information about the object being stored in the memory, from which it may be recalled at will. These events form an event-representation of the object. The model of forming such representations (in the context of remembering the temporal order of events) was presented in Chapter 1. Second is the mechanism of attraction, sketched in the section on texts to describe the process of changes of topics and developed further in this chapter to account for shifts in focal points of consecutive glances in an unrestrained "free" eye movements. Third is the mechanisms of utilization of the prior knowledge of the object; this mechanism shows how knowledge about the object determines the optimal path of inspection, that is, optimal sequence of glances. Finally, we have the mechanism of transportation, which plays the crucial role in comparisons, hence in constructing the "raw data" about the object. This mechanism, for the simpler case of comparing durations of stimuli, was presented in Chapter 1; here it will be extended to cover the effects of the locations of stimuli to be compared. This model leads in a natural way to certain modifications concerning both the memory and perception of some stimuli and the mental operations on them (Section 5.4).

Mixtures of such mechanisms as attractiveness, purposeful inspection, and transportation determine various perceptual pressures and conflicts. The notion of conflict is basic in the suggested theory; it allows us to analyze perceptual distortions, which in the simplest form appear as optimal solutions of conflicts (in optical illusions).

At this time it is worthwhile to introduce some informal intuitions related with various parts of the theory and show how they tie together.

Model of Building Event-Representations of the Object: Role of Memory in Generating Events from Pre-Events

The first component of the general model, as mentioned, was introduced in Chapter 1 on the occasion of temporal orders of events. Actually, this model concerns building event-representation of objects and explores the role of memory in this process. The most crucial item here is the mechanism of forming sequences of pre-events, which are simply the candidates for the events to be remembered. The candidate for an event becomes actually an event (i.e., becomes stored in memory) if it is preceded sufficiently recently by another pre-event of an appropriate type. The problem lies in building a model to describe the frequency of events, their types, and so on, that is, to describe the statistical features of what is being perceived, in the sense of storing the material to be processed later. It was shown in Chapter 1 that one may derive the probability distribution of the temporal spacings between consecutive events and that this distribution is asymptotically exponential, so that the storage times of events form an (approximately) Poisson process.

Model of Attraction Mechanism

The second component of the model concerns the attraction mechanism. To explain the exploratory eye movements over the object, the attraction function is introduced, representing the changes of attractiveness of various domains of the focal points. This function determines the eye movements (in much the same way as in Chapter 4 the attraction function described the changes of topic in a text); that is, the time of stay in a domain of a given focal point and the probability of passing to another domain. It is assumed that the attraction of the inspected domain decreases, while the attractions of the domains not inspected increase, with the rates depending possibly on the proximity to the inspected domain. The model postulates that the decision to terminate a glance concentrated at some focal point and start a glance concentrated at some other focal point is based on resolving a "conflict" between attractions for various focal points. More specifically, each focal point of the picture is characterized by its attraction force, which either increases or decreases, depending on which domain is actually inspected. Metaphorically, and with great simplification, the situation may be compared to watching TV and switching from channel to channel. When a channel with some interesting program (e.g., a basketball game) is not watched, the curiosity about the running score increases. This creates a desire to switch to that channel. However, as soon as one learns the score, the attraction diminishes, and one is tempted to turn to some other channel.

In general, we have here a continuous conflict which is resolved by changing the focal points of glances. According to this model, the process of consecutive glances is governed by some external forces (attractions to various domains).

MODEL OF OPTIMAL GLANCE PATH

On another extreme (as opposed to purely random movements of the eye being attracted to various domains), one can consider the glance process as controllable and designed to attain some specific goal, such as recognition and identification. In this case, the sequence of consecutive glances is chosen to optimize some criterion, such as recognition time. Here the model is based on the notion of recognition sets, and in particular minimal recognition sets (some aspects of this model have been presented in Chapter 3, when dealing with the problems of recognition of meanings of multimedial units). Human experience allows us to evaluate for its recognition the importance (weights) of fragments of the picture, or more generally, for various occasions and goals, and to determine some invariants of weights of fragments for classes of goals and objects, and also their transformations.

In the suggested model, one can formalize the problem to an extent that enables one to apply the Bellman equation to determine the optimal path of inspection of the figure.

As already mentioned, it may be conjectured that the actual glance process is a mixture of the above two: purely random walk governed by varying attractions and purely purposeful inspection governed by the intention to attain some specific goal.

MODEL OF TRANSPORTATION MECHANISM

Finally, as regards the mechanisms of transportation, the glance process may be assumed to induce the process of comparisons. Such comparisons require "transportation" of a fragment to the location of another; on the other hand, the results of these comparisons may be regarded as pre-events. It may be postulated that recognition, identification, and so on, require collecting "raw data" about the relational structure of the perceived object. Such raw data must involve, among others, the results of comparisons of values of attributes of various fragments. These comparisons, in turn, require that a glance at one point of the figure involve also a "transportation" of the image of some other fragment of the figure to a new location. Naturally, such transportations, or "translation," lead to a fuzzification and, hence, to some loss of precision in comparisons.

Under appropriate assumptions (similar to those introduced in Chapter 1 on the occasion of comparison of the duration of two stimuli), one may derive the formulas for the probabilities of errors, thus obtaining a clue to the parameters of the model. Also, which is more important, these formulas provide means for testing some intriguing hypotheses [see, e.g., Townsend and Landon (1983)] about parallel versus serial processing.

5.2 MEMORY WITH EVENT-TIME HORIZON

The main goal of this section will be to explain the fact that people may control (at least partially) the time of remembering, that is, the duration of time for which they remember a given thing.

This time is partially imposed by the temporal structure of events ("I should remember X until Y happens"). In particular, such an event Y may be simply the passage of a specific amount of time ("I ought to remember X for the next hour").

The internal control of memory will be identified with a tape of internal instructions, parallel to the memory input, and will be called *metamemory*. This determines the strength, direction, and horizon of memory. It is postulated that metamemory has primarily a linguistic character. It contains linguistic expressions pertaining to the strength with which a person wants to remember an event. The set of metamemory instructions is of a fuzzy character in the sense that with each instruction there is associated a set of some internal actions, each leading to a fuzzy set of outcomes. The event-time horizon set by metamemory is selected relative to the structure and organization of the event-space of a given person. In other words, the horizons of events in memory are implied by orders and plans imposed on events.

Specifically, in the model below the metamemory will cause a number of occurrences of *internal recalls* (to be abbreviated as IRCL) in specific memory compartments, each consisting of a number of memory units. At each IRCL the contents of memory units are copied down, so that the number of memory units containing a given item of information increases. At the same time, however, the memory units are subject to a risk of loss of their content. Such losses are assumed to occur at random moments.

Metaphorically, the operation of the model may be described as follows. Imagine a person who records the telephone numbers he needs in notebooks. For simplicity, let us idealize the situation by assuming that each notebook may contain just one phone number (plus identifying information, such as the name of the phone's owner.

The notebooks containing numbers become lost at a certain rate, and if all notebooks containing a given phone number are lost, the phone number itself is lost and is not recoverable. However, there is a supply of empty notebooks, and to protect himself against the possibility of losing all notebooks containing a given phone number, the person adopts a strategy of copying it into blank notebooks. Such a copying occurs from time to time and is aimed at keeping the number of notebooks containing a given phone number at a level that makes it unlikely that all of them become lost before the event that constitutes the horizon. The essential point here is that the process of losing the notebooks (forgetting) is random and beyond the control of the person in question; he can only control the process of "remembering" the numbers by continually copying them down.

Roughly, the above metaphorical description is the memory model to be analyzed in this section. Actually, two models will be suggested; in model 1 at each IRCL one unit is copied down, so that the number of memory units that contain the given information increases by one. In model 2 all memory units are copied down, so that the number of memory units with a given information doubles. These two represent, in a sense, the "extremal" cases of mechanisms of remembering for various classes of stimuli. It is conjectured that there exist biochemical mechanisms of stimulation of memory cells that may be responsible for the rate of copying of information and that these mechanisms underlying the strength of memory are related to the valuation of importance of the material to be remembered. Usually such a high valuation is connected with high emotional activation.

Naturally, in reality the information stored in a set of memory units is highly structured, so that loss in one memory unit may be more "damaging" than loss in another memory unit. Also the outside events, which serve as horizons for some memory compartments, may trigger IRCLs in some other memory compartments. At the beginning, however, considerations will concern a simple situation of a single memory compartment consisting of a number of units assigned by metamemory for storing and copying of one item of information.

At the end of this section, a certain heuristic dynamic model will be sketched with such concepts as multidimensional units and languages of communication actions and on the calculus of meanings based on algebras of goals and means. In this framework, metamemory will be treated as a certain subspace in the cognitive and motivational space, supplying modal frames over some motivational frames ("I want X," "I ought to remember that I want X," etc.).

However, in later parts of this section, a model will be presented that accounts to some extent for the structural properties of memory units and their interrelations. It will be assumed that loss in one memory unit changes the risk of loss in other units, so that the resulting process of total loss is "self-accelerating."

5.2.1   Assumptions of the Model

We shall assume that the memory (or, more precisely, that part of memory being modeled) forms a system

$$\langle M, C_1, C_2, \ldots \rangle \tag{5.1}$$

consisting of metamemory M and memory compartments $C_1, C_2, \ldots$. In turn, each C_i is a system of the form

$$C_i = \langle u_{i1}, u_{i2}, \ldots \rangle, \tag{5.2}$$

where u_{ij} is a function of time, describing the state of jth memory unit of ith compartment C_i at a given time. These units will be denoted by U_{ij}.

The basic interpretation is such that metamemory M decides about the occurrences of IRCLs in particular compartments. Each C_i is designed to store one item of information, say, I_i, perhaps in multiple copies, one copy in each of the units.

Accordingly, one may assume that each u_{ij} has only values 1 and 0, such that

$$u_{ij}(t) = \begin{cases} 1 & \text{if at time } t \text{ the unit } U_{ij} \text{ contains } I_i, \\ 0 & \text{otherwise.} \end{cases}$$

Observe that each unit of C_i contains either no information or the same information I_i. Consequently, what matters is only the number of units that contain I_i, and this justifies the following assumption.

ASSUMPTION 5.1   (Operation of C_i as a whole)   *The loss of I_i in C_i occurs if and only if all units lose I_i, that is,*

$$I_i \text{ is lost} \qquad \textit{iff} \qquad \sum_j u_{ij}(t) = 0. \tag{5.3}$$

Indeed, since each u_{ij} is either zero or one, the sum in condition (5.3) is simply equals to the number of u_{ij} equal to 1, that is, the number of units of C_i that contain information I_i.

The subsequent assumptions will concern the loss in particular units and also the mechanisms of "enhancing" the chances of remembering the information; the latter will be accomplished by increasing the number of units that store the information (number of copies).

ASSUMPTION 5.2   (Operation of individual units)   *Each unit U_{ij} is subject to the same constant risk of loss c, so that the probability that information I_i stored in a given unit at time $t = 0$ will still be present at time t is e^{-ct}.*

Thus if T denotes the duration of storage time in a given unit, then T has the probability distribution

$$P(T \le t) = 1 - e^{-ct}, \tag{5.4}$$

and $1/c$ is the average storage time in a unit.

The exponential distribution (5.4) reflects the property, mentioned in the introduction to this section, that individual memory units are not controllable and also, in a sense, "forget their past": no matter how long a given information was stored in a given memory unit, the probability that it will be lost during the next time interval of some length t is $1 - e^{-ct}$.

The third assumption concerns the mutual interrelations between the events in separate cells. We begin with the simplest of such assumptions, to be somewhat weakened in the later parts of this section.

ASSUMPTION 5.3 (Independence) *Transitions of units from state* 1 *to state* 0 *are independent.*

It is clear that the state of the memory compartment C_i at time t depends only on the number of units in state 1. Accordingly, we put

$$X_i(t) = \text{number of units in state 1 in } C_i \text{ at time } t. \tag{5.5}$$

We now impose the next assumption.

ASSUMPTION 5.4 (Initial condition)

$$X_i(0) = 1. \tag{5.6}$$

In the following we shall drop the subscript i: the considerations will concern an arbitrary but fixed memory compartment C_i.

5.2.2 Internal Recalls

We assume that forgetting is irreversible, that is, state $X = 0$ is absorbing. This means that, if at some time t we have $X(t) = 0$, then $X(t + t') = 0$ for all $t' \ge 0$. On the other hand, if $X(t)$ is positive at some t, then it is possible to increase it by internal recalls (in the example with copying down the phone numbers, an internal recall is just such a copy production). The fact that state $X = 0$ is absorbing means simply that when all notebooks with a given phone number are lost, one cannot make a copy.

Intuitively, at the time of an IRCL, the memory units that are in state 1 are copied down, in the sense of transfer of their content to other cells. Naturally, one may make various assumptions, of which two most natural and plausible will be considered. In what will be called Model 1, at the time of IRCL the number of units in state 1 is increased by one. On the other hand, in Model 2, the number of units in state 1 is doubled, which means that every unit in state is copied.

In terms of the metaphoric example, in Model 1, the person copies (at times of IRCL) just one of the notebooks, transferring its content to a blank notebook. In Model 2, he copies all the notebooks that contain a given number, so that the number of notebooks with a given number increases by factor 2.

We shall formulate these assumptions as follows.

ASSUMPTION 5.5a (Model 1) *Suppose that an IRCL occurs at time t, when the number of units in state 1 is $X(t)$. If $X(t) = 0$, then $X(s) = 0$ for all $s \geq t$. If $X(t) > 0$, then the value $X(t)$ increases to $X(t + 0) = X(t) + 1$.*

Alternatively, for Model 2 we postulate the following.

ASSUMPTION 5.5b (Model 2) *Suppose that an IRCL occurs at time t. Then the value $X(t)$ changes to $X(t + 0) = 2X(t)$.*

Let us observe that in Assumption 5.5b we do not need to separate the case $X(t) = 0$ and $X(t) > 0$: doubling the value $X(t) = 0$ again yields value 0.

5.2.3 Analysis of the Models

The main object of the analysis will be the probability that the information stored at time $t = 0$ will still be present in memory at the target time T if IRCLs occur at times

$$0 \leq t_1 \leq t_2 \leq \cdots \leq t_N < T. \tag{5.7}$$

Thus, we are interested in probability

$$P[X(T) > 0 \,|\, X(0) = 1, \text{IRCLs occur at times } t_1, \ldots, t_N]. \tag{5.8}$$

From (5.7) it may be seen that we also allow multiple IRCLs, that is, several IRCLs occurring at the same time, in particular at time $t = 0$. However, an IRCL at target time T would have no effect on whether $X(T)$ is positive. Thus, we assume that the last IRCL must occur strictly prior to the target time T.

It is clear that the knowledge of probability (5.8) is of crucial importance for our analysis, since it allows the solution of the optimization problem: at which times one should place the IRCLs so as to maximize the probability that the information will not be forgotten at the target time T.

In the following, $X(t_n + 0)$ will denote the number of units with the given information immediately after the IRCL at time t_n.

Since the only element under the subject's control are the times of IRCLs, we must calculate the probabilities of various transitions that may occur during the periods that are beyond control, that is, periods between the consecutive IRCLs. The final result will then be "composed" of these transitions.

Let

$$P_{ij}(t_n, t_{n+1}) = P[X(t_{n+1} + 0) = j \mid X(t_n + 0) = i] \tag{5.9}$$

be the transition probability from state i at the time immediately following the IRCL at t_n and the time immediately following the IRCL at time t_{n+1}. We have, first,

$$P_{0j}(t_n, t_{n+1}) = \begin{cases} 1 & \text{if } j = 0, \\ 0 & \text{if } j \neq 0. \end{cases} \tag{5.10}$$

This condition simply means that the state $j = 0$ is absorbing: if $X(t_n + 0) = 0$, that is, the information is absent at time t_n, then $X(t_{n+1} + 0) = 0$.

Denote for simplicity

$$p = \exp^{[-c(t_{n+1} - t_n)]}, \tag{5.11}$$

so that by Assumption 5.2, p is the probability that a unit in state 1 at time t_n is still at state 1 at time t_{n+1}.

Let us begin with the analysis of probabilities of the form (5.9) for Model 1. Assume that $i > 0$, that is, that at the time immediately following t_n there are exactly i units in state 1. We then have

$$P_{ij}(t_n, t_{n+1}) = 0 \qquad \text{for } j > i + 1. \tag{5.12}$$

This condition expresses the simple fact that, if at time t_n there are exactly i units in state 1, then the number of units in state 1 at the time following the next IRCL (at t_{n+1}) can be at most $i + 1$. Indeed, some units may lose their content before t_{n+1}, and at the time of the IRCL the number of copies is increased by 1 (if there is at least one unit that did not lose its content; otherwise the number of units in state 1 is 0 and remains 0).

Thus, at best no unit loses its content, and then the number of units in state 1 at the time immediately following t_{n+1} is $i + 1$.

We also have

$$P_{i1}(t_n, t_{n+1}) = 0. \tag{5.13}$$

This condition expresses the fact that it is impossible to have exactly one unit in state 1 at the time immediately following t_{n+1} or, generally, at any time immediately following an IRCL. Indeed, at the time immediately *preceding* an IRCL the number of units in state 1 may be arbitrary. If it is 0, it remains 0. If it is positive, it increases by 1, so that it may be $2, 3, \ldots$, but not 1.

Consequently, given $X(t_n + 0) = i > 0$, the only states that are possible at the time immediately following the next IRCL at t_{n+1} are $0, 2, 3, \ldots, i$ and $i + 1$.

Clearly, state 0 occurs if and only if all states lose their content by time t_{n+1}. Since the probability of *not* losing the content by a single unit between t_n and t_{n+1} is p [given by (5.11)], the probability of loss of all units is $(1-p)^i$. This is therefore the transition probability from state i to state 0.

Now let us consider the probability of reaching state j with $2 \le j \le i+1$. For that to happen we must have $j-1$ units in state 1 at the time immediately preceding the IRCL at time t_{n+1}. This in turn means that out of i units in state $1, j-1$ must have retained their state, while the remaining $i-(j-1)=i-j+1$ units must have lost their content between t_n and t_{n+1}. The probability of this event is given by the binomial distribution, in view of the assumed independence, and equals $(_{j-1}^{\ i})p^{j-1}(1-p)^{i-j+1}$. In this way we proved the following.

THEOREM 5.1   For Model 1, we have, for all $i \ne 0$,

$$P_{ij}(t_n, t_{n+1}) = \begin{cases} (1-p)^i & \text{for } j = 0, \\ 0 & \text{for } j = 1 \quad \text{and} \quad j > i+1, \\ (_{j-1}^{\ i})p^{j-1}(1-p)^{i-j+1} & \text{for } j = 2, 3, \ldots, i+1, \end{cases} \quad (5.14)$$

with p given by (5.11).

For Model 2 the situation is very similar. Clearly, if the state at the time immediately following t_n is $i \ne 0$, then with probability $(_k^i)p^k(1-p)^{i-k}$ there will be exactly k units in state 1 at the time immediately preceding t_{n+1}, hence $j = 2k$ units at the time immediately following t_{n+1}. Consequently, we have the next theorem.

THEOREM 5.2   For Model 2 we have

$$P_{ij}(t_n, t_{n+1}) = \begin{cases} 0 & \text{for } j \text{ is odd or } j > 2i, \\ (_{j/2}^{\ i})p^{j/2}(1-p)^{i-j/2} & \text{for } j = 0, 2, \ldots, 2i, \end{cases} \quad (5.15)$$

where p is again given by (2.11).

Theorems 5.1 and 5.2 give us the transition probabilities for passage between various states during the intervals between two consecutive IRCLs. Before combining these together, we still need the transition probabilities for the last interval of time, following the IRCL at t_N until the target time T. Thus, let

$$Q_{ij}(t_N, T) = P[X(T) = j \mid X(t_N + 0) = i]. \quad (5.16)$$

Proceeding as before, we put

$$q = \exp^{[-c(T-t_N)]}. \quad (5.17)$$

Since at the target time T there is no IRCL, hence no increase of the number of units, the formulas are the same for Models 1 and 2. Naturally, we must have

$$Q_{0j}(t_N, T) = \begin{cases} 1 & \text{if } j = 0, \\ 0 & \text{if } j \neq 0, \end{cases} \tag{5.18}$$

which expresses the absorbing property of the state $i = 0$: once this state is reached, it may never be left.

Now, if $i > 0$, then the possible states at time T are only $0, 1, 2, \ldots, i$ (in this case, state 1 is possible). To reach state j with $0 \leq j \leq i$, it is necessary that j units retain their constant and the remaining $i - j$ units lose it. The probability of this event is again given by the binomial distribution, so that we have the following.

THEOREM 5.3 *For Models 1 and 2 we have*

$$Q_{ij}(t_N, T) = \begin{cases} 0 & \text{for } j > i, \\ \binom{i}{j} q^j (1 - q)^{i-j} & \text{for } j = 0, 1, \ldots, i, \end{cases} \tag{5.19}$$

where q is given by (5.17).

Let us now try to combine the formulas from Theorems 5.1 and 5.3 (or 5.2 and 5.3 for Model 2) and evaluate the probability that at the target time the information is still present. We assume (Assumption 5.4) that at time $t = 0$ we have one unit with the information and that the IRCLs occur at times $0 \leq t_1 \leq t_2 \leq \cdots \leq t_N < T$. Let $j_1, j_2, \ldots, j_N$, be the numbers of units with the information in question at times immediately following the consecutive IRCLs and at the target time.

The information is not lost if $j > 0$. Obviously, this requires that $j_1 > 0$, $j_2 > 0, \ldots, j_N > 0$, since if at any time after an IRCL there are no units with the information required (i.e., $j_k = 0$ for some k), then all subsequent j's will be 0. Thus, a typical path leading to a state where the information is not lost will have the form

$$j_0 = 1, j_1, j_2, \ldots, j_N, j, \tag{5.20}$$

with all terms being positive. The probability of path (5.20) equals

$$P_{1,j_1}(0, t_1) P_{j_1, j_2}(t_1, t_2) \cdots P_{j_{N-1}, j_N}(t_{N-1}, t_N) Q_{j_N, j}(t_N, T). \tag{5.21}$$

The probability, say, $r(t_1, t_2, \ldots, t_N, T)$, that the information is still present at the target time T is obtained by summing all probabilities (5.21) for all indices $j_1, \ldots, j_N, j$ that are positive. Thus, we have the next theorem.

THEOREM 5.4 *Probability $r(t_1, t_2, \ldots, t_N, T)$ that the information is not lost at time T, given the IRCLs at times $t_1, \ldots, t_N$, equals*

$$r(t_1, \ldots, t_N, T) = \sum_{j > 0} \sum_{j_N > 0} \sum_{j_{N-1} > 0} \cdots \sum_{j_1 > 0} P_{1,j_1}(0, t_1) P_{j_1, j_2}(t_1, t_2)$$
$$\cdots P_{j_{N-1}, j_N}(t_{N-1}, t_N) Q_{j_N, j}(t_N, T), \tag{5.22}$$

where $Q_{j_N, j}(t_N, T)$ *is given in Theorem* 5.3, *and* $P_{j_{k-1}, j_k}(t_{k-1}, t_k)$ *are given by Theorems* 5.1 *or* 5.2, *depending on whether Model* 1 *or Model* 2 *is used.*

This theorem may be presented in a more streamlined form by use of the matrix notation. Let $P(t_k, t_{k+1})$ be the matrix of the transition probabilities $P_{i,j}(t_k, t_{k+1})$, and similarly with the matrix $Q(t_N, T)$. Then we have the following.

THEOREM 5.5 *Probability* $r(t_1, \ldots, t_N, T)$ *equals the term* $1 - p_{1,0}$, *where* p_{10} *is the entry in the matrix*

$$P(0, t_1)P(t_1, t_2) \cdots P(t_{N-1}, t_N)Q(t_N, T). \qquad (5.23)$$

5.2.4 Problems of Optimization

The basic question one could ask now is how to allocate the IRCLs to maximize the probability that $X(T) > 0$, that is, probability $r(t_1, \ldots, t_N, T)$ of remembering the information at target time T.

Without loss of generality we now assume that $T = 1$, which amounts to a simple change of scale. We shall solve the optimization problem only under the restriction that the total number of IRCLs is small. We begin with the case of one IRCL.

Let $p(x)$ be the probability that $X(1) > 0$, given that IRCL occurs at time x with $0 \leq x < 1$. Thus, in the notation of the preceding section, we have $p(x) = r(x, 1)$, that is, when $N = 1$ and $t_1 = x$.

Let us denote

$$p = e^{-cx}, \qquad q = e^{-c(1-x)}. \qquad (5.24)$$

Obviously, if only one IRCL is allowed, then the probability $p(x)$ will be the same for Model 1 and 2. We have then Theorem 5.6.

THEOREM 5.6 *For Models* 1 *and* 2

$$p(x) = P[X(1) > 0 \mid X(0) = 1, \text{ one IRCL at } x]$$

$$= p[1 - (1 - q)^2]. \qquad (5.25)$$

To prove this theorem, observe that p is the probability that the only one unit that is at $t = 0$ in state 1 is still in state 1 at time x of IRCL (this is a necessary condition for remembering). On the other hand, $1 - (1 - q)^2$ is the probability that out of the two units with the information existing at the time immediately following the IRCL at x at least one is still in state 1 at target time $T = 1$.

Differentiating with respect to x, we obtain

$$p'(x) = -ce^{-2c}e^{cx}. \qquad (5.26)$$

Consequently, the derivative is always negative, and we therefore have the following.

THEOREM 5.7 *If only one IRCL is allowed, then it is optimal to make it at once; that is, function p(x) given by (5.25) is maximized at x = 0.*

Let us now consider the situation when two IRCLs are allowed. Suppose that they occur at times x, y with $0 \leq x \leq y < 1$. Denote

$$p = e^{-cx}, \qquad q = e^{-c(y-x)}, \qquad r = e^{-c(1-y)}, \qquad (5.27)$$

and let $p(x, y)$ be the probability that $X(1) > 0$, given the IRCLs at times x and y. We then have the following.

THEOREM 5.8 *For Model 1 we have*

$$1 - p(x, y) = 1 - p + p[(1 - q)^2 + 2q(1 - q)(1 - r)^2 + q^2(1 - r)^3], \quad (5.28)$$

with p, q, and r given by (5.27).

For the proof, let us observe that $1 - p(x, y)$ is the probability that the information is lost by the time $T = 1$, if IRCLs occurred at times x and y. Figure 5.1 shows all possible ways in which such a loss may occur. In the figure the symbol $\oplus$ signifies the loss of information of a unit. Between 0 and x there are two possibilities depicted by two parallel lines: the upper line represents the loss of information in the original unit prior to the first IRCL at time x. In this case, the IRCLs have no effect: the information is already lost before x. In the second case, represented by lower line, the number of units with the information increases by 1 immediately after the IRCL at x. From that moment on, we have three possibilities, marked (a), (b), and (c). In case (a), both

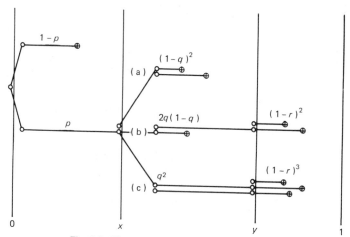

Fig. 5.1. Illustration of the proof of Theorem 5.8.

units lose their content before time y of the second IRCL, so that the information is lost before y. In case (b), one unit loses its content, and the other retains it until time y, so that at y, the number of units increases by one (to two). Finally, in case (c), both units retain their information until time y, hence at IRCL the number of units increases by one (to three).

If the information is to be lost by the target time, all units must lose their information: in case (b), this concerns two units, and in case (c) it concerns three units.

The probabilities of various events are marked in Fig. 5.1, and summing up all possibilities, we obtain the formula for probability $1 - p(x, y)$ of total loss.

The situation for Model 2 is very much the same. We have the following.

THEOREM 5.9 *For Model 2 we have*

$$1 - p(x, y) = 1 - p + p[(1 - q)^2 + 2q(1 - q)(1 - r)^2 + q^2(1 - r)^4], \quad (5.29)$$

with p, q, and r given by (5.27).

For the proof, we turn to Fig. 5.2, which represents various possibilities for the information to be lost by the target time. The reasoning is as in the preceding case. The only difference lies in the fact that in case (c), when both units resulting from doubling the number of units at the first IRCL last until the second IRCL, the number of units existing after time y is 4, not 3 as before. As a consequence, the probability of loss in all of them before the target time is $(1 - r)^4$.

It is clear that formula (5.29) will always give lower probabilities than formula (5.28). This follows from comparison of these formulas, and also from the direct interpretation of Models 1 and 2: the latter provides at least as many, and sometimes more, units with the required information.

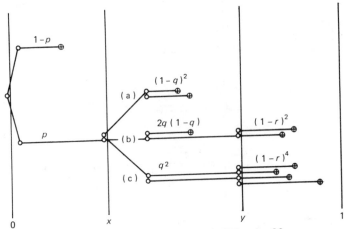

Fig. 5.2. Illustration of the proof of Theorem 5.9.

Tables I and II provide some numerical values of $p(x, y)$ for various x and y for Models 1 (upper entries) and Model 2 (lower entries). As may be seen from the upper entries in Table I (Model 1), it is optimal to take $x = 0$ and y about 0.25: this gives the value $p(x, y)$ about 0.7661 for the probability of remembering the information at time $T = 1$.

It may be checked that, for Model 1, if only two IRCLs are allowed, it is best to make the first IRCL at once (i.e., take $x = 0$ and the second IRCL somewhat later. The optimal placing of the second IRCL depends on the decay rate c; For example, for $c = 3$ (Table II) it equals about 0.39, with optimal $u = 0.166$.

Let us now inspect the lower entries (Model 2). Here again it is best to take $x = 0$, but the inspection of the columns reveals that it is also optimal to take $y = 0$. Thus, if two IRCLs are allowed, it is best to make them both at once.

Table I

Probabilities $p(x, y)$ of Remembering the Information by Target Time $T = 1$
If IRCLs Occur at Times x and y[a]

y	0.0	0.1	0.2	0.3	0.4	0.5	0.6	0.7	0.8	0.9
0.0	0.747									
	0.840									
0.1	0.759	0.716								
	0.829	0.793								
0.2	0.765	0.726	0.682							
	0.815	0.781	0.743							
0.3	0.765	0.730	0.690	0.646						
	0.800	0.768	0.733	0.693						
0.4	0.760	0.728	0.692	0.652	0.609					
	0.783	0.753	0.720	0.683	0.643					
0.5	0.749	0.720	0.688	0.652	0.613	0.566				
	0.762	0.735	0.704	0.671	0.633	0.592				
0.6	0.732	0.706	0.677	0.646	0.611	0.572	0.529			
	0.739	0.714	0.686	0.655	0.621	0.584	0.542			
0.7	0.709	0.686	0.660	0.633	0.602	0.567	0.530	0.488		
	0.712	0.689	0.664	0.637	0.606	0.573	0.535	0.494		
0.8	0.679	0.659	0.637	0.613	0.586	0.556	0.523	0.487	0.447	
	0.680	0.660	0.638	0.614	0.587	0.558	0.525	0.489	0.449	
0.9	0.643	0.626	0.607	0.586	0.563	0.538	0.510	0.477	0.444	0.406
	0.643	0.626	0.608	0.587	0.564	0.538	0.510	0.479	0.445	0.407

[a] The decay rate $c = 1$. Upper entries correspond to Model 1, and lower entries to Model 2.

Table II

Probabilities $p(x, y)$ of Remembering the Information by Target Time $T = 1$ If IRCLs Occur at Times x and y[a]

					x					
y	0.0	0.1	0.2	0.3	0.4	0.5	0.6	0.7	0.8	0.9
0.0	0.142									
	0.185									
0.1	0.153	0.140								
	0.183	0.180								
0.2	0.161	0.150	0.136							
	0.181	0.178	0.174							
0.3	0.165	0.157	0.146	0.132						
	0.178	0.175	0.171	0.165						
0.4	0.166	0.160	0.152	0.141	0.126					
	0.174	0.171	0.167	0.162	0.155					
0.5	0.164	0.159	0.153	0.145	0.134	0.119				
	0.169	0.166	0.163	0.158	0.151	0.142				
0.6	0.159	0.158	0.151	0.145	0.136	0.125	0.109			
	0.162	0.160	0.156	0.152	0.145	0.137	0.126			
0.7	0.151	0.148	0.145	0.140	0.134	0.125	0.113	0.097		
	0.152	0.150	0.147	0.143	0.138	0.130	0.121	0.107		
0.8	0.139	0.137	0.134	0.131	0.126	0.119	0.110	0.098	0.082	
	0.139	0.137	0.135	0.132	0.127	0.121	0.113	0.102	0.087	
0.9	0.121	0.120	0.118	0.116	0.112	0.108	0.101	0.093	0.081	0.066
	0.121	0.120	0.118	0.116	0.112	0.108	0.102	0.093	0.082	0.067

[a] The decay rate $c = 3$. Upper entries correspond to Model 1, and lower entries to Model 2.

As may be seen from Table II that the situation is very much similar in case $c = 3$, except that the probabilities of remembering are considerably smaller. This might have been expected if one observes that $c = 3$ means that, on the average, a unit stays in state 1 only up to one-third of the target time (while in Table I, the average time of remaining in state 1 is equal 1, i.e., equal to the target time).

Again, in both models the first IRCL ought to be made at once. In Model 2 also the second IRCL ought to be made at once, while in Model 1 the optimal time of placing the second IRCL is about 0.39.

Let us now consider the problem of optimal allocation of three IRCLs to be placed at x, y, z with $0 \le x \le y \le z < 1$. Let us denote

$$p = e^{-cx}, \qquad q = e^{-c(y-x)}, \qquad s = e^{-c(z-y)}, \qquad w = 1 - e^{-c(1-z)}. \quad (5.30)$$

The construction of the formulas for probability $p(x, y, z)$ that $X(1) > 0$, given that IRCLs occur at times x, y, and z is very much similar to the construction of the preceding formulas (for derivation, one can make diagrams similar to those presented in Figs. 5.1 and 5.2). We have the following.

THEOREM 5.10 *In Model 1 we have*

$$p(x, y, z) = p\{1 - (1 - q)^2 - 2q(1 - q)[(1 - s)^2 + 2s(1 - s)w^2 + s^2w^3]$$
$$- q^2[(1 - s)^3 + 3s(1 - s)^2w^2 + 3s^2(1 - s)w^3 + s^3w^4]\}, \quad (5.31)$$

while in Model 2

$$p(x, y, z) = p\{1 - (1 - q)^2 - 2q(1 - q)[(1 - s)^2 + 2s(1 - s)w^2 - s^2w^4]$$
$$- q^2[(1 - s)^4 + 4s(1 - s)^3w^2 + 6s^2(1 - s)^2w^4$$
$$+ 4s^3(1 - s)w^6 + s^4w^8]\}. \quad (5.32)$$

Tables III and IV give some selected numerical values for probabilities $p(x, y, z)$ in Models 1 and 2. As before, the upper entry refers to Model 1, and the lower entry to Model 2. To enable comparison of the profit that may arise

Table III

Probabilities $p(x, y, z)$ of Remembering the Information by Target Time $T = 1$, Given That IRCLs Occur at Times x, y, and z[a]

							z				
x	y	0.0	0.1	0.2	0.3	0.4	0.5	0.6	0.7	0.8	0.9
0.0	0.0	0.840	0.850	0.858	0.864	0.866	0.864	0.855	0.840	0.817	0.789
		0.975	0.971	0.966	0.960	0.953	0.944	0.932	0.917	0.898	0.873
	0.1		0.853	0.862	0.869	0.872	0.871	0.863	0.849	0.828	0.798
			0.957	0.952	0.946	0.939	0.930	0.918	0.903	0.885	0.860
	0.2			0.856	0.864	0.868	0.869	0.863	0.851	0.831	0.802
				0.934	0.928	0.921	0.913	0.901	0.887	0.869	0.846
0.1	0.1		0.791	0.800	0.807	0.811	0.811	0.806	0.794	0.776	0.750
			0.891	0.888	0.884	0.879	0.873	0.865	0.853	0.839	0.819
	0.2			0.803	0.810	0.814	0.815	0.811	0.801	0.784	0.759
				0.876	0.872	0.867	0.860	0.852	0.841	0.826	0.807
0.2	0.2			0.743	0.750	0.754	0.756	0.754	0.746	0.732	0.711
				0.812	0.810	0.807	0.803	0.792	0.790	0.779	0.764
	0.3				0.750	0.756	0.758	0.757	0.751	0.738	0.718
					0.799	0.796	0.792	0.786	0.778	0.768	0.753

[a] The decay rate $c = 1$. Upper entries refer to Model 1, and lower entries to Model 2. Maximal value equals 0.87238 for Model 1 (upper entries) for $x = 0$, $y \approx 0.12$, and $z \approx 0.43$.

Table IV

Probabilities $p(x, y, z)$ of Remembering of Information by Target Time $T = 1$, Given That IRCLs Occur at Times x, y, and z[a]

						z					
x	y	0.0	0.1	0.2	0.3	0.4	0.5	0.6	0.7	0.8	0.9
0.0	0.0	0.188	0.199	0.212	0.222	0.227	0.229	0.225	0.216	0.200	0.176
		0.335	0.333	0.329	0.325	0.318	0.309	0.298	0.282	0.259	0.228
	0.1		0.206	0.221	0.233	0.241	0.244	0.241	0.232	0.215	0.190
			0.328	0.324	0.320	0.313	0.305	0.294	0.278	0.256	0.226
	0.2			0.218	0.234	0.244	0.249	0.248	0.240	0.224	0.198
				0.317	0.313	0.307	0.299	0.288	0.273	0.252	0.222
0.1	0.1		0.180	0.193	0.205	0.213	0.217	0.216	0.209	0.195	0.172
			0.316	0.313	0.309	0.303	0.295	0.285	0.270	0.249	0.221
	0.2			0.199	0.213	0.224	0.230	0.230	0.223	0.208	0.185
				0.307	0.303	0.297	0.290	0.279	0.265	0.245	0.218
0.2	0.2			0.174	0.186	0.196	0.203	0.204	0.199	0.187	0.167
				0.292	0.289	0.284	0.277	0.268	0.255	0.237	0.211
	0.3				0.191	0.203	0.212	0.215	0.211	0.200	0.179
					0.281	0.276	0.270	0.261	0.249	0.232	0.207

[a] The decay rate $c = 3$. Upper entries refer to Model 1, and lower to Model 2. Maximal value equals 0.25021 for Model 1 (upper entries) for $x = 0$, $y \approx 0.24$, and $z \approx 0.55$.

from the right to make the third IRCL, the tables concern the same decay rates $c = 1$ and $c = 3$. The situation is practically the same as in the case of two IRCLs only. In Model 2 the optimal choice of times of IRCLs is $x = y = z = 0$,' that is, it is best to make all IRCLs at once. This is due to the fact that Model 2 gives the possibility of securing as many as eight units with the information at time $t = 0$, and this radically decreases the probability of loss by the target time.

On the other hand, in the case of Model 1, the situation is different. It is still best to make the first IRCL at once (at $x = 0$), but the second and third IRCL should be made at some time later.

To see how much the IRCLs, when properly placed, enhance the probability of recall at the target time, observe that for $c = 1$, the probability of recall equals (assuming the optimal placing of IRCLs):

0.37 if no IRCLs are allowed,
0.60 if one IRCL is allowed,
0.77 if two IRCLs are allowed,
0.87 if three IRCLs are allowed.

Analogous values exist for $c = 3$, hence for a "weaker" memory, where the decay rate is three times the one in the preceding case:

0.05 if no IRCLs are allowed,
0.10 if one IRCL is allowed,
0.17 if two IRCLs are allowed,
0.25 if three IRCLs are allowed.

The case of Model 2, shown in the accompanying tabulation, leads to still higher recall probabilities for $c = 1$ and $c = 3$, again under the assumption that IRCLs are placed optimally.

$c = 1$	$c = 3$	Number of allowed IRCLs
0.37	0.05	0
0.60	0.10	1
0.84	0.18	2
0.97	0.34	3

5.2.5   Abandoning the Independence Assumption

As mentioned, the crucial assumption of the model is the independence of losses in particular memory units. Thus, whatever happens to one memory unit does not influence the events in other units.

We shall present below a very simple model that abandons this assumption. The general hypothesis is that the decay intensities for particular memory units increase with the increase in the number of units which lost their content (passed to state 0). Qualitatively speaking, forgetting is a self-accelerating process.

Formally, the model will be described as follows. Suppose that at some time, say, $t = 0$, there are n units in state 1, labeled $1, 2, \ldots, n$. Then their decay intensities are $c_1, \ldots, c_n$ as long as all other units are in state 1 (retain their content). At some moment t there occurs the first transition, say, of unit number i, to the state 0. From that moment and until the next transition, the decay intensities of the remaining units $1, 2, \ldots, i - 1, i + 1, \ldots, n$ become $c_1(i), \ldots, c_{i-1}(i), c_{i+1}(i), \ldots, c_n(i)$, where generally $c_k(i) \geq c_k$ (decay intensities may only increase). At some time $t' > t$ the next unit, say, number j, passes to the state 0, and then the decay intensities for the remaining units become, $c_k(i, j)$, where $k = 1, \ldots, n$ with $k \neq i, k \neq j$. The process then continues in this way until all units lose their content. The model is therefore described by constants $c_k(i_1, \ldots, i_r)$, which represent the decay intensities of unit number k after the units numbered $i_1, \ldots, i_r$ lost their contents.

Naturally, there is not much chance of deriving the general formulas for the probability of loss in all units by time T. To see the degree of complexity, let us solve the problem for the case $n = 2$ units. As long as both of them are operating, the decay intensities are c_1 and c_2. If unit #1 loses its content as the first, then unit #2 begins to operate with decay intensity $c_2(1)$, while if unit #2 loses its content as the first, then the decay intensity for unit #1 becomes $c_1(2)$.

Let $p(T)$ denote the probability that both units lose their content by the time T.

THEOREM 5.11 *For $n = 2$, probability $p(T)$ equals*

$$p(T) = \int_0^T c_1 e^{-c_1 t} e^{-c_2 t} (1 - e^{-c_2(1)(T-t)}) \, dt$$

$$+ \int_0^T c_2 e^{-c_2 t} e^{-c_1 t} (1 - e^{-c_1(2)(T-t)}) \, dt. \tag{5.33}$$

If $c_1 + c_2 \neq c_2(1)$ and $c_1 + c_2 \neq c_1(2)$, then

$$p(T) = 1 - e^{-(c_1+c_2)T} + \frac{c_1 e^{-c_2(1)T}}{c_2(1) - c_1 - c_2} [1 - e^{-(c_1+c_2-c_2(1))T}]$$

$$+ \frac{c_2 e^{-c_1(2)T}}{c_1(2) - c_1 - c_2} [1 - e^{-(c_1+c_2-c_1(2))T}]. \tag{5.34}$$

The argument leading to formula (5.33) is as follows. If the loss in both units occurs by time T, then there must be a moment t preceding T at which one of the units loses its content as the first. The probability that this occurs to unit #1 equals $c_1 e^{-c_1 t} e^{-c_2 t} \, dt$, since $c_1 e^{-c_1 t} \, dt$ is the density of the time of loss of the unit 1 and $e^{-c_2 t}$ the probability that unit #2 lasts at least unit t. Next, term $1 - e^{-c_2(T-t)}$ is the probability that unit #2 loses its content sometime between t and T. This yields the first of the integrals in formula (5.33), and the second integral corresponds to the case when the first unit to lose its content at time t is unit #2.

Here $c_1, c_2, c_1(2)$, and $c_2(1)$ reflect the "structural" properties of the set of units: they may have different decay intensities, and what is more important, a loss in unit #1 may affect unit #2 in a different way than a loss in unit #2 may affect unit #1. The same is true in the general case, where the decay intensities $c_k(i_1, \ldots, i_r)$ reflect various structural properties of the system of units, for example, their interrelations.

In the simplest case of complete symmetry, we may have $c_1 = c_2 = a$ and $c_1(2) = c_2(1) = a + b$: the decay intensity is equal to a as long as the other unit retains its content and is the same for both units. After one unit loses its content, the remaining one operates with decay intensity $a + b$. In this case, formulas (5.34) yield the following.

THEOREM 5.12 *If $a \neq b$, we have*

$$p(T) = 1 + \frac{a+b}{a-b}e^{-2aT} - \frac{2a}{a-b}e^{-(a+b)T}. \tag{5.35}$$

If $a = b$, analogous reasoning yields

$$p(T) = 1 - (1 + 2aT)e^{-2aT}. \tag{5.36}$$

For the model with $b = 0$, hence with independence of losses in different memory units, we obtain

$$p(T) = (1 - e^{-aT})^2, \tag{5.37}$$

as expected.

For the case of three units, the reasoning is very similar. We shall present the formulas for the symmetric case, corresponding to formulas (5.35). Thus, we assume that

$$c_1 = c_2 = c_3 = a, \tag{5.38}$$

$$c_1(2) = c_1(3) = c_2(1) = c_2(3) = c_3(1) = c_3(2) = a + b, \tag{5.39}$$

$$c_1(2,3) = c_1(3,2) = c_2(1,3) = c_2(3,1) = c_3(1,2)$$

$$= c_3(2,1) = a + b + c. \tag{5.40}$$

These assumptions mean that as long as all three units retain their content, the decay intensity is the same in all of them and equals a. Next, as soon as one unit loses its content, the decay intensity in the two remaining units becomes $a + b$. Finally, if one of these remaining units loses its content, the decay intensity for the last unit becomes $a + b + c$. These constants are the same for all units and do not depend on which units and in which order their content is lost.

To calculate the probability of total loss in all three units (call them X, Y, and Z for simplicity), observe that there must be the first time, say, t (with $t < T$), when the first unit loses its content. The probability of this event occurring at t is $3e^{-2at}ae^{-at}\,dt$, where e^{-2at} is the probability of two units "surviving" beyond time t, factor $ae^{-at}\,dt$ is the loss density at time t, and factor 3 accounts for the fact that the first unit to lose its content may be any of the units X, Y, or Z. From time t on, the situation is as in the case of two units, and we may use formula (5.35), except that a is replaced by $a + b$, and b by c.

Let $p_2(T)$ denote the value of (5.35) or (5.36) with a replaced by $a + b$ and b replaced by c. Then we have the next theorem.

THEOREM 5.13 *Under conditions (5.38)–(5.40), probability $p(T)$ of loss of all units in memory, given that at $t = 0$ there are three units containing the* *information, is*

$$p(T) = \int_0^T p_2(T - t)3ae^{-3at} \, dt$$

$$= 1 - e^{-3aT} + \frac{3a(a + b + c)}{(a + b - c)(2b - a)} e^{-2(a+b)T}[e^{(2b-a)T} - 1]$$

$$+ \frac{6a(a + b)}{(a + b - c)(2a - b - c)} e^{-(a+b+c)T}[e^{(b+c-2a)T} - 1]. \quad (5.41)$$

Naturally, this formula is valid only if all the expressions that appear in the denominators are not zero. The cases when some of them are zero may be treated separately, in the manner described above.

Tables V and VI give selected values of probabilities of loss $p(T)$ for some T and selected values of parameters a and b (resp., a, b, and c) in cases of systems with two (resp., three) units. As may be expected, the probability of loss $p(T)$ increases with T, and also with the increase of parameters a, b, and c. In particular, the case $b = 0$ (resp., $b = c = 0$) corresponds to the case of independence of losses in memory units.

The symmetric case may be solved recursively as follows. Suppose that when n units retain their information, the decay intensity for each of them is the same and equals v_n. Thus, we have here, if originally there were N units,

$$c_k(i_1, \ldots, i_r) = v_{N-r} \quad (5.42)$$

for all k and all $i_1, \ldots, i_r$. Let $p_k(t)$ be the probability of loss by time t, given k initial number of units [so that we are interested in $p_N(T)$]. Conditioning on

Table V

Probabilities of Loss $p(T)$ for Selected Values a and b in the Case of Two Dependent Units[a]

					T			
a	b	1	2	3	4	5	8	10
0.1	0.0	0.009	0.033	0.067	0.109	0.155	0.303	0.400
0.1	0.05	0.013	0.048	0.096	0.153	0.214	0.401	0.513
0.1	0.1	0.018	0.062	0.122	0.191	0.264	0.475	0.594
0.1	0.25	0.029	0.098	0.186	0.280	0.373	0.610	0.724
0.5	0.0	0.155	0.400	0.604	0.748	0.843	0.964	0.987
0.5	0.1	0.180	0.450	0.661	0.801	0.886	0.980	0.994
0.5	0.5	0.264	0.594	0.801	0.908	0.960	0.997	1.000
0.5	0.75	0.307	0.652	0.845	0.935	0.974	0.999	1.000

[a] Case $b = 0$ corresponds to lack of dependence.

Table VI

Probabilities of Loss $p(T)$ for Case of Three Dependent Units

a	b	c	T 1	2	3	4	5	8	10
0.25	0.00	0.00	0.011	0.061	0.147	0.253	0.363	0.646	0.773
0.25	0.00	0.10	0.015	0.081	0.190	0.319	0.447	0.744	0.857
0.25	0.10	0.00	0.020	0.103	0.233	0.378	0.513	0.797	0.894
0.25	0.10	0.10	0.025	0.126	0.278	0.439	0.584	0.857	0.935
0.25	0.10	0.20	0.029	0.147	0.316	0.489	0.637	0.893	0.957
0.25	0.25	0.00	0.036	0.172	0.355	0.531	0.675	0.909	0.964
0.25	0.25	0.10	0.042	0.196	0.396	0.580	0.724	0.935	0.978
0.25	0.25	0.35	0.056	0.247	0.474	0.665	0.799	0.966	0.991
0.25	0.35	0.00	0.048	0.217	0.426	0.610	0.749	0.944	0.981
0.25	0.35	0.35	0.070	0.291	0.533	0.720	0.842	0.977	0.994
0.25	0.35	0.50	0.079	0.316	0.564	0.748	0.863	0.982	0.996

the moment of first loss of information by a unit, we prove easily the following theorem.

THEOREM 5.14   *Functions $p_k(t)$ satisfy the following recursive relations:*

$$p_1(t) = 1 - e^{-v_1 t}, \tag{5.43}$$

$$p_{k+1}(t) = (k+1)v_{k+1} \int_0^t e^{-(k+1)v_{k+1}s} p_k(t-s)\,ds, \tag{5.44}$$

for $k = 1, 2, \ldots$.

5.2.6   Optimization of IRCLs in the Case of Dependent Units

In this section the considerations will concern the problem of the optimal allocation of IRCLs in the case when the process of forgetting is "self-accelerating." We shall consider the "symmetric" case, when the decay intensity is the same for all units and depends only on the total number of units in operation. Moreover, we shall assume that the loss in any unit results in an increase of decay intensity in all remaining units by the same amount.

Thus, suppose that at some time there are k units operating. The decay intensity for each of them is equal to some constant, say, A_k. When one of these units loses its content, there remain $k - 1$ units, and now the decay intensity for each of them becomes A_{k-1}. It will be assumed that the difference $A_{k-1} - A_k$ is constant and does not depend on k (which is a formal expression of the assumption that each loss contributes the same amount to the decay intensity of the remaining units).

The parameters of the model are therefore just two constants: the decay intensity, say, A, when only one unit is operating and the value a, being the increase of intensity connected with the loss of one unit. Consequently, when j units are operating, the decay intensity in each of them equals $A - (j - 1)a$. For instance, when four units are in operation, the decay intensity is $A - 3a$; it increases to $A - 2a$ as soon as only three units remain; then it increases further to $A - a$ (when two units operate); and finally, when a single unit is left, the intensity becomes A.

To derive the formulas for the probability for the loss by target time T, we shall proceed much as before for the case of independent units. Let $F_k(j, u)$ denote the probability of loss in exactly j units in an interval of time of length u, given that at the beginning of the interval there were k units that contained the information.

Thus, $F_k(k, u)$ is the probability of the total loss of all k units during time u, while $F_k(0, u)$ is the probability that all units retain their information.

Suppose that we know probabilities $F_k(i, u)$ for all k, u and $i = 0, 1, \ldots, k$. Then the probability of loss by target time T may be calculated according to schemes such as presented on Figs. 5.3 and 5.4 for the cases of one and two IRCLs.

It is then clear that the probability of loss, say, $L(x)$, is given by the formula

$$L(x) = F_1(1, x) + F_1(0, x)F_2(2, T - x). \tag{5.45}$$

Similarly, for the case of two IRCLs, at times x and y, we enumerate all

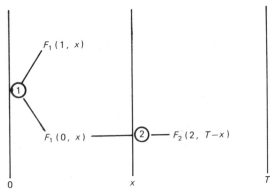

Fig. 5.3. The scheme for calculation of the probability of loss in the case of one IRCL.

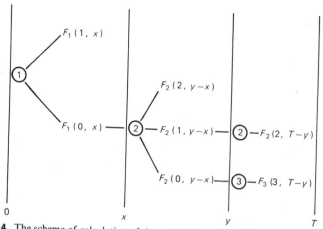

Fig. 5.4. The scheme of calculation of the probability of loss in the case of two IRCLs.

possibilities using Fig. 5.4. We have here

$$L(x, y) = F_1(1, x) + F_1(0, x)F_2(2, y - x)$$
$$+ F_1(0, x)F_2(1, y - x)F_2(2, T - y)$$
$$+ F_1(0, x)F_2(0, y - x)F_3(3, T - y). \qquad (5.46)$$

Now, probabilities $F_k(i, u)$ may be calculated inductively as follows. Observe first that we must have

$$\sum_{i=0}^{k} F_k(i, u) = 1 \qquad (5.47)$$

for any $k \geq 1$ and any $u \geq 0$. This follows simply from the observation that the probabilities in sum (5.47) exhaust all possibilities $(0, 1, 2, \ldots, k$ losses in the time interval of length u).

Next, we have

$$F_k(0, u) = e^{-k[A - (k - 1)a]u}. \qquad (5.48)$$

Indeed, 0 losses occurring means that all units retain their content throughout the interval of the length u. If there are k units operating, the loss intensity is $A - (k - 1)a$ for each of them, and the probability that a single unit retains its content is $e^{-[A - (k - 1)a]u}$. Since there are k units, raising to the kth power, we obtain (5.48).

In particular, for $k = 1$, formulas (5.47) and (5.48) yield

$$F_1(0, u) = e^{-Au} \qquad (5.49)$$

and

$$F_1(1, u) = 1 - e^{-Au}. \tag{5.50}$$

Finally, for $0 < i \leq k$, we have the identity

$$F_k(i, u) = \int_0^u k[A - (k - 1)a]e^{-k[A-(k-1)a]t} F_{k-1}(i - 1, u - t) \, dt. \tag{5.51}$$

To justify (5.51), observe that if a certain number $i > 0$ is to be lost during $[0, u]$, then there must be a certain time t, prior to u, when first one of the k unit loses its content. The density of this time is equal to $k[A - (k - 1)a]e^{-k[A-(k-1)a]t}$. Beginning with time t, we start with $k - 1$ units operating, of which $i - 1$ must be lost during the remaining time $[t, u]$; the probability of this event equals $F_{k-1}(i - 1, u - t)$.

Formulas (5.49)–(5.51) allow us, in principle at least, to calculate all probabilities $F_k(i, u)$ and, consequently, to calculate the loss probability for any allocation of IRCLs. The formulas become more and more involved with the increase of k. For the initial values of k, they are

$$F_2(2, u) = 1 - \frac{2(A - a)}{A - 2a} e^{-Au} + \frac{A}{A - 2a} e^{-2(A-a)u}, \tag{5.52}$$

$$F_2(1, u) = \frac{2(A - a)}{A - 2a} [e^{-Au} - e^{-2(A-a)u}] \tag{5.53}$$

$$F_2(0, u) = e^{-2(A-a)u}, \tag{5.54}$$

$$F_3(3, u) = 1 - \frac{3(A - a)}{A - 3a} e^{-Au} + \frac{3A}{A - 4a} e^{-2(A-a)u}$$
$$- \frac{A(A - a)}{(A - 3a)(A - 4a)} e^{-3(A-2a)u}, \tag{5.55}$$

$$F_3(2, u) = \frac{3(A - 2a)}{A - 3a} e^{-Au} - \frac{6(A - a)}{A - 4a} e^{-2(A-a)u}$$
$$+ \frac{3(A - a)(A - 2a)}{(A - 3a)(A - 4a)} e^{-3(A-2a)u} \tag{5.56}$$

$$F_3(1, u) = \frac{3(A - 2a)}{A - 4a} [e^{-2(A-a)u} - e^{-3(A-2a)u}], \tag{5.57}$$

$$F_3(0, u) = e^{-3(A-2a)u}, \tag{5.58}$$

$$F_4(4, u) = 1 - e^{-4(A-3a)u} - \frac{4(A-a)}{A-4a} e^{-Au} [1 - e^{-3(A-4a)u}]$$

$$+ \frac{6A(A-3a)}{(A-4a)(A-5a)} e^{-2(A-a)u} [1 - e^{-2(A-5a)u}]$$

$$- \frac{4A(A-a)}{(A-4a)(A-6a)} e^{-3(A-2a)u} [1 - e^{-(A-6a)u}]. \tag{5.59}$$

For the optimization problem, let us start with the case of one IRCL, say, at the point x. Without loss of generality, assume that $T = 1$. We have therefore that

$$L(x) = 1 - e^{-Ax}$$

$$+ e^{-Ax} \left[1 - \frac{2(A-a)}{A-2a} e^{-A(1-x)} + \frac{A}{A-2a} e^{-2(A-a)(1-x)} \right]. \tag{5.60}$$

Consequently, probability $P(x) = 1 - L(x)$ of retaining the information until target time $T = 1$ equals

$$P(x) = e^{-Ax} \left[\frac{2(A-a)}{A-2a} e^{-A(1-x)} - \frac{A}{A-2a} e^{-2(A-a)(1-x)} \right]. \tag{5.61}$$

Differentiating with respect to x we obtain

$$P'(x) = -\frac{2A(A-a)}{A-2a} e^{-A} [1 - e^{-2(A-2a)(1-x)}]. \tag{5.62}$$

Now, A-a must be positive, since it equals the decay intensity at the time when two units are operating, and after the IRCL, we may have two units containing the information. Quantity $A - 2a$, however, may be positive or negative (it is assumed to be nonzero, of course). In the case $A - 2a > 0$, the term in brackets is also positive, and the derivative is negative. In the case $A - 2a < 0$, the term in brackets is also negative, and so is the derivative. We conclude therefore that in the case of one IRCL it is best to make it at once, that is, at $x = 0$, since the probability $P(x)$ of retaining the information decreases with the increase of x.

In the case of two IRCLs, at times x and y, with $0 \le x \le y < 1$ we may again use formulas (5.53)–(5.58) and substitute them into (5.46). We then obtain the probability of loss by target time $T = 1$, and we may minimize it with respect to x and y. It appears that the minimum is again attained at $x = 0$; that is, the first IRCL should be made at once. This is no longer true, however, for the second IRCL. Figure 5.5 gives the optimal allocation of the second IRCL in the case when the decay intensity equals 2 (upper curve) and 1 (lower

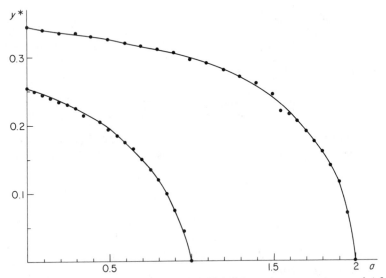

Fig. 5.5. Optimal allocations of the second IRCL (y^*) for various parameters a and A. In the upper curve we have $A = 2 + 3a$, and in the lower curve, $A = 1 + 3a$.

curve) at the times when there are three units operating and under varying a. Thus, the allocations of y on the curves correspond to values of parameters a and $A = 2 + 3a$ (upper curve) and $A = 1 + 3a$ (lower curve).

The model of this section may be regarded as a submodel of a larger one, describing generally the operation of metamemory and its internal organization, as well as stochastic and logical interrelations between various memory compartments. The model differs in many respects from the conceptions of memory advanced thus far [especially as regards recall; see, for instance, Bower (1977) and Glanzer (1977)].

First, it abandons to some extent the traditional division into a short-term and long-term memory [see, for instance, Montague (1977)], showing in which way the storage time may be subject to a partial control.

Second, despite the simplifications, the value of the model lies in the fact that it offers a novel mechanism of self-control of memory, a mechanism whose operation may be optimized. This opens two possibilities. One of them lies in testing and estimating in controlled experiments in which IRCLs are induced by the experimenter at certain times and one estimates the recall probability. The results of such experiments may show the extent of the adequacy of the model and differentiate between Models 1 and 2.

The second possibility lies in opening the ways of studying to which extent the subject applies automatically the optimal IRCL strategies and—if they deviate from optimality—what are the causes and directions of these deviations. In some sense, the situation is similar to that with decision theory, where one can observe the real behavior in decision situations, and knowing the optimal decisions, one obtains a powerful source of information from the data on observed deviations from optimality.

It seems also that the model presented in this section may be used in artificial intelligence to simulate systems that have imperfect memory controlled by metamemory. Another possibility of application of this theory is through the usage of the notion of metamemory as a controlling unit. Suppose that we have a number of systems (or subsystems), each generating a stream of events so that each system is representable as a stochastic process in which, however, time may be controlled. The actor may activate one process at a time, and the control problem consists of optimization (possibly with several objectives) of activation times of various processes.

Formally, suppose that we have k subsystems, $S_1, \ldots, S_k$, where the jth subsystem is representable as a stochastic process $X_j(t)$, except that time t may be "on" or "off." Control of the kth subsystem consists of a rule of activating of this process, with the requirement that at any given time at most one process may be active. If $U = \{0, 1, \ldots, k\}$, then $f: T \to U$, where T is the time axis of control, with the convention that $f(t) = i$ means that S_i is active at time t and that $f(t) = 0$ means that no process is active at time t. Of course, if the time is discrete, then rule f is a sequence of instructions.

If $f(t) = i$ and $j \neq i$, we may define $T_j(t) = \inf \{\tau > t : f(\tau) = j\}$ as the nearest time after t at which the process $X_j(t)$ is active. Thus, at time t the system "waits" for time $T_j(t)$ before becoming active. This waiting time may be fixed at t or may be undetermined at t, in the sense that it may be dependent on some other events to occur after t in S_i or some other subsystem.

The whole system operates under a number of constraints on the admissible functions f. If F is the class of all admissible controls, then with each f in F one may associate a loss $L(f)$, representing how well f performs the task, and the optimization of (one criterial) problem is to find f_0 in F with $L(f_0) \geq L(f)$ for all f in F.

The control process $f(t)$ involves a program with conditional and unconditional instructions about activation of various processes at given times.

Another application is the simulation on a computer of a number of simultaneous processes, where the problem lies in the fact that only one process (or one event) may be simulated at one time. Thus, one has to keep track of internal times in each process, which will differ, in general, from the real time. The next process to be activated (simulated) may be chosen from the set of these processes that are "ready," in the sense of meeting the appropriate constraints.

Such a control process is a good model of real human behavior when a person must organize (in the sense of sequentialization) a number of incompatible activities. One can think of the events in various activity domains as "queuing to occur" and the actor controlling the times of occurrences by activating particular systems. While in computer control processes such activation is obtained through specific instructions, for example, "wait with process X_i until...," "continue with process X_i until...," "use the data concerning the events....," human behavioral instructions (whether actually uttered or not) are often accompanied by modal frames, thus forming motivational sentences [see Nowakowska (1973)]. Perhaps this might lead to modal operations on programs and motivational-like calculus on programs by substitution of program-valued variables for propositional ones.

5.3 A MODEL OF MEMORY OF SENTENCES: APPLICATION OF THE MODEL OF VARIABLE STORAGE HORIZON

In this section we shall present a certain stochastic model of memory of sentences. The model will be based on the same idea as the model of the preceding section, namely, that of "copying" information from one memory unit to another to ensure higher probability of remembering by the target time (in the present case, the target time is determined by the termination of the sentence).

The main purpose of the model is to explain the phenomenon consisting of the fact that, statistically speaking, the words from the middle section of the sentence are more easily forgotten than the words from the initial and terminal parts of the sentence.

If the process of remembering the sentence is treated as a random phenomenon in which each of the consecutive words has a certain probability $p_1(t), p_2(t), \ldots$ of being remembered at time t, then the phenomenon we want to explain consists of the fact that probabilities $p_k(t)$ are higher for indices k corresponding to words that are close to the beginning or the end of the sentence.

In the present case, there is no sense in speaking of metamemory which controls the process of remembering, since the successive words enter the memory with too high a speed. Nevertheless, one can carry over to the present case the idea of internal recalls, resulting in "copying" some of the words, thus increasing their chance of remaining in memory for a longer time. In this case, however, copying would be caused not so much by conscious instructions as by some semantic interrelations between words.

In the next section, the assumptions of the model will be presented heuristically, and in Section 5.3.2 these assumptions will be given in a form enabling mathematical analysis. Finally, Section 5.3.3 will contain the description of the simulation model.

5.3.1 The Intuitive Background

The model presented in this section will be based on three groups of assumptions. The first group will concern the structure of the sentence to be remembered. Without going into details, it will be assumed that the sentence constitutes a certain structure in which some words are connected with a certain relation, say, R. In the process of storing the sentence into memory, we shall distinguish two stadia: the first, referred to as *storing*, and the second, called *strengthening*. Both of them will depend in a certain way on the structure of the sentence to be remembered.

Consequently, the second group of assumptions will concern the process of storage. Roughly, it will be assumed that at the moment when a given word is heard, two events happen: first, the word becomes stored in memory. The storage time is random, with the distribution of the storage time being one of the parameters of the model. Second, all preceding words, which are connected with the last word by relation R and are still remembered become "supported," or "copied." The detailed hypotheses concerning the latter process will be formulated in the next section; at this moment it is enough to state that the process of copying will enhance the probability of remembering the word copied.

Finally, the process of "strengthening" the sentence in memory will consist of successive copying of the last words, and the words connected with them by relation R.

Intuitively, one can expect that such assumptions should explain the phenomenon of the differences between probabilities of remembering particular words, as outlined at the beginning: the initial words will be copied more often, since their copying will occur whenever there appears a words connected with them. Statistically, this will give more copying of words from the initial parts of the sentence.

On the other hand, the last words are copied in the process of strengthening; moreover, they appear later than the remaining words, hence they have higher chances of being remembered at the recall time.

As regards the interpretation of relation R, which describes the structure of the sentence, it will be deliberately reduced so as to cover those and only those aspects that determine the statistical properties of the process of remembering, that is, the probabilities of remembering particular words.

Relation R, connecting pairs (x, y) of words of the sentence, will be interpreted as *any* connection between these words, which causes the "return" to the (earlier) word x upon hearing the (later) word y. Thus, relation R may be interpreted as covering the syntactic aspects, as well as (perhaps first of all) the semantic aspects, consisting of some connections between words x and y. Finally, relation R may be induced by the previous experience of the listener, resulting in "associations" of words x and y because of some previous events. From the point of view of the statistical characteristics of the process of storage of the sentence in memory, the only essential feature is that there exists *some* connection between words x and y, which causes supporting x when y is heard, while the origin of this connection is not relevant. Consequently, in the model, relation R will be treated as a sort of primitive concept and will not be defined. Moreover, since R is regarded as a subjective connection between x and y, without specifying the sentence or the subject, it will be assumed that relation R is random.

For the process of copying, we shall take into account not only relation R but also its transitive extension, that is, the relation that connects two words in the case when there exists a chain of R-related words that connects them. As a result, when y appears, the word x may be copied more than once, depending on the number of paths that lead from x to y or depending on the semantic power of y with respect to x.

As regards the mechanisms of copying, or strengthening, they may be described as follows. For simplicity, let us consider a single support of the word x, resulting from the appearance of some word y at a later moment. Suppose that the word x appears at time t. It is stored in memory for a random time X, that is, until time $t + X$. In the absence of support, after this time the word x becomes forgotten. The word y appears at some time t', later than t, and is stored for random time Y.

As regards the word x, there are two possibilities. First, we may have $t + X < t'$, which means that at t' the word x is already forgotten and cannot be supported (there is nothing to copy). Second, we may have $t + X \geq t'$, and in this case, at time t' the word x becomes "copied," and the copy is stored in the memory for time X'. Thus, out of two copies of the word x, one will be remembered until $t + X$ and the other until $t' + X'$. Consequently, the word will be remembered until the later of these two moments, that is, until

$$\max(t + X, t' + X'). \tag{5.63}$$

As already mentioned, $X, X', X'', \ldots$ are random variables with identical distribution. This distribution is a parameter of the model and may (in principle) be chosen in an arbitrary way.

Thus, the process of storage of a sentence consisting on N words $x_1, x_2, \ldots, x_N$ is as follows. At time t_1 there appears the first word, which becomes stored in memory for some random time. At time t_2 there appears the word x_2, which becomes stored for some random time, and also the word x_1

becomes supported, provided the following two conditions are met:

1. at time t_2 the word x_1 is still not forgotten;
2. the words x_1 and x_2 are connected by relation R.

At time t_3 there appears the word x_3, which becomes stored for a random time, and possibly there occur supports of the words x_1 and x_2. The word x_2 becomes copied if conditions analogous for the word x_1 are met. On the other hand, the word x_1 may become copied twice. First, there may exist a direct link between x_3 and x_1, and in this case, x_1 becomes copied, provided it is not yet forgotten. Second, there may exist an indirect connection between x_3 and x_1 through x_2. In such a case, x_1 receives another support, again provided it is not yet forgotten.

Finally, as regards the process of strengthening, it consists of supporting the words x_{N-1} and x_N and the words related to them; this support occurs at some moments after the termination of the sentence and the mechanisms are the same as described above.

5.3.2 The Assumptions of the Model

STRUCTURE OF THE SENTENCE

As mentioned, the primitive concept here will be relation R, which connects some words of the sentence.

Let $\prec$ stand for the relation "appears earlier than," so that $x \prec y$ means that the word x appears before the word y in the sentence under consideration. Let us now define the relation R' as

$$xR'y \quad \text{if} \quad xRy \text{ and } x \prec y, \tag{5.64}$$

so that R' is the restriction of R to the set of those pairs (x, y) for which $x \prec y$.

Next, let R^* be the transitive extension of R'. Formally, we define

$$xR'_1 y \quad \text{if} \quad xR'y \tag{5.65}$$

and

$$xR'_{n+1} y \quad \text{if} \quad (\exists z): xR'_n z \text{ and } zR'y. \tag{5.66}$$

Finally, we put

$$xR^*y \quad \text{if} \quad (\exists n): xR'_n y. \tag{5.67}$$

Thus, relation R^* holds between x and y if x is earlier than y, and moreover, x and y are connected by relation R', either directly or indirectly (i.e., through a chain of pairs, each connected by R').

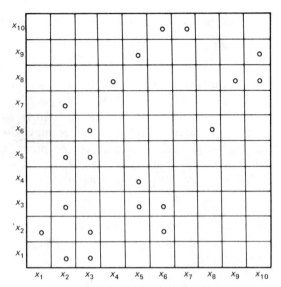

Fig. 5.6. Matrix of relation R.

As an example, suppose that the set of words forming the sentence consists of 10 elements, $x_1, \ldots, x_{10}$, with relation $\prec$ being consistent with the numbering of words: thus, $x_i \prec x_j$ if $i < j$ (so that the sentence has the form $x_1 x_2 \cdots x_9 x_{10}$).

Let us assume that the relation R comprises the pairs marked in the matrix from Fig. 5.6. It is assumed here that the rows correspond to the first and the columns to the last element of the pair. Thus, we have here $x_5 R x_2, x_3 R x_5, \ldots$.

Relation R need not be symmetric; for instance, in the matrix from Fig. 5.3 we have $x_4 R x_5$, but not $x_5 R x_4$.

Relation R' concerns only those pairs for which the first element of the pair precedes the second, that is, pairs (x_i, x_j) with $i < j$. This means that to relation R' we take only the pairs that lie above the main diagonal. In this case, these will be the pairs (x_1, x_2), (x_1, x_3), (x_2, x_3), (x_3, x_5), (x_3, x_6), (x_4, x_5), (x_6, x_8), (x_8, x_9), (x_8, x_{10}), and (x_9, x_{10}).

It will be convenient to represent relation R' graphically, arranging elements x_i in a sequence according to relation $\prec$ and marking the pairs that are in relation R' with arrows leading *to* the first element of the pair (see Fig. 5.7).

Relation R'_2 signifies a connection through *two* arrows, so that for instance we have

$$x_1 R'_2 x_3, \quad x_2 R'_2 x_6, \quad x_3 R'_2 x_8, \quad \ldots. \tag{5.68}$$

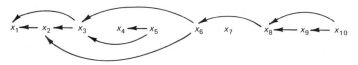

Fig. 5.7. Graph of relation R'.

Similarly, R'_3 means a connection through three arrows, so that

$$x_1 R'_3 x_5, \quad x_1 R'_3 x_8, \quad x_6 R'_3 x_{10}, \quad \ldots \quad (5.69)$$

Relation R^*, as mentioned, means a connection with a certain number (one or more) of arrows. Thus, we have

$$x_1 R^* x_2, \quad x_1 R^* x_{10}, \quad x_2 R^* x_8, \quad \ldots \quad (5.70)$$

On the other hand, we do not have $x_7 R^* x_{10}$ or $x_4 R^* x_{10}$: there are no arrows leading to x_7 at all, and there is no path leading from x_{10} to x_4 (since the connection must be following the direction of the arrows).

We shall now introduce the following definition, which will be useful later.

DEFINITION 5.1 By the *semantic power* $M(y \,|\, x)$ of word y with respect to word x we shall mean the number of paths leading from y to x.

Thus, in the above example (see Fig. 5.4) we have $M(x_6 \,|\, x_3) = 3$, since there exist three paths leading from x_6 to x_1, namely, (x_6, x_2, x_1), (x_6, x_3, x_1), and (x_6, x_3, x_2, x_1). Similarly, we have $M(x_{10} \,|\, x_6) = 6$, since we have the following paths leading from x_{10} to x_1:

$$(x_{10}, x_8, x_6, x_2, x_1), \quad (x_{10}, x_8, x_6, x_3, x_1), \quad (x_{10}, x_8, x_6, x_3, x_2, x_1),$$
$$(x_{10}, x_9, x_8, x_6, x_2, x_1), \quad (x_{10}, x_9, x_8, x_6, x_3, x_1), \quad (x_{10}, x_9, x_8, x_6, x_3, x_2, x_1).$$

As mentioned in the introduction to this section, the semantic power will play an essential role in the model: $M(y \,|\, x)$ will be equal to the number of copies, or "supports," received by x when y enters the memory.

In the model below, it will be assumed that relation R' is random, with all connections being equally likely. The probability of a connection will be one of the parameters of the model.

Formally, we express this as the following hypothesis.

HYPOTHESIS 5.1 *For a sentence consisting of N words, $x_1, x_2, \ldots, x_N$, the probability that the pair (x_i, x_j) with $i < j$ will be connected by relation R' is the same for all pairs.*

Let us observe that this hypothesis does not specify the character of possible dependence between the existence of connections between particular pairs. This dependence (or lack of it) may be characterized by various hypotheses, of which the two most natural will be presented below.

HYPOTHESIS 5.2a *For any two distinct pairs, the events consisting of connecting them with relation R' are independent.*

Under this hypothesis, the total number of pairs that are connected with relation R' is a random variable. One of the possible alternatives is to accept that the number of pairs connected by R' is fixed and that the randomness concerns only the identity of the pairs to be connected. This is described by the following hypothesis.

HYPOTHESIS 5.2b *The number of pairs connected with relation R' is fixed and equals K. The allocation of pairs that are connected is random, obtained by sampling K out of the possible N(N − 1)/2 pairs, with all possible allocations being equally likely.*

Thus, under Hypothesis 5.2a we have the following situation. Let p be the probability that a given pair will be connected by relation R'. Then the number K of pairs that are connected is a random variable with the binomial distribution

$$P(K = j) = \binom{N(N-1)/2}{j}p^j(1 - p)^{[N(N-1)/2]-j}, \qquad (5.71)$$

where $j = 0, 1, \ldots, N(N - 1)/2$.

Consequently, the expected number of connections is

$$E(K) = \tfrac{1}{2}N(N - 1)p \qquad (5.72)$$

and the standard deviation equals

$$\sigma_K = \sqrt{\tfrac{1}{2}N(N - 1)p(1 - p)}. \qquad (5.73)$$

For example, in the data simulated in the next subsections, we have $N = 10$ and $p = 0.2$. This means that the expected number of connections per sentence is $E(K) = 9$, with standard deviation $\sigma_K = 2.68$.

Under Hypothesis 5.2b the situation is somewhat different. The number of pairs connected is constant, hence the probability that a given pair is connected is

$$p = K/[N(N - 1)/2] = 2K/N(N - 1). \qquad (5.74)$$

THE PROCESS OF COPYING

We shall now present the hypotheses concerning the mechanisms of copying particular words of the sentence. For simplicity, let us assume that the sentence to be memorized consists of N words $x_1, x_2, \ldots, x_N$, with the first word x_1 appearing at time $t = 1$, the second at time $t = 2$, and so on. This corresponds to the choice of the unit of time equal to the average temporal distance between the words in a sentence. The assumption (implicit here) is that all words are of equal length, and it is an obvious simplification; it may be easily removed in the general model by assuming arbitrary times of appearances of particular words.

In the following, the symbols X, with indices such as X_i, will denote random variables with a given distribution f.

The intuitions connected with the copying process have been already presented in the preceding subsection. Roughly, a new word x_k becomes stored in memory for a certain random period of time, and also it causes a support, or copying, of all preceding words that are still not forgotten and are related to x_k by R^*, with the additional condition that a word is copied $M(x_k | x)$ times, where $M(x_k | x)$ is the semantic power of the word x to be copied with respect to the word x_k that stimulates copying.

The formal expression of this process is somewhat complex and will consist of an inductive definition of a sequence of random vectors

$$(T^k_1, T^k_2, \ldots, T^k_N), \qquad k = 0, 1, \ldots, N, \tag{5.75}$$

where T^k_j will be interpreted as the time until which the word x_j is to be remembered, after the appearance of the word x_k.

HYPOTHESIS 5.3   Sequence (5.75) satisfies the following relations:

$$T^0_j = 0 \qquad \text{for} \quad j = 1, 2, \ldots, N; \tag{5.76}$$

$$T^k_j = 0 \qquad \text{for} \quad j > k; \tag{5.77}$$

$$T^1_1 = 1 + X. \tag{5.78}$$

Suppose now that values $T^k_1, \ldots, T^k_N$ for some $k < N$ are already determined. Then

$$T^{k+1}_{k+1} = k + 1 + X, \tag{5.79}$$

and for $j = 1, \ldots, k$,

$$T^{k+1}_j = T^k_j \qquad \text{if} \quad T^k_j < k + 1, \tag{5.80}$$

$$T^{k+1}_j = \max[T^k_j, k + 1 + X_1, \ldots, X_{M(x_{k+1} | x_j)}] \qquad \text{for} \quad T^k_j \geq k + 1. \tag{5.81}$$

Here $M(x_{k+1} | x_j)$ is the semantic power of the word x_{k+1} with respect to the word x_j.

Assumption (5.76) simply describes the initial conditions: at time $t = 0$, hence before the appearance of the first word, none of the words is remembered.

Condition (5.77) asserts that the words that have not yet appeared cannot be remembered: at time k of appearance of word x_k, time T_j^k, until which the word x_j (later than the word x_k) is to be remembered, equal 0.

Finally, condition (5.78) asserts that, at the time when the first word enters, it becomes remembered for a certain random time X, hence (in the absence of support) it would be remembered until $1 + X$. Thus, after the appearance of the first word, the vector of the times until particular words are to be remembered is of the form

$$(T_1^1, T_2^2, \ldots, T_N^N) = (1 + X, 0, \ldots, 0), \tag{5.82}$$

where all coordinates except the first are zero, because of condition (5.77).

The remaining relations (5.79)–(5.81) concern the process of remembering that occurs after appearance of word x_{k+1}. Here the situation is as follows. As a result of the appearance of the first k words, we have already sampled some storage times $(T_1^k, T_2^k, \ldots, T_k^k, 0, \ldots, 0)$, where the coordinates with lower index $k + 1, k + 2, \ldots$ are zero because of condition (5.77), since the word x_{k+1} has not appeared as yet.

The latter word appears at time $k + 1$ and becomes stored for time X, hence until time $k + 1 + X$. This sampling is described by condition (5.79).

The remaining two conditions concern the process of copying, that is, supporting of the preceding words. Let us consider the word x_j, which appeared earlier. According to the times already sampled, this word is to be remembered until time T_j^k.

At time $k + 1$ (the appearance of word x_{k+1}), we have two possibilities: the word x_j may be forgotten (if $T_j^k < k + 1$) or it may still be remembered (if the opposite inequality holds). In the first case, the copying process does not occur, and therefore the time of storage of the word x_j does not change [this is described by condition (5.80)]. Finally, if at time $k + 1$ the word x_j is not yet forgotten, it is subject to the process of copying, with multiplicity equal to the semantic power of the word x_j with respect to the word x_k, and its new time of storage becomes equal to the maximum of the sampled times of storage. This is described by condition (3.81).

THE PROCESS OF STRENGTHENING

Finally, the last assumptions will concern the process of strengthening of the sentence, which occurs after the termination of the sentence. The mechanism here is, in principle, the same as in the process of copying upon the appearance of new words, with the only difference being that the strengthenings occur as a result of the stimulus in the form of the termination of the sentence. The latter becomes strengthened by copying several last words, and also all words that are connected with them. The hypotheses may be formulated in various ways, by specifying which words and at which moments these words are subject to copying.

In the simulation model presented in next section, it was assumed that the strengthening process concerns the last two words and occurs at time $t = N + 1$ for the last word and at time $t = N + 2$ for the penultimate word. Formally, this may be described by the following assumptions. After the appearance of the last word, at time $t = N$, we have the vector $(T_1^N, T_2^N, \ldots, T_N^N)$ of the storage times of particular words. This vector is subject to still two more transformations, leading successively to vectors $(T_1^{N+1}, T_2^{N+1}, \ldots, T_N^{N+1})$ and $(T_1^{N+2}, T_2^{N+2}, \ldots, T_N^{N+2})$. This is described by the following.

HYPOTHESIS 5.4 *For a given vector* $(T_1^N, T_2^N, \ldots, T_N^N)$, *the vector* $(T_1^{N+1}, T_2^{N+1}, \ldots, T_N^{N+1})$ *satisfies the following conditions: if* $T_N^N < N + 1$, *then for* $j = 1, \ldots, N$

$$T_j^{N+1} = T_j^N. \tag{5.83}$$

On the other hand, if $T_N^N \geq N + 1$, *then*

$$T_N^{N+1} = \max[T_N^N, N + 1 + X] \tag{5.84}$$

and for $j = 1, \ldots, N - 1$,

$$T_j^{N+1} = \max[T_j^N, N + 1 + X_1, \ldots, N + 1 + X_{M(x_j | x_N)}]. \tag{5.85}$$

Similarly, the last copying concern the word x_{N-1}, and is described by the following hypothesis.

HYPOTHESIS 5.5 *For the given vector* $(T_1^{N+1}, T_2^{N+1}, \ldots, T_N^{N+1})$, *the vector* $(T_1^{N+2}, T_2^{N+2}, \ldots, T_N^{N+2})$ *satisfies the following conditions:*

$$T_N^{N+2} = T_N^{N+1}, \tag{5.86}$$

if $T_{N-1}^{N+1} < N + 2$, *then for* $j = 1, \ldots, N - 1$

$$T_j^{N+2} = T_j^{N+1}, \tag{5.87}$$

and if $T_{N-1}^{N+1} \geq N + 2$, *then for* $j = 1, \ldots, N - 2$

$$T_j^{N+2} = \max[T_j^{N+1}, N + 2 + X_1, \ldots, N + 2 + X_{M(x_j | x_{N-1})}], \tag{5.88}$$

while

$$T_{N-1}^{N+2} = \max[T_{N-1}^{N+1}, N + 2 + X]. \tag{5.89}$$

The interpretation of these copyings is similar to the case of the preceding hypotheses: at time $N + 1$ copying occurs for the word X_N and all words connected with it, provided that this word is still remembered at $N + 1$. If not, there is no copying induced by the last word. Finally, at time $N + 2$, the word x_{N-1} and all words connected with it are copied in a similar way.

PARAMETERS OF THE MODEL

As mentioned, there exist various ways of generating the structure of sentence under which Hypothesis 5.1 is satisfied. The two most natural ways are by fixing the probability p of a connection and sampling for each possible pair, whether it is connected or not or by fixing the number K of connections and sampling K out of the set of all possible pairs.

The first case is described by Hypothesis 5.2a and the second by Hypothesis 5.2b. At any rate, one of the parameters of the model is p, the probability of connection (in the case of Hypothesis 5.2b, p is expressed through K and N, as already shown).

The second parameter is N, equal to the number of words in the sentence. In the simulation model, it was taken to be $N = 10$.

Finally, the model involves a probability distribution f according to which one samples all storage times of words. This distribution is a parameter of the model and may, in principle, be taken arbitrarily. For the purpose of simulation, it was assumed that this distribution is of the form

$$P(X \leq t) = \begin{cases} 0 & \text{for } t \leq d, \\ 1 - e^{-a(t-d)} & \text{for } t > d. \end{cases} \tag{5.90}$$

Thus, the density of the above distribution is

$$f(t) = \begin{cases} 0 & \text{for } t \leq d, \\ e^{-a(t-d)} & \text{for } t > d. \end{cases} \tag{5.91}$$

This means that the random variable X, equal to the time of storage of a word if it is not supported, may be represented as

$$X = d + Y, \tag{5.92}$$

where Y has the exponential distribution with parameter a.

In the particular case $d = 0$, we simply obtain the exponential distribution with parameter a.

This choice of distribution (5.90) seems justified on the following grounds. The exponential character of the storage time is consistent with the usual assumptions about the physiological nature of the memory process. In the present model, a somewhat richer class of distributions was allowed, by taking into account the additive constant d (so that the exponential case is obtained as a special case of $d = 0$). This is connected with the possibility that the exponential decay (disappearance from memory) may start not at once; rather, it may occur only after some time (e.g., needed to introduce the stimulus to memory).

The average storage time (without support) therefore equals

$$E(X) = d + (1/a), \tag{5.93}$$

and the variance is

$$D^2(X) = 1/a^2. \tag{5.94}$$

Consequently, the simulation model below involves four parameters, namely p, N, d, and a.

5.3.3   A Simulation Model

The model defined in the preceding section served as a basis for the construction of a simulation model of memory of sentences and the subsequent construction of a program and real simulation. The flowchart of this model is presented on Fig. 5.8; for convenience, the numbering of words starts with 0, so that the last word is that with index $N - 1$. The figure shows the general scheme, with particular subschemes presented on subsequent figures.

The process starts with generation of the structure of the sentence, according to the scheme of Hypothesis 5.2a (see Fig. 5.10 or according to Hypothesis 5.2b (see Fig. 5.11). This structure allows us, for each pair of words x_j, x_k, with x_j earlier than x_k, to determine the number $M_k(j)$ of paths leading from x_k to x_j. This process occurs in the block of Fig. 5.8 marked $M := M_k(j)$.

The process of remembering the sentence occurs as follows. At time $k = 0$ the first word x_0 becomes stored for a random time T_0, where T_0 is the sampled value of the random variable $X = d + Y$, with Y having exponential distribution with mean $1/a$. Next, there begins a loop, with the same procedure for words $x_1, \ldots, x_{N-1}$. For the word x_k, the cycle starts with sampling the storage time for the word x_k. This time equals

$$T_k = k + X, \tag{5.95}$$

where $X = d + Y$, with Y again sampled from the exponential distribution with mean $1/a$. (Addition of the constant k to the storage time is connected with the fact that the word x_k appears at the time k.)

At this stage another loop begins, leading to support of the words x_0, $x_1, \ldots, x_{k-1}$; the structure of this loop is presented on Fig. 5.9 and will be discussed below.

After going through all the words, up to x_{N-1}, we start the strengthening process, with its two stages. First, the strengthening concerns the word x_{N-1} at time N, and next, the word x_{N-2} at time $N + 1$.

If the word x_{N-1} is forgotten at time N, the process passes at once to the last stage, concerning the word x_{N-2}. Otherwise, the word x_{N-1} becomes supported once, and then the support occurs for all words related to x_{N-1}, after which the process passes to the last stage. This stage is analogous to the preceding ones.

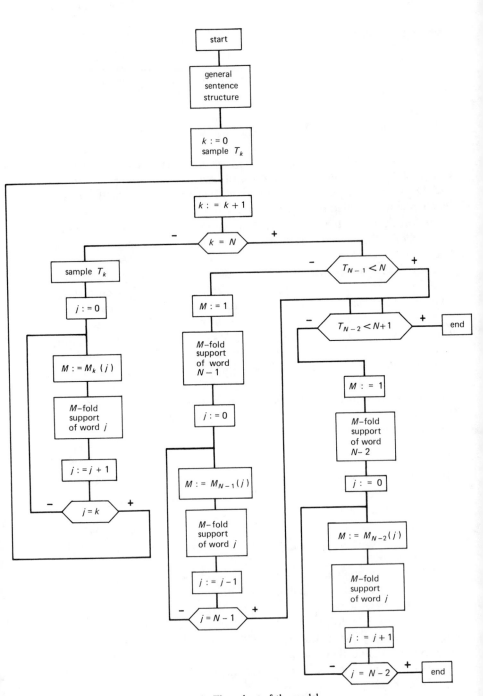

Fig. 5.8. Flow chart of the model.

The loop presented in Fig. 5.9 corresponds to the block marked "M-fold support of word j" in Fig. 5.8.

The first step here is to check, whether at time k the jth word is still remembered. If not, there is no process of support. If the jth word is still remembered at time k (i.e., T_j exceeds k), there is an M-fold loop being executed. Each time one samples the time, according to the previous scheme, that is, $X = d + Y$ with Y having the exponential distribution with mean $1/a$, this gives a "sample" new storage time until $k + X$. If the new storage time is better than the existing one, it becomes a new storage time. Otherwise, the old storage time remains unchanged. In each case, the process either ends or the loop begins anew.

Figures 5.10 and 5.11 show the flowcharts for the block in Fig. 5.8 marked "generate sentence structure." Figure 5.10 shows the sampling according to

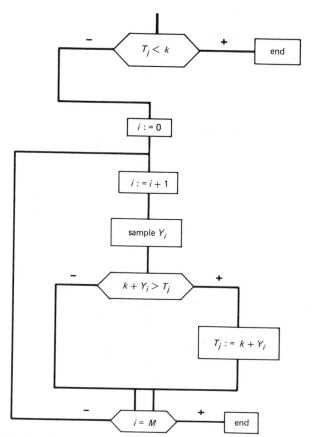

Fig. 5.9. The flow chart of the block marked "M-fold support of the word j" in Fig. 5.8.

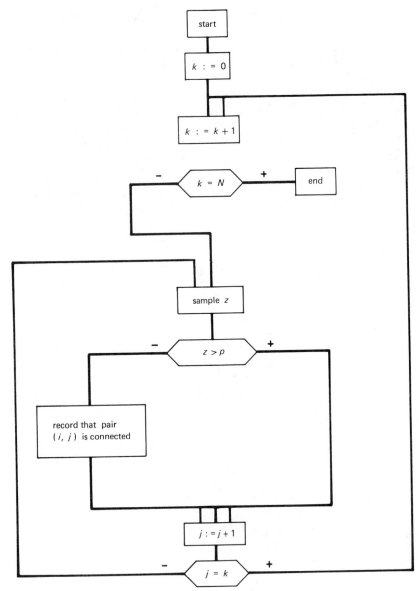

Fig. 5.10. The flow chart for generation of the structure of the sentence according to Hypothesis 5.2a.

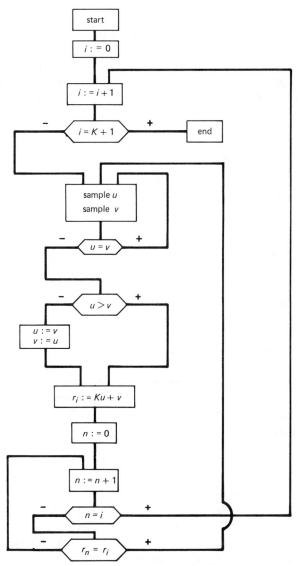

Fig. 5.11. The flow chart for the generation of the structure of the sentence according to Hypothesis 5.2b.

scheme from Hypothesis 5.2a, when the number of pairs connected is not determined in advance. Here for each possible pair one determines whether or not it becomes connected, and the latter event occurs with probability p.

In Fig. 5.11 it is shown how one may realize sampling according to the scheme from Hypothesis 5.2b, where we have the number K of connections to be made. Here the connected pairs are (u, v) for number $r = Ku + v$, which are obtained by simulation.

5.3.4 Empirical Results

In this section, we shall show the results of simulation of the model.

An example of simulated process of storage of a single sentence is as follows. The sampled sentence consists of 10 words (numbered from 0 to 9), connected as follows:

$$(0, 2), \quad (0, 6), \quad (1, 2), \quad (1, 5), \quad (2, 5),$$
$$(3, 5), \quad (3, 8), \quad (4, 5), \quad (4, 6), \quad (8, 9).$$

These results were obtained by using program for Hypothesis 5.2a, with probability of connection $p = 0.2$. Since the total number of pairs here is $10 \cdot 9/2 = 45$, the expected number of connections is $45 \cdot 0.2 = 9$. The sampled sentence has, therefore, one connection more than the expected number of connections.

The semantic powers for various words are in this case $M(1 \mid 5) = 2$, and for all other pairs the semantic power is 0 or 1. Indeed, there are two paths leading from 5 to 1: direct $(1, 5)$ and indirect $(1, 2), (2, 5)$. On the other hand, every other pair is either not connected or only connected directly.

The simulation was carried out for the parameter values $a = 0.1$ and $d = 2$. Thus the "elementary" storage time is $d + Y$, with Y having exponential distribution with mean 10. Consequently, the mean storage time is 12.

In four trials, denoted I, II, III, and IV, the storage times (after supports) of words $0, 1, \ldots, 9$ are as given in Table VII. For example, in trial IV, the first word (number 0) was remembered until the time 15.11 (counting from the moment of termination of the sentence) and the third word (number 2) was already forgotten when the sentence terminated.

As may be seen, there is a tendency to remember for a longer period those words from the initial and terminal parts of the sentence. This effect is seen better in the case of $n = 50$ sentences, each sampled separately. The results are presented on Fig. 5.12, in which we see the numbers of words remembered after time $t = 5$ (upper curve), after time $t = 15$ (middle curve), and after $t = 25$ (lower curve). On these graphs one can clearly see the decrease in probability of remembering for the words in the middle part of the sentence. This effect is

Table VII

Storage Times For Four Trials

Word number	Trial			
	I	II	III	IV
0	22.06	22.19	22.96	15.11
1	7.95	20.70	22.93	7.55
2	24.92	15.59	12.82	0.00
3	25.18	34.99	29.53	24.21
4	34.68	4.36	9.74	4.22
5	3.66	14.43	4.53	21.58
6	3.73	11.56	0.00	3.46
7	16.40	2.12	2.26	15.79
8	14.58	12.94	13.23	24.73
9	10.77	23.57	5.91	10.78

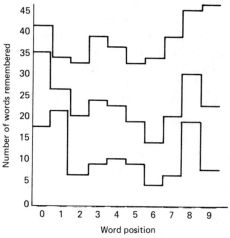

Fig. 5.12. Numbers of remembered words at a given position in 50 simulated sentences ($p = 0.2, d = 2, \alpha = 0.1$).

least visible for $t = 5$, that is, shortly after termination of the sentence, which is understandable, since at that time there may still be in the memory some of the words which received no support at all. As time passes, the words from the middle part of the sentence become less well remembered. For instance, word number 6, which for $t = 5$ was remembered in 36 out of 50 cases, is for $t = 15$ remembered in only 17 out of 50 cases.

There is an interesting effect of simulation that concern the last two words. The point is that the last word is remembered somewhat less well than the

Table VIII

Mean and Standard Deviation for 50 Sentences Simulated
under Parameters $p = 0.2$, $a = 0.1$, $d = 2$

Word number	Mean storage time	Standard deviation
0	22.97	19.21
1	17.89	16.88
2	12.86	11.57
3	16.44	13.26
4	16.56	14.74
5	14.69	13.80
6	13.05	11.94
7	14.42	10.43
8	21.43	13.75
9	16.58	9.99

penultimate word. This is connected with special assumptions about the process of strengthening accepted in the present model: the last word is supported only once, at time N, but the penultimate word is supported at later moment $N + 1$, and moreover, it may also be additionally supported at earlier moments if it is connected with the last word.

The means and standard deviations for storage times of particular words for 50 sentences simulated under parameters $p = 0.2$, $a = 0.1$, and $d = 2$, are given in Table VIII.

5.3.5 Discussion; Further Perspectives

The model of sentence memory presented in this section seems to represent reasonably faithfully the phenomenon of weaker memory for the words in the middle part of a sentence. Naturally, the results of simulation do not coincide with the empirical data, and fit is only qualitative. To simulate the actual data of the experiments on real sentences, one would have to estimate the parameters of the model, that is, find such values p, a, and d that would give the best (e.g., in the sense of least squares) fit to the data.

The simulation model suggested here may be used in several ways to obtain information about the mechanisms of memory storage by testing various empirical hypotheses. Thus, for instance, one could simulate the storage process for some concrete sentences. In other words, instead of separately generating the sentence structure, one could fix it in a way that would reflect the structure of the concrete sentence in question. One would obtain in this case a simulated process of storage of a concrete sentence that could then be compared with real data.

In addition, the above model may be fruitfully applied to simulate the storage process of lists, not sentences (e.g., lists of words, numbers, nonsense syllables). Here the structure is considerably poorer; on the other hand, list memory is a topic that has been extensively studied [see, e.g., Glanzer (1977) and Levelt (1978)] and a considerable amount of data about it may be found in the literature.

Here the model may serve as an alternative to the model suggested by Gilmartin, Newell, and Simon (1975), with an advantage consisting of the fact that the present model takes into account the stochastic aspects of memory operation (while Gilmartin *et al.* considered purely deterministic version).

Finally, it might be promising to modify the assumptions of the present model and compare the resulting models, both among themselves and with the empirical data. Among many possibilities, we shall mention two here, those we find most interesting and most promising.

It is best to illustrate the first possibility by an example. Let us consider three words, x_1, x_2, and x_3, and suppose that all three pairs (x_1, x_2), (x_2, x_3), and (x_1, x_3) are connected. Thus, the word x_1 is supported twice by x_3: directly, and also indirectly by x_2 (i.e., the semantic power of x_3 with respect to x_1 equals 2). In the present model, this means that at the time when x_3 appears, the word x_1 (if is not yet forgotten) receives a double support.

One may, however, modify the model, making the existence of nonexistence of the second support depend also on whether at that time the "intermediate" word x_2 is forgotten or not. In other words, the question is whether the existence of semantic connection through the intermediate word (x_2) always causes a support of x_1, or does such a support occur only if x_2 has not been forgotten at the time of support?

In the present model, the first possibility was assumed. It would be of some interest to compare the results with the results obtained under the alternative assumption.

Finally, another interesting problem here is connected with time. In the present model, it was assumed that copying occurs so fast that it terminates before the appearance of the next word, regardless of the number of copyings. Perhaps it would be better to assume that the time needed for copying is not negligibly short as compared with the temporal distances between words. In such a case, the copying process could be disturbed by the appearance of the next words.

The above remarks suggest only a few of the possible ways of modifying the model; other possibilities will undoubtedly appear in the process of testing various hypotheses. At any rate, it seems that the model, in its present form, describes reasonably adequately the process of sentence memory and therefore deserves careful attention as a possible source of information about the process.

5.4   MODELS OF PERCEPTION PROCESSES

5.4.1   Perceptual Organization: Model of Attraction Mechanisms

We start the analysis from the process of figure exploration. A simple way of representing the state of the process at any given time is to specify the position of the focus of the eye at time t, to be denoted $p(t)$. Thus, $p(t)$ is a bivariate process, $p(t) = [x(t), y(t)]$, where $x(t)$ and $y(t)$ denote, respectively, the horizontal and vertical coordinate of the eye focus at time t (the choice of the coordinate system is irrelevant).

We shall postulate that process $p(t)$ behaves in the following way: it consists of segments of continuous movements (fine eye movements), interrupted by jumps to some other areas of the figure. Accordingly, we shall make the following assumption about the figure inspected.

ASSUMPTION 5.6 (Partition of the figure)   *It is possible to distinguish in the figure a certain number of "focal points," say, $p_1, p_2, \ldots, p_n$.*

ASSUMPTION 5.7 (Partition of the process)   *At each time t process $p(t)$ belongs to the "domain of attraction" of one of the focal points.*

To formulate further assumptions, let $T_1, T_2, \ldots$ denote the times when process $p(t)$ changes the point of attraction and let $k_1, k_2, \ldots$ be the indices of attraction points in the consecutive intervals $[0, T_1), [T_1, T_2), \ldots$ (so that during $[T_{i-1}, T_i)$ process $p(t)$ is in the domain of attraction of the focal point p_{k_i}.

ASSUMPTION 5.8 (Fine eye movements)   *Between times T_{i-1} and T_i, process $p(t)$ is the Ornstein–Uhlenbeck process centered at p_{k_i}.*

For the precise definition of the Ornstein–Uhlenbeck process, see Feller (1968). At this place it suffices to say that it is a continuous path process such that the vertical and horizontal displacements are normally distributed in every interval of time, and with a force that "pulls" the process toward the central point p_{k_i}: if at some time the process is away from the central point, then the displacement in the following interval of time is more likely to bring it back toward the center than away from it.

To characterize the process under consideration, it remains to describe the mechanisms that generate the times T_i of changes in uninterrupted explorations of the domain of attraction of a particular focal point and also to specify the probability of the next focal point, if a change occurs at a given time.

ASSUMPTION 5.9 (Attraction function)   *With each focal point p_k there are associated two constants, $c_k > 0$ and $b_k > 0$, and a function $f_k(t)$ such that for $t \in [T_{i-1}, T_i)$, when $p(t)$ is in the domain of attraction of p_{k_i}, we have*

$$f_{k_i}(t) = f_{k_i}(T_{i-1}) \exp[-c_{k_i}(t - T_{i-1})] \tag{5.96}$$

and

$$f_j(t) = f_j(T_{i-1}) + b_j(t - T_{i-1}) \quad for \quad j \neq k_i. \quad (5.97)$$

This assumption means that as long as process $p(t)$ is in the domain of attraction of a given focal point, function f_k corresponding to this point decreases exponentially, while all other functions increase linearly. Functions f_k will be called *attraction functions*, associated with particular focal points.

The subsequent assumptions will connect the values of attraction functions with the probability of leaving a given domain, and also with the probability of choice of the next domain to inspect. Very roughly, the lower the attraction of a given domain is, the higher is the probability that it will be left, and then the process is more likely to move to domains with higher attraction functions.

Assumption 5.9 asserts therefore that the attraction of the domain actually inspected "wears off," while the attractions of all other domains increase.

One may intuitively expect that the vector of functions $[f_1(t), \dots, f_n(t)]$ will reach a sort of dynamic equilibrium: a component that would reach a high value (grow "too much") would likely start declining after the next change (when its domain is inspected). This mechanism will protect the components from indefinite growth, at the same time ensuring that every domain will be inspected, with returns to this domain when its attraction "rebuilds itself."

The last postulates can be used to describe precisely the role of attraction functions in determining the time of stay in a given domain of attraction and the probability of passing to another domain.

ASSUMPTION 5.10 (Termination of inspection of a domain) *Suppose that at some time t process $p(t)$ is in the domain of attraction of p_k. Then the probability that process $p(t)$ will leave this domain of attraction before time $t + \Delta t$ is*

$$\left[\sum_{j \neq k} f_j(t) \middle/ f_k(t) \right] \Delta t + o(\Delta t) \quad (5.98)$$

where $o(\Delta t)/\Delta t \to 0$ as $\Delta t \to 0$.

Let us observe that, if $f_k(0) \neq 0$, then $f_k(t) \neq 0$ for all t (since this function either increases linearly or decreases exponentially), so that (5.98) is always well defined.

ASSUMPTION 5.11 (Transition probabilities) *If at some time t process $p(t)$ leaves the domain of attraction of the point p_k, then the probability that it will move to the domain of attraction of point p_j ($j \neq k$) is*

$$f_j(t) \middle/ \sum_{i \neq k} f_i(t). \quad (5.99)$$

Assumptions 5.6–5.11 allow us to analyze in some detail the behavior of process $p(t)$ of inspection of the figure. In particular, Assumption 5.8 specifies completely the behavior of $p(t)$ in the domain of attraction of a focal point. Thus, we need only to analyze those aspects of process $p(t)$ that are connected with the jumps to other domains of attraction. Specifically, we shall analyze

(a) the "domain process," that is, the process of choices of consecutive domains of attraction for inspection, and the times of their inspection;

(b) the process of changes in attraction functions, that is, the dynamics of the vector of attraction functions.

Obviously, if we concentrate on the information about which domain is inspected at a given time, abstracting from the more specific information about the location of $p(t)$ in the domain, we deal in effect with the "domain process" $Z(t)$ defined by

$$Z(t) = k \qquad \text{if} \quad p(t) \text{ is in the domain of } p_k. \tag{5.100}$$

We have then the following theorem.

THEOREM 5.15 *Suppose that at some time process $Z(t)$ enters state i [i.e., $p(t)$ enters the domain of attraction of p_i], and let the values of attraction functions at the time of entrance be $f_1, \ldots, f_n$. Let T_i denote the time of uninterrupted stay in the domain of p_i. Then*

$$P(T_i \le t) = 1 - e^{-I_i(t)}, \tag{5.101}$$

where

$$I_i(t) = \frac{1}{f_i c_i^2} [(B_i c_i t + F_i c_i - B_i) e^{c_i t} + (B_i - F_i c_i)] \tag{5.102}$$

with

$$F_i = \sum_{k \ne i} f_k, \qquad B_i = \sum_{k \ne i} b_k. \tag{5.103}$$

For the proof see the Appendix at the end of this chapter.

The most important consequence of this theorem is that $Z(t)$ is *not* a Markov process (since the distribution of T_i is not exponential). In fact, differentiating (5.101) we see that the density of T_i is of the form $I_i'(t)e^{-I_i(t)}$, which (omitting for simplicity the index i) reduces to the form

$$(1/f) \exp[-(B - Fc)/fc^2](F + Bt) \exp(ct)$$
$$\times \exp\{-[(Fc - B + Bct)/fc^2] \exp(ct)\}. \tag{5.104}$$

Density (5.104) is either monotonically decreasing (i.e., has maximum at 0) or it reaches its modal value at some positive point t. For the latter case, qualitatively speaking, it is necessary that for small t the exponential terms

$$\exp\{-[(Fc - B + Bct)/fc^2] \exp(ct)\} \tag{5.105}$$

remains close to 1, while the term

$$(F + Bt)\exp(ct) \qquad (5.106)$$

grows relatively fast. This means that c and either F or B (or both) are relatively large. Now, under these conditions, for (5.105) to remain close to 1, the term $(Fc - B + Bct)/fc^2$ must be small. This necessitates Fc to be close to B and f to be large.

We have therefore the following qualitative conditions under which the distribution of time T_i (length of inspection of the domain of attraction of p_i) will have positive modal value:

1. The domain must have high initial attractiveness (f large) and also high "decay rate" c. This means that the domain has relatively few interesting points, or features; that is, after a short while, one feels that one has learned all that was to be learned about the domain.

2. The attractiveness of other domains, taken jointly, is increasing fast (large B), but at the beginning this attractiveness was not too high ($F \simeq B/c$).

This distribution is illustrated on Fig. 5.13 for values $c = 5$, $B = 20$, $F = 4$, and $f = 25$. As may be seen, the modal value for the time of inspection is about $t = 0.5$ (units of time in which the rates c and B are expressed).

Another form of the distribution of the inspection time T_i is illustrated on Fig. 5.14. Here the modal value is at $t = 0$; that is, the shorter times of inspection are more likely than the longer ones.

The values of the parameters in Fig. 5.14 are $c = 0.5$, $B = 15$, $F = 3$, and $f = 0.5$. This means that the domain is relatively rich in interesting elements (the decay rate is small, which means that the inspection exhausts the domain at slower rate). Furthermore, the initial value of interest in the domain is small ($f = 0.5$), while for the remaining domains, their joint attractiveness is $F = 3$,

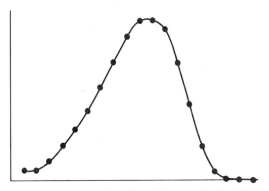

Fig. 5.13. Distribution of the inspection time T for $c = 5$, $B = 20$, $F = 4$ and $f = 25$ (horizontal spacing between points on the graph is $\Delta t = 0.05$).

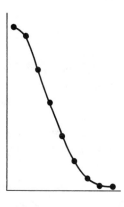

Fig. 5.14. A distribution of the inspection time.

and this attractiveness grows at a high rate, $B = 15$. Thus, the other domains exert increasingly higher pressure toward abandoning the inspection of the domain in question and moving somewhere else.

The properties of the distribution of the inspection time are best explained by the following simple theorem.

THEOREM 5.16 *The hazard function associated with the distribution of T_i is proportional to $(F + Bt)e^{ct}$, hence it is always strictly increasing.*

Thus, the distribution of T_i is in the class of the so-called distributions with increasing failure rate: the longer the inspection has lasted, the more likely it is that it will end in the next short interval.

The proof of Theorem 5.16 follows from simple differentiation, which yields $I_i'(t)$ as the hazard function.

Let us now analyze the dynamics of the transition probabilities. According to Assumption 5.11, if the eye leaves domain i at time t (counting, say, from the time $t = 0$ when this domain was entered), then probability $p_{ik}(t)$ of passing to domain k equals to ratio of the actual value of attraction function for the kth domain to the sum of attraction functions for all other domains (excluding the ith), that is,

$$p_{ik}(t) = f_k(t) \Big/ \sum_{j \neq i} f_j(t), \tag{5.107}$$

hence, if the initial attractiveness is $f_1, \ldots, f_n$, then

$$p_{ik}(t) = (f_k + b_k t)/(F_i + B_i t), \tag{5.108}$$

with F_i and B_i given by (5.103).

Denoting by $h_i(t)$ the density of T_i given by (5.104), we have, for the unconditional probability p_{ik} of passing from the domain i to the domain k,

$$p_{ik} = \int_0^\infty \frac{f_k + b_k t}{F_i + B_i t} h_i(t) \, dt. \tag{5.109}$$

We then have the following.

THEOREM 5.17   *Probabilities p_{ik}, $k = 1, 2, \ldots, n$, $k \neq i$, satisfy the inequalities*

$$p_{ik} \leq \frac{b_k}{B_i} + \left(\frac{f_k}{F_i} - \frac{b_k}{B_i} \right) \exp\left(-\frac{B_i}{f_i c_i^2} \right). \tag{5.110}$$

Some of the consequences of this theorem are as follows. Suppose that (other conditions being equal), c_i tends to 0. Then the exponential term on the right-hand side of (5.110) tends to 0, and we obtain $p_{ik} \leq b_k/B_i$. Summing with respect to k we obtain

$$1 = \sum_{k \neq i} p_{ik} \leq \frac{1}{B_i} \sum_{k \neq i} b_k = 1, \tag{5.111}$$

which shows that we must have

$$p_{ik} \approx b_k/B_i. \tag{5.112}$$

This means that, if c_i is small (the domain inspected is highly interesting, so that the decay in its attractiveness is low), then the major factor determining the probability of the next domain is the rate of increase of attractiveness of this domain: domains whose attractiveness grows faster when they are not inspected will have higher chances of being inspected next.

On the other hand, if c_i is large, then the exponential term in (5.110) is close to 1, and hence p_{ik} will be asymptotically equal to f_k/F_i. This means that, for domains with high c_i, hence with relatively little interest, the main factor determining the choice of the next domain is the initial value of attractiveness of this domain: domains whose initial attractiveness is higher will have higher chances of being inspected as next.

Therefore we have here an interplay among the initial attractiveness of the domains not inspected, the rates of increase of their attractiveness, and also the qualities of the inspected domain. Inspection of an interesting domain will likely last longer, and the next inspected domain will likely be the one whose attractiveness grew above the attractiveness of others (so that here the rates of increase play the dominant role). On the other hand, inspection of an uninteresting domain will likely be short, and then the next inspected domain will likely be the one with the highest initial attractiveness (so that the initial values play the dominant role). There is, therefore a general tendency to "satisfy the curiosity" of those domains for which the attractiveness grew up too much.

The rate of linear increase varies from domain to domain: a steeper increase corresponds to domains whose attractiveness builds more quickly. On the other hand, a steeper decline corresponds to those domains in which the inspection provides information at a higher rate.

One can think of the following example, which (metaphorically at least) represents the inspection process. Imagine a person, who sits in an armchair and watches TV. There are several programs he might watch, so he occasionally switches the channels.

The four main categories of domains, characterized by low or high b and low or high c may be described as follows.

1. A domain with both high b and c corresponds to a TV channel, call it A, that broadcasts a sports program, with the viewer highly interested in the current score but not especially keen on the spectator side of the sport. Then, as he watches the programs on other channels, he becomes increasingly curious about the current score on Channel A, and this curiosity grows fast (high b). Eventually, he switches to Channel A, but as soon as he learns the current score, his curiosity is completely satisfied (high c), since we assumed that he is not interested in the spectator aspects of this sport events. This argument suggests that Channel A will be switched *often but for brief periods*.

2. As a domain with high b and low c, one can think of a TV channel, say, B, that broadcasts an exciting film, full of action and unexpected events. Here the curiosity of what is happening on Channel B builds quickly when other channels are viewed (as in the case of Channel A), but—as opposed to the previous case—switching to Channel B does not lead to quick diminishing of the curiosity of events on this channel: one is interested not only in what happened but also in how it was happening (small c). Consequently, Channel B will be viewed *frequently and for longer periods of time*.

3. A domain with low b and high c corresponds to a channel, say, C, with a boring program (e.g., an interview with a person who has nothing of interest to say). The curiosity level for Channel C builds slowly during the viewing of other channels. When one switches to Channel C, the curiosity that has built up becomes quickly satisfied, and one returns to other channels. This suggests that the times of viewing Channel C will be *rare and short*.

4. Finally, a domain with low b and low c corresponds to a channel, say, D, that broadcasts a program that is of little interest as a whole but is "locally interesting." As examples one can think of a stupid comedy: it is not important to know what the plot is about, but even without understanding the whole context, it is fun to watch. As other examples, one can think of variety shows, quizzes, and so on. Here the curiosity level builds slowly (low b), so one seldom

Table IX

Data for $N = 500$ Simulated Transitions between
Four Domains[a]

Domain	Number of visits	Average stay in domain[b]	Average stay outside[b]
1	140	0.150(0.777)	0.774(0.4381)
2	159	0.435(0.2800)	0.374(0.3029)
3	84	0.096(0.576)	1.431(1.0371)
4	117	0.268(0.1757)	0.845(0.589)

[a] Domain 1: $b = 25, c = 10$ (high b, high c); domain 2: $b = 25, c = 1$ (high b, low c); domain 3: $b = 5, c = 10$ (low b, high c); domain 4: $b = 5, c = 1$ (low b, low c).

[b] The numbers in parentheses represent the standard deviations.
The transition matrix for $N = 500$ trials is:

	1	2	3	4
1	0	0.507	0.186	0.307
2	0.475	0	0.177	0.348
3	0.329	0.447	0	0.224
4	0.310	0.422	0.267	0

turns to Channel D, but once one switches to it, one is likely to remain there for longer time. This suggests that the periods of viewing Channel D will be *rare but last longer*.

Table IX gives some results of simulation of the times of inspections of four domains, characterized by low or high b and low or high c. As may be seen, the predictions specified above are confirmed.

5.4.2   Models of Transportation Mechanisms

Let us now analyze one of the processes that is preliminary to the recognition and conscious analysis of the figure. To carry on any meaningful analysis of the figure, it is necessary to first acquire some knowledge about it. Such knowledge may assume various forms in different contexts, but one can argue that its basic constituents consist of assertions about the identity or other relations between particular parts of the figure. For example, to recognize the meaning of a figure as a whole, it may first be necessary to establish that some fragments F_1 and F_2 are identical with respect to some attributes, such as size or color, or that F_3 is larger than F_4, or ....

It is not necessary that such a process of comparison be carried out on a conscious level: one could conjecture that, during the initial periods of exploration of the figure, such comparison processes are carried out, supplying the information to a central "processing unit," which then uses this information for recognition.

In this section we shall concentrate on one constituent part of such a process, namely on the comparison process, which contributes to the knowledge supplied by the glimpses by the exploration of the domains of the figure.

Thus, assume that two fragments of the figure, say, F_1 and F_2, belonging to different domains of attraction, are to be compared with respect to a number of attributes, say, $1, 2, \ldots, n$. Before formulating specific hypotheses, let us describe this process in intuitive terms. The subject inspects first one of the fragments, say, F_1, and then, to compare it with F_2, he has to "transport" it mentally to the location of the latter and "superimpose" it on F_2. In this process of "transportation" the perceived values of the attributes of F_1 undergo a certain fuzzification, due to fading of memory, and so on. We shall postulate that this fuzzification is representable by a Wiener process with the appropriate parameters, depending on the time used (or the distance separating the fragments) and on the type of attributes that serve for comparison.

We shall say that the attributes, say, i, of fragments F_1 and F_2, "match" if the values of the appropriate Wiener processes representing these attributes do not differ by more than a certain threshold at the time of comparison. We have therefore a set of n pairs of processes, and F_1 is perceived as identical to F_2 if all n pairs match (though perhaps with different thresholds). We shall derive the theoretical expressions for the probability that F_1 and F_2 will be perceived as identical, given the true values of their attributes.

Now, the main issue is the distinction between parallel and serial processing [studied extensively by various researchers, notably, Townsend; see, e.g., Townsend and Landon (1983)]. If the comparison is parallel, that is, all n pairs of processes are compared simultaneously, then (assuming independence of various attributes), the probability of F_1 being perceived as identical to F_2 is simply the product of the probabilities that the pairs match. If, on the other hand, that comparison is serial, the situation is different. First, a given attribute is compared, and if matching occurs, the next pair is compared, and so on, until either a nonmatching pair is found or all pairs are found matching. In this case, each pair is compared at a different time, and therefore the processes that are compared later undergo more fuzzification than the processes compared earlier.

We shall start by describing the assumptions about the process of fuzzification. Then we derive the formulas for the probability of a match for a given attribute, and finally, we derive the formulas for the probability of a particular outcome for n-fold comparison under the hypothesis of parallel and serial processing.

We assume that F_1 is inspected first, and then "transported" to the location of F_2. Next, F_2 is inspected, and then the process of comparison of the attributes occurs. It will be convenient to set $t = 0$ at the time when the inspection of F_1 terminates and the process of "transportation" starts. We shall denote by T_1 the duration of this process, so that at T_1 the inspection of F_2 begins, and it lasts until $T_1 + T_2$. The comparison starts at $T_1 + T_2 + T_3$. In the case of parallel comparison, time $T_1 + T_2 + T_3$ is the same for all attributes. In the case of serial processing, we assume that the comparison of each attribute takes the same amount of time T_4, so that the attribute that is compared first is compared at $T_1 + T_2 + T_3$, second at $T_1 + T_2 + T_3 + T_4$, third at $T_1 + T_2 + T_3 + 2T_4$, and so on. Generally, the attribute that is compared as kth in order is compared at time $T_1 + T_2 + T_3 + (k - 1)T_4$.

Let $x_i(t)$ and $y_i(t)$ be the sizes of the memory traces of ith attribute $(i = 1, 2, \ldots, n)$ of F_1 and F_2, respectively. Naturally, $y_i(t)$ is defined only for $t \geq T_1 + T_2$, that is, for times following the end of inspection of F_2. Let m_i and r_i denote the true sizes of the ith attribute of F_1 and F_2, respectively.

We shall make the following assumptions.

ASSUMPTION 5.12 *In the interval* $[0, T_1]$*, trace* $x_i(t)$ *of the* ith *attribute of* F_1 *is a Wiener process with*

$$E[x_i(t)] = m_1, \qquad \text{Var}[x_i(t)] = a_i^2 t, \qquad 0 \leq t \leq T_1. \tag{5.113}$$

ASSUMPTION 5.13 *In the interval* $[T_1, T_1 + T_2]$*, trace* $x_i(t)$ *of the* ith *attribute of* F_1 *is a Wiener process such that for all* t', t'' *with* $T_1 \leq t' \leq t'' \leq T_1 + T_2$ *we have*

$$E[x_i(t'') - x_i(t')] = 0, \tag{5.114}$$

$$E[x_i(t'') - x_i(t')]^2 = b_i^2(t'' - t'). \tag{5.115}$$

ASSUMPTION 5.14 *In the interval* $[T_1 + T_2, T_1 + T_2 + T_3]$ *(after inspection of* F_2 *and until the beginning of the comparison),* $x_i(t)$ *and* $y_i(t)$ *are Wiener processes such that*

$$E[y_i(T_1 + T_2)] = r_i, \tag{5.116}$$

and for all t', t'' *with* $T_1 + T_2 \leq t' \leq t'' \leq T_1 + T_2 + T_3$*, we have*

$$E[x_i(t'') - x_i(t')] = E[y_i(t'') - y_i(t')] = 0, \tag{5.117}$$

$$E[x_i(t'') - x_i(t')]^2 = E[y_i(t'') - y_i(t')]^2 = c_i^2(t'' - t'). \tag{5.118}$$

ASSUMPTION 5.15 *Suppose that* t' *and* t''*, where* $T_1 + T_2 + T_3 \leq t' \leq t''$*, are two times preceding the time of comparison of the* ith *attribute (i.e., until time* t''

some other attributes were compared). Then

$$E[x_i(t'') - x_i(t')] = E[y_i(t'') - y_i(t')] = 0 \tag{5.119}$$

and

$$E[x_i(t'') - x_i(t')]^2 = E[y_i(t'') - y_i(t')]^2 = d_i^2(t'' - t'). \tag{5.120}$$

These assumptions concerned, in effect, the character of the process of fuzzification. It is postulated to be a Wiener process, with varying variances (diffusion constants): during the transportation, variance of $x_i(t)$ increases proportionally to a_i^2; during the time when F_2 is inspected, this variance increases further, this time proportionally to b_i^2; following the time of inspection of F_2, the variance in both processes $x_i(t)$ and $y_i(t)$ increases proportionally to c_i^2; and finally, during the process of comparing other attributes, the increase of variance is proportional to d_i^2. The constants may be different, and it is reasonable to assume that b_i exceeds a_i and that d_i exceeds c_i.

The following assumption concerns the mechanism of comparison.

ASSUMPTION 5.16   *Figures F_1 and F_2 are preceived as identical if at the time t of comparison we have*

$$[x_i(t) - y_i(t)| \leq \varepsilon_i \quad for \quad i = 1, 2, \ldots, n, \tag{5.121}$$

where ε_i are some constants.

Finally, we impose the following assumption.

ASSUMPTION 5.17   *Processes $x_1(t), \ldots, x_n(t), y_1(t), \ldots, y_n(t)$ are independent.*

Let us first calculate the probability that figures F_1 and F_2 will appear identical on the ith attribute if the comparison occurs at time t. For simplicity, let us drop the index i of the attribute.

From the assumptions of the model, it follows that random variables $x(t)$ and $y(t)$ have normal distributions with means m and r. Let us denote their variances by A^2 and B^2, respectively. We then have, for the probability that F_1 will be regarded as identical (with respect to the given attribute), the following expression:

$$P(m, r, A, B, \varepsilon) = P[|x(t) - y(t)| \leq \varepsilon]$$

$$= P[y(t) - \varepsilon \leq x(t) \leq y(t) + \varepsilon]$$

$$= \int P[u - \varepsilon \leq x(t) \leq u + \varepsilon \,|\, y(t) = u] \, dP[y(t) \leq u]. \tag{5.122}$$

By the assumed independence of $x(t)$ and $y(t)$, we may write for the integrand in the last expression

$$P[u - \varepsilon \le x(t) \le u + \varepsilon] = P[(u - \varepsilon - m)/A \le (x(t) - m)/A \le (u + \varepsilon - m)/A]$$

$$= \Phi\left(\frac{u - m}{A} + \frac{\varepsilon}{A}\right) - \Phi\left(\frac{u - m}{A} - \frac{\varepsilon}{A}\right), \tag{5.123}$$

where Φ denotes the standard normal distribution function. Substituting into (5.122) we obtain

$$P(m, r, A, B, \varepsilon) = \frac{1}{B\sqrt{2\pi}} \int \left[\Phi\left(\frac{u - m}{A} + \frac{\varepsilon}{A}\right) - \Phi\left(\frac{u - m}{A} - \frac{\varepsilon}{A}\right)\right]$$

$$\times \exp\left[-\frac{1}{2}\left(\frac{u - r}{B}\right)^2\right] du. \tag{5.124}$$

Substitution of $u = r + Bz$ yields

$$P(m, r, A, B, \varepsilon) = \frac{1}{\sqrt{2\pi}} \int \left[\Phi\left(\frac{B}{A^z} + \frac{r - m}{A} + \frac{\varepsilon}{A}\right) - \Phi\left(\frac{B}{A^z} + \frac{r - m}{A} - \frac{\varepsilon}{A}\right)\right]$$

$$\times \exp\left(-\frac{1}{2}z^2\right) dz. \tag{5.125}$$

Now, under the hypothesis of parallel processing, the comparison occurs at time $T_1 + T_2 + T_3$ for all attributes, and hence the variances A^2 and B^2 are

$$A^2 = \text{Var}[x(T_1 + T_2 + T_3)] = a^2 T_1 + b^2 T_2 + c^2 T_3, \tag{5.126}$$

$$B^2 = \text{Var}[y(T_1 + T_2 + T_3)] = c^2 T_3 \tag{5.127}$$

[since process $y(t)$ starts only at $T_1 + T_2$].

Consequently, we have the following theorem.

THEOREM 5.18 *Under the hypothesis of parallel processing, probability $P(I)$ that F_1 and F_2 will be perceived as identical is*

$$P(I) = \prod_{i=1}^{n} P\left(m_i, r_i, \sqrt{a_i^2 T_1 + b_i^2 T_2 + c_i^2 T_3}, \sqrt{c_i^2 T_3}, \varepsilon_i\right), \tag{5.128}$$

with the factors given by (5.124).

Now let us analyze the serial comparisons. Suppose that the order of comparisons is given by a permutation $(i_1, i_2, \ldots, i_n)$ of numbers $1, \ldots, n$, to be interpreted so that attribute number i_k is compared as kth in order. Clearly, the first comparison occurs at time $T_1 + T_2 + T_3$, the second at $T_1 + T_2 + T_3 + T_4$, the third at $T_1 + T_2 + T_3 + 2T_4$, and so on. For a fixed permutation

$(i_1, \ldots, i_n)$, the probability of F_1 being indistinguishable from F_2 is

$$\prod_{k=1}^{n} P(m_{i_k}, r_{i_k}, \sqrt{a^2 T_1 + b^2 T_2 + c^2 T_3 + (k-1)d^2 T_4}, \sqrt{c^2 T_3 + (k-1)d^2 T_4}, \varepsilon_{i_k}).$$

$$(5.129)$$

Consequently, we have the following.

THEOREM 5.19 *Under the hypothesis of serial comparisons, the probability that F_1 will be perceived as indistinguishable from F_2 is*

$$P(I) = \frac{1}{n!} \sum_{(i_1, \ldots, i_n)} Q(i_1, \ldots, i_n),$$

$$(5.130)$$

where $Q(i_1, \ldots, i_n)$ is given by (5.129).

5.4.3 A Modification: Memory Storage of Unconceptualizable Stimuli

Let us now consider the following modification of the scheme of experiments from Section 5.4.2 concerning the mechanisms of translation. Generally, the task will be to perform some simple arithmetic operations on the displayed stimuli; namely form their sums or differences. We begin with describing the experiment and then formulate the hypotheses.

The subject is confronted with a panel; looking at it from the subject's side, the panel has no markings, except those indicating two endpoints of a imaginary horizontal line. A sliding window with a single mark is attached to the panel, so that the subject may move it to the right or to the left between the two marked points.

The sliding window may also be moved by the experimenter, who sits on the opposite side of the panel. Looking at it from his side, one may see markings indicating the distances from the endpoint. Thus, the experimenter may set the window at any desired distance x from one of the endpoints, and he may also ask the subject to indicate, by sliding the window, the midpoint (say) between the markings, and he may thus be able to determine the error in the subject's setting of the window.

At first the window is set by the experimenter at a point x (counting, say, from the leftmost endpoint as visible from the subject's side). The subject is asked to remember the distance between the mark in the window and the leftmost point so as to be able to reconstruct it later.

Next, after some pause, the window is set at another point y, and again, the subject is asked to remember its position. Finally, after some pause, the subject is asked to put the mark in the window, by sliding it appropriately, to the location $x + y$. The experimenter then records the error, that is, the deviation from the location indicated by the subject and the proper location of the point $x + y$.

The main hypothesis is that the stimuli may be partitioned into those that are conceptualizable and those that are not. The first type consists of stimuli that the subject may identify as one-half, one-third, or one-quarter of the distance between the marks and store the appropriate information in his long-term memory. Thus, for conceptualizable stimuli, it is not necessary to keep them in the "pictorial" part of the memory: they may be stored in verbal memory and then recalled and reconstructed at will. We conjecture that the conceptualizable stimuli are precisely those that correspond to a fraction of the total length, with the denominator equal to 2, 3, or 4. All other stimuli are called unconceptualizable, and it will be conjectured that they have to be held in the "pictorial" memory, where they are subject to distortions which increase with time.

To formulate the hypotheses, let us assume that the experimental scheme is such that the first stimulus x is displayed for time t_1, followed by a pause of duration t^*, and the by the display of stimulus y for duration t_2. Then, after another pause of length t^{**}, the subject is asked to make the sum $x + y$.

The control variables therefore constitute the vector $(x, y, t_1, t^*, t_2, t^{**})$; moreover, each of the stimuli x, y may be conceptualizable or not. Naturally, the sum $x + y$ cannot exceed the total length of the panel.

We shall make the following hypotheses concerning the properties of memory storage of stimuli.

HYPOTHESIS 5.6   *If stimulus x is of the conceptualizable type, this fact will be noticed by the subject after some threshold time D_x. Then the stimulus become stored in long-term memory and may be recalled at any time. If u_x denotes the reconstructed length of stimulus x, then u_x is a random variable with normal distribution $N(x, b_x^2)$.*

This hypothesis asserts, in effect, that when a conceptualizable stimulus, say, $x = \frac{1}{2}$, is displayed and later the subject is asked to reconstruct it, then his average error is 0 and variance is constant, depending possibly on x but not on the time elapsed.

The next hypothesis describes the changes in unconceptualizable stimuli that occur between the time they are stored in memory and the time they are used to reconstruct the size.

HYPOTHESIS 5.7   *If stimulus x is unconceptualizable, then its memory trace at time t after the end of exposure say, $u_x(t)$, is a random variable with normal distribution with $Eu_x(t) = x$ and $\operatorname{Var} u_x(t) = \sigma_x^2 t$.*

We shall now consider the error of the location of $x + y$ as set by the subject, depending on whether each of the stimuli is conceptualizable. These cases will be denoted by UU, UC, CU, and UU.

In the case UU, that is, when both stimuli are unconceptualizable, the variance of location of x is $\sigma_x^2(t^* + t_2 + t^{**})$, whereas the variance of the second stimulus y is $\sigma_y^2 t^{**}$. Consequently, the variance of the location of $x + y$ (as well as of $x - y$) is

$$\text{Var}_{x+y}(U, U) = \sigma_x^2(t^* + t_2 + t^{**}) + \sigma_y^2 t^{**}. \tag{5.131}$$

In the case CU, the variance of the location of x is b_x^2, whereas the variance of the location of y is $\sigma_y^2 t^{**}$. Consequently,

$$\text{Var}_{x+y}(C, U) = b_x^2 + \sigma_y^2 t^{**}. \tag{5.132}$$

In the case UC, the situation is similar, and the variance of the observed error is

$$\text{Var}_{x+y}(U, C) = \sigma_x^2(t^* + t_2 + t^{**}) + b_y^2. \tag{5.133}$$

Finally, in the case CC, we have

$$\text{Var}_{x+y}(C, C) = b_x^2 + b_y^2. \tag{5.134}$$

One can now set the ANOVA-type of experiment by varying x, y, and other parameters appropriately. This leads to testing various hypotheses about the parameters of the model.

The results of the preliminary experiments suggest that the error of $x + y$ does not depend on the value of the second stimulus. There exists, however, an interaction between the two stimuli ($p < 0.01$). This indicates that the second stimulus affects the memory of the first stimulus in a selective way, disturbing it more deeply in cases when the first stimulus is unconceptualizable.

The significance of these results lies in their directing the attention at various perceptual phenomena occurring in the so-called cross-modality matching [see, e.g., Krantz et al. (1971)]. Consequently, some of the findings obtained by the use of this technique [e.g., subadditivity of utilities, observed by Anderson and Shanteau (1970)] may in reality be artifacts.

5.4.4 Model of Optimal Glance Path

The model of Section 5.4.1 concerned eye movements in "free" inspection of the figure, idealized as a random walk guided by instantaneous impulses arising from the growing attractiveness of uninspected domains. On the other hand, the models of Section 5.4.2 concerned the process of comparison of features extracted from inspection of two domains.

Now, in reality, the process of comparison is carried out with some goal, conscious or not, such as recognition. Consequently, the inspection process is to some extent guided by this goal and is a mixture of purely random walk and purely deterministic inspection.

Thus it is worthwhile to study also the other extreme case of inspection process, namely the purely purposeful examination of the picture, aimed at recognizing and identifying it. Here the problem may be formulated as follows. Suppose that the picture is known (e.g., after preliminary inspection) to represent an object from a given class, and further inspection is needed to identify the particular member of the class that it represents (e.g., one knows that the picture represents a car and the goal is to identify the year, make, and model). Typically, the identification would consist of inspecting a number of "crucial" points $p_1, \ldots, p_n$ and identifying some attributes of fragments represented by these points.

Under additional assumptions about the frequency of objects of a given class (or alternatively, prior probabilities) and the probabilities of given attributes to be found at places $p_1, \ldots, p_n$, one can formulate the problem of inspection as an optimalization problem. The goal might be, for example, recognition in the least number of inspected points or in shortest time, and the control variables are the successive points $p_{i_1}, p_{i_2}, \ldots$ to be inspected.

The question may be generally posed as follows. With every permutation $i_1, \ldots, i_n$ and every object x, one may associate the value $C(i_1, \ldots, i_n; x)$ of the criterion function, for example the average time of identification of x under this permutation. If $q(x)$ is the prior probability that the object inspected is x, then

$$C(i_1, \ldots, i_n) = \int C(i_1, \ldots, i_n; x) \, dq(x) \tag{5.135}$$

is the expected criterion value at permutation $i_1, \ldots, i_n$. The objective is to find the optimal permutation, that is, such that $C(i_1, \ldots, i_n)$ is minimized.

The solution now reduces to one of the known schemes, either involving Bellman equation or some other optimization (e.g., salesman problem), depending on specific assumptions about the probabilities of finding "informative" attributes at specific points $p_1, \ldots, p_n$.

For example, the above general setup may be implemented as follows, leading to a specific optimization problem. Suppose that with each of the points $p_1, p_2, \ldots, p_n$ there is associated a feature, say, $f_1, \ldots, f_n$, that becomes apparent upon inspection of p_i with probability $\pi(i)$ (we assume here that one feature is associated with each point; generalization to more than one feature of a given point is obvious). Now let $F = \{f_1, \ldots, f_n\}$ be the set of all features; we may distinguish a class of subsets of F that are sufficient for recognition [of a given meaning z; see Nowakowska (1967) for the use of such fact in building a recognition model and defining weights of fragments]. Let $F_1, \ldots, F_r$ be all subsets sufficient for recognition. Finally, assume that it takes time T_{ij} to move the eye from the domain of p_i to the domain of p_j and inspect the latter.

About the class of sets sufficient for recognition, we shall make the following assumption. Let $F^* = \{F_1, \ldots, F_r\}$ be the class of all sets that are sufficient for recognition. Then

(a) for every subset S of F, there exists a set $F_k \in F^*$ such that $S \subset F_k$;
(b) if $A \in F^*$ and $A \subset B$, then $B \in F^*$.

The state (as regards recognition) at any given time may be described by set S of features already detected, where point x is inspected last. The problem is then to move the eye from point x to some other point y to minimize the loss, defined as the time used for recognition.

For state (S, x), let the total time spent until recognition, counting from the moment of leaving the point x, under optimal inspection strategy be $C(S, x)$. Clearly, we have

$$C(S, x) = 0 \qquad \text{if} \quad S \supset F_k \text{ for some } k. \tag{5.136}$$

This simply means that, if the set S contains any of the recognition sets in F^*, then the process of recognition is completed.

In general, for determining $C(S, x)$ and the optimal strategy of inspection, one may proceed as follows. Assume that in state (S, x) one decides to inspect the point $p_k = y$ and then proceed optimally. The time used for moving from x to y is T_{xy}. With probability $\pi(y)$, the inspection of y reveals the feature of this point. The next state is then $(S \cup \{f_y\}, y)$, and therefore the residual time needed for recognition is $C(S \cup \{f_y\}, y)$. On the other hand, with probability $1 - \pi(y)$ no feature is revealed, and the new state is (S, y), with the residual time needed being $C(S, y)$. Consequently, if one decides to move to y and then proceed optimally, the expected time used is

$$T_{xy} + \pi(y)C(S \cup \{f_y\}, y) + (1 - \pi(y))C(S, y). \tag{5.137}$$

Therefore the choice of optimal y in state (S, x) is determined from the Bellman equation as

$$C(S, x) = \max_{y} [T_{xy} + \pi(y)C(S \cup \{f_y\}, y) + (1 - \pi(y))C(S, y)]. \tag{5.138}$$

Clearly, if $S \subset S'$, then $C(S, x) \geq C(S', x)$ for every x. It follows easily that the choice of y in (5.140) may be restricted to points y such that $f_y \notin S$. This allows us to determine the optimal search pattern, that is, the optimal permutation of points to inspect.

5.4.5 Stochastic Model of Fine Eye Movements and an Explanation of the Müller–Lyer Illusion

Let us now offer some new explanation of the Müller–Lyer illusion (see Fig. 5.15), consisting of the fact that line AB appears shorter than line CD, even though they are of equal length. There is considerable amount of data

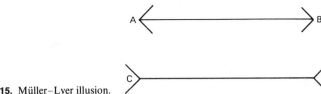

Fig. 5.15. Müller–Lyer illusion.

concerning this illusion; for a review of the literature on the subject and also some explanatory hypotheses advanced thus far, see Eijkman *et al.* (1981).

We shall present an explanation based on the assumptions about the eye movements. We postulate here that when the picture as on Fig. 5.15 is presented to a subject, stimuli *AB* and *CD* evoke some "traces," say, *ab* and *cd*. These traces result from activation by the retinal cells of a number of neurons in some locations in the brain. We need not be concerned here with determining the location in the brain where the traces of the stimuli are located, stored, and processed. We shall, in fact, use only the following postulate.

ASSUMPTION 5.18   *The size (in this case, length) of a stimulus is represented by its trace (e.g., number of neurons activated). A stimulus P is judged as larger (in this case, longer) than stimulus Q if the size of the trace of P at the time of comparison exceeds the size of the trace of stimulus Q.*

Because the judgment whether *AB* is shorter than *CD* results from the comparison of lengths of memory traces, the illusion will be explained when it is shown that the trace of *AB* is shorter than the trace of *CD*.

The mechanism of forming the trace is assumed to be the following.

ASSUMPTION 5.19   *When the image of the stimulus falls on the appropriate cells in the retina, the signal activates the corresponding memory cells assigned to store the memory trace. When the signal stops, these cells lose the stimulus after a random time, assumed to be exponentially distributed with parameter c (so that the mean time a cell remains activated after the stimulus ceases is equal to 1/c).*

We shall also assume, as in Section 5.4.1, that the eye, when focused at a certain point, performs some random movement in the vicinity of this point.

Let us now consider the "outward" arrow (see Fig. 5.16 for the enlargement of the endpoint). Without loss of generality, we may choose the coordinate system so that point *C* falls at the origin and the arrow extends in the positive direction along the *x* axis.

The movements of the eye inspecting a fixed arrow are equivalent to the movements of the arrow. We shall therefore assume that the arrow in Fig. 5.16 performs some process, to be more specific, the Ornstein–Uhlenbeck process, around its central position marked on the figure.

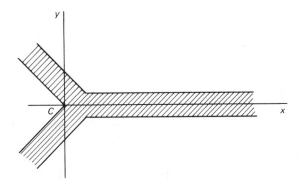

Fig. 5.16. Explanation of Müller–Lyer illusion in terms of a stochastic model, showing the "outward" arrow.

The intuitive explanation of the illusion is now as follows. Each point (x, y), sufficiently close to the arrow, is sometimes "covered" by it and sometimes not. The duration of time when the memory trace exists equals the time when the point is covered, plus the portion of time when it is not covered, but the trace has not yet faded.

Clearly, a point of the form $(x, 0)$ for small negative x will often be covered by the arms of the arrow and hence will generate the trace, even though there is no stimulus at $x < 0$. No such effect will be present in the "inward" arrow (see Fig. 5.17), whose memory trace will therefore be not deformed by such an effect.

To proceed formally, consider point (x, y) in the vicinity of the borderline of the arrow (i.e., such a point that the random movements of the eye will

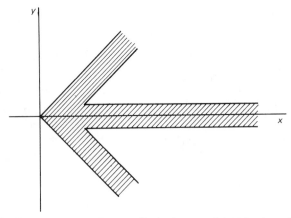

Fig. 5.17. Explanation of the Müller–Lyer illusion in terms of a stochastic model, showing the "inward" arrow.

sometimes cover and sometimes uncover this point). We may associate with this point a sequence of random times

$$U_1(x, y), V_1(x, y), U_2(x, y), V_2(x, y), \ldots \qquad (5.139)$$

representing the consecutive time lengths when point (x, y) is covered $[U_i(x, y)]$ and when it is not covered $[V_i(x, y)]$.

For simplicity, let us drop the index (x, y) and use the notation U_1, V_1, $U_2, \ldots$. Assume that all random variables U_i have the same distribution with mean A, and all random variables V_i have the common distribution function F with mean B so that

$$P(V_i \leq t) = F(t), \qquad E(U_i) = A, \qquad E(V_i) = B. \qquad (5.140)$$

We shall now determine the average time when point (x, y) will produce a memory trace in one "cycle" $U_i + V_i$. Point (x, y) will contribute to the memory trace throughout the whole period U_i, when (x, y) is covered by the stimulus, and throughout the period V_i^*, when the stimulus does not cover (x, y) but its trace is still in the memory (has not yet faded).

For given $V_i = v$ we have

$$P(V_i^* \leq t \mid V_i = v) = \begin{cases} 1 & \text{if} \quad t > v, \\ 1 - e^{-ct} & \text{if} \quad t \leq v, \end{cases} \qquad (5.141)$$

by the assumed exponentiality of the fading time of the memory trace in the absence of stimulus.

Consequently, for the expectation of the random variable V_i^* we may write

$$E(V_i^* \mid V_i = v) = ve^{-cv} + \int_0^v cte^{-ct}\,dt = \frac{1}{c}(1 - e^{-cv}). \qquad (5.142)$$

We have therefore

$$E(V_i^*) = E[E(V_i^* \mid V_i)] = \frac{1}{c}\int_0^\infty (1 - e^{-cv})\,dF(v)$$

$$= \frac{1}{c}[1 - F^*(c)], \qquad (5.143)$$

where

$$F^*(s) = \int_0^\infty e^{-vs}\,dF(v) \qquad (5.144)$$

is the Laplace transform of the distribution function F of V_i.

As a result, using (5.138), the average duration of the memory trace per one cycle $U_i + V_i$ is

$$L(x, y) = \frac{A + (1/c)[1 - F^*(c)]}{A + B}. \qquad (5.145)$$

When c approaches 0 (signal persists in memory for a long time), we have

$$\lim_{c \to 0} \frac{1}{c}[1 - F^*(c)] = \frac{dF^*(c)}{dc}\bigg|_{c=0} = B, \qquad (5.146)$$

and therefore $L(x, y)$ approaches 1. On the other hand, when $c \to \infty$ (memory traces fade fast), we obtain

$$\lim_{c \to \infty} (1/c)[1 - F^*(c)] = 0, \qquad (5.147)$$

and $L(x, y)$ approaches the value $A/(A + B)$.

Now, A, B, and $(1/c)[1 - F^*(c)]$ depend on point (x, y). Consider a point of the form $(x, 0)$ with small negative x, hence a point not on the arrow. In the case of the "outward" arrow, we may have $E(U_i)$ and $E(V_i)$ comparable to those for points $(x, 0)$ with positive x, hence points on the arrow. Consequently, in this case we may have a significant memory trace from points that do not belong to the stimulus. On the other hand, for the "inward" arrow, points of the form $(x, 0)$ with negative x will not produce such an effect.

5.4.6 Informal Analysis of Some Perceptual Illusions

Let us return to the Müller–Lyer illusion (Fig. 5.15), consisting of the fact that distance AB appears shorter than CD. According to the general principles of the model, perception is treated as an active dynamic process, where the eye produces an event-representation of the object. The eye not only moves several times along lines AB and CD, visiting their endpoints, but also projects shorter lines (arrows) on the longer ones. Generally, the illusion is due to the operation of context. The explication lies in the interaction of two processes: perception as a "mirroring" physiological process and perception as a construction process, which changes the parameters of the basic physiological process. The main parameters here are the angle α and the lengths r and a (see Fig. 5.18). The problem is to estimate the probability of shifting the endpoint A

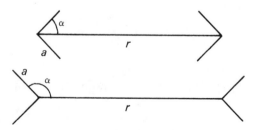

Fig. 5.18. Role of context.

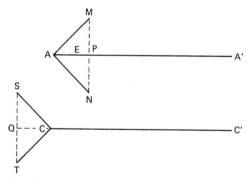

Fig. 5.19. Müller–Lyer illusion as a solution of a conflict: hypothetical construction process.

(see Fig. 5.19) in the context of AM and AN, and similarly for the "outward" arrow.

The process of visiting the endpoint A (or C), as well as projecting lines AM and AN on the horizontal line starting from A, leads to a fuzzy point P (or Q) or a distribution of points resulting from the fact that on each occasion the point P (or Q) is remembered at a somewhat different place. We assume that this distribution is bivariate normal, with mean at point P (or Q) and with some variances and correlation coefficient.

The mechanism above is consistent with the Gestalt law of closure of the triangle AMN (or CST). The final evaluation of length of the shaft of the arrow is produced relative to the fuzzy point P or Q. For the perceiver, the situation is as if the line had endpoints A and P (and corresponding points on the other end). As a result of a relatively dense event representation, point P "pulls" point A. Here the perceiver behaves as if he were applying the Gestalt law of equalization, choosing point E as a constructivistic endpoint of the line, point E being a fuzzy average of A and P.

The longer is arm AM, the less probable is the shift of A to E, so that

$$P(\text{shift of } A \text{ to } E) = f(r),$$

where f is a decreasing function of r.

In the case when intervals AM and AN are not equal, the hypothetical construction process of shifting A is as follows (see Fig. 5.20). One now has two points, P_1 and P_2, being the projections of M and N on the line starting from A. Perception may now be based on events from the path of the smaller triangle AMP_1 or larger triangle ANP_2. The tendency to simpler structure should imply more frequent use of the smaller triangle. At any rate, the perception of the length will be based on some function of points A, P_1, and P_2, with the larger weight attached to P_1 than to P_2.

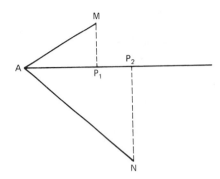

Fig. 5.20. Müller–Lyer illusion as a solution of a conflict: the role of parameters.

Another interesting object is when arms AM and AN are comparable with the total length of the shaft. One may conjecture that in this case the shift is inversely proportional to the length of the arms.

For the second situation in Fig. 5.19, the context of lines CS and CT requires, according to the mechanisms of continuation of figures, an extension of the line CC' and, symmetrically, determination of the fuzzy point Q, with respect to which one defines the shift of C.

The perceptual bias connected with the mechanism of interference of perception of the type "reaction to the stimulus" and the process of constructivistic contextual perception is more visible when the two lines, with the arms directed outward and inward, are presented simultaneously (for various r and α). Then the shift of A for the first case and the shift of C in the second case become evident because of their opposite directions. The subject may be under the impression that the difference in lengths is significant and may be of the order of several millimeters, depending on the parameters used, such as the lengths of exposed lines or angles.

For the analysis of the Poggendorf illusion (see Fig. 5.21), one should distinguish parameters such as angles, lengths of crossing lines, and lengths of lines subject to comparison.

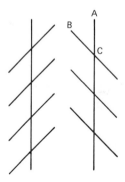

Fig. 5.21. Poggendorf illusion.

The paradoxical effect decreases with

(a)   a decrease in the number of crossing lines;
(b)   an increase of the angle;
(c)   the removal of interior arms.

On the other hand, it decreases even more with the removal of external arms (crossing lines).

The perceptual model is as follows. As before, perception will be regarded as an interference of two perceptual processes, the basic physiological process and the construction process connected with the operation of context and looking at the figure. The illusion, or perceptual bias, results from an attempt of finding a "compromise" process.

For each segment between the crossing arms, and in particular for the extreme ones, as a result of "event-representation" and especially because of the wandering of the eye between the points on the line and on the arms, there occurs the effect of line AC merging with the distracting arm BC. Consequently, line AC becomes fuzzy, with the average position somewhat in between lines AC and BC. This perceptual process dynamizes the basic line AA' in the context of the distractors. As a result, one obtains a set of segments, marked by dots in Fig. 5.22, and integration of it into one "compromise" line (marked by $+$) gives a slanted line, which explains the illusion.

Let us now consider the illusion of rotation (see Fig. 5.23): it consists of illusion of rotation of the circles, if the whole figure is subject to circular motion. As before, the explanation will consist of finding two perceptual systems: one (basic) to represent the perceptual work connected with the eye movement and the second, contextual.

The parameters of this illusion are the number of circles, their width and intensity, and the size of the figure. With an increase in the number of circles, the manifestation of the illusion becomes first stronger and, then, after passing the optimal number, gradually weaker. As regards the size, there again exists the optimal size of the figure, below and above which the illusion weakens. For the illusion, it is necessary that the figure be seen as a whole.

The basic process, when the figure is stationary, is simply the jumping of the eye from one ring to another, with higher probability of jumping to the center than away from it, as well as movements along the rings. Out of these moves, the most crucial ones are those between the rings; they are essential for an explanation of the illusion.

The contextual, or distractor, system consists of a circular motion of the whole figure. Here also we may have the optimal radius and velocity of motion, relative to the size of the figure, for which the illusion is most apparent.

To show how the illusion arises, it is enough to show the situation for one "elementary" event (see Fig. 5.24). Imagine that the eye has just moved along

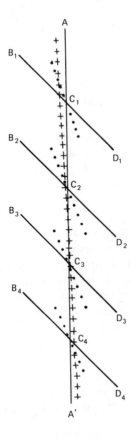

Fig. 5.22. Explanation of illusion.

Fig. 5.23. Rotation illusion.

line AB toward the center, leaving trace AB in memory. At the same time, the whole contextual system starts to work, giving a circular motion to the whole figure. To analyze the chosen event, let us analyze the shift of the points in interval AB in two positions: original AB and halfway through the motion, namely, $A'B'$. At position AB, the direction of the motion is upward, whereas in position $A'B'$ the motion is directed downward. This is marked in Fig. 5.24

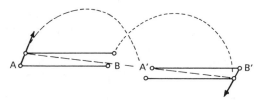

Fig. 5.24. Explanation of illusion of rotation as a solution of a conflict.

by two positions above and below lines AB and $A'B'$, representing the positions assumed shortly after positions AB and $A'B'$.

If the motion is sufficiently fast, every pair of lines on Fig. 5.24 leaves simultaneously existing memory traces. For small time intervals, these are two memory traces, one slightly below another. The resultant constructive system solves the perceptual conflict by introducing an "averaging" line (marked by dots on Fig. 5.24) that accounts for the impression of rotation when such "microeffects" are integrated for many lines. The effect here is similar to that on which line films are based, where a series of discrete pictures is integrated into one continuous motion.

This suggests that in the organization of memory one should take into account the existence of higher-order traces of a constructivistic character that allow us to register and approximate the direction of change and its magnitude. It seems that for perception of change and movement the essential roles played by such cognitive operations are translation and rotation.

This example of illusions illustrates (among others) the thesis that, for the coherent perception of structures, it is sufficient to have only some minimal number of perceptual events over these structures. This is possible because of the complementary role of knowledge, represented here by the principle of constructivism. In other words, fragmentary and discontinuous knowledge about the world becomes semantically continuous knowledge due to constructions. One may admire how economical the cognitive processes are. Moreover, one may admire how early in cognition, already on microlevel situations, there appear some elements of cognitive modeling in operations such as extension, addition, and approximation, as well as complementation of properties or rejection of them.

5.4.7   Relations between an Object and Its Verbal Copy

Imagine now that a picture has been described by the subject, that is, the subject produced a verbal copy of the picture. Let us first consider only that part of the verbal copy that consists of labels of fragments of the picture. Here the natural hypothesis is that the order of naming the fragments is connected with the recognition weights of fragments, introduced in Chapter 3.

If one assumes that the picture has a hierarchical structure, that is, it consists of fragments (first-level components), which in turn consist of parts (second-level components), and so on, then there are two natural hypotheses about the description: the hypothesis of "horizontal" and "vertical" order of description [see also Nowakowska (1967)].

In the horizontal order of description, the subject would exhaust all floors consecutively, descending only after completing the preceding floor. On each floor the order of description is determined by the weights of fragments, in the sense that the parts are named in decreasing order of weights. In the vertical order of description, the subject would commence at the top of the hierarchy and then follow the successive branches, starting from the most important ones, that is, with the one of highest weight. Each branch will be described down to the bottom before the next branch is commenced. Both the selection of branches and the selection of elements of these branches are determined by the order of decreasing weights.

Clearly, the actual description may be a mixture of the above-mentioned two orders. Each order of description may be regarded as a linear ordering of fragments of the picture, and with such an ordering there is the naturally connected relation "to be mentioned earlier than."

In actual observations one would, of course, have to take into account the effects of random deviations and repetitions and devise appropriate statistical tests for verification of the hypothesis that a given description follows some preassigned order.

Here one can formulate the following hypothesis about the order of description. In an abstract way, a description of a given picture may be regarded as a walk on the tree of hierarchy of this picture, where the nodes of the tree are endowed with weights. It might be worthwhile to study the properties of this walk, that is, relations between the weights and the transition probabilities. A tempting conjecture is that this random walk is a mixture of separate Markov chains: considering only the times when the walk visits a certain group of nodes connected with a given node (e.g., a floor of basic components), one obtains a no-return type of chain, with transition probabilities related monotonically to weights.

Formally, if S is the set of nodes in question, then the state of the chain may be identified with the set of nodes already visited, so that states are subsets A of S, including the empty set. The conjecture is that the transition probabilities are

$$P(A \cup \{f\} \mid A) = g_A[w_A(f)], \tag{5.148}$$

where f is a fragment not in A, g is some increasing function and the symbol $w_A(f)$ stands for the weight of f conditional upon knowledge of fragments in A, to be defined later. Here the left-hand side of (5.148) is the probability that fragment f will be mentioned next, given that the set of fragments already mentioned is A.

It might also be interesting to study the learning effects in connection with the experiments of observing a description. Thus, one could teach the subjects in advance something adverse to the weight structure of the picture (e.g., subjects may be rewarded for some orders of description but not for others). One could then observe the orders elicited from such experiments and compare them with "natural" orders induced by weights.

Another experiment may be of the game-type: two subjects play a cooperative game in which one of them is asked to draw a picture, knowing only the description of the picture given by the other subject. The amount of reward may depend on performance. In this way one could study the "information value" of weights of components and their fragments.

In connection with the description treated as a "walk" on the tree of object, one can state the following conjecture. The smaller is the variance of weights of the basic components, the more freedom of choice of the next fragment, and consequently, there will be more distinct permutations that occur in the population of observed verbal copies. The test of the hypothesis of the relation between the walk on the tree of the picture and the weight structure, based on observing the variance of weights and the number of distinct permutations occurring in the data, has the advantage that it does not depend on any specific assumptions about the transition probabilities. The conclusion on which the test is based depends only on the psychophysical laws: the smaller is the difference in the discriminated property (in this case weights) the more randomness there is in the choice.

Let us now consider some of the possible relations between fragments of the picture. First, consider the relation of meaning generating dominance. Naturally, the formal definition of this relation refers to weights: one fragment dominates another if it has a higher weight. However, the experimental procedure of determining this relation empirically will consist of pairwise comparisons instead of using the technique of evaluating all permutations and determining the pivotal elements. Thus, in pairwise comparisons, the observed relation need not be transitive, and the first hypothesis connects the number of intransitivities with the weight structure.

1. *If the relation of meaning-generating dominance is highly transitive (i.e., there are only a few cycles), then the weights of fragments that dominate fewer fragments will tend to be smaller.*

2. *If the relation of meaning-generating dominance is highly intransitive (i.e., there are many cycles), the weights tend to be poorly discriminated.*

The second relation, called *aesthetic dominance*, is also elicited experimentally by asking the subjects to make pair comparisons between fragments and to point out the fragment that they think is more important from the point of view of aesthetics.

We may then formulate the following hypothesis.

3. *If the relation of aesthetic dominance is highly transitive, the picture is more likely to be judged static; if it is highly intransitive, it is likely to be judged dynamic.*

4. *The more contradictory are the graphs of the dominance relation for pictures stripped of some of the their properties (e.g., color), the more cycles will appear in the relation of dominance for the final version of the picture and the less stable (inter- and intraindividually) these graphs will be.*

Thus, this hypothesis concerns the way in which various attributes, such as color, intervene in the overall relation of dominance.

The conclusion of the hypothesis agrees with the known psychological phenomena, namely that people are generally not capable of integrating conflicting attributes in a coherent way, and they show a tendency of taking into account only one attribute in making the judgment.

Another relation between the fragments, closely related to weights and to the process of recognition as contained in verbal copy in the form of a meaning assignment, is the relation of proper proportion. The implicit definition of this relation is as follows: fragments of a picture are in relation of proper proportions, if they are geometrically placed in such a way that does not prevent the picture from being recognized as intended by the experimenter. Examples are presented on Fig. 5.25.

We may then formulate the following hypothesis.

5. *Those fragments that must be drawn with least freedom of choice to preserve the relation of proper proportions have highest weights.*

Here the question is to determine experimentally the classes of transformations (in this case, deformations) of the picture under which the meaning remains invariant. The hypothesis asserts that those fragments that can be greatly deformed without affecting the recognition have small weights, and those fragments for which there is little freedom of choice have higher weights.

Finally, let us consider the following observable variables connected with verbal copies:

(a) the decision about the meaning of the picture;

(b) the aesthetic evaluation of it, that is, the decision about aesthetic value;

(c) latencies of these decisions, that is, the length of the part of the verbal copy preceding the verbalization of the decision.

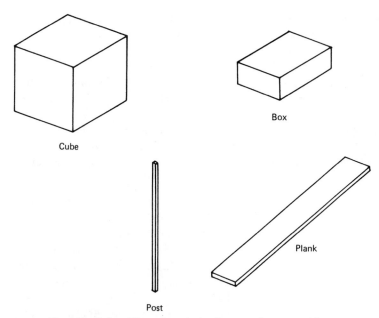

Fig. 5.25. Deformations of a cube leading to various recognitions.

(d)   the inter- and intraindividual variability of these decisions under repetition of the experiment, that is, variability in different productions of verbal copies of the same object.

The problem consists of connecting these variables with the structure of the picture (described object) by building a decision model and appropriate hypotheses. The decision model that accounts for the recognition and aesthetic judgment is a refinement of the model discussed in Chapter 3, namely connecting the decision about the meaning and the order of inspection. The refinement consists of inclusion of the following aspects:

1.   The basis for a decision may be not only the inspection of fragments but also the information produced by the subject himself. In the model, it will be referred to, in a picturesque way, as "information taken from the head."

2.   The decision making has a sequential character; the decision may be reached at any time during the process, not only at the termination of inspection of all fragments.

The assumptions of the model are as follows.

A.   *Information is drawn in portions, either from the object, or from the head.*

B. *The first portion of information is drawn from the object.*

C. *After drawing a portion of information, a trial decision is made, and the subjective probability of its correctness is assessed.*

D. *The level of this subjective probability determines whether* (i) *the decision is verbalized or* (ii) *the next portion of information is drawn. The decision is verbalized, if the subjective probability in C is high or the recent portions of information were such that the subjective probability did not change. In the opposite case,* (ii) *occurs, that is, the next portion of information is drawn.*

E. *If* (ii) *occurs, that is, the next portion of information is drawn, then it is drawn from the object if the subject expects it to be relevant; otherwise it is drawn from the head.*

The crucial points in these assumptions are those that specify when the decision is reached, and if it is not reached, whether the next portion of information is drawn from the object or from the head.

This still leaves open one question: if the information is taken from the picture, then which fragment is going to be inspected? The answer is, again, in terms of hypotheses combining the order of inspection and weights. However, it is necessary to modify somewhat the definition of weights given in Chapter 3, by introducing the concept of conditional weights: these are simply the weights of fragments that have not been inspected thus far, computed under the assumption that some fragments have already been inspected. The formal definition is, of course, based again on the notion of a decisive fragment in a permutation, except that now the class of permutations is restricted to those that begin with the fragments assumed to be known.

The conditional weights are defined as

$$w_z(f \mid f'_1, \ldots, f'_r) = B/(n - r)!, \tag{5.149}$$

where B is the number of permutations that start with fragments $f'_1, \ldots, f'_r$ in arbitrary order, where f is decisive in them.

The interpretation of the conditional weight (5.149) is such that it equals the importance (for recognizing the picture as z) of fragment f, given that fragments $f'_1, \ldots, f'_r$ are already drawn.

We have here the following hypothesis.

In the process of drawing successive portions of information from the object, in situations when the subject has the freedom of choice of fragment for inspection, he will choose that fragment whose conditional weight with respect to the previously inspected fragments is maximal.

This hypothesis, stated for simplicity in its deterministic version, asserts that the next inspected fragment is that with the highest conditional weight. Of course, for the purpose of analysis, one would have to use a probabilistic version of this hypothesis, asserting that the probabilities of the next fragments are related in an increasing way to the conditional weights. Incidentally, this hypothesis can be tested by a very simple experiment, whose version may be as follows [see also Nowakowka (1967)].

The subject is to recognize the meaning of a picture that is covered by paper with a hole in it, so that only a part of the picture may be inspected. The subject can move the paper. It may be conjectured that he will move the paper in such a way that he will be able to inspect the fragments with highest conditional weights, that is, are most informative, in the sense that they provide the best clues to differentiate various hypotheses about the meaning of the picture.

Here are some hypotheses about the model. The crucial ones for making the inference are the last three.

(a) *The order of drawing information from the object depends on the structure of the object and the weights of its fragments.*

(b) *The less clear is the object, that is, the poorer the differentiation of weights, the more often the information is drawn "from the head."*

(c) *If the subjective probability of correctness of the decision is high, then latency of decision is either very short or very long.*

(d) *If the subjective probability of correctness is low, the intraindividual variability is high, and conversely.*

(e) *There exist no objects for which the subjective probability of decision is low and latency of decisions short.*

Especially the third and the fifth hypotheses combined allow us to infer about the subjective certainty of the decision from the latency of this decision if it is short. If latency is long, one needs additional information about the variability.

Here is the logical scheme of inference from latency and variability. If the latency time is short, then subjective probability is high. If the latency is neither short nor long, then the subjective probability is low. If the latency is long and intraindividual variability is high, then the subjective probability is low; if the latency is long and intraindividual variability is small, then subjective probability is high.

The question now arises: what properties of objects can legitimately be inferred from such summary information as the latency and variability of decisions? Obviously, since one abstracts here from the content of the decision, the best one can hope is to make inference about some very general features of the object, namely only the features that may be expressed in terms of differentiation of weights, that is, clarity and difficulty in recognizing or making aesthetic judgments.

Weights of fragments	Differentiated	
	Well	Poorly
Differentiated well	1	2
Differentiated poorly	3	4

This scheme shows one type of categorization, which might possibly lead to inference (for aesthetic judgments) from latency and variability. The categories are obtained from two dichotomies: poor and good differentiation of weights of basic components and of their elements.

The hypotheses are as follows.

Type 1: *easily recognizable content, composed of easily recognizable elements (e.g., realistic paintings)*;

Type 2: *content difficult to recognize, composed of easily recognizable elements (e.g., surrealistic paintings)*;

Type 3: *easily recognizable content, fragments difficult to recognize (e.g., some impressionistic paintings)*;

Type 4: *content and meanings of fragments difficult to recognize (e.g., some abstract paintings)*.

Finally, we have the inference scheme for the two features of verbal copies: latency of decision about meaning, and variability.

Latency	Variability	
	Small	Large
Short	1	×
Medium	×	2
Long	3	4

The objects marked by × do not exist, in view of the hypotheses of the model. The hypotheses about inference are as follows.

Type 1: *clear meaning, easy recognition (e.g., objects of common use)*;

Type 2: *unclear, unfamiliar, judged unimportant*;

Type 3: *unclear, unfamiliar, judged interesting, finally classified*;

Type 4: *same as in type 3, except that there is no reliable classification achieved*.

Here is the same inference scheme, but for the aesthetic judgments.

Type 1: *well-known and recognized artistic objects and also objects of low aesthetic value*;
Type 2: *judged controversial, not interesting*;
Type 3: *judged important, controversial, interesting*;
Type 4: *same as in type 3.*

The difference between types 3 and 4 depends here on the personality characteristics of the subject. Observe also that the class corresponding to type 1 is not homogeneous: it contains two "extreme" categories, those of objects with low and high artistic value.

As regards the problems of meaning of an object or its fragment—defined an an invariant of some class of transformations—the meaning was not treated as a sum of the meanings of components. Already at the level of fragments, a series of mechanisms may be distinguished (as was done in Chapter 3), such as supporting or inhibiting a meaning, under the assumption of the existence of competitive meanings. Similar mechanisms operate, of course, on the level of objects. On the scale of degree of meanings, the values are bounded from below and from above, so that addition of the increments of meanings of the same sign give first a marginal increase and then a sudden reversal of sign, after exceeding a certain threshold. For instance, excessive expression of politeness becomes—when exceeding a threshold—a pejorative impoliteness.

If one considers, as in Chapter 3, the scale of fuzzy meanings, one obtains a combination of semantics with the models of scaling considered in psychophysics, and one may use the arsenal of means of this theory for empirical studies. Contemporary psychology of cognitive processes operates with the concept of cognitive or semantic representation. As a rule, such representation is built for expressions in the natural language, concerning a given situation, scene, and so on. The form of such a representation depends on the particular semantic theory used, on its sets of primitives, such as sememes or symbols, as well as on other metalinguistic entities.

The basic notions here would be "actor," "object," "place," "cause," and so on. In general, such representations are more or less developed graphs of relations, since some of the primitives are relational terms. The aim of these representations is to show the structure of the knowledge and thinking for a situation, problem, and so on. The result is a "cognitive map" on some level of abstraction, or "semantic model" of the situation, as reflected in the natural language, which is here the source of cognition, not its goal. The disadvantages of this approach are that such maps show the structure and not the dynamics of the cognitive process and also that there is no theory for analyzing such maps.

Here, as the discussion concentrated mainly on the study of relations between object structure and its perception, as reflected in the language, the analysis concerned relations between the order of the verbal copy and the structure of the object; the possibility of reconstructing some properties of the object described, from the properties of verbal copy, such as aesthetic judgments; and the properties of sets of verbal copies, taken as separate "languages" of objects.

If one assumes that there already exists a theory of semantic representations for sentences in the natural language (in the form of such structures or "semantic maps" built in some formalism with special symbols and primitives), one could introduce the "language of semantics," in the following way [see Nowakowska (1976b)].

First, one would have to accept some way (or some ways) of linearizing such representations. Then, to every sentence there would correspond one or more strings of symbols of the given formalism, which are linearizations of the structure of this sentence. The set of all such linearizations, for all sentences in the natural language would constitute, by definition, the language of semantics, that is, the class of strings of the considered alphabet of symbols. Thus, to each meaning there would correspond a string of symbols, and the set of all such strings would be the language of semantics. This language could be studied by means developed in formal linguistics, such as distributional classes, parasitic strings, or generative grammars, or by means of the formal theory of actions developed by Nowakowska (1973). The results would lead to a certain "syntax of semantics." Each string of such semantic language would represent a composite meaning, expressible in the natural language. Considering the primitive concepts on various levels of generality, one would obtain a hierarchy of such languages. In another approach, one could take as "letters" of the alphabet the complete representations and consider the language of semantics of texts by analyzing the strings of such representations.

It is also worth stressing that the notion of weights and decisive fragments allows us not only to identify the basic structure of the sign but also to empirically determine the minimal carriers of meanings, that is, such configurations of fragments that allow recognition. From a formal point of view, these minimal structures would be (in the terminology of voting theory) the minimal winning coalitions. This conception differs from the sometimes encountered idea of the existence of the minimal structure of a sign, since there would generally be more than one such minimal structure. Characterization of properties of a semiotic sign would then consist of specifying the whole class of such minimal coalitions, that is, substructures sufficient for recognition.

In this approach the weight of a fragment—the central notion of the suggested theory—acquires an interpretation as the number of minimal winning coalitions which contain this fragment.

At the end, it is worthwhile to discuss some of the theoretical consequences of the proposed model. The basic consequences are connected with the following question: what is the relation between the proposed model of perception and the Gestalt theory? The answer to this question may be expressed in the form of a "translation" of some laws of the Gestalt theory into the language of the proposed model built on the notion of weights of fragments. Specifically, this translation will consist of quantizing the notion of a "good" figure introduced by Gestalt theory, thus allowing an analysis of the problem of stability of pattern.

The Gestalt theory formulates some laws that, in relation to perception, describe the principle of "building" figures and the criteria of "goodness" of figure. The principle of building figures asserts that man recognizes as figures those configurations of elements that are near one to another (Law of Proximity), are similar (Law of Similarity), "close" the figure (Law of Closure), are continuations of one another (Law of Continuation), and are familiar to the perceiver (Law of Familiarity). As regards the criteria for good figures, the Gestalt theory distinguishes "good" and "bad" figures. In a "good" figure, the parts are well harmonized and well subordinated to the figure as a whole. Simplicity, harmony, and clarity are the properties of good figures. The basic notion of the Gestalt theory is that of equilibrium, expressed as a general tendency toward simplicity, which is equivalent (both in the process of perception and in the process of learning) to the tendency of forming the best Gestalt. This goal-directed tendency is its main law. According to this theory, three phenomena occur in the process of perception: leveling (i.e., tendency toward greater symmetry), sharpening (i.e., tendency toward accentuating the most important elements), and normalizing (i.e., tendency toward clarity and simplicity of the perceived figure). Thus the basic features of a good figure are symmetry, good accentuation, and simplicity.

In terms of the proposed model, the symmetric figures will have the property consisting of equality of weights of all symmetric elements of the picture. Good accentuation of the figure is the property of distinct differentiation of the weights of fragments on the floor of basic components. Finally, normalization of the figure, its simplicity and clarity, is expressed by the requirement that the tree of the hierarchy of the picture have few floors. In his tendency toward "good" figures, the perceiver therefore tends to form figures that are symmetric, with well-differentiated weights of the basic components and with a possibly small number of floors of the hierarchy tree.

As regards the structure of the verbal copy and the production of sign (assertion about the meaning or aesthetic value), the situation is as follows. First, the object perceived may appear to the subject as incomplete to some degree, at least in certain aspects. For instance, for a fixed position of the observer, the object may be seen only from one side. Next, on a picture, some parts of the figures may be without continuation, or covered by other parts, and so on. Because of that, the main mechanism in building the verbal copy and assigning the meaning is based on the process of complementation of lacking relations, properties, attributes, and so on, or even actions or events. The material for this complementation is taken "from the head," that is, from past experience, knowledge, reasoning, and so on, stored in the memory in the shape of "ideal" objects, schemes of events, or actions, and so on.

The complementation of the perceived picture or its fragments follows some laws, such as laws of the Gestalt theory (of proximity, similarity, continuation, and so on). In general, the complementation seems to follow the basic tendency of human perception to complement a fragment to an ideal good figure, that is, a well-balanced and simple figure. In other words, the process of complementation is based on the fact of existence of ideal objects stored in human memory. The ideal objects appear here as results of classes of transformations under which the objects retain their meanings. Thus, the meaning may be treated as an invariant of a large class of transformations (such as changes of perspective, rotations, or changes of proportions or dimensions. [Incidentally, the complementation is often automatic, to the extent that it is not given in introspection and is noted only in conscious decision making about the object (its meaning).]

Second, the complementation is parsimonious, in the sense that it is carried only to the extent needed for the conclusion. Thus, a verbal copy is, on the one hand, a description or linguistic representation of the perceived object and, on the other hand, has an inferential character.

A given verbal copy is, of course, chosen from the set of all possible verbal copies that may be meaningfully assigned to a given object. Intuitively, the verbal copy is simply a string of elements verbally representing the object, that is, its verbal linearization.

5.5 HEURISTIC MODEL OF MEMORY

To summarize, the main intention of this chapter was not only to introduce new memory models, but first of all, to show some new perception models that provide a relationship between problems of memory and perception. The second main point was to show partial controllability of these processes.

The connection between perception and memory was explored first in the model of memory of sentences, where the essential role for memory was played by perception of semantic relations between words. Also, another model presented showed the role of memory traces in remembering the unconceptualizable stimuli and in operations on them. However, the memory mechanisms appear to play the most essential role in their use in systemic explanatory and multimodel approach to visual perception. In these models—of fine eye movements (explanation of Müller–Lyer illusion), transportation (a model that explains the data concerning relations between attributes of objects), and changes of pre-events to events (choice of the object-representation to remember)—the memory processes are functionally related to the perception processes and thus provide elements of control.

Another essential feature of the approaches presented is the experimental access and possibility of simulation of perception processes. In addition, there exists a possibility of using these approaches in artificial intelligence and knowledge engineering, especially in building various perceptual devices based on new principles.

Let us now outline a heuristic model of memory by using the theories and notions introduced earlier in this and other chapters. This heuristic model uses the notions of (1) the multidimensional unit and language of communication, with dynamic fuzzy semantics in form of semantic calculus, (2) the ideal of an object and of a concept, defined through classes of meaning-preserving transformations, (3) the multidimensional gnostic unit, which memorizes the ideals of the objects and the concepts, (4) the algebra of goals and means, showing a method of constructing composite goals through logical operations on simpler goals, to which there correspond set-theoretical operations on sets of means of attaining these goals, (5) the representation of situation, understood as a description or linguistic measurement of situation, containing also motivational evaluations, (6) and the metamemory, understood as a certain subspace of cognitive or motivational space, supplying modal frames over some motivational frames (e.g., "I want X" and "I ought to remember that I ought to X").

In the heuristic model presented below, memory problems will be treated dynamically as certain calculus of meanings based on algebra of goals and means and leading to achievement of some internal or external goals. The first two concepts play key roles in recognition models. As shown, each multidimensional unit is a structure composed out of subunits, each carrying some meaning. The overall meaning is a result of these meanings. The unit has some internal constraints, both of syntactic and semantic type. A similar structure is assumed for multidimensional gnostic units. Recognition is then modeled through a random walk, where the decision about the meaning is identified with exit through one of the boundaries. The novelty here lies in the fact that the overall recognition random walk is built out of elementary random walks.

For the process of recognition, the crucial concept is that of the ideal. Intuitively, the ideal of an object or a concept is that "something" that enables one to recognize it despite the change of details. Thus, the ideal must be invariant with respect to change of details, that is, invariant with respect to some classes of transformations of multidimensional units. Naturally, the ideal need not be unique: there may be several ideals. The ideal of the whole unit is composed out of ideals of its submeanings, specific for various media.

For the model of recognition it is assumed that a gnostic unit is capable of processing a multidimensional unit and of deciding what the meaning of this unit is and to which degree.

The processing of a unit occurs through processing subunits on particular media. Each segment (subunit) is processed according to the principle of sequential comparisons, which define a certain random walk.

Formally, the ideal of a meaning of the unit is represented in form of a vector $(x_1, \ldots, x_N)$, and the unit is represented in form of another vector $(y_1, \ldots, y_N)$. The decision about meaning is attained through comparison of successive coordinates, which defines a random walk $u_0, u_1, \ldots$, with $u_0 = 0$, and $u_{n+1} = u_n + z_n$, where z_n is 1 or -1, depending on whether the coordinates x_n and y_n do or do not match. Thus, the value u_n changes by 1 either up or down. The meaning is decided to be s (of which $(x_1, \ldots, x_N)$ is the ideal), if the random walk exits through the upper boundary, and not-s, if the random walk exist through the lower boundary.

On the level of gnostic unit, there are many such processes occurring at the same time when the segment is tested for various meanings. We have therefore several simultaneous random walks and also various decisions about meanings $s_1, s_2, \ldots$, positive or not. These decisions are then integrated into the final decision about the overall meaning and the degree of this meaning. Here one can think about sort of voting, in which it is checked whether the main meaning is supported by the meanings carried by subunits or not, and if so, to which degree; whether it is canceled, and if so, whether the meaning may be maintained despite cancellation, and so on. After deciding about the maning and possibly its degree, the information from such a gnostic unit is sent to a gnostic unit of a higher order.

In this way, the calculus of meanings runs through various hierarchically arranged gnostic fields, which lead to a string of meanings expressed in the semantic language of the brain. Obviously, different levels of hierarchy contain ideals of meanings of appropriately different levels of generality. In this approach one suggests the existence of a certain algebra of goals and means on the strings of meanings used in the language of the brain.

Now, if one is to decide about the meaning of a string of multidimensional units—a fragment of behavior—the principle is the same: each multidimensional letter yields a support or inhibition of meaning s, based on many elementary random walks. Successive supports, when added together, yield fluctuating value—a new random walk—which serves for decision about the meaning of a string. Formally, this new random walk may be defined by the recursive formula $U_{n+1} = U_n + Z_n(s)$, where $Z_n(s)$ is the degree of support for s, based on processing a number of elementary random walks.

A theory of objects and their verbal copies, or, alternatively, on algebra of situations, is of interest for theories of memory, since it provides a background for them and also in view of the predominantly linguistic character of memory. The situation understood as configuration of objects with their attributes constitutes both the context and the territory of human actions as well as basic material that is stored in memory.

On the other hand, descriptions of situations (verbal copies) serve as the main source of information about the memory content and quality in the sense of the adequacy with which it represents real situations and objects. Consequently, the concepts of exactness and faithfulness of descriptions become the concepts dealing with the adequacy of memory with respect to a given situation. One of the functions of metamemory is the choice of not only the time horizon, but also the degree of faithfulness and exactness of the representation of object in memory.

The theory of objects and their descriptions constitutes, therefore, a broader context for a wider theory of memory and provides a formal description of the nature of more complex memory stimuli and the formal nature of subject's reports of memory contents. The decision about which features of the situation will be remembered, for how long and how strongly, and which will be neglected is determined by the valuation of situation on cognitive scales in motivational space. One assumes here that the cognitive space is mapped into the linguistic one, so that one may analyze the psychological states by observing the linguistic behavior. In other words, one assumes here a sort of homomorphism that enables one to make inference about the original from the observed values of the mapping (verbal behavior).

The relationship between the situation, understood as a vector of features $V = (V_1, \ldots, V_n)$, and the motivational space is such that to each particular V_i there corresponds a subset of language L, say, $H(V_i)$, which tells to which extent the features V_i are important, for how long they ought to be stored in memory, what the subject's attitude toward these features is, and so on.

Now, there is a set Q contained in L of those instructions that for some reasons (of sufficient importance, sufficient strength, etc.) imply that a given feature is to be remembered. Given a feature V_i of the situation, and assigned to it set $H(V_i)$, the feature V_i will be remembered if and only if $H(V_i) \cap Q \neq \varnothing$ and will not be remembered otherwise. Consequently, with every situation $V = (V_1, \ldots, V_n)$, there is associated a family of nonempty sets $H(V_{i_1}) \cap Q$, $H(V_{i_2}) \cap Q, \ldots, H(V_{i_k}) \cap Q$ (all other features have no intersection with Q). In such a case, features $V_{i_1}, \ldots, V_{i_k}$ of the situation will be remembered, and the sets $H(V_{i_j}) \cap Q$ will also contain specific instructions about remembering (for how long, how strongly, etc., thus providing strength, importance, direction, horizon, etc., of memory).

Denoting generally the family of the above intersections by $C(V)$ and by $D(V)$ the family of indices $i_1, \ldots, i_k$ associated with $C(V)$, the situation becomes mapped into the pair $[C(V), D(V)]$, which tells which features will be remembered and what the metamemory instructions about the storage are.

Given now a sequence of situations, say $V^{(1)}$, $V^{(2)}$,..., occurring to a given person, we have associated with it a binary process $[C(V^{(1)}), D(V^{(1)})]$, $[C(V^{(2)}), D(V^{(2)})]$,.... The first component of this process is of a linguistic character—these are multidimensional vectors of modal frames that determine the horizons, strengths, and so on. The second components concern the features that are to be remembered, that is, stored in the appropriate memory compartments.

Thus, metamemory orders facts and connects them, building the structures and streams of behavior. These streams may be semantically homogeneous or not. Moreover, metamemory determines the direction of memory operation and is based on fuzzy relations between various semantic fields; in short, it determines how memory "moves" within semantic space; that is, it determines the trajectories of the process described above.

The outlined notions and theories allow us to enrich and deepen the topics of memory, as well as to think of extending and modifying the approaches discussed in this chapter. This concerns, in particular, analysis of memory under partial conscious control as well analysis of unconscious memory, emotionally controlled through spontaneous intensifications of memory traces.

To study structural and semantic properties of motivational space as well for various concepts useful for the analysis of languages of the brain, see Nowakowska (1973). It is worth stressing that this book introduces and formally analyzes, among others, the concept of motivational consistency essential for the study of the relationship between verbal and nonverbal actions. This concept has somewhat more convenient methodological properties than the more elusive notion of rationality, which is subject to various interpretations, and therefore may ultimately prove useful in applications, among others, to robotics.

For the readers who are interested in the development, applicability, and means of absorption of concepts and theories in science, the following observations may be of some interest.

The notion of weights of fragments and their role in recognition in sequential decomposition of the picture reappears in psychological literature as late as the 70s [see, e.g., Normal and Rumelhart (1974)]. In the 80s, the notion of weight appears useful for machine vision in homomorphic mapping of a given object into its graph representation. Also, for a three dimensional description of an object [see, e.g., Marr (1982)], one introduces the decomposition of the whole shape into components, to be further decomposed into smaller parts, etc. This is additionally justified by the fact that processing of information by a computer should be split into a collection of small subprocesses, with a certain assumed structure. Naturally, for computer purposes, one allows various, sometimes quite radical idealizations leading, in particular, to an ordering of the subprocesses, and consequently, to the construction of a program.

As shown in this chapter, the process of perception is characterized by some interactions of processes rather than by their orderings and by some special, and still insufficiently known, forms of visual inference and reasoning based on approximate and qualitative data and operations.

It seems that cognitive AI will, in the future, tend to simulation of visual perception of a given object (picture) under assumed dynamic generating mechanisms.

The programs now available and the architecture for parallel processing may appear useful for future studies on reconstructibility of perception, but they do not lead directly to the necessary solutions.

Only recently have attempts been made in computational linguistics to relate the structure of description with the knowledge of certain properties of the structure of the situation (object) and actions. This may be essential in construction of knowledge and expert systems.

5.6   EYE CONTROL ALLOCATION FOR HAND MOVEMENTS IN MULTITASK SITUATIONS WITH SOME POSSIBLE APPLICATIONS TO THE FOUNDATIONS OF ROBOTICS

In perceptual robotics one usually considers multicontrolled actions [see, e.g., Arbib (1983, 1984) or Lee and Fu (1984)]. The question arises of economicity of control and time allocation for different types of control in a course of action.

A man has the feeling of physical distance and also has some sort of "measure" in the hand and arm, in the sense that even when he does not see the target (for example in darkness), he knows from experience how far and in which direction he should reach. In fact, he measures the distance "by eye," from (say) a hypothetical cup in the hand and the target—a cup on the table, remembers the speed of motion of the arm, and relies on the memory of the target and proprioceptive memory. This is probably done by remembering the speed of hand relative to various stationary and nonstationary objects. This suggests that a man may change from one type of perceptual control to another by using the memory (also proprioceptive) and knowledge of a situation, in particular, the memory of "languages of objects," that is, the actions admissible for a given object or relation between objects [for these concepts see Nowakowska (1973, 1983)]. A man may complete an action under apparently interrupted or weakened control of the eye and under attention shift. This is due to the anticipatory and measuring action of the eye. For instance, a soldier may shoot at the target "feeling" only the direction due to memory, and at the same time look in another direction for a new anticipated attack. As another example, one may take the following situation: the man is to put a cup on the table—he already sees the place to put the cup, that is, the target place. Suddenly there is a knock at the door. The man continues carrying the cup, and at the same time turns his head toward the door. It seems that the robot might combine actions in a way similar to those of the man—complete one action under lowered control, and start a new action during the first one.

In the examples considered, what is important is the ability to combine actions in the context of economical control, turning on and off the visual control, depending on the importance of actions, or of accepted priority in a multiaction situation (for instance, if the cup is very full, the visual control is more permanent). These classes of situations may lead to interesting studies of an experimental character, combining the records of eye movements in a given situation. With such data, and in particular with knowledge of the break points of visual control, one could try to model and simulate this process, i.e., try to reconstruct the values and assumptions of the neuropsychological processes that are involved in the process of multiaction situations.

For robotics such research would also have some significance, leading to the topics of optimalization of allocation of visual control in the situations of multichannel control and in simultaneous multiaction situations.

To be more specific, we shall analyze the following situation: the subject is to perform simultaneously two manual tasks, say T_1 and T_2. At any given moment, the visual control may be concentrated at one task only; at such a time, performing the other task depends on memory.

Specifically, we shall assume that each of the tasks involves moving the hand to the target location (perhaps combined with transporting some object to this location, or picking up the object, etc.).

If the visual control could be concentrated at one task without any interruption, the performance of this task would have been perfect. (This means that we assume that subjects are not impaired in any way and that the tasks under consideration are simple ones.)

Now, in the absence of visual control, the performance level deteriorates as the memory fades away (proprioceptive memory, as well as memory of the situation, of target location, of motion parameters, etc.; whatever is needed to perform the task). Thus, it becomes necessary to shift visual control from one target to the other.

The aim of the model in this section will be to build a model (or, to be precise, a class of models) of visual control and memory fading, providing an adequate description of the phenomenon studied, and thus provide means for determining the optimal policy of visual control.

5.6.1 Outline of the Model

The model will be built on some assumptions which describe the performance with and without visual control.

We shall denote by T_1 and T_2 the tasks, associated with two target locations, say p_1 and p_2, to be reached by the left and right hand respectively.

For simplicity, it will be assumed at the start that the optimal paths of the arms are straight lines to the targets (that is: there are no obstacles on the way). If the visual control could be executed in a continuous fashion, the arm would follow the straight line to the target.

Now, it will be assumed that when the visual control becomes interrupted, the location of target and the arm are stored in memory, and used to guide the motion. However, as these memory traces fade, the motion is subject to three kinds of deviations. First, the initial direction of the motion may deviate from the optimal. Second, the direction is subject to systematic change in time, and third, it is also subject to randomly fluctuating changes.

Formally, we assume the following model. In the presence of visual control, the trajectory is described by the equation

$$dp/dt = a, \tag{5.150}$$

where $p(t) = [x(t), y(t), z(t)]$, and $a = [a_1, a_2, a_3]$ is a constant velocity vector pointing from the initial point to the target. Consequently,

$$p(t) = p_0 + a \cdot (t - t_0), \tag{5.151}$$

where p_0 is the location at t_0.

In the absence of visual control, the motion is described by the equation

$$dp/dt = a + b(t) + dW(t), \tag{5.152}$$

where $b(t)$ is the systematic bias, and $dW(t)$ is a random disturbance. Here $W(t)$ is a Wiener process, so that $dW(t)$ is a white noise.

Integrating (5.152), we obtain

$$p(t) = p_0 + a \cdot (t - t_0) + \int_{t_0}^{t} b(u)\, du + W(t) - W(t_0). \tag{5.153}$$

Putting

$$B(t, t') = \int_{t}^{t'} b(u)\, du, \tag{5.154}$$

and observing that the distribution of $W(t) - W(t_0)$ is the same as that of

$W(t - t_0)$, we may write

$$p(t) = p_0 + a \cdot (t - t_0) + B(t_0, t) + W(t - t_0). \tag{5.155}$$

To make a closer analysis, suppose now that the initial locations of the left and right hand are p_L^0 and p_R^0, and let the target locations (to be reached at t^* simultaneously by both hands) be p_L and p_R.

Finally, assume that the visual control is initially directed at the left hand, and that the right hand will remain stationary until the visual control shifts to it.

Let $t_1, t_2, \ldots, t_N$, with $t_0 < t_1 < \cdots < t_N < t^*$ be the times of shift of the visual control. Thus, it is directed at the left hand in all time intervals that begin with even indices, that is, $(t_0, t_1), (t_2, t_3), (t_4, t_5), \ldots$, and so on. Similarly, the visual control is directed at the right hand in the interval with odd indices of the initial moments, that is, $(t_1, t_2), (t_3, t_4), \ldots$.

Equation (5.151) implies that at time t_1 of the first shift, the velocity vector $a_L^{(0)}$ of the motion of the left hand is

$$a_L^{(0)} = [p_L(t^*) - p_L^{(0)}]/(t^* - t_0) \tag{5.156}$$

and the location at time t_1 is therefore

$$p_L(t_1) = p_L^{(0)} + \frac{p_L(t^*) - p_L^{(0)}}{t^* - t_0}(t_1 - t_0). \tag{5.157}$$

Clearly, the initial velocity vector at t_1 is

$$[p_L(t^*) - p_L(t_1)]/(t^* - t_1), \tag{5.158}$$

which reduces to $a_L^{(0)}$ as it should.

Between t_1 and t_2, the motion of the left hand is not controlled visually, hence equation (5.153) holds. Consequently, for location at t_2 we have

$$p_L(t_2) = p_L(t_1) + a_L^{(0)}(t_2 - t_1) + B(t_1, t_2) + W(t_2 - t_1), \tag{5.159}$$

with $p_L(t_1)$ given by (5.157) and $a_L^{(0)}$ given by (5.156). The random variable $W(t_2 - t_1)$ has normal distribution with mean 0 and variance $c^2(t_2 - t_1)$. Here c^2 is the unit variance of the Wiener process $W(t)$.

We may now calculate the initial velocity $a_L^{(2)}$ at time t_2 for the interval (t_2, t_3) of control of the left arm, also being the initial velocity at time t_3 when control shifts to the right arm. Thus, we may also find the (random) location at time t_4.

In this way we may determine the trajectory of the left arm, with locations and velocity vectors being some random variables. The procedure for the right arm is analogous.

Suppose now that we are given the loss function (criterion of performance), assumed to be of the form

$$C[p_L(t^*), p_R(t^*)] + \int_{t_0}^{t*} F[p_L(t), p_R(t)] \, dt \qquad (5.160)$$

where C and F are some functions. Here the first component represents the loss connected with missing the target, so that one may assume

$$C(x, y) = 0 \quad \text{if} \quad x = p_L \quad \text{and} \quad y = p_R, \qquad (5.161)$$

with p_L, p_R being the target locations.

On the other hand, the function F represents the loss due to nonoptimal trajectory of the arm, that is, the trajectory deviating from the straight line.

Naturally, in each specific case, one would have to make precise assumptions about functions C and F, so as to be able to apply the known optimization techniques for obtaining the solution, such as the Bellman equation. etc.

If one determines theoretically the optimal policy of visual control in a given situation, one could find empirically the behavior of the subjects, in particular, determining how close their strategies are to the optimal ones, and what causes the deviations from optimality (if any).

APPENDIX

PROOF OF THEOREM 5.15

From Assumption 5.10 it follows that

$$P(T_i > t) = e^{-I_i(t)}, \qquad (A.1)$$

where

$$I_i(t) = \int_0^t \frac{\Sigma_{k \neq i} f_k(s)}{f_i(s)} \, ds, \qquad (A.2)$$

which, in view of Assumption 5.9, may be written as

$$I_i(t) = \int_0^t \frac{\Sigma_{k \neq i} f_k + \Sigma_{k \neq i} b_k s}{f_i e^{-c_i s}} \, ds$$

$$= \frac{1}{f} \int_0^t (F + Bs) e^{-cs} \, ds, \qquad (A.3)$$

where index i was suppressed and

$$F = \sum_{k \neq i} f_k, \qquad B = \sum_{k \neq i} b_k. \qquad (A.4)$$

By integrating (A.3) we obtain the assertion of the theorem.

6 STOCHASTIC MODELS OF EXPERTISE FORMATION, OPINION CHANGE, AND LEARNING

6.1 INTRODUCTION

The aim of this closing chapter of the book is to more deeply connect the cognitive sciences with the topics of expert systems and AI. The two groups of models considered here concern formation of opinions, in particular in expertise and learning material of a course. The superficial similarity of these groups of models lies in the fact that they postulate that the process under investigation (changes of expert opinion, or changes in acquired knowledge) is representable as a multidimensional "random walk": the state, at any given time, is supposed to be a vector with integer-valued coordinates, with transitions always leading to the "neighboring" state (differing only at one coordinate and by unit value).

The transition intensities are assumed to depend on the state, and possibly on control variables, and on an "environmental" process.

In the case of changes of expert opinions, the state vector represents evaluations on various scales; the control process may, for instance, represent the way in which the information is given to an expert, while the environmental process is the process of arrivals of new data items, which affect the opinion.

The aim of introducing and analysing the model is to get an access to the biases in expert's opinions. The latter is assumed to be the end value of the stochastic process defined by the model. In some sense, therefore, the model complements other models of expert decisions, which concern mostly the underlying logic [see, e.g., Shafer (1976), Zadeh (1979), or Doyle (1978)]. As opposed to these models, here it is not assumed that two experts given the same starting state and the same information should arrive at the same opinion. On the contrary, the process is assumed to be inherently stochastic, and the model concerns, in some sense, the interplay between situation and the expert's behavior.

The second part of this chapter concerns learning. It is namely assumed that knowledge acquisition occurs through "enlightenments," that is, instances of sudden understanding of some essential facts or relations, etc. The state of knowledge is assumed to be representable as the vector of numbers of enlightenments in various topics that occurred up to a given time.

In this case, the control parameter is the allocation of times that the instructors should spend on various topics, so as to maximize the rate of enlightenments, that is, rate of knowledge acquisition. On the other hand, the environmental process concerns different abilities of students (assumed to follow some distribution).

In both models, one of the central assumptions concerns the dependence between the components of the state vector. Typically, one may expect that they enhance one another. This idea, essentially of "synergy" between various components of learning or opinion processes, may in some instances be tested empirically. The last section of the chapter provides a plan of experiments for testing the "synergy" hypothesis.

6.2   A MODEL OF EXPERTISE FORMATION

Understanding the mechanisms of formation of expertises and their constraints and biases is of crucial importance in view of the fact that expertises are a basic tool of control of various domains of life, science, technology, and culture, in the sense of possible stimulating or inhibiting effects on development.

The existing computer advisory systems, AI systems, etc. utilize only some aspects of the problem [see, e.g., Hayes-Roth *et al.* (1983), Pearl (1984), or Sowa (1984)], and there exists no comprehensive theory of expertise. In particular, there is little or no research on limitations of expertises, and on consequences of these limitations, e.g., in science. The increasing specialization and fragmentation of science leads to a relative isolation of specialties, and sometimes to a certain standardization of thinking in some specialties, as well as to a related decrease of growth rate of knowledge under increasing costs.

It becomes very important, therefore, to have a dynamic model of expertise formation and, in particular, of learning of experts. This section will present a model of changes of opinion resulting from exposition to some factors. Such models can cover a variety of situations: first, the "opinion" may be interpreted also as knowledge about some subject, as attitude towards some issue, and so forth. Second, "factors" may be treated as some processes or events that are observed by the subject or as certain actions that constitute a part of the control process.

As special cases one can consider here problems such as optimal learning or teaching techniques, optimal manipulation of propaganda arguments, and optimal influencing of decision makers, e.g., a jury, panel of experts, constituency of voters.

In most general terms, the model will consist of specifying how the opinion (expressed as a suitable point in state-space) is affected by each of the available options (such as information release, use of certain arguments, use of such and such teaching techniques, etc., whatever the case may be) and also how it is affected by external events. The changes here are of a nondeterministic nature, with the opinion forming a certain multidimensional stochastic process.

6.2.1 The Model

In the sequel, we shall consider changes of opinion (knowledge, etc.) about some arbitrary but fixed subject. To simplify the terminology, the considerations will refer simply to changes of *opinion* (without reference to the subject of the opinion). It will be assumed that the opinion is representable as a vector

$$X = (x_1, \ldots, x_N), \tag{6.1}$$

with $0 \le x_i \le K$, $i = 1, \ldots, N$, the components x_i being integers.

The intended interpretation here is such that each of the components represents some aspect of the opinion, such as, for instance, evaluation on some attribute scale. The restriction to a bounded set of integers is of no serious consequence in the sense that by taking K large enough, one can always approximate a continuous scale.

The evolution of opinion x will be regarded as a certain stochastic process $X(t) = [x_1(t), \ldots, x_N(t)]$ whose laws of evolution may depend on some external control parameters, say θ, and on some other stochastic process $\{\Xi(t)\}$, to be referred to as random environment.

To formulate the hypotheses, it will be convenient to first introduce some notation.

If $X = (x_1, \ldots, x_N)$, then

$$X_i^{(+)} = (x_1, \ldots, x_i + 1, \ldots, x_N) \tag{6.2}$$

and

$$X_i^{(-)} = (x_1, \ldots, x_i - 1, \ldots, x_N), \tag{6.3}$$

so that $X_i^{(+)}$ and $X_i^{(-)}$ are, in a sense, the "neighboring" points to X.

Generally, the following hypothesis will be accepted.

HYPOTHESIS 6.1 *Suppose that the state of the environment at time t is $\Xi(t)$ and that the control variable applied is θ. Then the transitions between t and $t + \Delta t$ and their probabilities are as shown in the accompanying tabulation regardless of the history of the process prior to time t.*

t	$t^+\Delta t$	Probability
X →	$X_i^{(+)}$	$\lambda_i[X, t, \Xi(t), \theta]\,\Delta t + o(\Delta t)$
X →	$X_i^{(-)}$	$\mu_i[X, t, \Xi(t), \theta]\,\Delta t + o(\Delta t)$
X →	X	$1 - [\lambda_i + \mu_i]\,\Delta t + o(\Delta t)$
X →	any other	$o(\Delta t)$

Thus, conditional on the environment process, the opinion process is Markov, and λ_i and μ_i are its transition intensities, in the sense that we have

$$\lambda_i(X, t, \xi, \theta) = \lim_{\Delta t \to 0} \frac{1}{\Delta t} P[X(t + \Delta t) = X_i^{(+)} \mid X(t) = X, \Xi(t) = \xi, \theta]. \quad (6.4)$$

and

$$\mu_i(X, t, \xi, \theta) = \lim_{\Delta t \to 0} \frac{1}{\Delta t} P[X(t + \Delta t) = X_i^{(-)} \mid X(t) = X, \Xi(t) = \xi, \theta]. \quad (6.5)$$

The form of transition intensities (6.4) and (6.5) varies depending on the concrete situation that one wishes to describe. Generally, the "birth rate" λ_i of coordinate x_i depends on the value of this coordinate and possibly on values of other coordinates, and similarly for "death rates" μ_i. This dependence creates an intricate set of relationships between the processes $x_i(t)$ where they may enhance or inhibit one another.

Next, one may argue that each expert has some initial preconceptions in the form of prior probability distribution π on the state space, so that we have $P[X(0) \in A] = \pi(A)$.

Finally, at the target time T, the opinion $X(T)$ becomes expressed. This may be formally represented as the assumption that the expressed opinion is $B[X(T)]$, where $X(T)$ is the "true" opinion, while B is a bias function.

6.2.2 A Special Case

The model outlined in the preceding section is rather general and needs to be appropriately narrowed down if one wants to investigate a particular question. To illustrate these possibilities, we may consider the following situations.

(a) *Expert decision in a stationary state.* Assume that the expert has received all the data about the subject of expertise and possesses all the necessary knowledge of the theoretical issues involved. He has to evaluate the data and arrive at the final decision.

In this case it seems reasonable to assume that the environmental process is a constant (which amounts to the assumption that the environment has no effect) and also that there are no control parameters. Moreover, we may assume that the transition intensities do not depend on time, so that $\lambda_i = \lambda_i(X)$ and $\mu_i = \mu_i(X)$. In such a case, the transition coefficients reflect the structural aspects of the domain of expertise, that is, interrelationships between the scores.

Typical questions here may concern the variability of expertise, both between the experts (who may start from different initial distributions) and for the same expert under hypothetical repetitions under the same initial conditions.

(b) *Expert decisions in changing information.* Here one may distinguish various types of processes that affect the change of opinion and treat them as environmental processes. The most important among them are (a) changes in the factual knowledge about the subject of the expertise, (b) changes of the theoretical knowledge of the expert (i.e., changes of his microparadigmatic viewpoint, where a microparadigm is understood as a set of methods, hypotheses, theoretical convictions, etc. accepted by a scientist), (c) changes of attitudinal factors of expertise, and (d) effects of social pressures.

We shall now present a special model of the kind described in (b). It will be assumed that the "environmental process" is generated by a stream of events, each belonging to one of N categories. The general situation that the model is intended to represent is that a high frequency of events of a given category constitutes a premise to increase the coordinate corresponding to this category (there are as many categories of events as coordinates of opinion). On the other hand, a low frequency of events in the ith category is a premise to decrease the coordinate x_i.

In addition, the model will attempt to capture the "recency" effect: the frequencies will be counted only for events that occurred last (which may represent, say, the effects of memory fading). As a practical example of a situation of this kind, one may consider evaluations of various safety regulations, depending on the temporal distance from the most recent accident at work.

The general character of the transition intensities will be as follows. As long as the evaluation x_i on the ith attribute is of moderate value, the transition intensities for this coordinate are affected only by the frequency of events of the corresponding (that is, ith) category and are independent of evaluations and/or frequencies of events in other categories. However, when x_i approaches one of the extreme values 0 or K, the values of other coordinates and the corresponding frequencies start playing a role.

Specifically, it is assumed that $\Xi(t) = [Z_1(t), \ldots, Z_N(t)]$ is the environmental process of events, as specified below, while

$$\lambda_i[X, \Xi(t)] = \alpha(1 + x_i)(K - x_i)A[i, X, \Xi(t)] \tag{6.6}$$

and

$$\mu_i[X, \Xi(t)] = \beta x_i(K + 1 - x_i)B[i, X, \Xi(t)] \tag{6.7}$$

with the functions A and B defined as

$$A[i, X, \Xi(t)] = \begin{cases} Z_i(t) & \text{if } x_i \leq R, \\ \sum Z_j(t)U_j & \text{if } x_i > R, \end{cases} \tag{6.8}$$

where

$$U_j = \begin{cases} 1 & \text{if } x_j \geq R, \\ 0 & \text{otherwise.} \end{cases} \tag{6.9}$$

Similarly,

$$B[i, X, \Xi(t)] = \begin{cases} 1 - Z_i(t) & \text{if } x_i \geq C, \\ \sum [1 - Z_j(t)]V_j & \text{otherwise,} \end{cases} \tag{6.10}$$

where

$$V_j = \begin{cases} 1 & \text{if } x_j \geq C, \\ 0 & \text{otherwise.} \end{cases} \tag{6.11}$$

Here $\alpha > 0$, $\beta > 0$ are scaling constants, while R and C and constants such that $0 < C < R < K$.

From the above formulas it may be seen that the growth of the ith coordinate is logistic in nature (with endpoints 0 and K being nonabsorbing). As long as we have $C < x_i < R$, the transition intensities $x_i \rightarrow x_i + 1$ and $x_i \rightarrow x_i - 1$ are proportional to $Z_i(t)$ and $1 - Z_i(t)$, so that they depend only on the ith component of the environmental process. However, when we have $x_i \geq R$, the transition intensity for the transition $x_i \rightarrow x_i + 1$ equals the sum of all values of the processes $Z_j(t)$ for j such that $x_j \geq R$. A similar property holds for low values of x_i.

Before defining the process $Z_i(t)$, it is worthwhile to observe that the above assumptions imply that the transition intensity for the ith coordinate depends only on the ith component of the environmental process, as long as it oscillates around some values that are away from the extremes. However, as soon as this coordinate approaches one of the extreme values, it becomes dependent on all coordinates of the environmental process.

Let us now describe the latter process. In the model below, it is assumed that events occur according to a Poisson process with rate γ, and their categories are sampled independently from some underlying distribution. The ith coordinate $Z_i(t)$ is defined as the frequency of events of type i among the last s events prior to time t, so that $Z_i(t) = m(i, t)/s$, where $m(i, t)$ is the number of events of type i among the last a events preceding time t. We have therefore $\Sigma Z_i(t) = 1$.

The model depends therefore on the following parameters:

N — The number of attributes of the evaluation (and also the number of types of events)

K — Range of evaluation scales

γ — Rate of occurrence of events

q_i — Probability that an event will be of the ith type

α, β — Scaling parameters;

C, R — Thresholds for "extreme" opinions

M — Memory depth

The parameters α, β, γ should be chosen in such a way that one obtains a reasonable ratio of the occurrence of changes of the evaluations to the rate of changes in the processes $Z_i(t)$.

The most interesting parameters are the memory depth M and the thresholds R and C, below and above which the transitions begin to interact and affect one another. In some sense, therefore, C and R represent biases of an expert towards two extreme opinions: if (say) the threshold R is low (away from the extreme K), then his opinions begin to interact with one another early, providing a "drift" towards the extreme opinion $x_i = K$. A similar interpretation holds for threshold C.

It is of interest to study mutual relations between the frequencies of events of various types, memory depth M, and thresholds R and C.

Figure 6.1 shows the flowchart of the process (one loop), starting from a given state, described by the vector $(x_1, \ldots, x_N)$ of evaluations and the vector $(s_1, \ldots, s_M)$, where s_i is the type of ith event, counting the Mth event as the most recent.

The block labeled (1) represents the counting step, where one determines the values of the components of the environmental process, that is, components Z_i. This is attained by simply counting the numbers of events of each of the types, among the last M events, and dividing the counts by M so as to obtain the frequencies.

In the next step [labeled (2)], the coordinates of the opinion process are inspected and auxiliary vectors U_i and V_i are formed, indicating which of the coordinates are below the lower threshold and which are above the upper threshold.

In the block labeled (3), transition intensities are evaluated according to the formulas given in the model. These transitions are λ_i and μ_i, and their sums are denoted respectively by A and B so that the transition intensity towards any change of opinion (that is, any coordinate in the positive or negative direction) is $A + B$.

In the next step, two transition times T_1 and T_2 are generated with the use of random numbers. Here T_1 has exponential distribution with parameter γ, while T_2 has exponential distribution with parameter $A + B$. The comparison of these times determines which change is to occur: if T_1 is less than T_2 then the earlier change is that in the event process, and if T_2 is less than T_1 then the change concerns the opinion process. Next, an event with probability $A/(A + B)$ is generated: if this event occurs then the change is an increase of a coordinate (not yet specified), while if this event does not occur then a decrease of one of the coordinates occurs.

The three flowcharts shown on Fig. 6.1b correspond to generation of an increase or decrease of a coordinate of opinion x_i and to generation of a type of a new event. In each case, generation of a single random number (with uniform distribution on $[0, 1]$) suffices to determine the coordinate, or type of event, that is to be changed.

We shall now suggest somewhat more realistic assumptions concerning the latter process of opinion change, freeing it of the awkward assumptions that the number of types of events equals the number of coordinates of the opinion process and that only the last given number of events affects the process. The suggested assumptions will not only make the process more general, but also will simplify the simulation process.

The general idea is to retain the event process and use it to build an environmental process $\{\Xi(t)\}$.

We shall assume that there are M types of events, and that the process of their occurrences is a semi-Markov process, described by the transition matrix $P = [p_{ij}]$ and matrix of intensities $C = [c_{ij}]$. This means that if an event of type i occurred at time t, then the type of the next event is j with probability p_{ij}, and it occurs at time $t + T$, where T has exponential distribution with parameter c_{ij}, so that

$$P[T > s] = \exp[-c_{ij}s]. \tag{6.12}$$

We may now describe the environmental process $\{\Xi(t)\}$.

HYPOTHESIS 6.2   The environmental process $\{\Xi(t)\}$ is M-dimensional, i.e.,

$$\Xi(t) = [Z_1(t),\ldots,Z_M(t)], \tag{6.13}$$

where the component $Z_i(t)$ is defined as

$$Z_i(t) = \sum_{j:t_j<t} K_i\exp[-\alpha_i(t - t_j)], \tag{6.14}$$

where $t_1, t_2,\ldots$ are the times of occurrences of events of type j prior to time t.

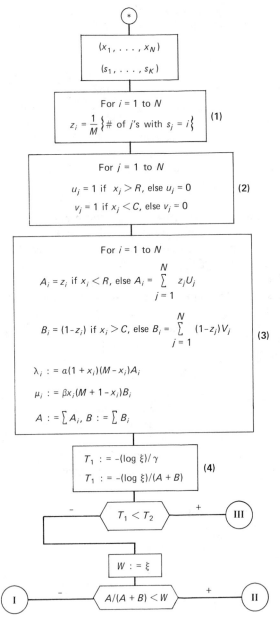

Fig. 6.1a. Flowchart for simulation. ξ is a random number from uniform distribution on $[0, 1]$.

The vectors $(K_1, \ldots, K_N)$ and $(\alpha_1, \ldots, \alpha_N)$ are called the impact vector and the decay vector, respectively.

Thus, if an event of type i occurs at some time, it contributes to the ith component of the environmental process. The initial size of the contribution is the impact K_i, and the contribution decreases exponentially, with decay α_i.

As a consequence of this definition, it is easy to see that the processes $Z_i(t)$ will oscillate around some stationary levels. To determine these levels, one can proceed as follows. Suppose that the stationary distribution of $Z_i(t)$ has been attained, and let L_i be the expected level of $Z_i(t)$ at the time prior to an occurrence of an event of type i. Further, let T_i be the expected waiting time for the next event of type i. We must then have

$$(L_i + K_i)\exp[-\alpha_i T_i] = L_i; \tag{6.15}$$

hence

$$L_i = \frac{K_i \exp[-\alpha_i T_i]}{1 - \exp[-\alpha_i T_i]}. \tag{6.16}$$

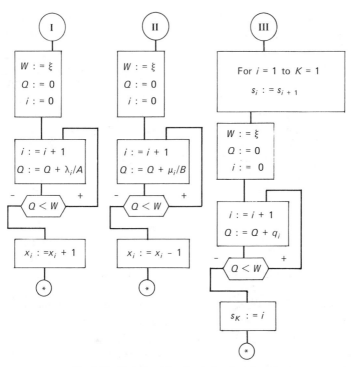

Fig. 6.1b. Flowchart for simulation (continued).

6.2.3 Prospects of Analysis

In order to be able to extract some information about the evolution of the opinion process (either by deductive inference or by simulation), one has to specify the functions λ_i and μ_i. Here we shall merely outline some classes of assumptions of this type.

As specified in Hypothesis 6.1, each of the functions λ_i and μ_i depends on the state $X = (x_1, \ldots, x_N)$, time t, state of the environment process $\Xi(t)$, and control parameter θ. The values of these functions represent the tendency of increase and decrease of the ith component of X.

As regards dependence on $X(t)$, the simplest form of assumption is that λ_i and μ_i each depend on X only through the coordinate x_i.

This assumption makes the component processes conditionally independent (given the sample path of the environmental process, and given the choice of control variables).

Naturally, conditional independence of the coordinates makes theoretical analysis feasible (otherwise, when the component processes interact, no theoretical analysis appears possible). Whether or not the assumption of conditional independence may be accepted as adequate is an intriguing question. A positive answer would mean that all observed mutual dependence of changes of various aspects of opinion is due to a common underlying process that affects this opinion.

Whether attained by simulation or not, the properties of the process of opinion, as defined in this section provide information about the evolution of opinions of an expert. In this sense, such results provide an important complementation of research on expert systems. This research, thus far, appears to be concentrated on the problems of how the opinions about various aspects of the phenomenon are (or should be) combined into one final opinion. This is the main objective of all decision support systems, diagnostic automaton systems, and so forth, where information is elicited from experts and combined into the "best" final whole, as well as the objective of various suggested logical inference schemes.

As opposed to that, the present model may provide an insight into another component of expertise, namely the process of evolution of an opinion on an individual level, biases of such opinions, their stability, and also the possibility of control by selection of information, i.e., by manipulation of the stream of events.

The model of change of opinion considered here is, in some sense, more general than the usual Bayesian model concerned with changes of probability of some event in light of incoming information about certain other events.

In the Bayesian theory of expertise one considers some distribution that is asserted by an expert; to simplify the presentation consider just the probability

of an event, say H_i, being one of a number of possible events H_1, H_2,...
(referred to sometimes as "states of the nature," "hypotheses," etc.).

Prior to any experimentation the expert has some probabilities of events,
say $\pi_i = P(H_i)$, $i = 1, 2, \ldots$, called prior probabilities. Then, in light of the
occurrence of some observed events $B_1, \ldots, B_n$, the assessment of $P(H_i)$
becomes

$$P(H_i \mid B_1, \ldots, B_n) = \frac{P(B_1, \ldots, B_n \mid H_i)\pi_i}{\Sigma \, P(B_1, \ldots, B_n \mid H_j)\pi_j}, \tag{6.17}$$

which expresses posterior probability of H_i in term of priors and conditional
probabilities $P(B_1, \ldots, B_n \mid H_j)$.

If these probabilities can be meaningfully assigned to events, Bayes' formula
provides the best description of opinion changes. However, often one does not
know how to interpret prior probabilities and even the conditional ones, i.e.,
$P(B_1, \ldots, B_n \mid H_i)$ may be doubtful. In this case, the model suggested provides a
conceptual scheme of opinion change (the fact that only changes by $+1$ or -1
are considered is of no consequence since by change of scale one can
approximate a continuous change).

In the present case, the changes of an opinion may be induced by some
external events and also by other opinions, not necessarily according to Bayes'
formula. The "environmental process" (playing the role of events B_1, B_2,... in
Bayes' formula) affects the birth and death rates λ_i and μ_i. Any values that
increase λ_i and/or decrease μ_i may be said to support the ith coordinate, while
in the opposite case, they may be said to inhibit it. Clearly, however, an event
from the environmental process may increase or decrease both λ_i and μ_i, and
thus be neither supportive nor inhibitive. The ultimate goal of the simulation
research suggested in this paper is to analyse the bias in expertise. The very
concept of bias is, however, rather elusive: one cannot use here the obvious
approach of defining bias as some systematic tendency towards deviation
between the actual values and those that "should" be, according to some
normative theory—mostly for simple reason that typically there is no
normative theory (if there were, one would not need to refer to experts). An
obvious attempt is to define an expert's bias by requiring some type of
sensitivity to specific kinds of information. A reasonable requirement would
be to demand that an unbiased expert should never change his opinion in the
direction "opposite to what is suggested by an event." For instance, if an event
supports some point of view, then an expert who would change his opinion
"against" would be biased. In other words, experts should behave in a
monotone way with respect to information. (Such a requirement is in some
way analogous to Arrow's postulate of consistency of individual and social
preferences). One can also find an analogue of Arrow's postulate of
sovereignity: the expert's opinion cannot be imposed by others. Also the

postulate of irrelevance of alternatives can be applied: an additional "neutral" fact should not cause changing of an opinion.

The trouble with such a definition of an expert's bias lies in deciding when an event "supports" a given point of view. In the most interesting cases, the evidence supplied by an event can be interpreted in either direction, "for" or "against," by different experts. Such situations are very frequent. They require analysis of patterns of facts, supported if possible by statistical analysis or additional modeling.

In general, this uncertainty of interpretation of facts is captured by the suggested model, where the environmental process may be ambiguous with respect to some of the coordinates. It might be possible to explicate the intuitive ideas about bias in expertise in terms of dependence of λ_i's and μ_i's on the present opinion and the environmental process, and collect the data from hypothetically biased and unbiased simulated experts.

At the end of this discussion, let us mention that what is modeled here is in fact a single expertise by an expert—as opposed to typical problems of creating a system that would provide expertises in various situations. Thus, this model concerns a single expertise that happens just once—for instance, an assessment of some future environmental impact or a choice of economic policy.

In this sense, the model concerns two processes: acquisition of knowledge (perception of data, etc.) by the expert, and use of this knowledge in the choice of questions and facts for use in assessments.

As the latter phenomenon is stochastic in nature, the model is also stochastic.

In fact, we have here a family of models, on varying levels of generality. This gives a flexibility of interpretations and applications, and allows us to capture various aspects of expertise formation.

The models may also be interpreted in terms of expressions in natural language, such as experts are using in evaluations of the degree of belief, credibility, confirmability, and so on. This opens up the possibility of using such approaches as those of Shafer and Doyle.

Incidentally, in AI the researchers are occupied mostly by the behavior of the above-mentioned functors (of belief, etc.). The book "Language of Motivation and Language of Actions" (Nowakowska, 1973), and also later books (Nowakowska, 1983, 1984), use a much wider set of functors and introduce the concept of motivational calculus, which also covers functors such as "I want," "I ought to," "I am glad that," and "I prefer." This is essential for the currently "hot issue" in AI, where one wants to analyze the relations between reasonings and actions, using more aspects than only belief.

Finally, a comment about the situation of the model proposed in this section from the point of view of the theory of observability. The model does not introduce the notion of an observer explicitly—but in some sense what is being modeled is the creation of an expertise, as seen by the observer. One can, however, treat the same model differently and consider an observer who forms an opinion about something that he perceives sequentially.

This approach might provide some empirical counterpart to theoretical considerations of observability [see Nowakowska (1982)], in particular, the concept of a mask defined as a temporal pattern of jointly observed variables.

6.3   TIME ALLOCATION TO TOPICS IN A COURSE OF STUDY

We shall now present a model, based on a similar idea as the model of opinion change of the preceding section, concerning some optimization in teaching. This model is based on a paper by Nowakowska et al. (1984). The intuitive background here is as follows.

The knowledge of a person grows as a result of his learning experiences. Some of these experiences are carefully structured, but there are many sources of such experiences. In formal education, teachers and books are the most common source. A problem common to many learning situations with diverse sources concerns the allocation of time. Relatively little is known about good ways to do that, despite its practical and theoretical importance.

Our primary object of inquiry is a randomly chosen student S who exposes himself to various learning experiences in order to make discoveries, thus adding to his knowledge. We call the elementary discoveries he makes for himself "enlightenments." These may be known to everyone else, but it is an increment of knowledge to him.

To formulate a tractable problem, we consider a one-semester course with many sections, each taught by another instructor. We assume that the syllabus is given and organized into n topics, $T_1, \ldots, T_n$. Each instructor is expected to spend t_i hours on topic T_i, so that the total number of hours is K. We ask what $\theta = (t_1, t_2, \ldots, t_n)$ should be so that $t_i > 0$, $i = 1, \ldots, n$, $\Sigma_{i=1}^{n} t_i = K$, and performance on a final examination is maximum.

The model to be analysed assumes that

(1)   the process of acquiring knowledge is stochastic;
(2)   students differ in their abilities;
(3)   teachers differ in their talents;
(4)   performance on the final exam accurately reflects how much knowledge has been acquired.

The purpose of this analysis is to conceptualize this kind of learning process and to use a computer simulation for determining an optimal strategy in some situations.

6.3.1 Assumptions of the Model

We assume that topics $T_1, T_2, \ldots, T_n$ are taught in the order listed. The knowledge of the student at time t is represented by the state vector

$$X(t) = [x_1(t), \ldots, x_n(t)], \tag{6.18}$$

where $x_i(t)$ is the number of enlightenments in topic T_i that occurred prior to time t.

It will be assumed that $x(t)$ is a Markov process, with elementary transitions consisting of an increase of one of the coordinates by 1. The initial state is $x(0) = (0, \ldots, 0)$.

To describe the transition intensities, suppose that at time t the state of the process is $x(t)$, and that topic T_k is taught. Then we have

$$P\{x_i(t + h) = x_i(t) + 1 \mid x(t)\} = \begin{cases} \lambda_k(x)szh + o(h) & \text{if } i = k, \\ \mu_{ik}(x)szh + o(h) & \text{if } i < k, \\ 0 & \text{if } i > k. \end{cases} \tag{6.19}$$

The last row in formula (6.19) implies that enlightenments may concern only the topic actually taught, or topics that were taught previously, but not the topics in the future parts of the course.

Symbols s and z stand respectively for the student's ability and teacher's talent.

Thus, formula (6.19) asserts that the ability s of the student and talent z of the teacher are (a) representable as a single number independent of the topic and (b) enter in a multiplicative way.

As regards (a), it would be perhaps more appropriate to represent the ability of the student as a vector $(s_1, \ldots, s_n)$, with s_i being his predisposition to the ith topic (and similarly for the teacher's talent). However, one may hope that a representation as a single number (somewhat akin to the old idea of the G factor in intelligence measurement) does not constitute too severe a restriction.

On the other hand, part (b) is not really binding: as long as one is willing to accept that a more talented student, or a student taught by a more talented teacher, will have a higher rate of enlightenments, the multiplicativity may always be attained by appropriate scaling. That is to say, if (other conditions being equal) student A has twice as high an enlightenment rate as student B, one can assign to him ability s_A equal to $2s_B$.

It remains to specify the functions $\lambda_k(x)$ and $\mu_{ik}(x)$. The first of them is defined as

$$\lambda_k(x) = \frac{[\alpha + x_k(t)][N_k - x_k(t)]}{\gamma D_k} e^{hQ}, \tag{6.20}$$

where

$$Q = \sum_{i=1}^{k-1} c_{ik} \left(x_i(t) - \frac{N_i}{2} \right). \tag{6.21}$$

The interpretation of these formulas is as follows. The rate of increase of $x_k(t)$ is proportional to the product $[\alpha + x_k(t)][N_k - x_k(t)]$, which implies that growth is roughly logistic, with N_k being the maximal possible number of enlightenments in topic T_k. Here α is some constant that makes it possible for the process of enlightenments in topic T_k to start.

Next, γ and h are scaling constants, while D_k is a measure of the difficulty of the topic T_k, so that the rate of enlightenments is lower for more difficult topics.

Finally, the factor e^{hQ} plays the following role. The sum Q given by (6.21) reflects the overall level of knowledge about topics $T_1, \ldots, T_{k-1}$ acquired previously, with differences $x_i(t) - N_i/2$ being positive or negative depending on whether more than half of the possible enlightenments in topic T_i occurred or not. Thus, Q is a weighted sum of acquisition levels of previous topics, where the weight c_{ik} reflects how helpful a good knowledge of topic T_i is in speeding up the rate of enlightenments in topic T_k (or, alternatively, how much the lack of knowledge of topic T_i impairs the rate of enlightenments in topic T_k). Consequently, weights c_{ik} reflect the internal structure of the domain taught.

The function $\mu_{ik}(x)$ is defined by the formula

$$\mu_{ik}(x) = \rho \beta^{k-i} \frac{[\alpha + x_i(t)][N_i - x_i(t)]}{\gamma D_i} \exp \left\{ hc_{ik} \left[x_k(t) - \frac{N_k}{2} \right] \right\}. \tag{6.22}$$

To see the effects of this assumption, observe that the growth of $x_i(t)$ at the time when topic T_k is taught is again approximately logistic, impaired or enhanced by the level of difficulty D_i of topic T_i, and acquisition level $x_k(t) - N_k/2$ of the topic taught. Here again ρ is a scaling factor, while β^{k-i} reflects "memory loss," depending on the number of topics T_j taught between T_i and T_k.

The choice of exponential factors in formulas (6.20) and (6.22) is admittedly arbitrary. If h is small enough, the last factor in (6.22) may be written as $1 + hc_{ik}[x_k(t) - N_k/2]$, which illustrates how the "excess" or "deficiency" in knowledge of the kth topic, as measured by $x_k(t) - N_k/2$, enhances or inhibits the rate of enlightenments, yet preserves the crucial condition that the rate must be nonnegative.

As regards the student's abilities and teacher's talents, one has to assume that they vary according to some probability law. Many choices are possible here: in particular, one can assume that s and z have gamma distributions, with density of the form

$$g(x) = [a^r/\Gamma(r)]x^{r-1}e^{-ax}, \qquad x > 0, \tag{6.23}$$

where a and r are the scale and shape parameters (possibly different for students and teachers). Consequently, the mean ability (talent) is r/a and the variance is r/a^2.

This is not a very restrictive assumption, as long as one is willing to accept that each of the above talent distributions is unimodal: the family of gamma distributions is sufficiently rich to provide a reasonable approximation to many "plausible" unimodal distributions. In particular, by choosing a and r, one can set both the mean and the coefficient of variation $1/r^{1/2}$ at any desired values.

6.3.2   Final Exam

The total knowledge acquired by the student at the end of the course is the criterion to be maximized by the choice of the decision variable $\theta = (t_1, \ldots, t_n)$. This total knowledge is represented by $x(K) = [x_1(K), \ldots, x_n(K)]$, where $K = \sum_{i=1}^{n} t_i$ is the total number of hours spent on all topics.

To formulate a criterion to be optimized by the choice of θ, we may proceed as follows.

The knowledge $x(K)$ acquired by a student is a random entity, with distribution depending on the decision variable θ; it also depends on the student's ability s, and on the talent z of the teacher. Thus, we may write

$$P\{x_1(K) = k_1, \ldots, x_n(K) = k_n\} = P(k_1, \ldots, k_n | s, z, \theta). \tag{6.24}$$

Typically, the vector $(k_1, \ldots, k_n)$ is not observable. Instead, one may observe the score ξ on the final exam, which may be regarded as a random variable whose distribution depends on $x = (k_1, \ldots, k_n)$ in a monotone way in the sense that

$$E[\xi | x_1(K) = k_1, \ldots, x_n(K) = k_n] \tag{6.25}$$

is an increasing function of each of the arguments $k_1, \ldots, k_n$.

We therefore have the expected final score for a student with ability s taught by a teacher with talent z:

$$E(\xi | s, z, \theta)$$
$$= \sum_{(k_1, \ldots, k_n)} E[\xi | x_1(K) = k_1, \ldots, x_n(K) = k_n] P(k_1, \ldots, k_n | s, z, \theta). \tag{6.26}$$

The problem may now be formulated as follows: *Find* $t_1, t_2, \ldots, t_n$, *subject to constraints*

$$t_i > 0, \quad i = 1, \ldots, n, \quad \sum_{i=1}^{n} t_i = K \tag{6.27}$$

such that

$$E(\xi \mid \theta) = \int_0^\infty \int_0^\infty E(\xi \mid s, z, \theta) g_1(s) g_2(z) \, ds \, dz \tag{6.28}$$

is maximum [here g_1 and g_2 are the densities of s and z, given by (6.23)].

6.3.3 Analysis

Two entities that are crucial here are the distribution (6.24) of the final attained knowledge and the expected score (6.25) on the exam, given the final knowledge. The latter quantity, incidentally, may depend on the student's ability s if the exam requires not only knowledge but also some creativity in applying it.

As regards (6.25), it is relatively easy to postulate a reasonable form of the relation between the expected final score on the exam and the knowledge of particular topics. The exam typically has a number of problems, each concerning one or more topics, and the probability of a correct answer may be postulated to be some simple function (e.g., logistic) of the number of enlightenments in the relevant topics.

As regards (6.24), the explicit solutions do not appear to be easily obtainable; however, one can easily simulate the process of knowledge acquisition directly from the hypotheses of the model, thus obtaining empirical access to the distribution (6.24), or to criterion (6.28). The simulation algorithm is based on the following theorems.

THEOREM 6.1 *Let t be such that*

$$t_1 + \cdots + t_{k-1} \leq t < t_1 + \cdots + t_k, \tag{6.29}$$

so that topic T_k is taught at t. Suppose that the state of knowledge of the student at t is $x(t) = (x_1(t), \ldots, x_k(t), 0, \ldots, 0)$. Then the probability that the next enlightenment occurs before time τ such that $t \leq \tau < t_1 + \cdots + t_k$ equals

$$1 - \exp[-(\tau - t)szV(x)], \tag{6.30}$$

and with probability

$$\exp[-(t_1 + \cdots + t_k - t)szV(x)], \tag{6.31}$$

there will be no enlightenments occurring while topic T_k is taught, where

$$V(x) = \lambda_k(x) + \sum_{i=1}^{k-1} \mu_{ik}(x). \tag{6.32}$$

THEOREM 6.2   *If an enlightenment occurs while topic T_k is taught, it concerns topic T_k with probability*

$$P_k = \lambda_k(x)/V(x), \tag{6.33}$$

and it concerns a previously taught topic T_i with probability

$$P_i = \mu_{ik}(x)/V(x). \tag{6.34}$$

PROOF   Let $P(\tau) = P(\tau; t, x)$ be the probability of no change of state x between t and τ. Then for h such that $t < t + h < t_1 + \cdots + t_k$ we have

$$P(\tau + h) = P(\tau)[1 - sz\lambda_k(x)h - sz \sum_{i=1}^{k-1} \mu_{ik}(x)h] + o(h)$$

$$= P(\tau)[1 - szV(x)h] + o(h), \tag{6.35}$$

by assumption (6.19). Dividing both sides by h and letting $h \downarrow 0$, we obtain

$$P'(\tau) = -szV(x)P(\tau), \tag{6.36}$$

which yields assertions (6.30) and (6.31). To prove Theorem 2, observe that if a transition occurs, then the probabilities of various types of transitions are given by the relative contributions to $V(x)$ from intensities $\lambda_k(x)$ and $\mu_{ik}(x)$.

6.3.4   Discussion

Despite the importance of the problem, there is so far no research on optimality of the time allocation for curriculum structuring. However, certain aspects of such research have been investigated, and one can find in the literature several relevant papers. For example, there were attempts at mathematical modeling of student testing for instructional purposes; e.g., in Pinsky (1970), psychometric methods were applied for instructional improvement and for selection of test items (including a selection algorithm) used for estimation of the desired parameters.

The present discussion will concern first, the assumptions underlying the model and their plausibility, and second, the problems of estimation of the parameters needed as input data in the simulation program aimed at optimizing the allocation of teaching times.

The main assumption that the accumulation of enlightenments can be counted requires some explanation, as does the assumption that learning takes place primarily in this way.

In practice, many high-level geometry students make no discoveries of their own at all, but merely memorize enough of what they think will be on the exam to pass it. Our use of "learning" in this paper is restricted, so as to exclude this. A student who learns in our sense might discover or come to see why the theorem of Pythagoras is useful, important, or true, or how to construct a line whose length is the square root of a given line. When we count the enlightenments by giving the same weights to (re)discovering the Pythagorean theorem and to the fact that 3, 4, 5 are the lengths of the sides of a right triangle, there is a distortion, for the former is of much greater importance than the latter.

In fact one may interpret the notion of an enlightenment in two ways. One is to regard an enlightenment as an assimilation of a piece of knowledge (e.g., memorizing the theorem of Pythagoras), without grasping the possible relationships with other pieces of knowledge. In this case, $x_i(t)$ could perhaps be operationalized, through listing all pieces of information deemed relevant and checking how many of them are known to the student at the time of taking the exam.

It is possible, however, to view the concept of enlightenment differently. The starting point here is the fact that students do not accumulate pieces of knowledge one at a time, but assimilate them into knowledge structures that make their minds prepared to accept them; at the same time, these assimilations enrich these knowledge structures and change their preparedness for new potential pieces of knowledge. Accordingly, we may view enlightenments as instances of grasping some previously not realized relationships between two distinct pieces of knowledge. Using a simple example, the enlightenments would be not the mere learning of the theorem of Pythagoras, and of the fact that the triangle with sides 3, 4, and 5 is a right angled one, but the realization that these two facts are closely related.

In this interpretation, the number $x_i(t)$ of enlightenments is not easily observable; it may, however, be postulated that it is monotonically related to the expected score on the exam.

In our model, the intention was to frame the assumption so as to cover the second interpretation.

This is closely related to our assumption that the process of accumulation of enlightenments is a Markov process, with only "upward" transitions possible.

As regards the second of these assumptions, it means that once an enlightenment occurs, it is never forgotten. This is, of course, an idealization of reality: students often forget the material they have learned. However, while it may be easy to forget an isolated piece of knowledge, forgetting something that resulted from a sudden instance of understanding is much less likely. Consequently, if one accepts the second of the above interpretations of enlightenments, then the assumption that they are irreversible may not be very farfetched.

The Markovian character of the process of enlightenments implies that the probability of the next enlightenment is independent of the time that elapsed from the last enlightenment. This neglects the effects of loss of zeal in studying due to discouragement, etc. However, the fact that a Markov process is "memoryless" (in the sense that given the present, the past values have no influence on probabilities of events in the future) does not imply that the model assumes lack of memory of a student. In fact, the specific assumptions about the enlightenment rates describe in some sense the student's memory and its role in learning, including some features of forgetting (through making enlightenments in temporally distant topics gradually less important for new enlightenments).

Now, the specific assumptions of the model concern the functional form of the enlightenment rates, given the state of knowledge of the student and the topic actually taught.

Basically, these rates imply a logistic growth in each topic, modified by the state of knowledge of other topics. These assumptions do not appear directly testable. However, the general logistic character may be defended on intuitive ground: at the beginning, the knowledge "builds on itself" in a more or less exponential fashion, as one grasps various easily accessible relationships. At later stages the growth rate declines, as one is required to grasp less immediate relationships.

There is probably little doubt that the state of knowledge of other topics may have an enhancing or inhibiting effect on enlightenment rates. Whether or not the modifying factor is indeed of the exponential form postulated in the model is an open question, and it is not clear whether the assumption is empirically testable. However, the functional form of enlightenment rates appears sufficiently flexible to approximate intuitively acceptable alternative functions.

A question that requires careful consideration here is as follows. At present, it is assumed that the state of knowledge of a given topic intervenes through the term $x_i(t) - N_i/2$. Thus, if less than one half of all possible enlightenments occurred in a topic, we have $x_i(t) < N_i/2$, and the term is negative, having therefore an inhibiting effect on the rates of enlightenments. If more than half of the possible enlightenments occurred, $x_i(t) - N_i/2$ is positive, and therefore has an enhancing effect. While it is reasonable to postulate an effect of such a form, there is little justification for selecting $N_i/2$ as the critical threshold. It is quite possible that these thresholds vary from topic to topic, and their choice should be made after analysing the subject taught.

6.3.5   Estimation

To use the simulation program, one needs to have estimates of certain parameters. First, the maximal possible numbers of enlightenments in various topics can be determined from the subject matter analysis: as an approximation of N_i, one may count the number of items on a list of what one can expect the top students to know and understand.

An experienced instructor could also provide assessments of the relative difficulty levels D_i of topics. These (as well as the coefficients c_{ik}) may be scaled arbitrarily, since it is only their ratios that matter (the magnitudes become absorbed by scaling factors).

As regards coefficients c_{ik}, they again may be assessed by experienced instructors. Roughly, c_{ik} may be measured by the number of items on a list of instances when some facts about the ith topic are recalled or used in teaching the kth topic.

As regards the difficulty of the topics, one could also try an empirical approach in the following way. Suppose we devise tests covering various topics in the course. Assume that a test for the kth topic contains R_k (binary, say) items, and the score of a student is the number of items that he answers correctly (one could, of course, modify this approach by considering partial scores, etc.). The data have the form of a matrix $[z_{ik}]$, where z_{ik} is the score of the ith student on the kth test (i.e., concerning the kth topic). This matrix allows us to gain some insight into the relative difficulty of the topics, by analyzing the average scores in various topics (averaging over the students). However, such data may serve at best only as a guideline, since the scores depend not only on the difficulties (which we want to measure) but also on the attained knowledge. Similarly, the averages of scores z_{ik} across the topics may provide some information about the distribution of the students' abilities. Here again, however, the data are confounded with the attainment levels, which cannot be separated from abilities.

It remains to outline the method of assessing the values of the remaining parameters, namely, the scaling values γ, h, ρ, and β, as well as the parameter α and the parameters of the distribution of the teacher's talents and the student's abilities.

Here the idea is to use the knowledge of learning rates, either known from the instructors' experience, or acquired from carefully designed experiments.

Suppose that the difficulties D_k and coefficients c_{ik} have already been chosen and the values N_k are known. The scaling of D_k and c_{ik} is, as mentioned, arbitrary (e.g., one may assign $D_k = 100$ to the most difficult topic, and smaller values to the remaining topics, so as to express the ratios of difficulty).

Suppose now that we take an average student's ability and an average teacher's talent to be 100 (say). To determine the values of α and γ imagine that an average student taught by an average teacher acquired about one half of the possible knowledge of previous topics, and that at time t he starts to learn a new topic with difficulty D_k. We have, therefore, $x_i(t) \cong N_j/2$ for $j < k$; hence $Q = 0$ and $x_k(t) = 0$. The enlightenment intensity for the kth topic is therefore, using (6.20),

$$\lambda_k = (\alpha N_k/\gamma D_k)100 \times 100;$$

hence the average time until the first enlightenment in the kth topic is $1/\lambda_k$. If we now find (e.g., from some experiment, or from the instructor's experience) that an average student, taught by an average teacher, with average knowledge of previous topics, should have his first instance of understanding the topic of difficulty D_k after, say, 20 minutes of learning, then $1/\lambda_k = 0.33$ (hours), which gives an assessment of the ratio $\alpha/\gamma \cong 0.33 \times 10^4 N_k/D_k$. Suppose now that the same student, at some later time, acquired about one half of the knowledge of the kth topic while it was still being taught. His learning rate is now fastest, and we can expect, say, the average time between enlightenments to be only 10 minutes (i.e., about six "graspings" of the material per hour of learning). We have now

$$\lambda_k = \frac{(\alpha + N_k/2)N_k/2}{\gamma D_k} \times 10^4,$$

and taking $1/\lambda_k = 1/6$, we obtain a second equation for α and γ.

After choosing α and γ from the knowledge of average times to enlightenments for an average student with average previous knowledge, we can assess h by considering how much improvement is gained as a result of previous knowledge. Thus, suppose that we have two students, with the same abilities and taught by the same teacher, one with average knowledge of past topics (so that $x_i(t)$ is about $N_i/2$ for all past topics) and the other with a "good" knowledge, say $x_i(t) = 0.75N_i$. The value Q for the first student is 0, and for the second, it may be computed by knowing the constants c_{ik}. If the rate of enlightenments of the first student is λ, that of the second is λe^{hQ}, so that the ratio of the rates, hence the ratio of average interenlightment times is e^{hQ}.

Similar reasonings, concerning only average enlightenment times in past topics, may lead to the assessment of constants ρ and β.

Finally, an assessment of the parameters of the distribution of teachers' talents and students' abilities may be obtained by considering the amounts of variability of learning results (known from experience; as the means are set at the value 100, only one parameter needs to be determined for each of these distributions).

6.4 INFORMATIONAL SYNERGY

Both models presented in the preceding sections were based on tacit assumptions that the components of the state process (evaluation on a given attribute or number of enlightenments on a given topic) interact in some way. This assumption is, of course, plausible on a purely intuitive level. Nevertheless, one should like to be able to subject it to an empirical test. In this section, we shall present such a testing procedure, applicable in some context. [See also Nowakowska and Kochen (1986).]

The main issue, of course, lies in finding suitable data. This might be possible in the context of learning. In the process of teaching, a student learns some items of information (facts, techniques, theorems, etc.). Each of them increases the student's knowledge, hence also increases his level of preparedness for a given task. Suppose that we can measure this increase (for a specified task). The question, in a simplified situation of two items of information, may be posed as follows: suppose that information A increases the level of preparedness by x, and information B increases it by y. Now, if both A and B are known, the preparedness increases by some value z. Is z equal the sum of $x + y$ or not? In the case $z > x + y$ we may think of *synergy* of information; knowledge of both A and B is worth more than the sum of the values of A and B alone.

The broad framework outlined in this section has to be specified in order to make the question of synergy meaningful. The first problem lies in defining the notion of level of preparedness in a quantitative way, making it subject to observation and measurement, at least in some broad statistical sense. Second, we shall have to allow for individual variability of students' abilities, prior knowledge, etc. Thus, we must formulate the hypotheses in a way that allows testing the (sub)additivity versus the synergy hypothesis, despite the variability of individuals' levels of preparedness.

Third, we must overcome the difficulties connected with the impossibility of "unlearning."

6.4.1 Level of Preparedness

To make the solution feasible (by keeping the number of parameters under control), the analysis will be restricted to two items of information, say A and B. We assume that each of them may be comprehended separately (that is, knowledge of A is not vital to understand B, and vice versa). Each of A and B is helpful in attaining some task.

Imagine that we have two tasks, G_1 and G_2, of the same level of difficulty, and such that attaining of one of them does not facilitate attaining the other.

In practical situations of experiments, tasks G_1 and G_2 may be some mathematical problems, while A and B are some theorems helpful for solution.

Moreover, for ensuring empirical access to the hypotheses that we want to test, we assume that tasks G_1 and G_2 are binary (they are either attained completely or not at all), so that the only measure of level of attainement is the time it takes to solve the respective problems. Consequently, we shall take as level of preparedness for a task simply the time it takes to attain it or—more precisely—the appropriate parameter of the distribution of the time it takes to attain the task.

6.4.2 The Experiment

In the sequel, we assume that we have a group of $m + n$ students, who initially do not know either A or B. It might be helpful to try to make this group homogeneous with respect to some possibly confounding variables, such as abilities or prior knowledge. The model, however, will not assume such homogeneity, and the hypotheses will be tested in the presence of nuisance parameters representing the factors described in the preceding section.

Out of $m + n$ students, m are subject to the following procedure:

(1)   They are taught A (informed about A, etc.) and then asked to solve G_1. The solution times $x_1, x_2, \ldots, x_m$ are recorded.

(2)   The students are then taught B (so that they know both A and B), and are asked to solve G_2. The solution times are now $y_1, y_2, \ldots, y_m$, so that we have m pairs of observations (x_i, y_i), $i = 1, \ldots, m$.

The remaining group of n students is subject to the same procedure, except that they are taught B in the first stage, and A in the second. The recorded times are now $z_1, \ldots, z_n$ (times to solution under knowledge of B only), and $w_1, \ldots, w_n$ (times to solution under knowledge of both A and B).

6.4.3 Assumptions

We now make the following assumptions, which will enable us to express the hypotheses tested in parametric form and also to design statistical procedures for testing and estimation.

ASSUMPTION 6.1   *Each student is characterized by his level of talent, prior knowledge, etc., to be denoted generally by s. The values of s are not observable; they are assumed to follow a gamma distribution, with shape parameter r and scale parameter β.*

Consequently, the density of s is

$$h(s) = \frac{\beta^r}{\Gamma(r)} s^{r-1} e^{-\beta s}, \, s > 0. \tag{6.37}$$

In the sequel, we shall treat r and β as nuisance parameters of the model.

ASSUMPTION 6.2   *Given the value of s, the times (x, y) for students in the first group (who are taught A first and then B) are independent and exponentially distributed, with parameters sa and sc, so that the joint density of (x, y) is*

$$f(x, y \mid s) = sae^{-sax}sce^{-scy} = s^2ace^{-s(ax+cy)}. \tag{6.38}$$

Similarly, the joint density of (z, w) for the second group of students (who are taught B first and then A) is

$$g(z, w \mid s) = s^2bce^{-s(bz+cw)}. \tag{6.39}$$

We therefore have five parameters. First, a, b and c pertain to times of solutions under knowledge of A alone (parameter a), knowledge of B alone (parameter b), and knowledge of both A and B (parameter c). The remaining two parameters r and β are nuisance parameters, pertaining to the distribution of factors other than knowledge of A and B, that may affect the observed times of solution.

Note here that the marginal distribution of y in the first group of students is the same as the marginal distribution of w in the second group: both concern the times of solution for those who know both A and B (in practical terms, this means that order in which one acquires knowledge of A and B is immaterial).

We shall be concerned with the estimation of parameters, and also in testing the null hypothesis

$$H_0: \quad a + b \geq c, r, \beta \quad \text{(arbitrary)}$$

against the alternative

$$H_1: \quad a + b < c, r, \beta \quad \text{(arbitrary)}$$

(the synergy hypothesis).

6.4.4   Analysis

We start from deriving the joint density of times x, y. We have here

$$f(x, y) = \int_0^\infty f(x, y \mid s)h(s)\, ds$$

$$= \int_0^\infty acs^2 e^{-s(ax+cy)}\frac{\beta^r}{\Gamma(r)}s^{r-1}e^{-\beta s}\, ds$$

$$= \frac{ac\beta^r}{\Gamma(r)}\int_0^\infty s^{r+1}e^{-s(ax+cy+\beta)}\, ds$$

$$= \frac{ac\beta^r\Gamma(r+2)}{\Gamma(r)(ax+cy+\beta)^{r+2}}, \tag{6.40}$$

so that

$$f(x, y) = \frac{ac\beta^r r(r + 1)}{(ax + cy + \beta)^{r+2}}. \tag{6.41}$$

Similarly, the unconditional density of (z, w) is

$$g(z, w) = \frac{bc\beta^r r(r + 1)}{(bz + cw + \beta)^{r+2}}. \tag{6.42}$$

We may now write the likelihood of the sample (x_i, y_i), $i = 1, \ldots, m$, (z_j, w_j), $j = 1, \ldots, n$. We have here

$$\begin{aligned}
L &= \prod_{i=1}^{m} \frac{ac\beta^r r(r + 1)}{(ax_i + cy_i + \beta)^{r+2}} \prod_{j=1}^{n} \frac{bc\beta^r r(r + 1)}{(bz_j + cw_j + \beta)^{r+2}} \\
&= a^m b^n c^{m+n} \beta^{r(m+n)} r^{m+n} (r + 1)^{m+n} \prod_{i=1}^{m} (ax_i + cy_i + \beta)^{-(r+2)} \\
&\quad \times \prod_{j=1}^{n} (bz_j + cw_j + \beta)^{-(r+2)}, \tag{6.43}
\end{aligned}$$

so that

$$\begin{aligned}
\log L &= m \log a + n \log b + (m + n) \log c + r(m + n) \log \beta \\
&\quad + (m + n) \log r + (m + n) \log(r + 1) - (r + 2) \\
&\quad \times \left[\sum_{i=1}^{m} \log(ax_i + cy_i + \beta) - \sum_{j=1}^{n} \log(bz_j + cw_j + \beta) \right]. \tag{6.44}
\end{aligned}$$

Differentiating with respect to the parameters, we obtain

THEOREM 6.3 *The maximum likelihood estimators of the parameters a, b, c, β, and r are given by the equations*

$$a = \frac{m}{(r + 2)P_2}, \qquad b = \frac{n}{(r + 2)Q_2}, \qquad c = \frac{m + n}{(r + 2)(P_3 + Q_3)}, \tag{6.45}$$

$$r = \frac{2\beta(P_1 + Q_1)}{m + n - \beta(P_1 + Q_1)}, \qquad \beta = \exp\left[\frac{P_4 + Q_4}{m + n} - \frac{1}{r} - \frac{1}{r + 1} \right], \tag{6.46}$$

where

$$P_1 = \sum_{i=1}^{m} \frac{1}{ax_i + cy_i + \beta}, \qquad Q_1 = \sum_{j=1}^{n} \frac{1}{bz_j + cw_j + \beta}, \tag{6.47}$$

$$P_2 = \sum_{i=1}^{m} \frac{x_i}{ax_i + cy_i + \beta}, \qquad Q_2 = \sum_{j=1}^{n} \frac{z_j}{bz_j + cw_j + \beta}, \tag{6.48}$$

$$P_3 = \sum_{i=1}^{m} \frac{y_i}{ax_i + cy_i + \beta}, \qquad Q_3 = \sum_{j=1}^{n} \frac{w_j}{bz_j + cw_j + \beta}, \tag{6.49}$$

$$P_4 = \sum_{i=1}^{m} \log(ax_i + cy_i + \beta), \qquad Q_4 = \sum_{j=1}^{n} \log(bz_j + cw_j + \beta). \tag{6.50}$$

The solution of the above system of equations may be obtained numerically, e.g., by iteration techniques.

To test the synergy hypothesis, let L^* stand for the maximum of the likelihood taken over all parameter space, so that L^* is the value of the likelihood (6.43) at the solution of equations (6.45–6.46).

One may then use the likelihood ratio test. What is needed is the value L^{**}, being the maximum of likelihood (6.43) under the constraint $a + b = c$. Thus, the logarithm of likelihood becomes

$$\log L = m \log a + n \log b + (m + n) \log(a + b) + r(m + n) \log \beta$$

$$+ (m + n) \log r + (m + n) \log(r + 1)$$

$$- (r + 2) \left\{ \sum_{i=1}^{m} \log[a(x_i + y_i) + by_i + \beta] \right.$$

$$+ \left. \sum_{j=1}^{n} \log[b(z_j + w_j) + aw_j + \beta] \right\}. \tag{6.51}$$

Elementary differentiation now leads to a system of four equations for unknowns a, b, r, and β, which are solvable by numerical methods similar to those in the theorem in this section. Substituting the solution to (6.43), we find the value L^{**}, and for the test of the synergy hypothesis we may use the statistic

$$X = -2 \log(L^{**}/L^*), \tag{6.52}$$

which has asymptotically a chi-square distribution with one degree of freedom.

6.5 COMMENTS

Production systems in cognitive psychology [see, e.g., Anderson (1980, 1983), Newell and Simon (1972)] and cognitive AI (expert systems, knowledge representation) [see, e.g., Hayes-Roth *et al.* (1983)], in view of their methodological similarities—construction of programs simulating some human behavior, or generating machine action that simulates human behavior—are facing similar criticism. Thus, it is difficult to sharply define the value criteria allowing evaluation and comparison of programs. Such "natural" criteria as correctness, efficiency, and parsimony, do not solve the problem. It is difficult to verify the logical correctness of a program built on the basis of accepted rules of reasoning. The latter may allow derivation of inconsistent or contradictory inferences, or may lead to a large number of correct but irrelevant inferences. Additional knowledge is needed to allow guidance in the application of these rules.

In cognitive psychology, the interest in production systems is connected with their unifying value—all higher-order cognition processes may potentially be expressed as programs and their hierarchy. Even if the production systems do not lead to unique predictions and have implicational form, connecting sometimes a very large set of productions with the observed behavior, it is still possible to choose a smaller set of most likely productions, using the actual learning mechanisms. The latter are also appreciated in computer science and AI [see, e.g., "Machine Learning," Michalski *et al.* (1983)]. It seems, however, that—as opposed to AI—the methodological difficulties and restrictions of the production system approach are incomparably higher in cognitive sciences—especially as regards cumulation and synthesis of knowledge. The latter also constitute a problem in AI.

It appears that in cognitive sciences, as well as in AI, one could obtain new results—as shown in this book—by putting more stress on observability, experiment, formation of judgments and opinions, and their variability, problems of descriptions and texts, as well as stressing basic structural and functional properties of knowledge and reasoning (especially justification and explanation) in science. For the latter analysis, see Chapter 3 of "Theories of Research" (Nowakowska, 1984). Perhaps this is a way that would lead to an extension and enrichment of various modal calculi simulating the reasoning by experts.

In other words, one of the possible ways of deepening the theoretical foundations of expert systems is through an understanding of the logical structure and dynamics of the development of a given domain of knowledge, both by the constructor of the system and by its user. This will allow us to show not only how the information about new facts or new knowledge may affect an expert's opinion but also to better understand how a scientist, in particular an expert, can change the area of knowledge and its content by the rejection and introduction of new concepts, hypotheses, or theories, which better explain the collected facts and hypotheses. To put it differently, one can show how an expertise changes the state of information in a domain or problem by design of change or by keeping the status quo if it is considered optimal. Consequently, the automatization of expertise in science or technology (as opposed to expert systems built for medical applications) would have to take into account to a larger extent certain wider characteristics of the domain (e.g., trends, controversial issues, hypotheses tested thus far, models or methods used). Moreover, among others, the constructors of expert systems must be well acquainted with the process of judgment and opinion formation, as well as with the cognitive limitations and biases connected with these processes. In particular, it is important to understand the distortions of judgments connected with the difficulties of discrimination and identification, implying variability of judgments and opinions in time. It is worth stressing that the statistical properties of judgments and opinions were, until now, almost entirely neglected in many important areas of research, such as decision theory, experimental research on subjective probability, and in general, measurement theory. In recent publications concerning expert systems [see, for example, Hayes-Roth (1983), Pearl (1984), Sowa (1984)], while there exists an awareness of the importance of these topics (not only in the construction of expert systems but also in the evaluation of their efficiency), there is no deeper analysis of the process of expertise formation—the basic cognitive, ethical, and social processes involved in it.

Observability is, for the constructor of an expert system, another important group of problems. In particular, in scientific expertise the way of obtaining the data base is essential, because of the possibility of many sources of errors.

APPENDIX

A.1 RELATIONS

Given two sets A and B a *relation* between elements of A and B is identified with a set $R \subset A \times B$. If $(x, y) \in R$, we say that x and y are in relation R and denote this fact by xRy. If $(x, y) \notin R$, we write $\sim xRy$.

To give some examples, let $A = B = $ set of all people and let

$$R = \{(x, y) \in A \times A : x \text{ is the father of } y\}.$$

Observe that when a relation is represented in the form of a set of pairs, it is important to specify the underlying sets A and B. For instance, in this example, if $(x, y) \in R$, then y is either a son or a daughter of x. If $A = B = $ set of all men, then $(x, y) \in R$ means that y is a son of x.

More generally, an *n-ary relation* between elements of sets $A_1, A_2, \ldots, A_n$ is a set

$$R \subset A_1 \times A_2 \times \cdots \times A_n,$$

the elements of R being n-tuples $(x_1, x_2, \ldots, x_n)$ with $x_i \in A_i$, $i = 1, 2, \ldots, n$. If $(x_1, x_2, \ldots, x_n) \in R$, we say that $x_1, \ldots, x_n$ are in relation R.

To give examples of ternary relations, let $A_1 = A_2 = A_3$ be the set of points on the plane and let $(x, y, z) \in R$ if x is at the same distance from y as from z. Operations in the numerical domain, such as addition $x + y$, may be represented as ternary relations: taking $A_1 = A_2 = A_3$ to be the set of real numbers, we put $(x, y, z) \in R$ if $x + y = z$.

Quarternary relations occur most often when pairs are compared. Thus, with appropriate sets A_i, we may have $(x, y, z, w) \in R$ if the distance from x to y is larger than the distance from z to w, and so on.

Functions

Let $R \subset A \times B$ be such that

(i) for every $x \in A$ there exists $y \in B$ with $(x, y) \in R$;
(ii) if $(x, y_1) \in R$ and $(x, y_2) \in R$, then $y_1 = y_2$.

Then R is called a *function* that maps A into B. For each $x \in A$, the (unique) $y \in B$ with $(x, y) \in R$ is identified with the value of the function, say, f, and is denoted $f(x)$. Relation R consists then of all pairs $(x, f(x))$, and we use the notation $f: A \to B$.

If for any $y \in B$ there exists an $x \in A$ such that $y = f(x)$, the function f is said to map A *onto* B. If $x_1 \neq x_2$ implies that $f(x_1) \neq f(x_2)$, we say that f is *one to one*.

Images, Inverse Images, and Projections

Let $R \subset A \times B$ be a binary relation. For any $x \in A$, let

$$R_x = \{y \in B : xRy\};$$

and for any $y \in B$, let

$$R_y^{-1} = \{x \in A : xRy\}.$$

More generally, for $A' \subset A$ we define

$$R(A') = \{y \in B : xRy \text{ for some } x \in A'\};$$

and for $B' \subset B$ we put

$$R^{-1}(B') = \{x \in A : xRy \text{ for some } y \in B'\}.$$

Then $R(A') = \bigcup_{x \in A'} R_x$ and $R^{-1}(B') = \bigcup_{y \in B'} R_y^{-1}$. The sets $R(A')$ and $R^{-1}(B')$ are called, respectively, the *image of* A' and *inverse image of* B' (under R), or simply the *projections* of sets A' and B'.

If R is a function that maps A into B, then each R_x consists of just one point, namely, the value of the function at the point x. If the function is one to one, then R_y^{-1} is either empty or consists of just one point (the point mapped into y). The projection of B equals A, since every point in A has some image in B. On the other hand, the projection of A is strictly contained in B, unless the function is onto, in which case it is equal B.

Isomorphism and Homomorphism

A set with a system of relations defined in it (binary, ternary, etc.) is called a *relational structure*. The notions of isomorphism and homomorphism concern the underlying intuitive notion of similarity between two structures.

To take the simplest example, let $\langle A_1, R \rangle$ and $\langle A_2, S \rangle$ be two relational structures, with $R \subset A_1 \times A_1$ and $S \subset A_2 \times A_2$ being binary relations. We say that these two structures are *isomorphic* if there exists a function $f: A_1 \to A_2$ that is one to one and onto, such that for all $x, y \in A_1$ the condition $(x, y) \in R$ holds if and only if $(f(x), f(y)) \in S$.

Naturally, this definition extends easily to the case of structures that involves more than one relation and also relations that are not binary. Thus, two structures are isomorphic if the elements of their sets may be put into one-to-one correspondence, which preserves all relations.

If $\langle A_1, R \rangle$ and $\langle A_2, S \rangle$ are two relational structures and there exists a function $f: A_1 \to A_2$ such that whenever $(x, y) \in R$, then $(f(x), f(y)) \in S$, we say that f establishes a *homomorphism* between these structures. Here f need not be one to one or onto.

Operations on Relations

Now let $R \subset A \times A$ so that R is a relation between elements of the same set.

DEFINITION The *converse* $\hat{R}$ of relation R is defined by the condition $(x, y) \in \hat{R}$ if and only if $(y, x) \in R$.

Let $R \subset A \times A$ and $S \subset A \times A$ be two binary relations on A. Then their *sum* and *product* are defined simply as the union $R \cup S$ and intersection $R \cap S$. Thus, $x(R \cup S)y$ if either xRy or xSy (or both), whereas $x(R \cap S)y$ holds if both xRy and xSy.

To take an example, let A = set of all people, let $R = \{(x, y) \in A \times A : x$ is the father of $y\}$, and let $S = \{(x, y) \in A \times A : x$ is the mother of $y\}$. Then $R \cup S$ is the relation of parenthood, that is, $x(R \cup S)y$ if x is either the father or mother of y. Relation $R \cap S$ is empty, since no person can be both father and mother. The converse of relation R is the relation of being a child of, so that $x\hat{R}y$ if x is a child of (the man) y.

DEFINITION The *composition* of relations R and S, denoted by $R \circ S$, or simply RS, is defined as $(x, y) \in RS$ if there exists $z \in A$ such that xRz and zSy.

In particular, $R^2 = RR$ is defined as xR^2y if there exists $z \in A$ such that xRz and zRy. Again, if R is the relation of being the father, then R^2 is the relation of being the paternal grandfather.

More generally, let

$$I = \{(x, x) : x \in A\},$$

so that I is the *diagonal* in the set $A \times A$. We may now define

$$R^0 = I, \qquad R^{n+1} = R^n R, \qquad n = 0, 1, \ldots.$$

DEFINITION The relation $R^* = R^0 \cup R^1 \cup R^2 \cup \cdots$ is called the *closure*, or *transitive extension*, of R.

Thus, xR^*y if xR^ny for some n, that is, either $x = y$, or xRy, or there exists an $n \geq 1$ and a sequence $z_1, \ldots, z_n$ of elements of A such that xRz_1, $z_1Rz_2, \ldots, z_{n-1}Rz_n$, and z_nRy.

Equivalences

Let $R \subset A \times A$ be a binary relation on A.

DEFINITION We say that R is *reflexive* if $I \subset R$, and *antireflexive* if $I \cap R = \varnothing$.

Thus, reflexivity means that xRx for every $x \in A$, that is, that every element of A is in relation R with itself. Antireflexivity means that no x is in relation R with itself, so that $\sim xRx$.

DEFINITION Relation R will be called *symmetric* if $R = \hat{R}$; it will be called *asymmetric* if $R \cap \hat{R} = \varnothing$; and *antisymmetric* if $R \cap \hat{R} = I$.

Thus, for a symmetric relation, xRy implies yRx. For asymmetric relations, whenever xRy, then $\sim yRx$, whereas for antisymmetric relations, whenever xRy and yRx, then $x = y$.

Examples of asymmetric and antisymmetric relations in the numerical domain are $<$ and $\leq$, respectively.

DEFINITION Relation R is called *transitive* if $R^2 \subset R$.

This means that whenever xRy and yRz (so that xR^2y), then xRy. Clearly, for any R, the closure R^* is transitive.

DEFINITION Relation R, which is reflexive, symmetric, and transitive, is called an *equivalence*.

Let R be an equivalence, and for any $x \in A$ let

$$[x] = \{y \in A : xRy\}.$$

The set $[x]$ is called the *equivalence class* of x.

For any $x, y \in A$ we have either $[x] = [y]$ or $[x] \cap [y] = \varnothing$, the first case when xRy and the second when $\sim xRy$. Indeed, suppose that xRy and let $z \in [x]$. Then xRz, hence by symmetry zRx, and by transitivity we obtain zRy, so that yRz also, which means that $z \in [y]$. Thus $[x] \subset [y]$, and similarly we obtain $[y] \subset [x]$, so that $[x] = [y]$.

Now let $\sim xRy$, and suppose that $z \in [x] \cap [y]$. Then xRz and yRz, which implies xRy, contrary to the assumption. The above argument shows that each equivalence relation determines a partition of A into equivalence classes of its elements. This set of equivalence classes is denoted A/R. Conversely, if $A = A_1 \cup A_2 \cup \cdots$ with sets A_j disjoint, then relation R defined by $(x, y) \in R$ iff x and y belong to the same class of the partition is an equivalence. It generates the same partition, so that $A/R = \{A_1, A_2, \ldots\}$.

Order Relations

DEFINITION   We say that R is a *quasi-order* if R is reflexive and transitive, and *strict partial order* if it is antireflexive, asymmetric, and transitive.

Let R be a quasi-order in A. We may then define two relations, E and R', as follows:

$$xEy \qquad \text{iff} \qquad xRy \text{ and } yRx,$$

$$xR'y \qquad \text{iff} \qquad xRy \text{ and } \sim yRx.$$

Thus, $E = R \cap \hat{R}$, and $R' = R - \hat{R}$. It is easy to show that E is an equivalence relation, while R' is a strict partial order.

Consider now the set of equivalence classes of relation E, to be denoted $A_1, A_2, \ldots$ (so that xEy if $x, y \in A_i$ for some i). We may now define a strict partial order, say, S, on the set of equivalence classes of E. We put $A_i S A_j$ if $xR'y$ for some $x \in A_i$, $y \in A_j$. To see that this definition is correct, one needs to show that the condition $A_i S A_j$ is independent of the choice of $x \in A_i$ and $y \in A_j$.

Indeed, suppose that for some $x \in A_i$, $y \in A_j$ we have $xR'y$, and let $x' \in A_i$, $y' \in A_j$. We then have $x'Ex$, $y'Ey$ and from the chain $x'Rx$, xRy, yRy' we obtain $x'Ry'$ by transitivity. It remains to show that $\sim y'Rx'$. Indeed, if we had $y'Rx'$, then we could write the chain yRy', $y'Rx'$, $x'Rx$, and by transitivity we would obtain yRx, contrary to the assumption that $xR'y$.

This shows that S is well defined, and it remains to show that S is a strict partial order. If we had $A_i S A_i$, then for some $x, y \in A_i$ we would have $xR'y$, hence $\sim xEy$, which contradicts the definition of equivalence classes A_i. Similarly, if we had $A_i S A_j$ and $A_j S A_i$, then for some $x, x' \in A_i$, $y, y' \in A_j$ we would have $xR'y$ and $y'R'x'$ with xEx', yEy'. This implies xRy, and combined with $x'Rx$, yRy' we obtain $x'Ry'$ by transitivity of R, contrary to the condition $y'R'x'$. This shows that S is asymmetric. Finally, transitivity of S is an immediate consequence of transitivity of R.

Strict partial orders, whether defined directly or elicited from quasi-orders, allow for the possibility that some elements are left not comparable (i.e., not connected by the ordering relation). We therefore introduce the following definition.

DEFINITION   Relation R is called *connected* in A if for every $x, y \in A$ we have either xRy or yRx (or both).

DEFINITION If R is transitive and connected, it is called a *weak order.*

Since in this case R must be reflexive, it is also a quasi-order, and the construction presented above allows us to define equivalence E, strict order R', and relation S ordering the equivalence classes of E. In this case relations R' and S are connected.

A.2 FUZZY SETS

Fuzzy sets were introduced by Zadeh (1965) as a means to handle in a precise way the vague concepts, especially those that appear in natural languages. The time-honored examples of such concepts, which may be found in almost any text introducing fuzzy sets, are "tall," "old," "very old," and so forth.

The central idea lies in introducing graded membership in a set, so that the relations $x \in A$ and $x \in -A$ may both hold in some degree.

The formal foundations of the theory are as follows. Let X be a (nonfuzzy, or *crisp*) set, which constitutes the *universe of discourse* (this means that all considerations will be restricted to subsets, fuzzy or not, of X).

DEFINITION A *fuzzy* subset A of X will be identified with a function

$$f_A : X \to [0, 1],$$

to be called a *membership function* of the set A.

The intended interpretation is that $f_A(x)$ represents the *grade of membership* of x in A. If $f_A(x) = 1$, then x belongs to A "fully"; if $f_A(x) = 0$, then x does not belong to A at all, while the intermediate cases represent partial membership.

Set-Theoretical Operations

Now let A and B be two fuzzy subsets of X, with membership functions $f_A(x)$ and $f_B(x)$.

DEFINITION Sets A and B are *equal*, $A = B$, if $f_A(x) = f_B(x)$ for every $x \in X$.

DEFINITION Set A is said to be *contained* in B, to be denoted $A \subset B$, if $f_A(x) \le f_B(x)$ for every $x \in X$.

Thus, as in the case of crisp sets, $A = B$ iff $A \subset B$ and $B \subset A$.

DEFINITION *Complement* $-A$ of set A is the set with membership function

$$f_{-A}(x) = 1 - f_A(x).$$

DEFINITION   *Union* $A \cup B$ is the fuzzy set with membership function

$$f_{A \cup B}(x) = \max[f_A(x), f_B(x)].$$

DEFINITION   *Intersection* $A \cap B$ is the fuzzy set with membership function

$$f_{A \cup B}(x) = \min[f_A(x), f_B(x)].$$

The operations of union and intersection can be extended to any finite family of fuzzy sets and also to any infinite family if max and min are replaced by sup and inf, respectively.

Clearly, the operations on fuzzy sets satisfy the corresponding laws for crisp sets; that is, they are commutative, associative, distributive; they also satisfy idempotence and De Morgan's laws.

In particular, $A \cup B = B$ iff $A \subset B$ and $A \cap B = A$ iff $A \subset B$, and the class of all fuzzy subsets of X is a lattice.

DEFINITION   A fuzzy set A is called *empty* if $f_A(x) \equiv 0$.

DEFINITION   A fuzzy set A is called *normal* if $\sup_{x \in X} f_A(x) = 1$.

Fuzzy sets are a generalization of the usual (crisp) sets in the following sense. Let $F(X)$ be the class of all fuzzy subsets of X, and let $F^*(X)$ denote the subclass of $F(X)$ consisting of all those fuzzy sets whose membership function assumes only the extreme values 0 and 1. Clearly, $F^*(X)$ is closed under all set-theoretical operations.

If $f \in F^*(X)$, let

$$Q(f) = \{x \in X : f(x) = 1\}.$$

Then $Q: F^*(X) \to 2^X$ establishes an isomorphism between the class $F^*(X)$ and the class 2^X of all crisp subsets of X, in the sense that, if f_A, $f_B \in F^*(X)$, we then have

$$Q(f_{A \cup B}) = Q(f_A) \cup Q(f_B), \qquad Q(f_{A \cap B}) = Q(f_A) \cap Q(f_B),$$
$$Q(f_{-A}) = X - Q(f_A).$$

With every fuzzy set A with membership function f_A, one may associate a family of crisp sets A_α, $0 \le \alpha \le 1$, called α-*level sets* by putting

$$A_\alpha = \{x \in X : f_A(x) \ge \alpha\}.$$

An important special case occurs when the underlying universe X is the real line or its subset, so that we have the linear ordering relation $\le$ for elements of X. We may then introduce the following definition.

DEFINITION   A fuzzy subset A of X is called *regular* if its membership function f_A satisfies the property: for all $x_1 < x_2 < x_3$, if $f_A(x_1) > f_A(x_2)$, then $f_A(x_2) \ge f_A(x_3)$.

This means that f_A may have at most one peak: it is either monotone increasing, monotone decreasing, or there exists a point x_0 such that the function f_A is increasing (more precisely, nondecreasing) to the left of x_0 and decreasing (more precisely, nonincreasing) to the right of x_0.

The class F^r of all regular fuzzy sets is closed under the operation of intersection: if $A, B \in F^r$, then $A \cap B \in F^r$.

Fuzzy Relations

A fuzzy (binary) relation between elements of (crisp) sets A and B is a fuzzy subset $R \subset A \times B$ given by membership function

$$f_R : A \times B \to [0, 1],$$

where $f_R(x, y)$ is the degree to which the elements $x \in A$ and $y \in B$ are in relation R.

Generally, a fuzzy n-ary relation R between elements of sets $A_1, \ldots, A_n$ is a fuzzy subset R of the Cartesian product $A_1 \times \cdots \times A_n$, given by membership function

$$f_R : A_1 \times \cdots \times A_n \to [0, 1].$$

If R is a fuzzy binary relation on $A \times B$, given by membership function f_R, and A', B' are fuzzy subsets of A and B, respectively, with membership functions $\psi_{A'} : A \to [0, 1]$, $\psi_{B'} : B \to [0, 1]$, then the image of A' and inverse image of B' under R are usually defined as follows.

DEFINITION The *image* of A' under R is a fuzzy set $R(A')$ in B with membership function

$$f_{R(A')}(y) = \sup_{x \in A} \min [\psi_{A'}(x), f_R(x, y)], \qquad y \in B.$$

Similarly, the *inverse image* $R^{-1}(B')$ of B' under R is a fuzzy subset of A with membership function

$$f_{R^{-1}(B')}(x) = \sup_{y \in B} \min [\psi_{B'}(y), f_R(x, y)], \qquad x \in A.$$

These concepts reduce to the concepts of image and inverse image for crisp sets, if the sets A', B' and relation R are crisp.

Possibility and Necessity

One of the most important concepts that may be defined in terms of notions of fuzzy set theory is that of possibility; consider too the related notion of necessity. Both these notions serve as a base for Zadeh's (1978) theory of semantics.

Let X be the universe of discourse, and let u be a variable which takes values in X. Let p be a certain proposition or set of propositions (typically, forming our initial data or representing our knowledge). Assume that p restricts the values of U to some (fuzzy or not) subset K of X, and let μ_K be the membership function of K. It will be convenient to identify sets with attributes of elements of X and represent p as the proposition "U is K."

Now let B be a fixed subset (fuzzy or not) of X, described by the fuzzy membership function f_B. One may then ask the following question: given that we know p (i.e., we know that U is K), how possible it is that U is B?

The possibility postulate of fuzzy set theory defines the latter value as

$$\text{Poss}(B\,|\,p) = \sup_{x \in X} \min[\, f_B(x), \mu_K(x)].$$

Similarly, one may ask the question: given that we know that U is K, how necessary it is that U is B?

The answer is

$$\text{Nec}(B\,|\,p) = \inf_{x \in X} \max[\, f_B(x), 1 - \mu_K(x)].$$

To appreciate the significance of these definitions, first observe that, if B is nonfuzzy, then the formula for the possibility of B given K becomes

$$\text{Poss}(B\,|\,p) = \sup_{x \in B} \mu_K(x),$$

and for necessity we obtain in a similar way

$$\text{Nec}(B\,|\,p) = \inf_{x \notin B}[1 - \mu_K(x)] = 1 - \sup_{x \notin B} \mu_K(x) = 1 - \text{Poss}(-B\,|\,p).$$

In short, given p, the possibility that U is B (for nonfuzzy sets B) is the maximum possibility values that $U = x$ for some x in B.

On the other hand, given p, the degree of necessity of B is determined by the degree of possibility that U is not B.

As regards p, that is, the statement that determines the set K, the most important cases occur when

(a) the knowledge is nonfuzzy and exact, so that $K = \{x_0\}$; that is, $\mu_K(x) = 1$ or 0 depending on whether $x = x_0$ or $x \neq x_0$.

(b) the knowledge in p is nonfuzzy but inexact; that is, K is a crisp set containing more than one element. In this case $\mu_K(x) = 1$ or 0 depending on whether $x \in K$ or $x \notin K$.

(c) the knowledge given in p is fuzzy; in this case K is a fuzzy set.

To give examples, suppose we are interested in human height, so that X is the set of possible heights, say, in centimeters. Suppose that p is an assertion about John's height. In case (a), p might be "John's height is 182 cm"; in case (b), the information might be "John's height is above 180 cm"; in case (c), the information might be "John is tall."

Let B be a set with membership function $f_B(x)$. In case (a), we have $\text{Poss}(B \mid p) = f_B(x_0)$, that is, the degree of membership of x_0 in B. In the case when B is crisp, $\text{Poss}(B \mid p)$ is 1 if $x_0 \in B$ and 0 if $x_0 \notin B$.

In case (b), when K is crisp, we have $\text{Poss}(B \mid p) = \sup_{x \in K} f_B(x)$. If B is also crisp, then $\text{Poss}(B \mid p) = 1$ if $B \cap K \neq \varnothing$ and 0 otherwise. Thus, B is possible if it intersects with K, otherwise the possibility of B is zero.

Finally, in case (c), when the set B is crisp, we have $\text{Poss}(B \mid p) = \sup_{x \in B} \mu_K(x)$.

For an excellent exposition of the foundations of possibility theory, see Yager (1980). For a general exposition of fuzzy set theory and its application, the reader is referred to Dubois and Prade (1980). Applications to semantics are given in Zadeh (1978), and the development of the theory and various applications may be found in Gupta, Ragade, and Yager (1979). Finally, a complete bibliography of fuzzy set theory until about 1975 may be found in Gaines and Kohout (1977).

A.3 PROBABILITY

This section contains some basic information about stochastic processes. Generally, they are probabilistic representations of the random evolution of some systems. In most cases, the state of the system at any given time is representable by a number, so that the corresponding stochastic process is a numerical random function.

The main issue is, as a rule, to derive (from the assumptions characterizing a given class of stochastic processes) probabilities of various events pertaining to the future behavior of the system, given specific information about the present and past.

In this appendix, we present some basic information about three classes of stochastic processes.

Markov Chains

Consider a system that at any moment t may be in one of a number of states, $E_1, E_2, \ldots, E_m, \ldots$ Suppose that changes of state occur only at specific time moments, say, $t = 1, 2, \ldots$ Denote by X_n the index of the state of the system immediately following the transition at $t = n$.

DEFINITION   We say that the process of transitions, or the process $X_0, X_1, \ldots$ of state indices, forms a *Markov chain* if for every n and integers $i_0, \ldots, i_n, i_{n+1}$ the following relation holds:

$$P\{X_{n+1} = i_{n+1} \mid X_n = i_n, X_{n-1} = i_{n-1}, \ldots, X_0 = i_0\}$$
$$= P\{X_{n+1} = i_{n+1} \mid X_n = i_n\}.$$

This condition asserts that, given the "present" state E_{i_n}, the transition probability to future states does not depend on the past states (prior to time $t = n$).

Denote

$$p_{ij} = P\{X_{n+1} = j \mid X_n = i\}.$$

Then $[p_{ij}]$, $i, j = 1, 2, \ldots$ is called the *transition matrix* of the Markov chain. Obviously, $p_{ij} \geq 0$ and

$$\sum_j p_{ij} = 1 \qquad \text{for every } i.$$

Let $\{a_j\}, j = 1, 2, \ldots$, be the probability distribution of the initial state, so that $a_j = P\{X_0 = j\}$. For any sequence $j_0, j_1, \ldots, j_n$, the probability of a history given by the indices of this sequence is

$$P\{X_0 = j_0, X_1 = j_1, \ldots, X_n = j_n\} = a_{j_0} p_{j_0 j_1} \cdots p_{j_{n-1} j_n},$$

in view of the Markov property, which makes the transition probabilities for a given state independent of the history leading to that state.

Let $p_{ij}^{(m)}$ be the m-step transition probability, that is,

$$p_{ij}^{(m)} = P\{X_{n+m} = j \mid X_n = i\},$$

which, in view of temporal homogeneity, is also equal to $P\{X_m = j \mid X_0 = i\}$. Then

$$p_{ij}^{(2)} = \sum_k p_{ik} p_{kj}$$

and, generally,

$$p_{ij}^{(n+m)} = \sum_k p_{ik}^{(n)} p_{kj}^{(m)}.$$

It follows that the matrix $[p_{ij}^{(n)}]$ is the nth power of the transition matrix $[p_{ij}]$. Moreover, the *absolute* probability of a given state, that is, $a_j^{(n)} = P\{X_n = j\}$ is given by

$$a_j^{(n)} = \sum_i a_i p_{ij}^{(n)}.$$

The most interesting properties of Markov chains are the so-called *ergodic* properties, concerned with the behavior of the probabilities $p_{ij}^{(n)}$ as $n \to \infty$. One may expect here that, as the number n of transitions increases, the influence of the initial state "wears off." This indeed is true under some rather general assumptions, as expressed by the following ergodic theorem.

THEOREM *Assume that the numbers of states is finite, and that the transition matrix* $[p_{ij}]$ *is such that, for some m and j, we have* $p_{ij}^{(m)} > 0$ *for all i. Then*

$$\lim_{n \to \infty} p_{ij}^{(n)} = \pi_j$$

exists and is independent of i. Moreover, the limits π_j *satisfy the system of equations*

$$\sum_v \pi_v p_{vj} = \pi_j, \qquad j = 1, 2, \ldots,$$

$$\sum_v \pi_v = 1.$$

The assumption of the theorem means in effect that there exists at least one state, say, E_j, that is attainable in m steps from any other state.

The ergodic probabilities π_j may be interpreted as the probabilities of finding the system in state E_j if a large number of transitions has already occurred, regardless of the initial state. Another interpretation is provided by the following theorem. Let T_j be the time until first return to state E_j, that is,

$$T_j = n \qquad \text{if} \quad X_0 = j, X_1 \neq j, \ldots, X_{n-1} \neq j, X_n = j.$$

THEOREM *Under the assumptions of the ergodic theorem, we have*

$$E(T_j) = 1/\pi_j$$

Thus the average time for returning to a given state is the reciprocal of the ergodic probability of finding the system in this state.

Poisson Process

Poisson process is a probabilistic representation of a stream of events occurring at random moments (examples here are times of customer arrivals at a service counter, times of incoming telephone calls, etc.).

The postulates for Poisson process are as follows.

I. *the numbers of events occurring in two nonoverlapping intervals are independent;*

II. *the probability of an event occurring in the interval* $[t, t + h]$ *is* $\lambda h + o(h)$, *while the probability of two or more events in this interval is* $o(h)$, *where* $o(h)/h \to 0$ *as* $h \to 0$.

Let $P_n(t)$ be the probability of exactly n events occurring in the interval $[0, t]$. We may then write, using Postulates I and II,

$$P_0(t + h) = P_0(t)(1 - \lambda h) + o(h)$$

and

$$P_n(t + h) = P_n(t)(1 - \lambda h) + P_{n-1}(t)\lambda h + o(h), \qquad n = 1, 2, \dots.$$

Forming the differential ratio and passing to the limit with $h \to 0$, we obtain

$$P'_0(t) = -\lambda P_0(t),$$

$$P'_n(t) = -\lambda P_n(t) + \lambda P_{n-1}(t), \qquad n = 1, 2, \dots,$$

a system that is to be solved for the initial condition $P_0(0) = 1$, $P_n(0) = 0$, $n = 1, 2, \dots$. The solution is easily seen to be

$$P_n(t) = \frac{(\lambda t)^n}{n!} e^{-\lambda t}, \qquad n = 0, 1, \dots,$$

which is the Poisson distribution with mean λt.

Birth and Death Processes

The Poisson process from the preceding section is a special case of the following process. Consider a system that at any time may be in one of the states E_0, E_1, E_2, ... At each moment, it may move to one of the "neighboring" states, so that from state E_n it may move to state E_{n+1} or E_{n-1} (if $n > 0$). The transitions are governed by the following postulate.

Given that the state at time t is E_n, the probability of transition to E_{n+1} during the time interval $[t, t + h]$ is $\lambda_n h + o(h)$, probability of transition to E_{n-1} is $\mu_n h + o(h)$, while probability of transition to any other state E_j, $j \neq n$, is $o(h)$. These probabilities do not depend on the history of the process prior to the time t.

Clearly, this is a generalization of the Poisson process, for which we have $\lambda_n = \lambda$ for all n, and $\mu_n = 0$ (so that transition to E_{n-1} is impossible).

If $P_n(t)$ is the probability that the system is in state E_n at time t, then for $n > 0$ we have

$$P_n(t + h) = P_n(t)(1 - \lambda_n h - \mu_n h) + P_{n-1}(t)\lambda_{n-1} h + P_{n+1}(t)\mu_{n+1} h + o(h).$$

A similar identity may be written for state E_0. We may then derive the system of differential equations

$$P'_0(t) = -\lambda_0 P_0(t) + \mu_1 P_1(t),$$

$$P'(t) = -(\lambda_n + \mu_n)P_n(t) + \lambda_{n-1} P_{n-1}(t) + \mu_{n+1} P_{n+1}(t),$$

where $n = 1, 2, \dots$.

By specifying parameters λ_n and μ_n one obtains various types of birth and death processes. (The name is connected with the fact that, when $\lambda_n = n\lambda$,

$\mu_n = n\mu$, we obtain a process that well describes the development of a population in which death rate and birth rate are proportional to the actual size.)

The system of differential equations given above is to be solved under initial conditions $P_i(0) = 1$, $P_n(0) = 0$ for $n \neq i$ if E_i is the initial state.

Typical questions concern the limiting behavior of probabilities $P_n(t)$ as $t \to \infty$ (which corresponds to ergodic properties of Markov chains).

Martingales

The concept of a martingale originally concerned the topics of fairness of games. Typically, a sequence of wins and losses accumulated after a number of participations in some fair games has the property that the expected accumulated fortune after the participation in the next game is the same as the fortune before the game.

Formally, a sequence $\{X_n, n = 0, 1, \ldots\}$ is called a *martingale* if

$$E(|X_n|) < \infty \qquad \text{for all } n,$$

and

$$E\{X_{n+1} \mid X_0 = x_0, X_1 = x_1, \ldots, X_n = x_n\} = x_n$$

or, in a more compact version,

$$E\{X_{n+1} \mid X_0, X_1, \ldots, X_n\} = X_n.$$

Martingales have a number of properties that make them an extremely useful and powerful tool in studying the behavior of stochastic processes. We give here only the property that was used in the text. We may write

$$E(X_{n+1}) = E\{E(X_{n+1} \mid X_0, X_1, \ldots, X_n)\} = E(X_n),$$

so that by induction we have

$$E(X_n) = E(X_0) \qquad \text{for all } n.$$

An excellent exposition of Markov chains and Poisson and birth and death processes is given in Feller (1957). For martingales, the reader is referred to Feller (1968) or Karlin and Taylor (1975).

REFERENCES

Anderson, J. R. (1980). *Cognitive psychology and its applications.* San Francisco, California: Freeman.

Anderson, J. R. (1983). *The architecture of cognition.* Cambridge, Massachusetts: Harvard Univ. Press.

Anderson, N. H., and Shanteau, J. C. (1970). Information intergration in risky decision making. *Journal of Experimental Psychology,* **84,** 441–451.

Arbib, M. A., Iberall, T., and Lyons, D. (1983). Coordinated control program for movements of the hand. COINS Technical Report, pp. 83–25. Univ. of Massachusetts at Amherst, Amherst, Massachusetts).

Arbib, M. A., Overton, K. J., and Lawton, D. T. (1984). Perceptual systems for robots. *Interdisciplinary Science Reviews* **9,** 31–46.

Arrow, K. J. (1963). *Social choice and individual values.* New York: Wiley.

Balmes, J. (1848). *Filosofia fundamental.* Barcelona: Brusi.

Barr, A., and Feigenbaum, E. A. (1982). *The hanbook of artificial intelligence.* Stanford, California: HeurisTech Press.

Bower, G. (1977). A multicomponent theory of the memory trace. In G. Bower (Ed.), *Human memory.* New York: Academic Press.

Caelli, T. (1981). *Visual perception.* London: Pergamon.

Carnap, R. (1981). On the dependence of properties of space upon those of time. In A. Benson (Ed.), *R. Carnap, essays in philosophy of science 1921–1928.* Dordrecht: Reidel.

Chomsky, N. (1957). *Syntactic structures.* The Hague: Mouton.

Costa de Beauregard, O. (1965). Irreversibility problems. In Y. Bar-Hillel (Ed.), *Proceedings of the 1974 international congress of logic, philosophy and methodology of science* (pp. 313–342). Amsterdam: North-Holland.

Debreu, G. (1958). Stochastic choice and cardinal utility. *Econometrica,* **26,** 440–444.

Doyle, J. (1978). Truth maintenance systems for problem solving. MIT AI Laboratory Report AI-TR-419, January 1978. Cambridge, Massachusetts.

Dubois, D., and Prade, H. (1980). *Fuzzy sets and systems: theory and applications.* New York: Academic Press.

Dubois, D., and Prade, H. (1982). A class of fuzzy measures based on triangular norms. *International Journal of General Systems,* **8.**

Eijkman, E. G. J., Jongsma, H. J., and Vincent, J. (1981). Two dimensional filtering, oriented line detectors and figural aspects as determinants of visual illusions. *Perception and Psychophysics,* **29,** 352–358.

Feller, W. (1957). *An introduction to probability theory and its applications* (Vol. 1). New York: Wiley.

Feller, W. (1968). *An introduction to probability theory and its applications* (Vol. 2). New York: Wiley.

Gaines, B. R., and Kohout, L. J. (1977). The fuzzy decade: a bibliography of fuzzy systems and closely related topics. *International Journal of Man–Machine Studies,* **9,** 1–69.

Gilmartin, K. J., Newell, A., and Simon, H. A. (1975). A program modeling short-term memory under strategy control. In C. N. Cofer (Ed.), *The structure of human memory.* San Francisco: W. H. Freeman.

Ginsburg, S. (1968). *Mathematical theory of context-free languages.* New York: Academic Press.

Glanzer, M. (1977). Storage mechanisms in recall. In G. Bower (Ed.), *Human memory.* New York: Academic Press.

Gödel, K. (1949). A remark about relationship between relativity theory and idealistic philosophy. In P. A. Schlipp (Ed.), *Albert Einstein: philosopher–Scientist* (pp. 557–562). Evanston, Illinois Northwestern: Univ. Press.

Grossberg, S. (1982). *Studies of mind and brain.* Dordrecht: Reidel.

Grünbaum, A. (1973). *Philosophical problems of space and time* (2nd ed., Vol. 12). In R. S. Cohen and M. M. Wartofsky (Eds)., *Boston studies in the philosophy of science.* Dordrecht: Reidel.

Gupta, M. M., Ragade, R. K., and Yager, R. R. (Eds.). (1979). *Advances in fuzzy set theory and application.* Amsterdam: North-Holland.

Hayes, J. R. (1978). *Cognitive psychology.* Homewood, Illinois: Dorsey Press.

Hayes-Roth, F., Waterman, D. A., and Lenat, D. B. (Eds.). (1983). *Building expert systems.* Reading, Massachusetts: Addison-Wesley.

Hinton, G. E., and Anderson, J. A. (Eds.). (1981). *Parallel models of associative memory.* Hillsdale, New Jersey: Lawrence Erlbaum Assoc.

Hubel, D. H., and Wiesel, T. N. (1977). Brain mechanisms in vision. *Scientific American,* **237** (6), 108–128.

Karlin, S., and Taylor, H. M. (1975). *A first course in stochastic processes* (2nd ed.). New York: Academic Press.

Klement, E. P. (1980). Fuzzy σ-algebras and fuzzy measurable functions. *Fuzzy Sets and Systems,* **4,** 83–93.

Klir, G. J. (1972). *Trends in general systems theory.* New York: Wiley.

Kosslyn, S. M. (1980). *Image and mind.* Cambridge, Massachusetts: Harvard Univ. Press.

Krantz, D. H., Luce, R. D., Suppes, P., and Tversky, A. (1971). *Foundations of measurement.* New York: Academic Press.

Kwakernaak, H. (1978). Fuzzy random variables. I. Definitions and theorems. *Information Sciences,* **15,** 1–29.

Kwakernaak, H. (1979). Fuzzy random variables. II. Algorithms and examples in the discrete case. *Information Sciences,* **17,** 253–278.

Lee, C. S. G., Gonzales, R. C., and Fu, K. S. (1983). *Tutorial on Robotics.* Silver Spring, Maryland: Computer Society Press.

Lechalas, A. (1896). *Etude sur l'espace et le temps.* Paris: Alcan.

Lee S. H. (Ed.). (1981). *Optical information processing fundamentals.* Berlin: Springer-Verlag.

Levelt, W. J. M. (1978). A survey of sentence. In W. J. M. Levelt and G. B. Flores d'Arcais (Eds.), *Studies in the perception of language.* New York: Wiley.

Lindsey, P. H., and Norman, D. A. (1977). *Human information processing: an introduction to psychology.* New York: Academic Press.

Lotze, H. (1887). *Metaphysic.* (2nd ed.) B. Bosanquet, Ed.). Oxford: Clarendon Press.

Luce, R. D. (1959). *Individual choice behavior.* New York: Wiley.

Luce, R. D., and Raiffa, H. (1957). *Games and decisions.* New York: Wiley.

Marr, D. (1982). *Vision.* San Francisco, California: Freeman.

Mehlberg, H. (1981). Time, causality and quantum theory. In R. S. Cohen (Ed.), *Studies in the philosophy of science.* Dordrecht: Reidel.

Michalski, R. S., Carbonell, J. G., and Mitchell, T. M. (Eds.). (1983). *Machine Learning,* Palo Alto, California: Tioga.

Minsky, M. L. (1975). A framework for representing knowledge. In: P. H. Winston (Ed.), *The psychology of computer vision.* New York: McGraw-Hill.

Montague, W. E. (1977). Elaborative strategies in verbal learning and memory. In G. Bower (Ed.), *Human memory.* New York: Academic Press.

Muir, A. (1981). Fuzzy sets and probability. *Kybernetes,* **10,** 197–200.

Neiser, U. (1967). *Cognitive psychology.* New York: Appleton.

Newell, A., and Simon, H. A. (1972). *Human problem solving.* Englewood Cliffs, New Jersey: Prentice-Hall.

Nilssen, N. J. (1980). *Principles of Artificial Intelligence.* Palo Alto, California: Tioga.

Norman, D. A., and Rumelhart, D. E. (1975). *Explorations in cognition.* San Francisco, California: Freeman.

Nowakowska, M. (1967). Quantitative approach to dynamics of perception. *General Systems,* **12,** 81–95.

Nowakowska, M. (1973). *Language of motivation and language of actions.* The Hague: Mouton.

Nowakowska, M. (1975). Teoria działania—Algebra celów i algebra sposobów. *Prakseologia,* **53,** 5–14.

Nowakowska, M. (1976a). Action theory—algebra of goals and algebra of means. *Design Theories and Methods,* **10,** 97–102.

Nowakowska, M. (1976b). Towards a formal theory of dialogues. *Semiotics,* **17,** 291–313.

Nowakowska, M. (1977). Methodological problems of measurement of fuzzy concepts in the social sciences. *Behavioral Science,* **22,** 313–326.

Nowakowska, M. (1979a). Fuzzy concepts: their structure and problems of measurement. In M. M. Gupta, R. K. Ragade, and R. R. Yager (Eds.), *Advances in fuzzy set theory and application* (pp. 361–387). Amsterdam: North-Holland.

Nowakowska, M. (1979b). New ideas in decision theory. *International Journal of Man–Machine Studies,* **11,** 213–234.

Nowakowska, M. (1979c). Foundations of formal semiotics: objects and their verbal copies. *Ars Semeiotica,* **2** (2), 133–148.

Nowakowska, M. (1979d). Verbal and nonverbal communication as a multidimensional language [in Polish]. *Studia Semiotyczne,* **9,** 181–196.

Nowakowska, M. (1980a). Comments on Longacre's paper. *Proceedings of the Nobel Symposium on Text Processing.* Göteborg.

Nowakowska, M. (1980b). A model of memory with storage horizon control. *International Journal of Man–Machine Studies,* **13,** 213–221.

Nowakowska, M. (1980c). Verbal copies. *Bulletin of the Section of Logic,* **9** (1), 23–29.

Nowakowska, M. (1980d). Semiotic systems and knowledge representation. *International Journal of Man–Machine Studies,* **13,** 223–257.

Nowakowska, M. (1981a). Logical and stochastic aspects of discussions. In A. Lange-Seidl (Ed.), *Zeichenkonstitution (Akten des 2. Semiotische Kolloquiums Regensburg 1978* (Vol. 2, pp. 98–109). Berlin/New York: De Gruyter.

Nowakowska, M. (1981b). New model of memory with event-time horizon. In F. Klix and J. Hoffman (Eds.), *Cognition and memory: knowledge and meaning comprehension as functions of memory.* Amsterdam: North-Holland.

Nowakowska, M. (1981c). A model of internal decisions in answering questions. In J. E. Morse (Ed.), *Organization: multiple agents with multiple criteria* (pp. 265–282). Berlin/ Heidelberg/New York: Springer-Verlag.

Nowakowska, M. (1981d). Temporal systems and time theory. *International Journal of Systems, Measurement and Decisions*, **1**, 22–43.

Nowakowska, M. (1982a). New theory of time: fuzzy temporal relations and stochastic processes in fuzzy time. *Proceedings of the Twenty-sixth Annual Meeting of the Society for General Systems Research and the American Association for the Advancement of Science*. Louisville, Kentucky: Institute of Systems Sciences.

Nowakowska, M. (1982b). Some problems in the foundations of fuzzy set theory. In M. M. Gupta and E. Sanchez (Eds.), *Fuzzy information and decision processes*. Amsterdam: North-Holland.

Nowakowska, M. (1983). *Quantitative psychology: Some choosen problems and new ideas*. Amsterdam: North-Holland Publ.

Nowakowska, M. (1983). Dynamics of perception: some new models. *International Journal of Man-Machine Studies*, **18**, 175–197.

Nowakowska, M. (1984). *Theories of research*. Seaside, California: Intersystems Publications.

Nowakowska, M. (1984). Dynamic theory of expertise. In: *Proceedings of Conference of Society for General Systems Research, May 1984*, New York.

Nowakowska, M., Cox, J., and Kochen, M. (1984). Time allocation to topics in a course of study. *Mathematical Social Sciences*, **7**.

Nowakowksa, M. (1985). Erkennungspotenz: Grundlagen Einer Theorie der Grapheme. *Zeitschrift fur Semiotik*, **7**, 1/2, 27–34.

Nowakowska, M. (1985). Fundamentals of expert systems. I: Judgement formation and problems of description. *Mathematical Social Sciences*, **9**.

Nowakowska, M. (1985). Fundamentals of expert systems. II: Communication. *Mathematical Social Sciences*, **10**.

Nowakowsa, M., and Kochen, M. (1986). Informational synergy and mental preparedness. (in preparation).

Pearl, J. (1984). *Heuristics*. Reading, Massachusetts: Addison-Wesley.

Pfanzagl, J. (1968). *Theory of measurement*. New York: Wiley.

Pinsky, P. D. (1970) A mathematical model of testing for instructional management purposes. *Conference Paper, Annual Meeting of American Educational Research Association*, Minneapolis, Minnesota, March, 1970.

Posner, M. I. (1973). *Cognition: An introduction*. Glenview, Illinois: Scotland Foresman.

Reichenbach, H. (1965). *The direction of time*. Berkeley: Univ. of California Press.

Reichenbach, H. (1969). *Axiomatization of the theory of relativity*. Berkeley: Univ. of California Press.

Reichenbach, H. (1978). The causal structure of the world and the difference between past and future. In M. Reichenbach and R. E. Cohen (Eds.), *H. Reichenbach, Selected Writings*, 1909–1953. Dordrecht/Boston: Reidel.

Robb, A. (1914). *A theory of time and space*. Cambridge: Cambridge Univ. Press.

Roberts, F. S. (1979). *Measurement theory*. Reading, Massachusetts: Addison-Wesley.

Roberts, F. S., and Luce, R. D. (1968). Axiomatic thermodynamics and extensive measurement. *Synthese*, **18**, 311–326.

Rumelhart, D. E. (1977). *An introduction to human information processing* New York: Wiley.

Russell, B. (1927). *The analysis of matter*. London: Kegan Paul.

Sambuc, R. (1975). *Fonctions-floues. Application a l'aide au diagnostic en pathologie thyroidienne*. Unpublished doctoral thesis, University of Marseilles.

Schefe, P. (1980). On foundations of reasoning with uncertain facts and vague concepts. *International Journal of Man–Machine Studies*, **12**, 35–62.

Schlegel, R. (1961). *Time and the physical world*. East Lansing, Michigan: Michigan State Univ. Press.

Shapley, L. S., and Shubik, M. (1954). A method of evaluating the distribution of power in a committee system. *The American Political Science Review*, **48**, 787–792.

Shafer, G. (1976). *A mathematical theory of evidence*. Princeton, New Jersey: Princeton Univ. Press.

Shank, R. C., and Abelson, R. P. (1977). *Scripts, plans, goals and understanding: An inquiry into human knowledge structure*. Hillsday, New Jersey: Erlbaum Associates.

Shepard, R. N., and Cooper, L. A. (1982). *Mental images and their transformations*. Cambridge, Massachusetts: MIT Press.

Skvoretz, J., and Fararo, T. J. (1980). Language of grammar of action and interaction: a contribution to the formal theory of actions. *Behavioral Science*, **25**, 9–22.

Sowa, J. F. (1984). *Conceptual structures: Information-processing in mind and machine*. Reading, Massachusetts: Addison-Wesley.

Swinburne, R. (1968). *Space and time*. London: Macmillan.

Townsend, J. T., and Ashby, F. G. (1983). *Stochastic modelling of elementary psychological processes*. London and New York: Cambridge Univ. Press.

Townsend, J. T., and Landon, D. E. (1983). Mathematical models of recognition and confusion in psychology. *Mathematical Social Sciences*, **4**, 25–71.

Ullmann, S. (1979). *The interpretation of visual motion*. Cambridge, Massachusetts: M.I.T. Press.

van der Zouwen, H., Nowakowska, M., and Dijkstra, W. (1979). Simulation model for answering questionnaire items. *Proceedings of the Conference on Systems, Modeling and Control*. Zakopane.

Watanabe, S. (1966). Time and the probabilistic view of the world. In J. T. Fraser (Ed.), *The voices of time* (pp. 527–563). New York: Braziller.

Winston, P. (1983). *Artificial intelligence*. Reading, Massachusetts: Addison-Wesley.

Yager, R. R. (1979a). *On the measure of fuzziness and negation. Part II: Membership in the unit interval* (Technical Report # 79–01, Iona College, New Rochelle, New York).

Yager, R. R. (1979b). *On the measure of fuzziness and negation. Part II: Lattices* (Technical Report # 79–02, Iona College, New Rochelle, New York).

Yager, R. R. (1979c). A measurement-information discussion of fuzzy union and intersection. *International Journal of Man–Machine Studies*, **11**, 189–200.

Yager, R. R. (1980). On a general class of fuzzy connectives. *Fuzzy Sets and Systems*, **4**, 235–242.

Zadeh, L. A. (1965). Fuzzy sets. *Information and Control*, **8**, 338–353.

Zadeh, L. A. (1978). PRUF—a meaning representation language for natural languages. *International Journal of Man–Machine Studies*, **10**, 395–460.

Zadeh, L. H. (1979). A theory of approximate reasoning. Hayes, Michie and Mikulich (Eds.). *Machine Intelligence*, **9**.

Zadeh, L. A. (1981). Possibility theory and soft data analysis. In L. Cobb and R. M. Thrall (Eds.), *Mathematical frontiers in the social and policy sciences* (pp. 69–129). Boulder, Colorado: Westview Press.

Zimmermann, H. J., and Zysno, P. (1980). Latent connectives in human decision making. *Fuzzy Sets and Systems*, **4**, 37–51.

INDEX